# Disarmed

PRINCETON STUDIES IN AMERICAN POLITICS:

HISTORICAL, INTERNATIONAL, AND COMPARATIVE PERSPECTIVES

Ira Katznelson, Martin Shefter, and Theda Skocpol, series editors

# Disarmed

## THE MISSING MOVEMENT FOR GUN CONTROL IN AMERICA

*Kristin A. Goss*

PRINCETON UNIVERSITY PRESS

PRINCETON AND OXFORD

Library of Congress Cataloging-in-Publication Data

Goss, Kristin A., 1965–
Disarmed : the missing movement for gun control in America / Kristin A. Goss.
p. cm.—(Princeton studies in American politics)
Includes bibliographical references and index.
ISBN-13: 978-0-691-12424-7 (hardcover : alk. paper)
ISBN-10: 0-691-12424-8 (hardcover : alk. paper)
1. Gun control—United States. 2. Firearms and crime—United States—Prevention.
3. Violent crimes—United States—Prevention. I. Title. II. Series.
HV436.G653 2006
363.330973—dc22          2005034121

British Library Cataloging-in-Publication Data is available

This book has been composed in Sabon

Printed on acid-free paper. ∞

pup.princeton.edu

Printed in the United States of America

1  3  5  7  9  10  8  6  4  2
10  9  8  7  6  5  4  3  2  1

*For my dad*
*Douglas K. Goss*
*(1934–2002)*


*and my mom*
*Georgia B. Goss*

# Contents

# Figures

# Tables

# Acknowledgments

THE TRAJECTORY of our lives is powerfully influenced by the people who show up at critical forks in the road. In the years that I worked on this project, these people were there: Nili Abrahamsson, Barbara Asnes, Stephanie Barys, Anthony Braga, Stuart Bratesman, Andrea Campbell, Zoe Clarkwest, Susan Crawford Sullivan, Karena Cronin, the DeLio family; E. J. Dionne, Charlotte Ellertson, Joel Fleishman, Bob Frank, Marshall Ganz, Joe Gates, Harry Gomes, Harrison Gomes-Porter, Lilia Halpern-Smith, Bert Johnson, David Kennedy, Louise Kennedy, Bom Kim, Alma Kuby, Les Lenkowsky, Jens Ludwig, Jane Mansbridge, Jerry Mayer, Eileen McDonagh, Suzanne Mettler, Josh Mitchell, Stacy Palmer, Abby Peck, David Reingold, Bob Resling, Rick Richardson, Mark Rom, Rick Rosenfeld, Cathy Rudder, Tom Sander, Phil Semas, Maria Snyder, Bob Spitzer, Shannon Steenburgh, Thom Wall, Dick Waltz, Peggy White, and Ronda Zakocs.

Part of my research entailed a survey of nearly eight hundred participants in the Million Mom March. Without the following people, who graciously agreed to help collect the data, the survey would never have happened: Kristin Amerling, Anne Lowrey Bailey, Beth Blaufuss, Eva Jacobs, Jennifer Marien, Jessica Marien, Kiki McGrath, Bruce Millar, Brent Mitchell, Lew Pulley, Kristin Smith, Liz Stanley, and Lisa Zimmer-Chu. I am deeply grateful, as well, to the hundreds of people who agreed to answer my surveys, sometimes more than once, and to be interviewed about their experiences with gun control activism. We hear that Americans are oversurveyed, but all these respondents were eager to share their thoughts and experiences. Social science would be nowhere without people like this.

This study concerns many individuals who have dedicated their lives to advancing a policy idea that they believe will spare lives and heartbreak. Whether you agree or disagree with the efficacy of gun regulation, there is no doubt that its advocates are overworked and, relative to their counterparts in the for-profit sector, underpaid, yet they generously gave of their time to help me understand their world. I owe a huge debt of gratitude to these people: Roseanna Ander, Gerry Anderson, Mike Beard, Mike Berkey, Frieda Bernstein, Mary Leigh Blek, Robin Carnahan, Simon Chapman, Talmadge Cooley, Jack Corbett, Matt Fenton, Scott Harshbarger, Dennis Henigan, Barbara Hohlt, Toby Hoover, Kathleen Hopkins, Josh Horwitz, Carolynne Jarvis, Kelly Johnston, Wendi Kaplan, Mark Karlin,

Becca Knox, Patricia Koldyke, Julie Leftwich, Marj Levin, Brian Malte, Thom Mannard, Florence McMillan, Nadine Onodera, Teresa Patterson, Mark Pertschuk, Ron Pinciaro, Gail Powers, Lisa Price, Dana Quist, Sue Ann Schiff, Joe Sudbay, Rene Thompson, Sherry Tippett, Marion Towne, Bob Walker, Jeannie Weiner, Hilary Wendel, and several others whose confidentiality was assured. Of the many advocates who helped on this project, I owe extraordinary thanks to three in particular: Donna Dees-Thomases, founder of the Million Mom March; Kathy Zartman, whose archives from Illinois greatly enhanced this book; and David Steinberg, a national gun control pioneer who is also the causes's chief archivist.

This book began as a Ph.D. dissertation. Graduate school can be, um, unpleasant, but I was mercifully blessed by a spectacular set of advisers: Philip J. Cook (Duke University); Mark Harrison Moore (Harvard University); Robert D. Putnam (Harvard University); and Theda Skocpol (Harvard University). From start to finish, each of them was a tough critic and a responsive, generous mentor. As I was typing the last sentence of the last chapter of the dissertation, two weeks before I was set to defend, I got a call that my father had died, suddenly and without warning. The kindness, flexibility, and sacrifices that Phil, Mark, Bob, and Theda offered then merely underscored how many other times each of them had come through. Every graduate student should be so lucky. I would also like to thank three teachers who have been my role models over the years: Bill Bradley (Cherry Creek High School, Englewood, Colo.); Mike McElroy (North Carolina State University); and Dalene Stangl (Duke University). I cannot count the number of times I have asked, What would Bill, Mike, and Dalene do? The example they have set will last a lifetime.

I likewise owe an enormous debt of gratitude to the anonymous reviewers who insightfully identified the weaknesses and gaps in my argument and challenged me to make the product better. Thank you. Portions of chapter 4 were published in Women & Politics 25, no. 4 (2003): 83–118. Much of chapter 5 appeared in the Fordham Law Review 73, no. 2 (2004): 681–714. I am grateful to the publishers of both journals for their early support and permission to republish portions of those articles here. The study on which this book is based was supported by grants from the Harvard University Department of Government, the National Science Foundation, and the Hauser Center for Nonprofit Organizations at Harvard University.

Chuck Myers at Princeton University Press believed in this project from the start, provided numerous suggestions that made the manuscript infinitely more readable, and shepherded it (and me) through the review process with gentle and exquisite care. His reputation as a wonderful editor is richly deserved. I also thank Nathan Carr and Jennifer Nippins for guiding the book's production and the Editorial Board for taking a chance on this unusual project.

A core group of friends and family members have displayed an exceptional generosity and good humor that have sustained me: Marie Morris; Sally and Doug Caraganis; Laura Cratin; Rebecca Kramnick; Dave, Heather, Kaela, and Brenna Goss; Liz Stanley; Imy and Bill Williams; Jim Bulman and Beth Watkins; Zeta Graham; and Bunny and Puffin Goss-Williams. All of them epitomize the goodness to which all human beings should aspire.

Finally, I would like to thank three special people. My mother, Georgia Goss, played a critical part in this project from start to finish. Besides cheerfully assuming the role of my multistate clipping service and conscientiously mailing me hundreds of articles about the gun issue, Mom provided constant moral and intellectual support. She also spent many days scrupulously editing and proofreading the final manuscript. Words cannot express my gratitude to her.

This book would not have been possible—and that is literally true—without my beloved husband, Grant Williams. In our many years together, he has buoyed me in every respect, including during two stints in graduate school that kept us apart by 275 and 475 miles. (Perhaps it would be appropriate at this moment to thank USAirways for fabulous service over the years.) When I arrived back in Washington, he provided me with a home, allowed me to spread scores of manila folders all over the floor, and never once asked when I was going to be done. He always referred to this book as "your paper," as in, "I'll lie on the couch and read while you work on your paper." When I finished, he read my paper—in fact, several times—while I lay on the couch. Grant is funny, generous, and kind. I wake up every morning wondering how I could be so lucky to be married to him. He is my life and my love, and always will be.

Finally, I would like to thank my father, Douglas Keith Goss. In what would turn out to be his last week of life, he spent Thanksgiving with us in Washington. He refused to go sightseeing, and in a moment of obvious desperation, I said, "Uh, well, you wanna read my paper?" It took him four days, and even as I begged him to stop, he insisted on getting through the whole thing. He made insightful comments in the margins, and as he finished each chapter, he put a check mark at the top. He said this was his job, and he was going to finish his job. Dad was a western Colorado farm boy, a military veteran, and a passionate gun rights supporter. He also lived five miles from Columbine High and was traumatized by the massacre. The hours and hours of conversations we had in the three years after Columbine profoundly shaped my thinking at each stage of this project. As everyone who knew him will attest, Doug Goss was kind, generous, and loving to a fault; he treated people with dignity and provided a moral compass to everyone he met. He was my dad, but he was also my friend. The void that his death left defies words.

# Disarmed

# CHAPTER ONE

# The Gun Control (Participation) Paradox

ON APRIL 20, 1999, two alienated teenagers armed with an arsenal of semiautomatic firearms calmly made their way into their suburban Denver high school and began shooting indiscriminately. The young gunmen shot fellow students as they ate lunch on the school lawn, as they ran for cover in the school cafeteria, and as they crouched in terror in the school library. When the shooting spree at Columbine High School was over, one teacher and fourteen students (including the shooters) lay dead, and another twenty-one were wounded. With satellite trucks and cameras stationed outside the besieged school, coverage of the massacre was beamed live to television stations across the nation.

Columbine, the Colorado state flower and the massacre's ironic shorthand term, may have been the deadliest school shooting in U.S. history, but it was not the first. Between 1997 and 2000, there were three dozen mass shootings in schools, workplaces, and other seemingly safe spaces across the United States. But Columbine seemed "different," as one gun control leader noted at the time. "The focus on gun control seems to be more immediate and more lasting."[1]

On April 20 and in the weeks that followed, the nation indeed was galvanized to confront gun violence. Newspapers and talk radio featured impassioned testimonials about the historically tragic role of guns in America. Amid a popular outcry, pro-gun legislators' efforts to ease access to firearms stalled in state legislatures, including Colorado's. President Bill Clinton renewed calls for congressional passage of modest gun control measures, and previously reluctant lawmakers made tentative moves in that direction. Donations poured in to national gun control organizations, and their memberships grew.[2] And thousands of people, including students from Columbine and other Denver-area high schools, gathered for an unprecedented protest against the nation's mighty champion of gun rights, the National Rifle Association (NRA), whose long-planned annual meeting was held in Denver two weeks after the Columbine shootings.

As it turned out, Columbine *was* different in some ways—but sadly routine in others. The aftermath of Columbine looked a lot like the aftermath of many other high-profile shootings in American history: collective outrage, followed by a momentary flurry of unorganized calls and letters and donations from thousands of individuals, and then a quick return to the status quo.[3] In the months after Columbine, Americans witnessed four particularly traumatic shootings: a white supremacist's racially motivated killing spree in Illinois and Indiana in July 1999 that killed two people and wounded nine; an indebted day trader's massacre at his home and two Atlanta brokerage houses later that month (thirteen dead, including the shooter's wife and children, and twelve injured); a white supremacist's attack in August 1999 on a Jewish Community Center in Granada Hills, California (five injured), and on a Filipino postal worker (who died); and a six-year-old boy's fatal shooting of his classmate in February 2000 at an elementary school near Flint, Michigan. If ever the country had been primed to confront its gun violence problem, this was the time.

Within two years of Columbine and the traumatic shootings that followed, leading American newspapers decided to investigate the political fallout from these dramatic national events. What they found was not the stuff of banner headlines. Instead, headline after headline told a story of mass political quiescence. "New Gun Control Politics: A Whimper, Not a Bang," concluded the *New York Times*.[4] "Hill Reaction Muted on Latest Shooting; Lawmakers Largely Silent on Gun Control," the *Washington Post* reported.[5] "Rampages Elicit Little Outcry for Gun Control," sighed the *San Francisco Chronicle*.[6] Even though Columbine had seemed different, like a watershed moment that would radically alter the history of gun politics in America, in fact very little had happened legislatively or electorally. The nation seemed to have returned to normal, with Columbine and the other shootings nothing but a terrible memory.

The headlines notwithstanding, Columbine and the other high-profile shootings that followed appear to have accomplished what countless other gun violence traumas failed to do. These shootings planted the seeds of a sustained, visible, grassroots, nation-spanning gun control effort. New leaders emerged, new tactics were pioneered, and new interest groups formed. Whether a full-fledged movement will arise remains to be seen; that question is best left to future scholars. But Columbine bequeathed the present generation of scholars an equally engaging question: If a gun control movement were to arise in America, why didn't it happen before Columbine? Where was this missing movement?

Columbine was a shock but not a surprise. The United States witnesses sensational shootings with numbing regularity. The nation also experiences an epidemic of gun violence about once a decade. In recent surveys, roughly one in three American adults reported that someone "close" to them "such as a friend or relative," had been shot.[7] This means some 63 million American adults have been secondary victims of gun violence.[8] More to the point, polls back to 1973 consistently have found that about 20% of Americans have been threatened by a gun or shot at. Thus, in any given year, *between 25 million and 46 million people* report having had a close call with a gun at some point in their life.

Perhaps not surprisingly, public opinion polls routinely show crime and violence to be at or near the top of Americans' list of problems facing the nation. Polls also show crime and violence to be one of the issues citizens most want the government to address. For the seventy years that scientific surveys have been conducted, Americans have strongly and consistently favored at least one approach to the violence problem: stricter government regulation of firearms. And yet, decades of poll findings notwithstanding, each high-profile shooting or violence epidemic produces little more than a brief flurry of citizen outrage—a burst of emotion followed by a return to political normalcy. To be sure, millions of Americans bemoan the loss of life and the breakdown of moral order that these events reflect, and a small fraction of those citizens go so far as to write letters of protest to their local newspaper or their Congress member. In Congress and in state legislatures, a few elected officials invariably use the opportunity to advance gun control legislation. But most political leaders lie low, assuming that the public agitation will prove fleeting, just as it has so many times before. And prove fleeting it inevitably does.

Studying the gun control issue in the early 1970s, Hazel Erskine observed: "It is difficult to imagine any other issue on which Congress has been less responsive to public sentiment for a longer period of time."[9] That insight is at the heart of the well-known "gun control paradox": Most people want strict gun laws, but they don't get them—why? This book argues that there is a deeper puzzle: Most people want them, but they don't mobilize to get them—why? I refer to this as the "gun control participation paradox." This book seeks to explain that puzzle. To put the question in stark, if overly simplistic, terms, Why is there no *real* gun control movement in America?[10]

The answer, as it turns out, is multifaceted and far reaching, encompassing an array of structural constraints, historical developments, and organizational choices. But if there is one overarching explanation it is this: Gun control advocates were not nearly as successful as their opponents were in using American federalism to advance their cause. Sometimes this was the result of choices made by gun control proponents; sometimes it was the result of roadblocks that their opponents placed in the way; and sometimes it was the result of factors that systematically favor certain types of groups over others. In the end, the gun control case illustrates a stubborn lesson: The framers of the Constitution rigged the U.S. political system to frustrate the ambitions of bold policy reformers and to reward those who build consent from the ground up. Their plan succeeds to this day.

This introductory chapter serves several purposes. It outlines the scope and nature of gun violence in America, presents the core research question, and justifies the question in quantitative terms. The chapter then couches the question in theoretical terms and dispenses with some of the "obvious" explanations. Finally, the chapter presents a summary of the argument that unfolds in the chapters to come.

## AN AMERICAN GUN CULTURE?

Between 1992 and 2001, more than 336,000 Americans died by gunfire,[11] and more than 5.4 million were threatened or injured by gun-wielding robbers or other assailants.[12] More than one-third of the deaths occurred on the tail end of what the press and public health officials dubbed an "epidemic" of firearms violence, which lasted from 1988 through 1994. During that time, the annual gun fatality rate reached 15 deaths per 100,000 people—only a small fraction of the deaths from heart disease, but more than the rate of death from common afflictions such as leukemia, liver disease, or AIDS.[13] Even in "nonepidemic" years, the firearms death rate in the United States is considerably higher than that in any other advanced industrial nation. For example, the rate at which Americans were killed by guns in 1997 (a relatively peaceful year in the United States) was thirty-four times the rate of gunshot deaths in the United Kingdom, and more than three times the rate in Norway or Australia.[14]

On top of the hundreds of thousands of "everyday shootings" each year, the United States has regularly witnessed high-profile killings that have garnered significant public attention. One-third of the U.S. presidents since the Civil War (nine of twenty-seven) have been assassinated or threatened by assailants with guns, and many other high-profile Americans—politicians, civil rights leaders, entertainers—have been felled by bullets. In the late 1990s, even as the overall gun violence rate was declining, the United States witnessed a series of "rampage shootings" in schools, workplaces, and other "safe spaces." Between 1997 and 2001, at least thirty-six such incidents attracted widespread media coverage.[15] Together, these episodes resulted in the death of 139 people, including more than 30 schoolchildren, and the wounding of at least 188 students and adults.[16]

It is often argued that, relative to other advanced industrial nations, the United States has unrestrictive gun laws. For example, Canada passed a comprehensive scheme of gun registration after a man killed 14 women and wounded 13 others at a Montreal university in 1989. Australia outlawed semiautomatic and automatic assault weapons, and imposed strict registration and owner licensing for other firearms, after a man killed 35 and wounded 18 at a tourist spot in Tasmania in 1996. The United Kingdom banned private possession of handguns after a gunman killed 16 schoolchildren and a teacher in Dunblane, Scotland, also in 1996.

Guns are less tightly regulated and more easily purchased in the United States than in other Western nations. To be more specific, American firearms regulations are comparatively less restrictive in at least five senses. First, the laws have concentrated more on penalizing misuse than on controlling access; the laws are post hoc (punitive) more than ex ante (preventive). Second, broad availability has been taken for granted. Thus, regulations have focused on *keeping guns from* certain groups (minors, felons, addicts, the mentally ill) rather than *restricting availability to* a small class of potentially vulnerable individuals who can show a particular need to own a firearm (security guards, small-business owners in high-crime areas, women threatened by stalkers). Third, the laws have been relatively decentralized; as a result, gun control regulation has varied widely across jurisdictions, with strict controls concentrated in a handful of cities and states and most places having relatively few restrictions. Fourth, regulation has centered on sales conducted through primary markets, such as federally licensed gun stores; relatively few policies have sought to regulate or circumscribe informal sales. Fifth, laws have been subject to political compromise, leaving multiple "loopholes" whose shortcomings can be exploited by both gun control and gun rights advocates. The modern gun control forces' most far-reaching achievement in twenty-five years—the Brady Law, enacted in 1993—did little more than plug part of an existing loophole by requiring criminal background checks on a limited category of gun buyers.

The pattern of firearms regulation in the United States, coupled with its high gun violence rate, led historian Richard Hofstadter to proclaim America the quintessential "gun culture."[17] Interestingly, the popular image of America as a gun culture is at odds with more than fifty years of public opinion polls, which have found both widespread concern about gun violence and overwhelming support for measures to restrict access to firearms. Summarizing the findings, Tom W. Smith observed: "One of the few constants in American public opinion over the last two decades has been that three-fourths of the population supports gun control."[18] For example, in more than two dozen surveys conducted between 1959 and 1994, roughly 70% to 80% of respondents have favored "a law which would require a person to obtain a police permit before he or she could buy a gun."[19] In polls going back to 1968, similarly large majorities have supported a federal law to require registration of all gun purchases.[20] Milder proposals, such as requiring gun buyers to take a safety course and restricting youths' access to guns, have received support from a larger fraction of the population.[21] Only a ban on gun possession has not drawn majority support over the past several decades, though 30% to 40% of the population, and a larger share of American women, have consistently supported a handgun ban.[22]

The image of America as a gun culture is also at odds with attitudes toward gun ownership. In a survey conducted every year from 1975 to 1998, only about 20% of Americans generally or definitely thought there should be a gun in every home. That fraction has been dropping steadily since the early 1980s, to about 16%. By contrast, between 50% and 60% of respondents generally or definitely *did not* believe every home should have a gun, and that percentage has been rising.[23] Likewise, roughly 45% of Americans think guns in the home reduce safety,[24] compared with 41% who think a gun makes the home safer. At least since the early 1970s (when data began to be collected in a systematic way), gun possession in the United States has been declining. The fraction of people reporting a gun in the home in the late 1990s ranged from 37% to 43%, down from 48% to 54% in the mid-1970s (see figure A-1 in appendix A).[25] There is no doubt that there is a gun *sub*-culture in the United States, but it does not necessarily comprise a majority of gun owners. Indeed, one of the most persistent findings in public opinion research is that a majority of *gun owners* support moderate gun control measures.[26]

## The Gun Control Paradox, Properly Understood

Most people want strict gun control, but they don't get it. Why? The textbook answer to the gun control paradox is straightforward. American gun owners are intense, well organized, and willing to vote for or against candidates purely on the basis of their position on gun control. Gun owners' groups, notably the National Rifle Association and its state affiliates, provide an array of incentives to attract members and then turn those membership dues toward political action.[27] America's political system, with its multiple layers and divided powers, favors committed and well-organized groups such as the NRA, even if only a small minority of citizens embrace their views.[28] As Robert Spitzer notes, "The nature of interest-group politics is such that the energized and intense backers of the NRA have repeatedly proven the axioms that a highly motivated, intense minority operating effectively in the interest-group milieu will usually prevail in a political contest over a larger, relatively apathetic majority."[29]

The traditional answer to the gun control paradox focuses on the strength of gun control's opponents. However, in any contest one side is only as strong as the other side is weak. This is a seemingly obvious point. But, in the case of gun control, scholars have focused almost exclusively on explaining why the gun rights side is strong while assuming away the more interesting and challenging question of why the gun control side is so politically weak. In focusing exclusively on the anti–gun control forces, the "textbook answer" to the gun control paradox has two core problems. First, it may be partially incorrect. The pro-control majority may not be apathetic so much as lacking in meaningful opportunities to reveal intensity. Second, far from settling matters, the "unorganized majority" explanation begs—but is silent on—the more interesting question, Why are gun control sympathizers unorganized?

In challenging the textbook answer, I do not dismiss its core insight: Gun rights forces are intense, vocal, well organized, and capable of blocking policy proposals. My argument is simply that a single-minded focus on the strength of the gun rights side makes little sense, because in a pluralist democracy one cannot understand outcomes without considering the actions of all the players. There may be a connection between one side's strength and the other side's weakness; the two variables may not be independent. But merely demonstrating that one side is strong does not illuminate whatever causal connection may exist between that strength and the other side's weakness. That is, the mechanisms through which the gun lobby plies its organizational advantage have been underexplored. More important, a single-minded focus on the strong side needlessly distracts our attention from the potentially important dynamics on the weaker side. As this book will demonstrate, gun control advocates have played a role in suppressing their own movement.

In a larger sense, this book argues that the "gun control paradox" itself is misspecified. In its classic formulation the paradox has seized on the discrepancy between polls, which favor strict gun control, and policy outcomes, which do not. But polls alone don't usually change policy; political action does. Thus, I argue that the true paradox is the discrepancy between what people tell pollsters ("We want strict gun control") and what people's actual behavior suggests ("We are indifferent"). The gun control paradox properly understood is: *Why do Americans who want strict gun control not mobilize, in large numbers in a sustained way, to get it?*

Oddly, the participation paradox does not appear to have been explored before, at least in any systematic way. Rather, scholars have assumed the presence of a "movement" without questioning the many ways in which gun control advocacy does not resemble a conventional movement at all.[30] Given the American public's apparent concern with gun violence, why aren't citizens mobilized on a broad and sustained scale to control firearms? Why does the gun control movement (assuming that the various advocacy efforts qualify as a movement) bear so little resemblance in scope or drama to the great movements of the last century: movements against alcohol and smoking, for example, or for civil rights and women's equality? Any good intellectual puzzle has the potential to shed light on political questions far broader than the one at hand. And so it is in this case. The curious absence of broad public participation in what has been called "the great American gun war"[31] may tell us something interesting, not only about the politics of gun control in America, but also about patterns of political activism in the late twentieth and early twenty-first centuries.

## MOVEMENTS VERSUS LAWS

This is a study of participation around the gun control cause in America from the 1960s to 2000. I have introduced two paradoxes—the gun control paradox and the gun control participation paradox—to guide the study. Both, of course, are simplifications of reality. The gun control paradox notwithstanding, America *does* have gun laws; and the participation paradox notwithstanding, Americans *do* participate in favor of gun control. Although both the laws and the participation have one common feature—they are constrained relative to what one might expect—they should not be confused. Before moving on to tackle the gun control participation paradox, it is important to clarify two fundamental, important questions: What about all those gun laws? And what exactly constitutes a movement?

### Participation and Laws Are Not the Same

This is a study of popular participation, or lack thereof, around the issue of firearms control. It is not a study of gun laws. Participation, not policy, is the dependent variable. One must be careful not to conflate participation and policy; they are not the same thing, though, as I later demonstrate, they can be causally related. Equally important, one must be careful not to assume that, because there are gun laws, a mass movement must have been in place to put them there. Social movements are not necessary for policy change. Many laws—including, as it turns out, gun control laws—have passed with little or no organized prodding from citizens. Elites simply take it upon themselves to champion legislation.

Consider state gun control laws. In a sweeping study, Jon Vernick and Lisa Hepburn estimated that by the beginning of 2000, there were 275 state gun control laws on the books, ranging from handgun permit requirements to gun-crime sentencing provisions.[32] Interestingly, nearly 40% of those laws had been put in place before 1970, well before gun control supporters began to organize; they were not movement-inspired laws. Of the laws put in place since, there is no clear pattern that would suggest the presence of a mass movement behind them.

For example, during the 1970s, when gun control groups began to form, there was indeed a spurt in gun-related lawmaking—but it was focused on mandatory minimum sentences and sentencing enhancements for gun crimes, neither of which was a policy focus of early gun control leaders. During the 1980s, very few state gun laws passed. During the early 1990s, when there was a pronounced rise in gun law passage, most of the states that were responsible for the legislation (states such as Utah, Kentucky, Nebraska, Delaware, and New Mexico) had no gun control organizations, or particularly weak ones, suggesting again that these laws were not movement inspired. (For a graph showing the incidence of gun laws from 1970 to 1999, see figure A-2 in appendix A.) Indeed, both quantitative and qualitative evidence makes clear that gun control lawmaking has been driven by events far more than by organized citizen prodding. The increase in early 1990s lawmaking, for example, came on the heels of an epidemic of juvenile gun violence that had gripped most major cities since the late 1980s. The laws of this era were focused on restricting youths' access to firearms, particularly in states that had permissive laws and weak or non-existent citizens' gun control groups. Over all, the pattern of state gun control lawmaking in the 1970–1999 period suggests two conclusions. The vast majority of the laws were modest measures, and as a rule they were instigated by elected officials, not grassroots movements.

Although movements are not required for legislation to pass, movements matter in important ways. Movements increase the probability that elected officials will act and that the proposed reforms will be substantive instead of merely symbolic. Movements are particularly important for policy proposals that, like gun control, are (1) broadly popular but face well-organized opposition, and (2) can be portrayed as challenging political-cultural values. Always looking to the next election, American politicians are reluctant to take policy risks. Popular participation provides them with reliable information about their constituents' preferences and with the political cover to cast difficult votes. Movements also facilitate policy making by conducting research, disseminating new ideas aimed at changing social norms, recruiting citizen advocates, and lobbying legislators. Thus, although movements are not necessary for lawmaking, they make it much more likely. It is telling that the foundation of American national gun laws, the Gun Control Act of 1968, came in response to an unprecedented nationwide organizing effort on behalf of individuals affected by the back-to-back assassinations of Martin Luther King Jr. and Robert F. Kennedy. The law strengthened the federal licensing system for firearms dealers, providing among other things that only federally licensed dealers could ship firearms across state lines; required federally licensed dealers to keep sales records; banned dealers from selling guns to high-risk persons (e.g., drug addicts, mentally disabled people, youths);

prohibited interstate sales of handguns; and barred imports of small weapons not meant for sporting purposes (i.e., "Saturday night specials," though not their parts).[33] With the exception of the Brady Law, which required a background check to enforce the "prohibited persons" provision, the 1968 act's core provisions have remained largely unchanged.

At the state level, there has been more activity, including scattered victories for pro-control forces. But taken as a whole, the pattern of state firearms lawmaking in the 1980–2000 period signals, if anything, the presence of an *anti*–gun control movement, coordinated by the NRA and carried out in cooperation with its state and local affiliates. Under intense pressure from the gun rights movement, scores of states passed laws removing law enforcement's discretion over who may obtain a permit to carry a concealed weapon, stripping from local governments the right to regulate firearms, and barring lawsuits against gun manufacturers. Unlike the pro-control laws, which were ad hoc, fitful, uncoordinated, and driven largely by events, these anticontrol laws were pushed through systematically, legislature by legislature, in a series of well-financed, well-organized, nationally coordinated grassroots campaigns. Gun rights advocates' quick success provides telling evidence of the weakness of the gun control "movement." While gun control advocates have been organized and successful in a small handful of states, they have been no match for the decades-long antiregulatory movement spearheaded by national, state, and local gun rights organizations.

Most movements worthy of the name are successful. They may not get everything they want (in part because goals tend to expand with success), but history shows that strong movements eventually achieve most of what they initially sought. The Prohibition movement secured a constitutional amendment banning alcohol sales; the civil rights movement dismantled segregationist laws and spurred a significant decline in white racism; the antismoking movement turned cigarette use from a glamorous norm to a heavily regulated form of deviance. Although movements are not required for policy making, any exploration of policy outcomes—or nonoutcomes—must include an examination of the scope and nature of popular participation around the issue in question.

## What Is a "Movement"?

The online humor magazine the *Onion* once lamented in a headline that a protest march had fallen one person short of success.[34] Although clearly facetious, the headline inadvertently captures an important truth, not only about protest marches, but also about social movements more generally. Deciding whether a mobilization does, or does not, count as a movement would seem to require some sort of quantitative measure of "movement," some magic threshold beyond which the mobilization clearly qualifies. But for any particular situation, what is that numerical threshold? How many people, or actions, or events, must be involved? What kinds? How long must mass mobilization be sustained? If it is geographically bounded—say, limited to one city or state—is that a movement? One can immediately see the problem: Trying to provide a quantitative answer to those questions would involve pulling numbers out of a hat, and surely there would be no consensus about what those numbers should be. Thus, for perfectly understandable reasons, scholarly definitions of "movement" dodge the fundamental question: At what point does a mobilization become a movement?

In practice, there have been two answers to that question. The first is, "When advocates call themselves a movement," which is most of the time. The second is, "When the term 'movement' becomes commonly accepted by the media and other public commentators as a way of describing a mobilizing effort." In short, the term "movement" is subjective, not objective; post hoc, not ex ante; qualitative, not quantitative. Movements are collective judgment calls. We know a movement when we have seen it.[35] In that tradition of judgment calls, I will state my opinion up front: There has not been a true gun control movement in America. Reasonable people may disagree; indeed, even gun control leaders themselves come down on both sides of the question. But regardless of whether one concludes that there has, or has not, been a gun control movement, most observers agree that the effort has been at best a movement constrained. This is a study of how and why a popular issue has failed, mostly, to become a popular movement.

Even if "movement-ness" is inherently nonquantifiable, a baseline definition is necessary to lay out the core *qualitative* features. William A. Gamson and David S. Meyer define a movement as "a sustained and self-conscious challenge to authorities or cultural codes by a field of actors (organizations and advocacy networks), some of whom employ extra-institutional means of influence."[36] *Thus, social movements are (1) organized, (2) sustained, (3) visible, and (4) locally rooted forms of political action aimed at (5) changing norms and laws.* While it is convenient to speak in shorthand, dichotomous terms—in terms of movements and nonmovements—mass mobilization is of course a fluid concept, a continuous variable. Recognizing this fact allows one to move beyond endless definitional disputes (she says it takes seven protests to count as a movement, but he says it only takes six) and to tackle the question at hand. Thus, this study borrows from E. E. Schattschneider's concept of expansion in the scope of political conflict, or more simply "conflict expansion."[37] Conflict may expand along three dimensions: breadth (the number and types of people involved); depth (the intensity of their engagement); and length (their commitment over time). This book examines the difficulties that gun control advocates have had in widening, deepening, and lengthening citizen involvement in their cause. For the sake of ecumenicalism, I will use the terms "nonmovement" and "constrained movement" interchangeably.

## How Do You Know a Nonmovement When You See One?

Consider the following mental exercise. If you wanted to affect gun control policy, what would you do? Although this question has never been asked of a representative sample of Americans, an informal poll suggests that the answer would be "send money to Sarah Brady." Five years after her husband, White House press secretary James Brady, was shot in the head in the assassination attempt on President Reagan in 1981, and shortly after her five-year-old son found a loaded handgun in a friend's truck, Sarah Brady joined the board of Handgun Control, Inc., a Washington-based lobbying organization. Soon thereafter, she became the public face of gun control, appearing before Congress, headlining fund-raising events, and affixing her name to millions of direct-mail solicitations.[38] That "Sarah Brady" has become synonymous with gun control activism in America dramatizes a central assertion in this book. In terms of paradigms of policy change, gun control fits an interest-group model (a small cadre of elites working through staff-driven nonprofit organizations to push legislative change in Congress) far better than it fits a social-movement model (elite-directed masses pushing social as well as policy change in multiple private and governmental arenas).

Indeed, when surveying news reports on gun control, especially at the state and local level, the first thing one notices is not what is in the story but rather what is missing from it: evidence of broad-based citizens' groups pushing the issue. Even in states where gun control policies are under active consideration, and where some sort of gun control organization is known to exist, there is seldom evidence that the citizens' group initiated the policy debate or is visibly mobilizing citizens behind the proposal. Often, leaders of citizen groups are not even quoted. This is a reflection not of reporter bias but of the reality that gun control battles typically are led by lone legislators, not by social-movement organizations. In gun control debates, elected officials act on behalf of an unorganized public, rather than at the behest of an organized one.

This book readily concedes that gun control has attracted a small but committed group of activist leaders who have tried to change laws over the years; indeed, gun control activism has been institutionalized in the

TABLE 1.1
Media Adoption of "Movement" Mantle

| # Mentions (per year) | Gun Control MVT | | Antiabortion MVT | |
|---|---|---|---|---|
| | WP (1977–2002) | WP & NYT (1980–2002)[a] | WP (1977–2002) | WP & NYT (1980–2002) |
| Median | 0 | 1 | 16 | 33 |
| Mean | 0.7 | 1.4 | 16 | 35 |
| Mode | 0 | 0 | 17 | 29 |
| Range[b] | 0–4 | 0–5 | 7–38 | 13–68 |
| Total (all years) | 19 | 33 | 412 | 797 |

[a] *New York Times* (NYT) and *Washington Post* (WP) counts for 6/1/80–4/29/02 (NYT came online in June).

[b] The year 2002 is not included, because counts are for less than half the year. The upper bound figures for gun control (4 and 5 mentions) appeared in 2001; the lower bound (0) was found in many years covering all four decades under study.

nation's capital since the mid-1970s. And, at least since the 1930s, America has witnessed uncoordinated bursts of activism around gun control. But these bursts of popular outrage—and often the local and state voluntary groups they have nourished or given rise to—have quickly faded into quiescence. Even as gun control policies are debated regularly in the nation's legislatures, popular involvement has been contained and fleeting. Whatever gun control "movement" might exist at any time, or in any given locality, it has never reached the size, scope, or duration of the Prohibition, civil rights, environmental, and women's movements. Relative to its potential, the gun control "movement" has underperformed.[39] The gun control movement is a movement constrained, a movement that does not move very far very often. The constraints are captured by the following five measures.

*Media (Non) Adoption*

If there had been a gun control movement in America, surely it would have been acknowledged by reporters and editorialists. Yet the phrases "gun control movement" or "movement for gun control" have appeared infrequently in major U.S. newspapers, such as the *New York Times* and the *Washington Post*.[40] Table 1.1 summarizes the findings. For comparison's sake, I have included counts of references to "antiabortion movement," "pro-life movement," and "movement against abortion."

As the table shows, the "movement" label was affixed to antiabortion advocacy approximately twenty-four times as often as it was affixed to gun control advocacy. Figure 1.1 shows the data in longitudinal terms. It is clear that, even in down years, the antiabortion forces have merited far more movement affirmation than have the gun control forces.

The findings on gun control—usually zero "movement" mentions, or on average fewer than one or two per year—are particularly surprising in that both the *Times* and the *Post* for decades have keenly focused on the gun issue. Both newspapers have long taken a strong pro–gun control stance in their editorial pages; are based in a city where gun control routinely makes the political agenda; cater to a largely pro-control urban audience; and cover political affairs across the nation, not just in the home city. In other words, for at least four different reasons, if there were a vibrant gun control movement in America, the *New York Times* and the *Washington Post* surely would have noted it by bestowing on gun control advocates the movement mantle and covering their noteworthy activities. As I demonstrate below, the gun control coverage was there, but the recognition of a gun control "movement" basically was not.

### *(Lack of) Scholarship*

The leading scholarly books on the gun control issue, even those purporting to be about "the gun control movement," contain scant evidence of any such movement. Indeed, these books center on other aspects of the gun control issue: the strength of the NRA, the dynamics of public opinion, the various congressional debates, and so forth. There are no comprehensive chronicles of the gun control "movement" that would be comparable, for example, to the civil rights movement studies of Doug McAdam, Aldon Morris, and David Garrow or to the women's rights movement studies of Jo Freeman and Anne Costain.[41]

For example, Alexander DeConde's *Gun Violence in America: The Struggle for Control* (2001) repeatedly refers to the "gun control movement" but never really describes the identity, scope, organization, or activities of the putative movement. Although interested in the struggle *for* control, the book's attention is primarily focused on the struggle *against* control, led by organized gun owners. Another history, Gregg Lee Carter's *Gun Control Movement* (1997), spends just 30 pages, only about one-fourth of the text, exploring the subject in the book's title. Those pages focus almost exclusively on the legislative activities of three Washington-based interest groups, stretching the "movement" definition beyond reasonable bounds. Probably the best analytic history of the gun control issue, William J. Vizzard's *Shots in the Dark: The Policy Politics, and Symbolism of Gun Control* (2000), spends just 2 pages out of 184 describing gun control advocacy groups, all in Washington, and includes only a scattered few paragraphs on campaigns to secure new gun laws. Robert J.

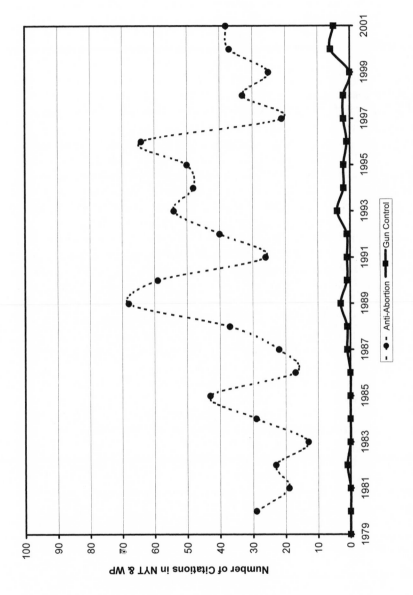

Figure 1.1. "Movement" Label in Major Newspapers: Gun Control *vs.* Antiabortion. Source: Nexis search.

Spitzer's *Politics of Gun Control* (1998) likewise devotes just 2 pages (out of 153) to a discussion of the pro-control side, in this case a quick overview of one Washington-based interest group.

### (Gaps in) the Agenda

The third "nonmovement" indicator concerns the relative infrequency of mentions of gun control activism in news stories about gun control politics. The logic behind this indicator is that, when an issue is on the agenda of political leaders, we should expect issue advocates to be prominently featured. This is so because advocates are often responsible for pushing issues onto political leaders' agendas, and even when advocates have not initiated action, they are likely to intensify their public efforts once leaders are paying attention. To measure the agenda gap, I constructed a data set consisting of a count of all stories on gun control in the *New York Times Index* between 1958 and 2000.[42] Figure 1.2 shows, year by year, the number of stories about the gun control issue juxtaposed with the number of stories within that larger group that provide some evidence of a mobilized public. I defined "evidence" quite broadly: If a Washington-based interest group testified in a congressional hearing or wrote a letter to the editor, the action counted; if a store decided to stop selling guns, that action also counted. As the graph shows, although gun control has been on the agenda since the early 1960s, citizen mobilization has remained low and relatively flat, although it began to inch up in the second half of the 1990s.

The graph shows that the *New York Times* ran an average of 76 stories per year about the gun control issue, with a range of 1 (1962) to 385 (1999). However, the number of stories citing some evidence of a mobilized citizenry averaged just 10 per year, with a range of 0 (various years) to 82 (1968). Of the 3,247 stories published, just 13% of them (418) mentioned citizen engagement. If we exclude two peak years (1968 and 2000), the number of mentions drops to 272, or 8% of the total stories. The graph is consistent with the conclusion that gun control is an elite-led issue: It appears to secure and maintain agenda status because of the efforts of legislators and other political leaders, not because of an organized and mobilized citizenry.

### Individual Participation

The fourth measure of "nonmovement-ness" revolves around the relatively low level of individual participation in organized gun control efforts. These measures are some of the hardest to obtain, so the findings must be considered with care. Here, I weigh one salient measure: membership in advocacy groups.

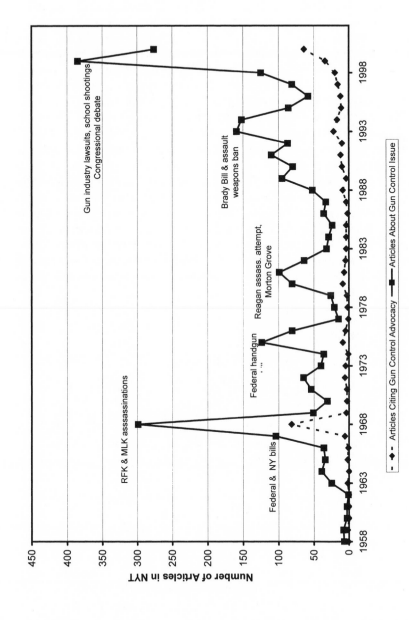

Figure 1.2. An Issue without a Movement. Source: *New York Times Index*, 1958–2000.

Consistent with the constrained-movement thesis, membership in the two leading national gun control groups (the Brady Campaign to Prevent Gun Violence and the Coalition to Stop Gun Violence) pales in comparison with membership in organizations at the forefront of other social-reform campaigns. In 2005, the Brady Campaign reportedly had fewer than 200,000 members, and the Coalition another 20,000. Assuming, as the groups do, that there is a 10% overlap in their membership rosters, that equals at most 218,000 national-group members.[43] In addition, my 2002 survey of state gun control groups suggests that the best-organized groups typically had 500 to 1,500 members apiece. In a sample of ten well-established groups, the average membership in 2002 was 1,700 people, and the median was 1,150. The combined membership for all state gun control groups probably numbers fewer than 50,000 people.[44] Assuming that these figures are not wildly exaggerated, and assuming (surely wrongly) that there is no membership overlap between the state and national groups, total membership in gun control organizations would be at most 268,000 people and almost certainly fewer. That means that gun control groups have just 8% of the membership that the anti-drunk-driving movement had in the mid-1990s (Mothers Against Drunk Driving, 3.2 million, 1995) and 7% of the membership in the National Rifle Association (approximately 4 million, 2004).

*Supporter Assessments*

The final measure of constraint is the assessments of gun control advocates and opponents. Both sides have an incentive to brand gun control efforts a "movement" —the advocates because the word suggests an appealing degree of solidarity and vitality, the opponents because the word conveys a threat around which to rally their forces. Indeed, both sides routinely do refer to gun control advocacy as a movement. But the term appears to be used principally for purposes of rhetorical shorthand. In interviews with leading gun control advocates, the question "Is the gun control movement a movement?" generally meets with a tellingly lengthy pause followed by a highly qualified answer.

One of the striking features of the history of the gun control issue is the degree to which the same arguments and observations echo from decade to decade. In 1964, journalist Carl Bakal, one of the earliest and most vociferous campaigners for gun control, wrote in *Harper's* magazine: "The vast majority of our citizens, including those who own guns for sports or other legitimate purposes[,] have expressed themselves as being in favor of firearms controls. But they are unorganized and, as memories of the Kennedy assassination recede, increasingly apathetic."[45] In

1975, Representative John Conyers (D-Mich.), who spearheaded the gun control campaign in the mid-1970s, called gun control supporters "a lumbering silent majority."[46] In 1978, the *Christian Science Monitor* reported, "Neither the Carter Administration nor the professional gun controllers have been able to mobilize the consistent public opinion majority in favor of handgun curbs . . . into practical political support for legislation."[47]

By the early 1980s, the line was much the same. The *Washington Star* noted in 1981 that the "mass sentiment" in favor of gun control "is not well articulated and is no match, at the trench-warfare level, for the singleminded lobbying and spending of the National Rifle Association and other groups."[48] Around the same time, a longtime gun rights advocate asserted, "There is no gun-control movement worthy of mention. There are a few isolated situations, but no large movement of people."[49] Two years later a state gun control advocate tried to rouse the public with the admonition, "It is time for the sleeping giant to awaken."[50]

By the 2000s, the gun control forces continued to be described as a latent public, rather than a social movement. Representative Carolyn McCarthy (D-N.Y.), whose husband was killed and son badly wounded in a 1993 mass shooting aboard a Long Island Railroad train and who won a seat in Congress by vowing to secure stricter gun laws, lamented in 1999, "Even though we had been working with an awful lot of gun-control groups, they don't have the money and they don't have the organizational skills that the NRA has."[51] Likewise, a gun control organizer in California lamented, "There's only one grass-roots movement on guns in America, and that's the NRA—but there need to be two."[52] The following year, Housing and Urban Development secretary Andrew Cuomo reached much the same conclusion, wondering why poor people, public health professionals, and other gun control supporters could not equal the power of the NRA: "There are three million public housing residents. Why don't they have the same impact that the three million members of the NRA have? There are three million nurses. Why don't they have proportionate impact? It's because the NRA is a focused force."[53] Speaking in Washington, D.C., a year after Columbine, Cuomo went on, "You are going to have to win the battle outside of this town. Awaken the sleeping giant— the American people. And the American people are starting to rustle."[54] And in 2001, after a four-year spike in school shootings and other so-called rampage killings, a national gun control advocate lamented, "There just (isn't) a whole lot of outrage. . . . I'm worried that people are seeing this as just part of living in America."[55] Around the same time, asked if there is a gun control movement in America, a state gun control advocate observed, "It's a movement, but obviously not a movement that's real well organized."[56] The equivocal assessment of insiders suggests the following consensus: Yes, various individuals and organizations are pushing hard for gun control in America, but do they add up to a movement? Maybe, but probably not.

## CAN YOU STUDY A "NONEVENT"?

Before exploring the substantive challenges facing gun control advocates in America, it is important to justify this book's motivating question, which is both nontraditional and perilous. Why does something *not* happen? I refer to such questions as "negative-outcome questions." Social science is in the business of studying phenomena that have happened— the observable, the countable, the tangible. It is not at all clear how one is to study, let alone explain, something that has not happened—the unobservable, the noncountable, the intangible.

Negative-outcome questions require inductive reasoning in a deductive-reasoning discipline. When the potential answers are limitless, where does one look begin to look for the "right" one? How does one know that her induction is correct? Behind the "right answer" problem lurks an even larger issue: Is the question itself valid? After all, there is a potentially infinite universe of woes that have not inspired mass political action, and so there must be a clear rationale for singling out any one of these problems for study. It is not particularly interesting, for example, to ask, "Why is there no antibullfighting movement in Manhattan?"[57]

In "Silver Blaze," Sir Arthur Conan Doyle's fictional detective Sherlock Holmes discovers that the solution to his mystery lies in a nonevent: a dog that "did nothing" when it should have been expected to bark. Following Holmes, this book's core insight is that one cannot understand the emergence and development of movements without also considering *nonmovements*, the nonbarking dogs of American politics. Social science has traditionally focused on the barking dogs: why phenomena start, how they grow. It has almost completely ignored the "silent" questions: why phenomena do not start, why phenomena do not expand, why phenomena end. But studying negative outcomes is fundamental to developing a solid theoretical account of movement formation. As social scientists going back to John Stuart Mill in the mid nineteenth century have understood, causal processes cannot be properly identified unless the outcome to be explained varies from case to case.[58] There must be variation on the dependent variable. Using case studies of works on economic growth, social revolutions, and class conflict, Barbara Geddes shows the perils of violating the convention. She concludes that positive cases "cannot test the theories they propose and, hence, cannot contribute to the accumulation of theoretical knowledge."[59] Yet, amazingly, the canonical social-movement literature consists entirely of positive cases—movements that have happened. As Maurice Jackson and his colleagues noted in 1960: "Without studies of unsuccessful movements there can be no assurance that the crucial conditions have been properly identified in the study of successful movements."[60]

By studying only movements that have happened, we risk misunderstanding the causal processes behind those movements. There are two possible sources of error. First, by focusing only on positive cases, we risk attributing causal significance to factors that were merely correlates (thereby upwardly biasing those factors' importance). Second, and conversely, we risk overlooking variables that are in fact important. Only by studying "nonmovements" can we hope to produce valid causal models. A handful of creative scholars have bucked the social-science establishment by taking on "dog that didn't bark" questions.[61] Tellingly, these orphan works have become some of the most widely cited material in political science, and they powerfully guide this book.

Understanding the gun control participation paradox, or any negative-outcome question, requires a triangulated research design and the blending of a wide variety of data. The research design, described in greater detail in the next chapter, has three prongs: matched case comparisons, in which gun control is compared with three other issues that are comparable to it along theoretically relevant dimensions; a longitudinal, qualitative analysis of "movement moments" in which the gun control movement had the structural potential to emerge but did not; and a natural (real life) "experiment" in which a gun control entrepreneur attempted to create a national movement. The study uses five categories of empirical data:

1. Secondary literature. This book draws on dozens of historians' and social scientists' case studies of movements for social reform.
2. Two massive, never-before-used archives of primary materials relating to gun control. These archives, which were amassed by gun control leaders in Chicago and Washington, comprise thousands of documents, including personal correspondence, confidential strategy memos, records from congressional hearings and debates, interest-group pamphlets and direct-mail pieces, and research reports. Material in one archive dates to the early 1960s and in the other to the early 1970s.[62]
3. Newspaper archives. I used the Lexis-Nexis database and the *New York Times Index* to create summary measures of the nature of the discourse surrounding gun control and its status on the political agenda.
4. Interviews. I conducted semistructured interviews with roughly seventy current and past gun control activists and spoke informally with many others over the course of three years.
5. Survey data. I carried out a survey of roughly 800 participants in the nation's first major gun control demonstration, held in Washington in May 2000. In

addition, I resurveyed roughly 220 of those people six to nine months after the march. Besides these original surveys, I made use of national surveys conducted by the National Opinion Research Center, Gallup, and others.

## Isn't the Answer Obvious?

Whether one is at a dinner party or a scholarly meeting, all questions about gun control politics seem to boil down to the same, three-letter answer: N-R-A. The conventional wisdom holds that gun owners and their main interest group are culturally and politically invincible, while the pro-control majority are indifferent or otherwise unmotivated. The conventional wisdom is so powerful and pervasive that it must be considered here. Isn't "the mighty NRA" the solution to the gun control participation paradox? Isn't the answer obvious? The answer is no. A careful deconstruction of the conventional wisdom, including its various components and tangents, shows that it cannot explain the gun control participation paradox. Below, I consider the conventional arguments and show why they are at best incomplete and at most flat-out wrong.

### Lack of Intensity?

One of the most persistent claims is that members of the pro–gun control majority are only weakly supportive of the cause and that it is not very important to them. A variation of this explanation is that gun control supporters care about many causes but gun rights supporters care about only one. According to this account, the "participation gap" stems from an "intensity gap," in which anti–gun control forces care passionately enough to organize but gun control supporters do not. This explanation is incomplete at best and flat wrong at worst. While some gun owners certainly are intense—as anyone who has seen them at gun control hearings can attest—there is no reason to believe that they are more passionate than those affected by gun violence: the mothers, fathers, siblings, and spouses who show up to plead for gun control laws and in some cases devote their lives and fortunes to volunteer groups lobbying for the cause. Gun rights supporters appear to be more intense because they are better organized and because people tend to experience threatened losses more intensely than potential gains.[63] Contrary to conventional wisdom, a landmark study found that the fraction of gun control advocates who are passionate about their cause was slightly *higher* than the fraction of gun rights advocates who are passionate about theirs.[64] What's more, because pro-control forces outnumber anticontrol forces by about two to one, the *number* of intense gun control advocates far exceeded the number of intense gun rights supporters. Likewise, a national survey found that 20% of gun permit supporters said "the gun control issue" was "one of the most important" to them, compared with just 12% of gun permit opponents who felt similarly strongly.[65]

The difference between the two groups appears not to be in self-reported intensity but in actual political action on the gun issue. Howard Schuman and Stanley Presser found that gun rights supporters were slightly more likely than pro-control individuals to say that gun control was "one of the most important" issues in how they voted in congressional elections, and gun rights supporters were far more likely to have written a letter and/or given money on the gun issue.[66] The same pattern continued to appear through the 1990s, but the "action gap" had narrowed. My analysis of the 1996 National Gun Policy Survey found that gun rights supporters were about twice as likely as gun control supporters to have taken some action, such as joining an organization or writing a Congress member, to further their cause. Thus, the "participation gap" may not reflect a difference in intensity as much as a difference in organization. Tellingly, a 1987 poll found that 9% of respondents cited "pro gun control" as an issue that concerned them enough to "take an actual personal role in a movement," roughly equal to the 10% percent who said they cared enough about *opposing* gun control to get involved. That equal fractions on both sides want to take an active part, while the actual rate of participation is far greater on the gun rights side, suggests that there is, indeed, an organization gap.

Even if we disregard poll evidence and assume that gun control is not a top priority for many people, we still are left without an answer to the participation paradox. No mass movement has ever required all citizens to see the issue as their top priority. Rather, movements require only a committed core of activists and a wider circle of individuals who will show up at demonstrations and take part in other ways. One of the chief tasks of these movement activists and entrepreneurs is precisely to persuade sympathetic bystanders to get involved in the political fray and to provide them opportunities that will motivate them to stay involved. Put another way, commitment does not necessarily precede organization. And, in fact, good organization will nurture commitment.

### Racism?

Another common claim is that gun control has failed to inspire a movement because gun violence disproportionately affects members of minority groups and the white majority is sufficiently insulated that it can avoid involvement. According to this theory, white Americans do not feel any personal connection to gun violence or do not think anything can be done to change what they may secretly see as minorities' proclivity for violence. The racial explanation is at least superficially plausible. African-American and Latino males are disproportionately involved in gun violence, both as victims and as perpetrators.[67] Virtually all the epidemic increase in gun violence that swept the nation between 1985 and 1993 is attributable to nonwhite males under twenty-five.[68] Swings in gun violence are clearly more prevalent in urban areas than they are in small towns and rural areas.

However, the racial argument appears to be another account that ultimately does not hold up under scrutiny. The strongest argument against the white-racism claim is that, in fact, lots of whites are personally affected by gun violence. A Gallup poll conducted in 1993 found that roughly one-third of white American adults said someone "close" to them, "such as a friend or relative," had been shot in circumstances other than military combat.[69] This translates into approximately 50 million whites who have been secondary victims of gun violence. Likewise, polls suggest that roughly 20% of white Americans have been threatened by a gun, or shot at.[70]

There are other reasons to doubt the racial explanation. For one, gun control activism was stronger in the 1970s, when white racism was more prevalent, than in the early 1990s, when racism was at historic lows. Moreover, a cynic might argue that the racism explanation would actually favor a gun control movement: If whites believe that blacks are prone to violence, wouldn't whites rise up in favor of gun control, raising the cost of firearms ownership and burdening those at the lower end of the income spectrum? Indeed, the fact that gun control activism is strong in northern cities with large black populations is consistent with the cynical interpretation but inconsistent with the "uninterested whites" explanation.

### Issue-Attention Cycles

High-profile shootings do not happen every day, or even every month. And crime comes in waves. Perhaps advocates have trouble sustaining a movement because the problem is short lived and self-correcting, rather than stable and in need of policy interventions. Again, there are reasons to doubt this explanation. For one, even during down years, gun violence in America remains quite high by international standards. Second, other social movements have arisen in nonepidemic periods. Liquor consumption was actually declining when the Prohibition movement took off, and smoking had been declining for more than a decade before the antitobacco movement gained its footing in the 1980s.[71] A third reason to doubt the cyclical explanation is that the endemic level of violence alone should produce enough primary and secondary victims to fill movement ranks.

*Futility?*

The futility theory comes in two parts. The first is that Americans do not rise up for gun control because doing so would be pointless given the political strength of gun rights forces. The difficulty with this explanation is that, almost by definition, social movements start from a position of weakness. The civil rights movement, to cite a clear example, began in the virulently segregated South, where the state and white citizens' groups not only politically stifled but also violently repressed movement activism. Although conditions were liberalizing at the national level, the civil rights movement was strongest in the region most resistant to change.

The second dimension of futility has to do with perceptions of whether gun control, as a policy, would be effective. This explanation holds that Americans doubt whether gun control would work, thereby diluting their willingness to spend time and energy on a gun control movement. Judging whether Americans believe gun control would be effective depends on how the survey question is worded.[72] Generally speaking, polls suggest that Americans do not see gun control as *the solution* to criminal violence, but they do believe that significant reductions in criminal violence are not possible without stricter gun laws. They see gun control as an imperfect remedy, but a useful and necessary one. For example, a 1993 Yankelovich survey asked, "Do you think [stricter gun control laws in general] would decrease the amount of violent crime in this country a great deal, a fair amount, only a little, or not at all?" One-third (35%) said a great deal; 25% said a fair amount; 19% said only a little, and 17% said not at all. In other words, 60% thought that gun control would do a decent amount of good. Likewise, when asked whether "legislation designed to reduce the amount of violent crime in this country can do so without imposing stricter gun control laws," fully 65% said that new gun laws were necessary; only 28% said violent crime could be reduced without stricter gun control.[73]

*Rational Self-Interest?*

This explanation, usually forwarded by gun control opponents, holds that Americans don't really want gun control, because it is against their self-interest in two ways. First, many Americans own guns, and therefore firearms regulations that applied to the existing stock would impose new costs and burdens on law-abiding citizens. Second, the explanation goes, Americans view guns as necessary for self-defense. They therefore would oppose gun control on the grounds that they might need to use a gun someday and would therefore want firearms to be unregulated and readily accessible. There are several problems with these explanations. First, taking the reasonable assumption that most gun owners would never join a gun control movement, we are still left with half the population (the non–gun owners) who are presumably available for recruitment. No movement in history has been launched on the basis that the entire population is likely to join. Indeed, if there were that much consensus, a movement would hardly be necessary. The second objection—the "just in case" self-protection scenario—makes sense only insofar as the public also believes that gun control legislation would, in fact, deprive them of obtaining or using a gun when necessary. In a 1996 survey, respondents were asked how concerned they were that "if people were required to register their handguns, the government would use the information to try to confiscate the handguns of law-abiding citizens."[74] Only 16% of gun control supporters were very concerned about this possibility. Fully 47% were not concerned at all.

### Responsive Federalism?

Finally, perhaps the gun control movement has foundered because the "right amount" of gun control already exists at the state level. While there is a significant correlation between the weakness of gun laws and the strength of pro-gun sentiment across the states, statistical analysis shows that state gun laws are far from a perfect reflection of citizen preferences.[75] Perhaps more important, it is not clear that there should be a strong correlation between laws and activism. For example, states with weak gun laws and a strong gun culture might indeed suppress pro-control activism—because the pro-control partisans are few in number and might view theirs as a lost cause. But weak laws and a strong gun culture might also *encourage* activism, because gun control partisans could see the pervasiveness of guns as a "problem." Likewise, residents of states with a weak gun culture and strong gun laws might be encouraged by their victories to pursue ever stricter laws at the state level, and such local success might buoy them to lead a movement for national restrictions. In middle-ground states, with a more even split between pro-gun and pro-control sentiment, one might expect activism on both sides because the "middle ground" laws would not satisfy either.

### The Free-Rider Problem?

If none of the above explanations will suffice, perhaps the answer lies not in the peculiarities of the gun issue itself but in the principles of collective action generally. The characteristics of public policies structure the political dynamics that surround them.[76] By implication, policies will vary in their amenability to mass mobilization. Two policy categories that face particular challenges in this regard are policies seeking "social regulation" and policies advancing "public goods." Social-regulatory policies are those that govern individual behavior and communal relations; public goods are those that benefit everyone indiscriminately. Advancing either requires infringing individual liberty. Gun control fits into both categories, and so gun control advocates—and advocates for policies like gun control—face not one challenge but two. These challenges are formidable, but creative entrepreneurs have found ways to surmount them.

The first challenge is that America is imbued with a classical liberal political culture derived from the Founding Fathers and their philosophical patron, John Locke. Contemporary advocates for policies that seek to regulate individual behavior in the name of the commonweal invariably run up against Americans' faith in the twin tenets of individual liberty and a small central state.[77] Americans resist social regulation as an affront to their natural rights, and politicians risk an electoral penalty if they seek to deny or even infringe these Creator-endowed, constitutionally enshrined liberties. Consequently, as Anthony King notes, *the state plays a more limited role in America than elsewhere because Americans, more than other people, want it to play a limited role.*[78] Advocates asking the state to play a larger role in social relations face an uphill battle.

Besides being a social-regulatory policy, gun control also is designed to deliver a public good: public safety. As Mancur Olson notes in his classic study, public (or collective) goods also are difficult to mobilize around, but for a different reason—having to do not with communal political beliefs but with individual rationality.[79] By economists' definition, a public good has two core characteristics: jointness of supply and impossibility of exclusion.[80] Jointness of supply means that one person's consumption does not reduce anyone else's; nonexclusion means that everyone benefits, not just those who agitate for the good. Economic theory suggests that public goods will be undersupplied: The market will not produce the socially optimal amount. Because everyone receives an equal share of the good, regardless of whether he has helped to secure it, it is rational for each individual to free ride on the efforts and expenditures of others— "let someone else take care of it." Of course if everyone rationally abstains, the free market will not provide the good absent some form of coercion (say, conscription or taxation). The free-rider problem can be overcome under certain circumstances.[81] But it remains a stubborn problem for collective idealists.

The difficulty with these theoretical solutions to the gun control participation paradox is that we know that history is fraught with examples of movements for social regulation and public goods. Scores of volumes have been written about movements that defy the logic of collective inaction:

the antitobacco movement, the antiabortion movement, and, most spectacularly, the Prohibition movement.

These movements in fact will prove critical to understanding the gun control nonmovement. The next chapter provides a quick sweep of the modern history of gun control politics in America. I have already demonstrated that gun control has never provoked a true grassroots movement, even as gun violence spiraled out of control. The next chapter will demonstrate that, according to conventional social theories of social-movement formation, gun control should have produced a movement. The chapter will then derive the theoretical framework that will guide the rest of the book. The theory situates collective action in a framework of individual costs and benefits. It argues that vigorous movements have always found a way to spread (or socialize) the costs, to concentrate (or personalize) the benefits, and to increase the individual's expectation that his personal costs will result in social benefits (or boost the participation payoff). To derive the theory, the next chapter offers brief case studies of issues that are comparable to gun control except that they *have* inspired true social movements.


## Why No Real Gun Control Movement in America?

Even as the United States has suffered through murders of public figures, workplace rampages, schoolroom massacres, and regular epidemics of "everyday" gun violence, the nation has never witnessed a vigorous, nation-spanning social movement to control access to firearms. This is not because Americans are indifferent to gun violence or lack support for enhanced gun control measures. It is not because gun control laws, or the effort to secure them, would be futile. Rather, gun violence has not inspired a mass mobilization in part because the leaders of the pro-control majority have lacked external resources to underwrite such a movement and in part because these leaders have chosen political strategies that are anathema to movement building.

To mount a movement, gun control leaders need external patrons. But these patrons have been largely unavailable. As chapter 3 documents, this is so in part because of the structure of American tax laws, which facilitate giving to charity but enact barriers to philanthropic foundations' support for political advocacy. It is also due in part to the shifting interests of a key set of potential patrons: women's voluntary associations. In an earlier day, female reformers would have provided volunteers and funds to social causes such as gun control; but by the 1970s, when gun control organizing began, women's groups were being diverted toward feminism and its agenda. Finally, gun control advocates have been denied patronage from government institutions. Gun rights supporters have successfully lobbied for a slew of laws over a thirty-year period that have denied gun control advocates a foothold in sympathetic bureaucracies. Thus, for a host of reasons, socializing the costs of participation has been formidably difficult.

Personalizing gun control has been equally elusive, at least until recently. But unlike the stumbling blocks surrounding patronage, this difficulty is not so easily attributed to the conscious actions of anti–gun control organizations. Instead, as chapter 4 shows, gun control advocates themselves have failed to frame their issue in ways that would activate their mass base of supporters. Seeing their cause as self-evidently good, gun control advocates have framed their policy argument in terms that appeal more to policy experts than to everyday citizens. In particular, advocates have portrayed gun control as a means of crime control, thereby conferring "issue ownership"[82] on criminal-justice professionals rather than, say, business leaders and parents. This frame has helped to ensure that gun control would be an issue for elite politics rather than mass politics. If issue advocates do not legitimate the authority of lay citizens, why would these citizens think their participation would count? To underscore the argument, chapter 4 documents gun control forces' recent attempts to reframe their cause in terms that are more compelling to everyday Americans and shows quantitatively that this effort has spurred broader and more intense mass participation.

To complete the argument, chapter 5 documents how national gun control organizations have forgone the opportunity to alter the prospective cost-benefit ratio of participation in a favorable way. Unlike leaders of other reform movements, leading gun control advocates shunned incremental strategies and instead adopted a "rational national" model of policy change to which they remained largely committed through at least the mid-1990s. From the start, they chose to emphasize good policy at the expense of good politics, sacrificing mass pressure and elevating the role of insider expertise. In a sense, then, there has been no sustained, national gun control movement in America because gun control leaders chose, perhaps unwittingly, not to have one. To the extent that some gun control advocates, particularly at the state and local levels, tried to embrace a vision of movement-building incrementalism, their gun rights adversaries used institutional, electoral, and cultural resources to undermine these campaigns. Thus, because they lacked the opportunity to build outward, and certainly upward, gun control advocates had trouble turning mass sympathy into sustained engagement. However, when gun control leaders experimented with incremental approaches, popular participation did expand as the theory would predict. Chapter 6 documents three such cases with a clear, quantifiable link between incrementalism and mobilization.

In broad terms, chapter 7 concludes that the answer to the gun control participation paradox boils down to which side has better exploited the American political system to alter the costs and benefits of individual participation. I argue that the opponents of gun control have accommodated themselves better to the stubborn realities and political inconveniences of a fragmented, federalist system than have the supporters of gun control, whose strategies may have been rational in a policy sense but were politically naive. The struggles of the gun control "movement" stem both from choices that leaders made and from choices that were thrust upon them by a politically savvy and implacable foe. At the same time, the gun control case illuminates a broader set of issues in contemporary American politics. In particular, it highlights the seductive lure of elite politics. Modern liberals, including gun control advocates, model themselves on the civil rights movement, but in doing so they misread the lessons of history. The civil rights movement's national legislative triumphs, which outlawed discrimination in all public places (1964) and put the weight of federal law enforcement behind local voting rights (1965), came after decades of local organizing around modest measures—changing seating patterns on a bus route or at soda fountains, for example. The civil rights movement stands for the proposition that there are no quick fixes in American politics, but contemporary liberal reformers draw from the movement exactly the opposite conclusion. The gun control case serves as a cautionary tale. The Founding Fathers meant for political reform to be slow and difficult. Movements that adapt their strategies to that reality will expand; movements that do not adapt will falter.

# CHAPTER TWO

# A Movement in Theory

EARLIER, I MADE TWO BROAD CLAIMS: that social-movement theories are derived from a research approach that is flawed because it relies only on positive cases, and that the "movement" for gun control is not much of a movement at all. Here I connect those two insights by demonstrating that conventional social-movement theory cannot explain the nonmovement for gun control. Through a brief sweep of history, I show that gun control appeared to have all the makings of a social movement, not just once, but at a handful of pivotal points in time. Yet no movement arose. From this exercise, I conclude that there is something missing from conventional movement theory. But what?

In the second part of the chapter, I develop a theory capable of answering that question. The theory is derived from an analytical case comparison of three issues that have inspired movements and one issue that has not. Gun control is the negative case. The three positive cases are the movements against alcohol, against smoking, and against abortion. These three cases were selected because they are similar to gun violence along key dimensions, except that they have clearly inspired movements. These cases, and the theory derived from them, are the subject of this chapter. Readers who are interested in gun control more than social-movement theory may read the section in this chapter dealing with gun control's "movement moments" and then skip to chapter 3.

## CONVENTIONAL SOCIAL-MOVEMENT THEORY

Social-movement theory is derived from studies of social movements. At first glance, this seems quite logical. After all, theory is derived from observable actions. Yet, the scientific method tells us that good theory depends crucially on variation in what is observed. Traditionally, social-movement scholars have obtained variation by examining the waxing and waning of activists' success over time. These scholars have assumed that the background condition—group-based grievances—is more or less steady. Given human beings' penchant for oppressing other human beings, there is no shortage of *potential* movements. The research question therefore becomes, What factors must be in place to cause a potential movement to become an actual movement? Social-movement theory is rich and varied, but a gathering consensus based on numerous case studies suggests that three factors are fundamental to this shift: collective *efficacy*; mobilizable *resources*; and political *opportunities*.

Collective efficacy comes when disenchanted individuals, first, recognize themselves as a group with a shared grievance and, second, believe that collective action can reduce or eradicate the source of that grievance. William Gamson refers to these two prongs as *identity* and *agency*.[1] Doug McAdam refers to them as "cognitive liberation."[2] When groups possess collective efficacy and are thus primed to act, social-movement theory holds that they require resources to translate emotion into collective action. Typically, "resources" refers to money, volunteers, and the nongovernmental organizations that provide them.[3] More recent studies have broadened the understanding of resources. John McCarthy refers to "mobilizing structures," which include not only formal organizations but also activist networks, affinity groups, memory communities, protest communities, and movement schools.[4] Sidney Tarrow likewise sees informal resources as central to movement formation.[5] These include social networks, temporary assemblies, and connective structures. Synthesizing these perspectives, William Gamson and David Meyer note that a social movement is a "range of actors pursuing numerous strategies," an amalgam of "organizations and advocacy networks," and "a field of actors, not a unified entity."[6] Although some scholars have argued that institutionalization is the death knell of social movements, most accept that organizations are fundamental to sustained campaigns for political change, for without an organizational infrastructure, the expression of mass grievances is limited to quick outbursts of anger rather than sustained, strategic political pressure for legislative and social reform.[7]

Finally, possessing collective efficacy and access to human and financial resources, social-movement leaders require a political opportunity when collective action stands a better-than-average chance of paying dividends.[8] In a synthesis of various social-movement theories, Doug McAdam argues that there are two types of opportunity that matter for movement-building purposes. The first is political opportunities: "(1) The relative openness or closure of the institutionalized political system; (2) The stability or instability of that broad set of elite alignments that typically undergird a polity; (3) The presence or absence of elite allies; and (4) The state's capacity and propensity for repression."[9] The second type is cultural opportunities: "(1) the dramatization of a glaring contradiction between a highly salient cultural value and conventional social practices; (2) 'suddenly imposed grievances'; (3) dramatizations of a system's vulnerability or illegitimacy; (4) the availability of an innovative 'master frame' within which subsequent challengers can map their own grievances and demands."[10] In essence, political opportunities involve government leaders, and cultural opportunities involve the mass public.

As scholars have looked back on social movements that have arisen, they have found all three elements to be present. Civil rights leaders, for example, could take advantage of black group identity forged through centuries of repression and group agency encouraged by favorable government and court decisions from the 1930s through the 1950s; could tap historically black colleges and churches for volunteers, money, leadership, and other movement resources; and could take advantage of political opportunities occasioned by growing black electoral strength, increasing support for civil rights, and Cold War pressures.[11] Thus, there has been a strong correlation between the presence of these three movement catalysts and the presence of a movement itself. Although "nonmovement" eras typically receive little explicit analysis, movement studies imply that they are marked by the absence of one or more of these catalysts. The standard research design—seeking variation over time—is theoretically sound. At first glance, it is a workable way to create variation out of a single positive case, and thus to avoid selecting on the dependent variable of interest—movements that *have* happened.

But the history of gun control suggests that looking over time to find case variation is not sufficient to produce a robust theory. In fact, history shows that gun control advocates, like advocates for other movement causes, have had critical moments when all the social movement elements were in place. Yet unlike other issues that produced movements when the theory would have predicted, gun control did not. Thus, the gun control case suggests that models derived from seeking variation over time may not be adequately specified. The theories are good: They contain important variables not contradicted here. But these theories are not as robust as they could be. To understand why movements form, one must study nonmovements.

## APPROACHES TO THE QUESTION

Building on the insights of social-movement and interest-group scholars, this chapter argues for a refined model of when mass, sustained participation takes root. First, I demonstrate the contention stated above that, according to conventional social-movement theory, which is derived from observed changes in causal variables over time, the gun control issue should have produced at least one true social movement, and probably more than one. Thus, my first method of analysis is a longitudinal, qualitative examination of five "movement moments" in which gun control had the potential to crystallize into a movement but did not.

To understand why it did not—why gun control is the perennial negative case—I next follow traditional movement scholarship in examining positive cases, social movements that have occurred. However, rather than drawing on the rights-based movements that have been so influential in social-movement theorizing, I examine six shadow cases, all involving issues that are comparable to gun control in key ways. From these six cases—which cover three issues, each at two points in time—I derive a series of testable hypotheses about why those movements arose. Hence, like other social-movement theorists, I derive my theory from positive cases, but unlike them, I test my theory against a negative case that is comparable to the positive case in theoretically relevant ways. Thus, the second method employed is the case-control method.

Finally, I examine the gun control case more closely by examining localized efforts to broaden mass participation—what John Gaventa refers to as "relevant counterfactuals."[12] The intuition is that, if the causal variables that I have pinpointed as critical to movement formation are present even in fleeting or limited ways, we should expect to see participation increase; by extension, when they are present in a more comprehensive way, a movement might well break through. In particular, I examine an important natural experiment in movement building that unfolded during the course of this research: the Million Mom March for gun control in May 2000.

Thus, my own theory is derived—and tested—using not one, but three, types of variation.

- *Variation across issues:* The cases are based on three issues that have inspired movements and one issue that has not.
- *Variation across time:* The gun control case is examined over a thirty-year period, and the other three movement issues are examined in two eras—the late nineteenth century and the late twentieth century—thereby ensuring that the theory is not the product of a particular historical moment.
- *Variation across space:* The gun control case, which unfolds in chapters 3–6, includes localized counterfactual examples demonstrating that, in the presence of causal variables overlooked by conventional movement theory, participation expands in ways that my refined theory would predict.

## "MOVEMENT MOMENTS" WITHOUT A MOVEMENT

The premise of this study is that the American gun control "movement" has been surprisingly weak and probably not a movement at all. Yet judging from established theories of social movements, gun control should have spurred a full-fledged movement, and probably more than one. This is so because all the requisite movement elements, as identified in the literature, have been in place many times, over more than three decades. At the individual level, gun control advocates have had a constituency group (what social scientists call an "issue public") with shared grievances and determination to make a difference, or *collective efficacy*. At the intermediate level, they have had individual and organizational supporters with *resources* to contribute to the cause. And at the structural level, advocates have had numerous political *opportunities* to mobilize. These three elements—efficacy, resources, and opportunities—have all come together at least five times between 1963 and 1993, and yet the gun control "movement" failed to emerge in a way that conventional movement theory would have predicted. I refer to these as "movement moments." Typically, these moments have been prompted by a particularly traumatic shooting or wave of gun violence. This is in keeping with Robert Spitzer's observation that the politics of gun control is cyclical, touched off by an event that provokes mass outrage.[13] The movement moments came in 1963, 1968, the early to mid-1970s, the early 1980s, and the late 1980s to early 1990s. They are considered briefly, in turn.

## Movement Moments 1963–1993

### Moment 1: 1963

The first movement moment is, of course, the assassination of President John F. Kennedy on November 22, 1963. The assassination engulfed the nation in sorrow and defined a generation of Americans. Young people, Democrats, and Roman Catholics found special solidarity in the loss of the president. Their shared grief became their collective grievance. After the assassination many Americans wrote letters to Congress protesting the availability of military firearms through the mails, and newspapers alleged a connection between gun violence and the lack of gun control laws. A poll taken seven weeks after the assassination found that 78% of Americans supported mandatory handgun permits.[14] Support was high in all regions of the country: from 72% in the South to 90% in the East.[15] Only 18% opposed such permits, and the fraction of Catholics opposed was even lower, 13%.[16]

Although gun control supporters lacked a single-issue pressure group, they did not lack resources in the broader sense. Because Kennedy's appeal was particularly strong among young people and Catholics, gun control supporters might have tapped colleges and churches for movement resources, as the civil rights movement was doing at that very time. Local police were also ready to take up the cause.[17]

The assassination was a dramatic focusing event that had the potential to translate an increasingly favorable political climate into a true political opportunity. In the early 1960s, foreign-made guns were flooding the U.S. market and being sold by mail-order houses, undercutting the domestic firearms market and alarming congressmen from the New England states, where most domestic manufacturers were located. These Congress members had both electoral incentives and constitutional authority to restrict the international and interstate firearms trade. What's more, the assassination came on the heels of an increase in youth violence, which had been severe enough to spur the creation of a Senate Subcommittee on Juvenile Delinquency in 1953. Carl Bakal noted that, although overall homicide rates had declined, juvenile offenses were on the rise, particularly in the late 1950s.[18] Between 1955 and 1960, the increase in young people arrested for carrying guns was nearly twice as great as the increase in the youthful population.[19] Finally, Congress had built a policy case for stricter firearms laws. Under the leadership of Senator Thomas Dodd (D-Conn.), the Subcommittee on Juvenile Delinquency had spent more than two years conducting a wide-ranging investigation into firearms accessibility and produced the first body of research on firearms markets and gun control laws. "No other firearms bill in our history was based on such extensive research as the measure that was to become known as the Dodd Bill."[20]

The product of the subcommittee's research and hearings was S. 1975, introduced in August 1963, three and a half months before John F. Kennedy's assassination. The bill would have required people wishing to purchase concealable guns by mail to provide a notarized statement that they were over eighteen, that they were not a convicted felon, and that the purchase would not violate state or local gun laws.[21] The bill was amended after the assassination to include not only handguns but rifles and shotguns as well. The Johnson administration and key congressional leaders supported the bill, but Senator Warren Magnuson (D-Wash.), chairman of the Senate Commerce Committee, delayed the measure by holding hearings, thereby giving gun rights supporters time to mobilize. "Members reported receiving mail in the ratio of eight to one in favor of the bill. But the tide changed during and after the hearings with an onslaught of letters against the bill."[22]

On August 11, 1964, the Commerce Committee decided, without a roll-call vote, to postpone action on the Dodd Bill, thereby eliminating any possibility of its passage.[23] According to one observer of the nonvote, "There was an overwhelming sentiment for doing nothing."[24] Dodd attributed the bill's demise to "almost hysterical attempts to kill this legislation" engineered by "a loud and well-organized hard-core minority" using "big lie" strategies.[25] On the other hand, "Dodd failed to stir up a public demand," according to a Senate spokesman.[26] In the aftermath of

Kennedy's assassination, 18 gun control bills were introduced in Congress, and at least 150 were introduced in state legislatures.[27] All had vigorous support from President Johnson. Yet none of the congressional bills passed, and only one state changed its gun laws. The gun rights supporters seemed to perceive, accurately as it turned out, that the hue and cry for gun control would quickly fade as the aroused but unorganized citizens returned to their everyday lives.

### Moment 2: 1968

The next movement moment came in 1968, with the back-to-back murders of two of America's most prominent political leaders: the Reverend Martin Luther King Jr., father of the modern civil rights movement, and Senator Robert F. Kennedy (D-N.Y.), who was campaigning for the job that his slain brother had held. Again, the standard movement model would have predicted collective action. The nation was gripped by grief and outrage, and opinion polls found support for gun control to be at or above 70%, regardless of race or region.[28] Despite the traumas of April and June, Americans were not culturally fatalistic about gun violence. In a survey taken two weeks after Robert Kennedy's assassination, two-thirds of Americans rejected the notion that "we have violence because it is built into our pioneer tradition"; only one in five agreed.[29]

In the year before the 1968 assassinations, a leading magazine had characterized the pro-control forces as "an amorphous, virtually fundless coalition of citizens, clergy, judges, police chiefs, and other public officials."[30] Although they may have lacked a well-funded, single-issue organization, this coalition did not lack movement resources. The first element of the coalition, everyday citizens, possessed time, money, and energy. In 1968 and in the decades to come, gun control drew disproportionate support from white-collar professionals, who were especially rich in these civic resources. The second element, clergy members, had moral, financial, and volunteer resources at their disposal. The third element, judges, had intellectual authority and access to networks of elites. The fourth element, police chiefs, spoke authoritatively on crime issues and oversaw squads of officers who were well organized and politically influential. Finally, public officials could provide movements with resources such as political leadership, policy ideas, grant money, and access to elite networks. All these resourceful constituencies would play a role in the brief burst of gun control activism that followed the 1968 assassinations.

The groundwork for the institutionalization of gun control advocacy was laid in 1967 with the formation of the National Council for a Responsible Firearms Policy. Although cumbersome, the name reflected a calculated decision by the founders to avoid inciting the National Rifle Association;

thus, "responsible firearms policy" sounded less threatening and less political than "gun control."[31] The council's founders included James V. Bennett, who had recently retired after a distinguished thirty-year career as director of the Federal Bureau of Prisons; J. Elliott Corbett, who was head of the United Methodist Church's General Board of Christian Social Concerns, the church's Washington-based social-action wing; and David J. Steinberg, a Washington-based trade policy advocate. All three had had a long-standing interest in gun control. In his career overseeing prisons, Mr. Bennett had become convinced that gun availability encouraged lethal crime and had testified before the Dodd committee in the early 1960s. Mr. Corbett had presided over the Methodist Church's 1965 resolution to support national gun control legislation. Mr. Steinberg had been a one-man "citizens' lobby," testifying before the Dodd panel as a private individual disturbed by a notorious teenage shooting not far from his suburban northern Virginia home in 1962. The council was always a small operation. It had a prestigious board of government officials with expertise in criminal justice, but it never acquired a mass membership. At the time of the 1968 assassinations, it had no chapters. Instead, the council was a group of experienced policy experts focused on changing national laws.

After Robert Kennedy was assassinated, the council proved critical in harnessing and directing the spontaneous and intense desire on the part of many Americans to express their support for gun control. The council's first step was to begin a petition drive. Working through existing networks of churches, voluntary associations, and businesses, the council eventually collected more than one million signatures in less than one month; when Mr. Bennett presented the boxes of petitions to Congress in July, the photo was splashed across the top of the front page of the *New York Times*. The council also provided material support and policy expertise to the Emergency Committee for Gun Control, an effort by Robert Kennedy's aides and supporters to rally public support for the stalled legislation.

The Emergency Committee was chaired by the astronaut John Glenn and made up of more than three dozen women's, religious, law-enforcement, labor, and business organizations. The committee brought together resourceful, politically savvy, idealistic young people united through local and state Kennedy campaign committees and mobilized federated voluntary associations encompassing millions of more seasoned civic organizers. Glenn said the committee would urge the pro-control majority "to send millions of letters and post cards, telegrams and petitions, and make telephone calls and personal visits to the Congress and to the White House."[32] The council's and the Emergency Committee's actions apparently paid off. Newspaper reports at the time showed that key members of Congress who had historically blocked gun control bills had agreed, under a barrage of pro-control mail from constituents, to switch their votes.[33]

Gun control legislation had been introduced in state legislatures and in Congress throughout the 1960s, but the bills had lacked mass pressure for passage. After Robert Kennedy's assassination came the political opportunity for passage. Indeed, two major gun control bills were enacted, the first significant federal firearms statutes in three decades. The 1968 laws, which would be both weakened and strengthened on rare occasions over the next three decades, included the provisions that Senator Dodd had sought since before the first Kennedy assassination, as well as new provisions added by the Johnson administration.

In 1968, national grief, resourceful groups, and political openings came close to producing a national gun control movement. However, the passage of national gun control laws may have undercut the burgeoning movement through a process that Murray Edelman calls "symbolic reassurance."[34] Satisfied with having secured passage of a mild national gun control law, the Emergency Committee closed its doors, thereby casting local and state supporters adrift and agendaless. The council continued to operate until 1989, pushing a more ambitious gun control agenda through congressional testimony, press releases, and letters to the editor. But it never had a full-time staff, a mass base, or more than a few thousand dollars in the bank. Meanwhile, gun rights supporters began almost immediately to press for legislation that would weaken or repeal the 1968 gun control laws, which they viewed as excessive and grossly unfair to law-abiding sportsmen. There was no mass movement to oppose their efforts.

## Moment 3: Early to Mid-1970s

The third movement moment came in the early 1970s, again because of the shooting of high-profile politicians and a run-up in gun-related violence. On May 15, 1972, presidential candidate George Wallace (D-Ala.) was shot and paralyzed from the waist down by a would-be assassin during a campaign stop in Laurel, Maryland. Eight months later, on January 30, 1973, Senator John Stennis (D-Miss.) was shot and seriously wounded in an attempted robbery in front of his house in a fashionable Washington neighborhood. After the Wallace shooting, the major news media devoted considerable attention to the gun control issue. The *New York Times* noted "the spreading terror of political assassination" and the "appalling" level of gun "abuse." The *Times* stated, "There is simply no rational excuse for continued failure to pass effective Federal gun control legislation."[35] Chicago Mayor Richard Daley asked, "When in God's name is Congress going to wake up to the need to outlaw handguns?"[36]

Congress in the early 1970s did not seriously consider any major gun legislation. Then, in 1975, came back-to-back assassination attempts against President Gerald R. Ford. On September 5, while the president was greeting well-wishers outside a hotel in Sacramento, Lynette "Squeaky" Fromme, a follower of the murderous cult leader Charles Manson, aimed a .45-caliber handgun at the president and pulled the trigger at point-blank range; she missed only because the gun misfired and she was tackled to the ground. On September 22 in San Francisco, an unemployed bookkeeper named Sara Jane Moore fired a single shot from a .38-caliber revolver as the president emerged from a downtown hotel; the bullet might have struck him but for the quick action of a former marine who grabbed her arm as she was about to pull the trigger. Representative John Murphy (D-N.Y.) asked, "How many more attempts on the lives of our Presidents must we endure before we enact sane gun control measures?"[37]

On top of assassination attempts, the rate of "ordinary" gun violence continued to climb during the first half of the 1970s. Authoritative accounts blamed the rise on handguns. The rate of murders committed with handguns nearly doubled between 1966 and 1972, and the rate of aggravated assaults with handguns more than doubled.[38] Of particular concern, as evidenced by the political debate, was the increase in police officers shot and killed in the line of duty. An estimated 75% of police officers killed in 1971 were felled by handguns.[39] At the same time, government officials were expressing concern that soldiers from the Vietnam War were unleashing a "veritable flood" of guns into the United States, particularly automatic rifles.[40]

By the beginning of 1975, the nation had reached the highest rate of gun violence ever recorded: 16.1 shooting deaths per 100,000. Included in that figure was the mother of Martin Luther King Jr.; she was gunned down while playing the organ at Sunday morning church services in June 1974. The 1974 death rate attributed to firearms was nearly twice that of twenty years before. The increase was driven mainly by interpersonal violence (as opposed to accidents and suicides). The rate of homicides committed with guns had doubled over ten years, to 7.5 per 100,000. Figure 2.1 shows the spike that peaked in the mid-1970s.

As gun violence rose during the 1970s, opinion polls found a steady increase in the fraction of Americans who were afraid to walk alone near their home.[41] Polls also continued to show support for gun control: 73% of Americans favored a national law requiring registration of all handgun purchases, for example, and 64% said that failing to regulate guns contributes to violence.[42] Three-quarters of Americans agreed that people should have to obtain a police permit before buying a gun.[43]

During this period, the first real burst in gun control organizing took place. It was a period of intensive resource mobilization. Between 1974 and 1976, five national gun control groups were established, including the two that would go on to lead the gun control forces for the next

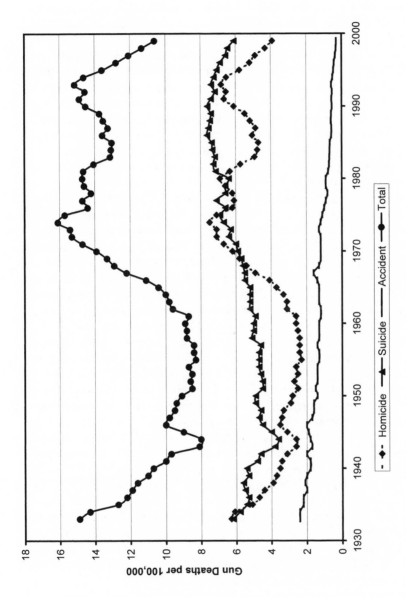

Figure 2.1. Firearms Death Rates, 1933–1999. Sources: 1933–1961 data from Division of Vital Statistics, U.S. Department of Health, Education, and Welfare, cited in Bakal (1968), appendix 3; 1962–1981 data from Centers for Disease Control and Prevention (CDC), cited in Ikeda et al. (1997); data from 1981–1999 derived by the author from CDC's online data retrieval system, WISQUARS. Rates are age-adjusted.

twenty-five years: the National Coalition to Ban Handguns (NCBH) and the National Council to Control Handguns (NCCH), both founded in 1974.[44] In addition, the number of state gun control groups more than doubled in the mid-1970s, from five groups in 1973 to eleven in 1975.[45] Even though they had little money and were run purely by volunteers, these groups had a presence in eight geographically diverse states by 1975. The nascent handgun control movement was also beginning to come together: twenty-four state and national leaders had met in Detroit in 1974 to exchange information for the first time, and leaders would meet again in greater numbers in 1975 in Los Angeles and 1976 in Boston. Not since 1968 had there been such a grassroots surge in organizing for stricter gun laws. Calling together his own advocacy coalition of interest groups and lawmakers in October 1975, Representative Abner Mikva (D-Ill.) noted, "For the first time there is some sense of citizen involvement."[46]

Although their names and initial policy goals were similar, the two leading national groups were quite different in both organizational structure and strategies. NCCH, founded by a newly minted Ph.D. who had been mugged at gunpoint during graduate school in Chicago, was modeled on Common Cause, the self-styled citizens' lobby. NCCH sought individual (as opposed to organizational) members through a massive direct-mail campaign. Like Common Cause, it wanted national regulation that would protect the "public interest" against the "special interests." NCCH engaged in both direct lobbying by staff and board members and grassroots letter writing by the "citizen activists" it had identified in the 435 congressional districts. NCCH was organized as a social-welfare advocacy group under section 501(c)(4) of the Internal Revenue Code, meaning that it could engage in unlimited legislative advocacy but could not receive tax-deductible contributions, including foundation grants, for that work. In terms of strategy, NCCH was singularly devoted to lobbying Congress for strict national gun control, including a ban on civilian handgun possession. NCCH quietly retreated from that position in 1977 or 1978.[47] In 1979, NCCH changed its name to Handgun Control, Inc., and in 1983, it created a sister organization, the Center to Prevent Handgun Violence. The center was organized under section 501(c)3 of the Internal Revenue Code as a public charity focusing on research and education. In 2001, the organizations were again renamed: the advocacy group became the Brady Campaign to Prevent Gun Violence, and the educational arm became the Brady Center to Prevent Gun Violence.[48]

The National Coalition to Ban Handguns, of which NCCH was originally a member, was an association of organizations, not of individuals. It was established at the behest of J. Elliott Corbett, the director of the United Methodist Church's Board of Church and Society. Initially, NCBH included roughly two dozen political, religious, women's, and labor organizations. The group's founding document indicates a decentralized approach to gun control policy. NCBH would, first, try to place handgun-ban initiatives on as many state ballots as possible and, second, would work "in close relationship" with local, state, and national groups to "mobilize their constituencies."[49] NCBH began as a 501(c)(3) educational organization, but it lost its charity status in 1977, becoming a 501(c)(4) advocacy group in that year.

Besides NCCH and NCBH, there was another national organization that would be instrumental in organizing gun control sentiment in the mid-1970s: the U.S. Conference of Mayors. Two years after passing a resolution supporting handgun control, the mayors' organization sought and received private foundation funding for a Handgun Control Project, which ran from late 1974 through 1981. The project had four objectives: "(1) create new leadership on the handgun control issue; (2) educate and stimulate other key organizations and individuals; (3) create an intensive and continuing dialog at the national policy level and at the state and local levels; (4) create a network of organizations which together can influence the attitudes of key policy-makers, opinion leaders, and the general public."[50] During its seven-year existence, the project held several national conferences of handgun control advocates; produced books on gun control laws, policy questions, and organizational strategies; and disseminated a regular newsletter to inform local gun control advocates of developments in other states and in Washington.[51]

Thus, the early to mid-1970s were marked by at least two movement catalysts: shared grievances in the form of rampant gun crime and resourceful organizations poised to lead the gun control campaign. As it turns out, the potential movement also had political opportunities during this era. First, Congress had changed. More than twenty gun rights members had retired or been defeated in the 1974 midterm elections, and the Watergate backlash had swept into office a number of "young Turks" who were more pro-control than the members of Congress whom they had replaced. When the new Congress convened in January, John Conyers, a Democrat who represented the crime-ravaged Detroit area, declared gun control legislation would be the "most urgent" priority of the House Judiciary Committee's newly formed Subcommittee on Crime, which he chaired.[52] Over the course of 1975, Conyers's committee held gun control hearings in seven cities, producing eight volumes of testimony from more than two hundred witnesses. His efforts were well timed. They would produce significant legislative proposals in a nonelection year and thus spare members from having to defend controversial decisions while on the campaign trail.

Second, the White House appeared willing to support certain gun control measures, even as President Ford was reluctant to take a lead role in the political battle. Early in his administration, the president had indicated that he supported limited gun control, including a ban on so-called Saturday night specials, the short-barreled, cheaply made handguns that were prevalent in urban areas. Ford hailed from a state where gun rights supporters were vocal and organized, but as House minority leader he had voted for the 1968 gun control legislation. Gun control supporters were heartened when Edward Levi, president of the University of Chicago, replaced William Saxbe as U.S. attorney general in February 1975. Saxbe had called gun control "another of our idealistic dreams that fails in practice."[53] Levi appeared more optimistic that some sort of gun control would be effective. In July, the White House presented to a Senate subcommittee a proposal to ban Saturday night specials, prohibit federally licensed dealers from selling more than one gun to any given customer, require dealers to increase efforts to verify that would-be buyers were eligible to own a gun, and tighten federal licensing and oversight of gun dealers. It did not include two provisions that Ford opposed—and that would become a central goal of gun control supporters for the next twenty-five years: federal licensing of all gun owners (or at least handgun owners) and national registration of all guns (or handguns).

The day after the second assassination attempt on President Ford, Representative Conyers introduced a bill that would have banned civilian possession of handguns. He said he had not arrived at his proposal lightly but had become convinced that such a ban was necessary.[54] Representative Conyers some months earlier had assumed a milder gun control stance, and he admitted that he did not expect his bill proposing an outright banning of handguns to pass the House. But he said it would be "hypocritical" to propose a bill that would "not deal with the problem."[55] Besides Conyers's own legislation, at least fifty other bills had been introduced to tighten firearms regulation at the national level. "This may be the year when Congress, after years of dispute and compromise, finally passes a law imposing tight nationwide controls over handguns," noted an article in *US News & World Report* magazine.[56] Mr. Conyers's bill failed, as expected, but so did all other gun control bills during the Ninety-fourth Congress.

One could argue that, if a gun control movement were going to emerge at any time in the second half of the twentieth century, 1975 would have been the year. Collective grievances, optimism, resources, and opportunities were clearly plentiful. But the movement did not happen. Instead, the emerging gun control campaign fractured. Decisions made during this time—over policy, strategy, and organization—would undermine the gun control campaign for decades. In many ways, the case of gun control in the 1970s holds the key to understanding both the failure of a gun control movement to arise and the failure of social-movement theories to explain its absence.

*Moment 4: Early 1980s*

The next political opportunity arose in the period from late 1980 through early 1981. In December 1980, one of the world's most famous musicians, John Lennon, was shot to death in front of his New York City home. In March 1981, only two months into his first term, President Ronald Reagan and several in his entourage were shot and critically wounded outside a Washington hotel. Gun-related street crime was also on the rise. The overall rate increased by more than 20% between 1976 and 1981; the gun homicide rate increased by 10%.[57] As in past years, support for gun control remained strong. Roughly 70% of Americans supported mandatory police permits before buying a gun.[58]

By the early 1980s, the national gun control groups had fully institutionalized, and the shootings of Lennon and Reagan added strength to the gun control campaign. After the Lennon killing, the membership of Handgun Control, Inc., increased by 25%, and it saw an increase in giving of close to $200,000.[59] The National Coalition to Ban Handguns also enjoyed substantial increases in members and donations. In Massachusetts, advocates organized Citizens for Handgun Control, which was active until the late 1980s. In addition, in memory of his slain friend, the editor of *Rolling Stone* magazine created the Foundation on Violence in America, which sought to use police officers to change public attitudes toward handgun ownership.[60]

At the same time, the state gun control groups were also trying to organize a movement. In 1979 they had formed the National Alliance of Handgun Control Organizations to facilitate the exchange of information among existing groups and to create new ones.[61] The association included fourteen organizations and held several national meetings in the early 1980s. However, most of the state groups were purely volunteer run; only those in Chicago and Cleveland had any paid staff. Thus, by 1980, the alliance had concluded that its members were not in a position to help create more state or local movement organizations, and by 1983, the alliance had just $257 in the bank and had resolved not to engage in political advocacy.[62] In mid-1983, the alliance and the Chicago Committee for the Study of Handgun Misuse secured a $50,000 matching grant from a private foundation to bring together people concerned about gun violence in several cities, with an eye toward creating "educational" groups to advance the gun control cause.[63]

The political opportunities for gun control at the national level were not favorable, but state and local opportunities abounded. Nationally, the United States was entering a period of conservative ascendance. The month before Lennon had been shot, national elections had handed the White House to a conservative opponent of gun control and had put the

Senate in Republican control. The gun control measures proposed in 1980 by Senator Edward M. Kennedy (D-Mass.), and by Representative Peter Rodino (D-N.J.) in the House, were destined to fade away after Kennedy lost his Judiciary Committee chairmanship to conservative Senator Strom Thurmond (R-S.C.), who was sympathetic to some limited gun control measures but not likely to champion the cause. Equally important, the White House was in the hands of Ronald Reagan, the first presidential candidate ever officially endorsed by the NRA. After his shooting, President Reagan stuck to his anti–gun control stance, arguing that firearms regulations would not have prevented the attempt on his life. A longtime gun control advocate told a reporter, "That knocked the ground out from under us."[64]

As advocates for national legislation despaired, there was considerable momentum at the subnational level. State and local advocates saw openings in the political opportunity structure and pushed for new laws. In 1981, Morton Grove, Illinois, drew national attention when it banned possession of handguns; and in 1982, San Francisco and Chicago outlawed future sales. This momentum, however, did not snowball into a trans–locally rooted gun control movement.

Once again, despite the familiar pattern of high-profile killings, increased crime rates, efforts to mobilize resources, and political openings, no gun control movement emerged in the early 1980s. By 1985, the state-by-state organizing project had stalled, and in 1986, gun rights forces secured the Firearms Owners' Protection Act, a sweeping bill that repealed significant parts of the landmark 1968 gun control law.

### Moment 5: Late 1980s to Early 1990s

The last political opportunity in the three decades after John F. Kennedy's assassination came in the late 1980s and early 1990s. During that period, America witnessed an unprecedented increase in gun-related violence. The firearms homicide rate rose by 40% between 1987 and 1994; the rate of gun-related robberies rose by nearly 30%; and the rate of aggravated assaults with firearms rose by 37%.[65] Journalists and others labeled the uptick an "epidemic" of gun violence, and scholars noted that it was largely concentrated in inner-city areas. On top of the increase in street shootings, the late 1980s and early 1990s featured three particularly noteworthy mass shootings: at a Stockton, California, school playground in January 1989 (five dead, thirty wounded); at a Killeen, Texas, cafeteria in October 1991 (twenty-three dead, twenty-three wounded); and aboard a Long Island Railroad train in December 1993 (six dead, nineteen wounded). A 1993 Harris poll found that 27% of Americans cited crime as "one of the two most important issues for the government to address."[66] Likewise, surveys continued to show high levels of support for stricter firearms regulation.[67]

Gun control also experienced another burst of resource mobilization during this time. From 1993 to 1995, as the seven-year gun violence epidemic was cresting, at least twenty-six state and local gun control groups formed. The national gun control groups by then were well institutionalized, with full-time staffs, paid lobbyists, and sophisticated direct-mail campaigns.

The late 1980s and early 1990s presented national political opportunities for gun control advocates. In response to the mass shootings, in particular at the Stockton playground, there was bipartisan support for restricting access to so-called assault weapons, the military-style firearms that had been used in the mass shootings and were associated with gang warfare. In 1989, the George H. W. Bush administration barred imports of 43 makes and models of foreign-made assault weapons.[68] By 1994, with the Democrats in charge of both houses of Congress and pro-control president Bill Clinton in the White House, federal lawmakers passed a federal ban on the possession or transfer of 175 types of assault weapons manufactured after September 13, 1994. During this time, the Brady Bill, which required a waiting period and background check for purchases of handguns from federally licensed dealers was introduced in both chambers of Congress. In 1990, the House Judiciary Committee approved the Brady Bill, but the bill did not make it to the House floor. In 1991, the bill passed the House and the Senate, but Senate Republicans blocked a vote on the conference report.[69] The bill finally emerged from Congress in 1993 and went into effect in 1994.

The late 1980s and early 1990s provided gun control advocates with the richest set of cultural and political opportunities in at least fifteen years. The media were dramatizing gun violence. Gun control had strong advocates in Congress and, after Bill Clinton's election in 1992, in the White House, as well. National gun control groups secured several significant laws. However, except for the campaign to pass the Brady Bill, there was very little movement for gun control on the ground. State and local groups, while proliferating, were little more than letterhead organizations, run by a handful of dedicated volunteers, often relatives of gun violence victims. These state and local groups had little support from above or coordination among themselves. Many were short lived.

## Movement Moments without a Movement

In the case of gun control, catalytic events, organizations, and opportunities—the necessary formative elements identified by social-movement theory—were present, but the expected movement did not arise from them. In the period from 1963 to 2000, America witnessed countless assassinations and other high-profile shootings—President Kennedy, Dr. King, Senator Robert Kennedy, Senator Stennis, Govenor Wallace, President Ford, President Reagan, John Lennon—and scores of mass shootings in workplaces and schools. The United States also experienced regular epidemics of street violence, fueled by the easy availability of handguns. In response, voluntary organizations formed with increasing regularity to mobilize resources and press for stricter gun laws. Indeed, gun control drew support from a wide range of resourceful and politically powerful organizations: religious denominations, women's associations, labor unions, medical and health associations, law enforcement organizations, and good-government groups. What's more, gun control has always appealed to a particularly resourceful segment of the population: urban and suburban professionals and their families, which have money, networks of powerful friends, access to political elites, and civically useful skills. The civil rights movement was far more vigorous, and accomplished far more, with a far less resourceful issue public.

Gun control organizations likewise had numerous opportunities to break through. As Figure 2.2 makes clear, gun control advocates always had public opinion on their side. During the whole period in question, roughly 70–80% of Americans supported a law requiring people to obtain a police permit before purchasing a gun.

Besides public opinion, gun control advocates never lacked for elite supporters. Presidents Johnson, Ford, Carter, and Clinton supported gun control to varying degrees. Congressional advocates from Thomas Dodd to John Conyers to Edward Kennedy championed the cause. Many governors and most big-city mayors and police chiefs were reliable allies.

Clearly, the conditions favoring a movement's emergence were stronger in some eras (e.g., the early 1970s) than in others (the early 1980s). But the conditions were there nonetheless, if not always at the national level, then certainly at the subnational level. According to standard social-movement theory, gun control long ago should have coalesced into mass, sustained collective action. Instead gun control was, and still is, distinguished by its missing movement. What happened? Most gun control leaders attribute their nonmovement status to factionalization within their ranks, including deep conflicts over personality, donors, philosophy, and tactics. While these divisions may inhibit coordinated action, they are not the primary reason that the gun control "movement" has floundered. All social movements are internally divided. Indeed, as the civil rights and antiabortion movements demonstrate, having many organizations with different structures and strategies is more likely to be movement enhancing than movement constraining. Another theory is that gun control advocates have trouble gaining movement momentum either because the passage of mild national legislation diffuses the sense of urgency—the "symbolic reassur-

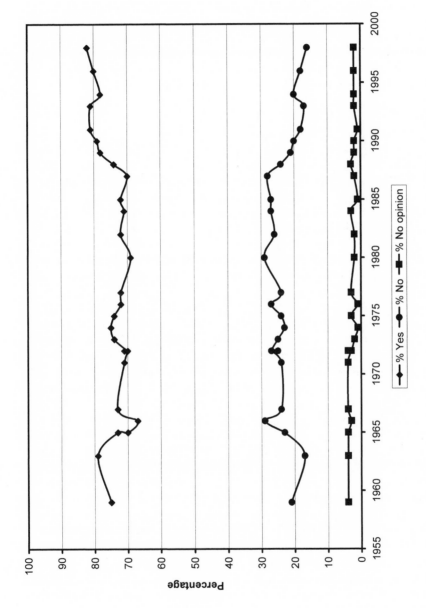

Figure 2.2. Public Support for Gun Permits. Source: General Social Survey, National Opinion Research Center.

ance" argument that Murray Edelman advanced forty years ago—or, on the other hand, because national gun laws are so difficult to pass.

The problem with these explanations is that they leave no room for movements to emerge: Movements cannot emerge when legislation is likely to pass, nor when it is unlikely to pass. The real reasons why the gun control groups have failed to generate a true grassroots movement are considered more fully in the next four chapters, but first we must derive the theory that guides the rest of the book.

## THE COSTS AND BENEFITS OF MASS MOBILIZATION

Freedom from gun violence is a public good, and gun control is a policy approach that many experts believe would further this end. Yet gun control proponents face serious challenges. As a means to securing a public good, gun control is inherently vulnerable to the free-rider problem. Likewise, gun regulation imposes clear costs on a well-organized minority. Gun control also defies America's classical liberal values. Thus, gun control advocates must find a way around problems of individual interest and collective values. How might they surmount these challenges?

To answer that question, I examine three issue campaigns whose advocates have faced similar challenges but have managed to mount sustained, vigorous social movements. To explain their successes in forging movements, I adapt a framework proposed by James Q. Wilson in a slightly different context. In his study of the politics of policy making, Wilson argued that all policies confer benefits and impose costs.[70] Whether those costs and benefits are concentrated or dispersed will determine the nature of the politics surrounding the issue. I borrow Wilson's cost-benefit approach and apply it to participation. Just as policies impose costs and confer benefits, so does mass advocacy for or against those policies. On the cost side, political participation consumes time, money, and emotional reserves; at the same time, it can also provide psychological and practical benefits, both short and long term. However, in the case of public goods, the individual citizen typically perceives the marginal costs of participation as outweighing the marginal benefits flowing from his or her efforts. Thus, the central challenge to issue entrepreneurs who want to mobilize the public is to alter individuals' cost-benefit calculation in a way that will increase the odds of participation. To do so, issue entrepreneurs must turn the cost-benefit calculation on its head, by concentrating the benefits of participation at the individual or small-group level and distributing the costs to the broader society.

There are three principal methods by which this reversal can be achieved. The more that movement leaders can do to achieve the goals of all three at the same time, the more they will succeed in expanding participation. To mobilize around public goods, particularly of the social-regulatory variety, advocates must (1) socialize the costs of participation; (2) personalize the benefits; and (3) boost the subjective likelihood that personal costs will yield social benefits (what I term "increasing the participation payoff," for short). These three strategies are logical responses to the cost-benefit dilemma facing advocates for public goods, particularly those that require behavioral regulation. These strategies are, in a sense, theoretical implications of a theoretical dilemma. In turn, these three implications combine to form a theory of collective action. If the theory is correct, we would expect to see successful pursuit of these three strategies in positive cases (movements) but not in negative cases (nonmovements).

Below, I present cases of movements for social regulation that have arisen not only once but at least twice in post–Civil War America. These cases will serve both as the first test of the theory and as a means of elaborating on it. That is, these cases will illuminate the specific mechanisms by which advocates have socialized costs, personalized benefits, and increased the participation payoff in ways that favored mass mobilization. With a richer understanding of how these issue advocates have accomplished these tasks, the book turns to the gun control issue itself to test the newly elaborated theory against a negative case.

The three positive cases—campaigns against alcohol, smoking, and abortion—involve movements at two points in time: in the late twentieth century and roughly a century earlier. The cases were chosen because they are similar to gun control in three theoretically important respects: (1) each movement championed policy proposals that would regulate individual behavior and hence restrict liberty; (2) each movement faced intense, well-organized, and politically potent opponents; and (3) each movement took on a practice that was widespread and, to its critics, posed a significant social problem. For obvious reasons, the case studies analyzed below are far from exhaustive histories of these movements, but they are faithful renditions. In each case, the presence of collective efficacy, resources, and opportunities is assumed. My aim is simply to demonstrate that these factors do not fully explain how the observed movements formed and flourished. To breathe life into my cost-benefit theory, the issue studies are nested within each theoretical proposition. Here, I illustrate each proposition with a case study from only one of the three issues. Appendix B shows that the theory works for the other two issues, as well.

## STRATEGY 1: SOCIALIZING THE COSTS OF PARTICIPATION

By "socialize," I mean distribute the costs to a larger group or transfer them to an outside entity, such that the individual participant's costs are reduced. Thus, Proposition 1:

Movements for public goods must have *patrons* to socialize the costs of participation.

"Patrons" is a broad term, and intentionally so. Patronage support can come from three categories of sources: (1) the state; (2) voluntary membership associations (e.g., social clubs and churches); and (3) individual or organized philanthropy. Patronage can take many forms: authoritative research, policy or political expertise, coalition leadership, volunteers, and legitimacy (a "seal of approval"). Of course, the most important form of patronage is money.

In an important study of public interest groups, Jack Walker and his colleagues found that those linked to social movements typically "were created by political entrepreneurs operating with the support of wealthy individuals, private foundations, or elected political leaders who act as their protectors, financial supporters, and patrons."[71] Patrons "provide the crucial seed money needed to mount the expensive campaigns required to convince thousands of people to affiliate with these fledgling organizations."[72] In effect, institutional patrons subsidize the costs of individual membership, thereby allowing groups to claim a large following without having to provide costly material incentives to achieve it. With institutional patronage, public-good organizations can attract members at little cost and thereby train organizational resources on the social-change project at hand. "Patrons stand at the center of a common solution to [the] collective goods dilemma."[73]

### State Patronage: The Antismoking Movement

The state has long been recognized as a solution to the collective-action problem.[74] Typically, this means that the state coerces resources from individuals so that it may supply public goods—for example, drafting individuals into the army to provide for the common defense. But recent research has shown that the state has a less coercive, more facilitative role in resolving collective-action dilemmas, as well. The state has supported, even catalyzed, movements for social reform by sponsoring and disseminating authoritative research, offering expert leadership, providing financial subsidies, and convening outside issue advocates for coordinated political action.

The central involvement of the state in forming and nurturing collective action is a function of the growth of the state itself, particularly since the early 1960s. Government at the national and state levels was more extensively involved in social welfare and social regulation in the early twenty-first century than it was fifty or one hundred years before. With the increases in the scope and complexity of government responsibilities has evolved a professionalized bureaucracy filled with issue advocates. The antismoking movement illustrates the central role that state patronage has played in socializing the costs of issue advocacy.[75]

The political battle over smoking policy has been at root a battle over state patronage. Beginning in the 1960s, antismoking activists had two chief goals: to remove state patronage of pro-tobacco interests and to secure that state patronage for the antismoking cause. In both cases, they were largely successful. The transfer of state resources to the antismoking side allowed it to nearly eliminate smoking in enclosed public places, recast cigarette consumption as an aberrant behavior, and help cut by half the fraction of Americans who regularly light up.[76] The breadth (and success) of the modern antismoking movement owes as much to the transfer of state patronage as to any other factor.

From 1890 to 1930, fifteen states banned the sale, manufacture, possession, and use of cigarettes, and at least twenty-two other states and territories pondered such bills.[77] The U.S. Supreme Court gave its blessing to such laws in 1900, when it voted to uphold a Tennessee cigarette ban. However, the Progressive Era antismoking movement foundered with America's entry into World War I, when the tobacco growers were given an unexpected infusion of state patronage. The U.S. government provided members of the armed forces with cigarette rations and encouraged soldiers to smoke to stay calm and out of trouble. "As the single greatest tobacco buyer in the world, the American government shipped an average of 425 million cigarettes a month to France alone. . . . During the last nine months of the war, the entire production of Bull Durham—the most popular roll-your-own brand—was consigned to the Subsistence Division of the War Department."[78] The connection between state-supported smoking and the decline of the antismoking movement was clear: "The *New York Times* . . . did not carry a single item on the activities or pronouncements of anticigarette groups during 1918. Instead the *Times* reported activities of citizen groups that sent cigarettes to soldiers, and they carried statements by army personnel on the need for tobacco."[79]

State provision of cigarettes to soldiers continued through World War II, the Korean conflict, and the Vietnam War. In addition, since 1933, the federal government has provided subsidies to tobacco farmers, allowing them to stay profitable even as the demand for their products declined; in 2000, the subsidy totaled $340-million.[80] Thus, the challenge to antismoking advocates was, not only to win over legislators and other potential state patrons, but also to end the government's deeply entrenched, decades-long support for cigarette companies and tobacco farmers.

By the time it began to coalesce in the late 1960s, the antismoking movement could count on the patronage of at least two federal agencies: the Office of the Surgeon General and the Federal Trade Commission. In 1964 a surgeon general's report, synthesizing seven thousand articles about smoking and disease, declared, "Cigarette smoking is a health hazard of sufficient importance in the United States to warrant appropriate remedial action." The report was ranked as one of the top news stories of the year.[81] The next year, Congress passed a law that would lay the groundwork for state support of antismoking activists. The law (1) created a National Clearinghouse for Smoking and Health to assemble research and data and educate the public about the link between smoking and disease; (2) required official government health warnings, albeit mild ones, on cigarette packages; and (3) demanded that the Department of Health, Education, and Welfare submit annual reports to Congress on the health hazards of smoking. As Richard Kluger noted, "for the first time, the federal government had acted against the perils of cigarette smoking."[82]

Although the Federal Cigarette Labeling and Advertising Act of 1965 did not provide direct financial support to the antismoking movement—which did not even exist at that time—the law did offer valuable resources to the movement as it developed in the coming years. By requiring warning labels, the government in effect subsidized the antismoking movement's public-education costs. Through legal coercion, cigarette companies were required to put a "don't smoke" message in front of the target audience of smokers. More important, in creating a federal advocacy office and requiring authoritative annual reports from the surgeon general, the law subsidized the antismoking movement's information-gathering and dissemination costs for decades to come. Antismoking groups needed only to cite the federal findings, which had the sort of credibility that no interest group could produce and, on top of that, were disseminated at taxpayer expense. The law created governmental advocates with a more or less steady income stream. These government advocates in turn provided authoritative information to movement groups, thereby freeing them from research and dissemination so that resources could be used on other movement activities. It is hard to overstate the role of the annual surgeon general's reports, in particular, in providing moral and material support to the antismoking movement.

As time passed, indirect forms of patronage expanded to include more direct support, not only at the national level but at the state and local levels, as well. In 1988, California voters passed Proposition 99, which raised cigarette taxes by twenty-five cents per pack, producing "$150 million to educate state residents on the perils of smoking and help them quit—a figure fifty times as high as the total for those purposes in the other forty-nine states."[83] With this tax subsidy, three hundred public health advocates provided training and oversight for local antismoking programs in all fifty-eight counties and one thousand school districts.[84] Tax dollars also directly subsidized mass participation. In 1990, the pro-industry Tobacco Institute complained, "Using state allocated Prop 99 funds earmarked for anti-smoking purposes, local governments create citizens committees designed to further the stated goal of a smoke-free society by the turn of the century. More often than not these committees come back to their city councils or boards of supervisors with a proposed smoking ordinance."[85] With Proposition 99 funds, the state also sponsored a year-long, $30-million advertising campaign involving hundreds of media outlets.[86] Massachusetts followed with its own ad campaign that was so successful it was syndicated nationally. As Richard Kluger concludes, "The smoking control movement, starved for funding nationwide and surviving through the dedication of a handful of workers, suddenly found itself awash in California gold."[87] In 2001, the states distributed $218 million from tobacco excise taxes to support antismoking initiatives run by state agencies and social-movement groups.

The antismoking movement also benefited from direct federal support. In 1991, the National Cancer Institute, part of the National Institutes of Health, began the American Stop Smoking Intervention Study for Cancer Prevention (ASSIST), bringing "federal involvement in tobacco control advocacy to a new level."[88] Done in cooperation with the nonprofit American Cancer Society, the project cost $165 million over seven years and provided funds to seventeen states. During the first year of ASSIST, states reported a 250% increase in spending on tobacco control.[89] As Mark Wolfson's study of Minnesota suggests, much of that money went to grassroots organizations, such as local chapters of Americans for Nonsmokers Rights, the American Lung Association, and the Smoke-Free Coalition.[90] Wolfson concludes that federal agencies—such as the National Cancer Institute, the Centers for Disease Control, and the Center for Substance Abuse Prevention in the Department of Health and Human Services—"provide funding for literally hundreds of state and local coalitions involved in tobacco control advocacy."[91] In addition to providing funding, the federal government assisted the Minnesota antismoking movement by (1) sponsoring and producing scientific knowledge; (2) devising movement tactics and promoting their use; and (3) helping movement organizations to develop effective political strategies.[92]

Finally, and perhaps most significantly, the antitobacco movement saw an infusion of state patronage as a result of the settlement of lawsuits brought by the states to recoup the Medicaid costs of treating smoking-related illnesses. Through the Master Settlement Agreement, which covered forty-six states, and individual settlements with the remaining four states, the major tobacco companies agreed to pay an estimated $246 billion over twenty-five years. The states were to use the money for smoking-prevention programs, many of which would be run by social-movement organizations. For example, Mississippi used its $62 million in settlement funds to create a nonprofit organization, the Partnership for a Healthy Mississippi, which included hundreds of state government agencies, churches, medical associations, and voluntary associations.[93] In addition, the settlement provided $1.45 billion to create a national nonprofit, the American Legacy Foundation, which has run antitobacco advertisements and provided millions of dollars to community groups to develop antismoking programs. In 2001, the states spent $655 million from the settlement money on antismoking programs.[94]

Based on the tobacco-control case, Wolfson argues that the social-movement literature's "depiction of 'the state' as a passive target, separate from the movement, is misleading."[95] Far from being passive targets, his case study suggests, "[s]ubdivisions of the state are often active participants—even collaborators, and sometimes instigators—in the movement's efforts to obtain desired changes in public policy."[96] In Wolfson's account, government agencies and social-movement organizations were locked in a relationship of "interpenetration" rather than mere facilitation. In particular, federal and state government agencies financed and disseminated scientific studies on smoking's adverse effects, trained and advised private antismoking advocates in successful strategies, and offered direct monetary support to antismoking groups.[97] Even when the state money and expertise went to buttress voluntary-sector educational programs, as opposed to legislative advocacy, these patronage resources nonetheless helped the political side of the movement to expand by influencing public opinion and social norms.

Why is state patronage important? Because of their power to tax, states typically command resources not available to organizations forced to rely on voluntary support. States have money. Likewise, because budgets are sticky, state funds are reliable. Once started, patronage is unlikely to end abruptly. State patronage also serves a signaling function. State support legitimizes a cause and thereby allows it to attract additional resources, including media attention, political support, private donations, and volunteer labor. In sum, whether supporting or leading social-change efforts, the state is an important ally. Issue advocates thus should be expected to cultivate relationships with state officials, while opponents will try to undermine those relationships.

### Associational Patronage: The Antiabortion Movement

Scholars have long appreciated the role that voluntary associations play in social movements. Indeed, in the traditional "resource mobilization" model of social movements, the resources that were mobilized came from voluntary groups.[98] However, traditional social-movement theories do not fully explore how and why voluntary associations generate patronage resources for social movements. I suggest that associations are important social-movement benefactors because they have social-capital resources that can be easily diverted to political causes.

To understand how social capital can be turned to political action, it is necessary to understand where voluntary associations get their civic resources in the first place. James Q. Wilson proposed that people join membership associations to obtain material, solidary, or purposive benefits.[99] Material benefits are tangible goods that enhance economic or professional well-being; solidary benefits are "intangible rewards created by the act of associating"; and purposive benefits are "intangible rewards that derive from the sense of satisfaction of having contributed to the attainment of a worthwhile cause."[100] Material and solidary benefits appeal to people's self-interest, while purposive benefits appeal to people's sense of altruism. People most readily respond to material and solidary incentives, and so many successful voluntary associations have been built on those appeals. But once members have paid their dues, associations turn these resources toward purposive goals that are of interest to the members. Theda Skocpol has demonstrated empirically how associations oriented around the provision of material and solidary incentives, especially veterans' and women's groups, have profoundly influenced the political agenda and social policy.[101] I refer to the diversion of material and social resources toward political activity as "associational cross-subsidies." This concept is similar to Mancur Olson's "byproduct theory" of collective action.[102]

The modern antiabortion movement provides a vivid example of patronage through associational cross-subsidies. In this case, the donor association has been organized religion, a network of voluntary associations (churches) that individuals join for reasons other than political activity. In the case of the antiabortion movement, the organizational subsidies came first from the Roman Catholic Church and later from evangelical Protestant denominations, as well. Indeed, one key to the movement's vigor and staying power is the ability of religious leaders to bundle millions of altar-plate contributions into patronage grants.

The modern antiabortion movement began in earnest after the Supreme Court's 1973 Roe v. Wade ruling, which found a constitutional right to abortion, subject to certain conditions. Kristin Luker argues that the ruling "shocked and horrified" abortion opponents, particularly Catholic professionals situated in institutions such as Catholic voluntary associations, professional groups, universities, and church organizations.[103] Within six months of the ruling, the National Conference of Catholic Bishops had created the National Right to Life Committee (NRLC), which grew to fifty state chapters and three thousand local affiliates. "Since that time the Catholic church has been a major financial contributor both to the NRLC and its individual state affiliates."[104] The NRLC, including its educational and electioneering arms, had a combined budget of $16.5 million in the early 2000s.[105] Although the pro-life movement has many organizations, the NRLC is widely considered the strongest, most influential, and best organized among them.[106]

In his study of the pro-life movement in three states, Ziad Munson finds that church organizations serve as patrons at the subnational level, as well.[107] Individual churches hold special fund-raising drives for pro-life organizations, provide meeting space for movement organizations, distribute pro-life advocacy materials during church services, include pro-life information in newsletters and bulletins, and allow pro-life groups to recruit during church services. Perhaps more important, individual churches and ministry associations provide seed money to create social-movement organizations themselves. Although the role of churches should not be overstated—many priests and pastors who are sympathetic to the pro-life cause stay away from it because it is controversial—there is little doubt that "the pro-life movement has been rooted in church institutions."[108]

Voluntary associations provide important political resources. These groups encompass large numbers of civically skilled, politically engaged, and generally like-minded individuals—a particularly resourceful slice of the "latent public." Although they may not lead a movement on a given issue, they command forces that, when engaged, have the potential to generate precisely the sort of action that influences elected officials: letters, protest marches, media coverage, interpersonal suasion, campaign contributions, and voting decisions. In contemporary terms, associations have the potential to turn social capital into political power. Thus, the extent to which incipient movements expand may hinge on the availability and health of mass-based, multipurpose voluntary associations.

### Philanthropic Patronage

In his important study of interest-group formation, Jack Walker notes: "One of the most important reasons for the rapid increase in the total number of groups and the increasing prominence of citizen groups during the 1960s and 1970s was the emergence of many new patrons of political action who were willing to support efforts at social reform."[109] Walker supports these arguments with data showing that philanthropic foundations were an important source of start-up funding for what he called "citizen sector" organizations and that foundations contributed to a lesser extent to groups' ongoing operations. By 2003, there were an estimated sixty-five thousand grant-making foundations in America, and they give away nearly $30 billion in that year.[110] However, federal law explicitly limits, and in most cases proscribes, the sort of philanthropic patronage that social-movement organizations most need: money for political advocacy. Philanthropic foundations are recognized under section 501(c)(3) of the Internal Revenue Code, meaning that they are legally classified as charitable organizations. This alone would severely limit their involvement in advocacy campaigns, but foundations also are subject to separate constraints under the Tax Reform Act of 1969. Under that law, foundations cannot provide money for legislative advocacy, either direct lobbying of lawmakers or grassroots mobilization efforts aimed at legislative change. Nor can foundations get involved in electoral campaigns. The legal framework thereby shifts private patronage resources away from overtly political projects and toward those legally classified as "charitable."

However, even as tax laws constrain overtly political grant making, these laws do not entirely deprive social-movement organizations of private patronage. Foundations can provide money for certain activities that social-movement organizations commonly pursue: litigation, development of sympathetic policy research, and dissemination of cause-friendly information ("public education"). Thus, the now-defunct DeRancé foundation spent at least $1.3 million on pro-life movement activities in the early 1980s.[111] The New Jersey–based Robert Wood Johnson Foundation allocated $426 million through mid-2004 to the antismoking cause, including $70 million in start-up funding for one of the major social-movement organizations, the Campaign for Tobacco-Free Kids.[112] In an earlier era, industrialists such as John D. Rockefeller, Cornelius Vanderbilt, and J. P. Morgan underwrote the monthly magazines of the National Temperance Society, which sought to convert individual drinkers to sobriety.[113]

Financing nonpolitical movement activities is perfectly acceptable under the law, but in many issue areas, resources are limited. This is so because most movements—especially those that seek to regulate individual liberty—are controversial, and foundations labor under a policy legacy that has inhibited their involvement in politically contentious issues. The Tax Reform Act of 1969 has been described as "a traumatic event in foundation history" that created a climate in which "fear of congressional hearings and new restrictions is part of the collective DNA of the foundation community, passed on as a cautionary tale to successive generations of program officers."[114] The 1969 act had a chilling effect on philanthropic foundations, leading them to concentrate their resources in areas where there was broad public consensus. As a result, controversial issues, those most likely to foment a social movement, were unlikely to benefit in meaningful ways from philanthropic patronage.

The legal constraints on philanthropic patronage have two results. First, and most obviously, they limit the pool of financial resources available to mobilize citizens politically for collective goods. And, second, tax laws encourage nonprofit organizations to restructure their priorities based on the availability of funds—that is, to shun political activities in favor of charitable activities such as public education programs. In these ways, the structure of U.S. tax laws actually encourages the depoliticization of social change. Thus, far from helping to solve free-rider problems associated with advocacy for public goods, the legal regimen actually may exacerbate the organizational difficulties by providing incentives for activities other than collective political action. Although philanthropic patronage may have an impact in certain strategic respects—and is thus important to this study—its role in movement formation may exist more in theory than in reality.

## Strategy 2: Personalizing the Benefits of Participation

To mobilize citizens, issue advocates must make the issue hit home. As Jane Mansbridge observes, "If an organization has no effective means of coercion at its disposal, it can try to link the public good to an individual good."[115] Causing individuals to see a public good as an individual good involves three steps. First, the issue must be constructed such that individuals *recognize* the problem that the public good would ameliorate. Second, individuals must feel *entitled* to get involved in the policy battle to secure the public good. And third, individuals must feel *obligated* to act. Thus, Proposition 2:

> Movements for public goods must *frame* the issue to transform diffuse public interest into compelling, actionable self-interest.

Henry Brady has perceptively noted that "most people get involved in politics because they care about some issue or cause, but most models of participation give short shrift to issues."[116] Thus, to understand mass mobilization we must first understand what causes people to care enough to overcome the natural free-rider impulse. Economic interest is one answer, but many of the most salient policy debates in America revolve around noneconomic considerations such as identity, justice, morality, or security.[117] In such cases, where self-interest is not readily quantifiable, the policy debate is more amenable to what Joseph Gusfield calls the "social construction" of problems.[118] As he wisely observes:

> Human problems do not spring up, full-blown and announced, into the consciousness of bystanders. Even to recognize a situation as painful requires a system for categorizing and defining events. All situations that are experienced by people as painful do not become matters of public activity and targets for public action. Neither are they given the same meaning at all times by all peo-

ples. "Objective" conditions are seldom so compelling and so clear in their form that they spontaneously generate a "true" consciousness.[119]

Thus, issue entrepreneurs must construct the problem. But they also must construct self-interest. Problems may dictate that someone should care; collective-action frames tell us who and why. Frames make the threat personal and legitimize involvement, creating what Gusfield calls "ownership" of those problems.[120] But constructing the problem and constructing self-interest are not enough. The final challenge to movement entrepreneurs is to frame issues so as to (1) compel action (2) from a broad and politically important swath of the population (3) over a sustained time period. As Mark Moore notes,

> Ideas simultaneously establish the assumptions, justifications, purposes, and means of public action. In doing so, they simultaneously authorize and instruct different sectors of the society to take actions on behalf of public purposes. The ideas create a reason for someone to take action by setting out the public value or necessity of the act and by giving the action a social meaning that is accessible to both the person who takes the action and others who are its audience or object. In this way ideas both motivate and direct action.[121]

Different scholars have used different terms to describe what I have called collective-action frames: master frames;[122] issue images;[123] public ideas;[124] value connection, value conversion, and value creation;[125] problem definition;[126] and causal stories.[127] No matter which term is used, the assumption is the same: The rhetorical construction of an issue affects who participates politically around the issue, how intensively, and for how long. As Roger Cobb and Charles Elder argue: "Whether or not the scope of a conflict will be expanded will depend in large measure upon the definition of the issues involved."[128] Indeed, Frank Baumgartner and Bryan Jones assert that *"mobilization typically occurs through a redefinition of the prevailing policy image."*[129]

Those who want the government to regulate individual behavior face formidable obstacles, notably that the United States is culturally and institutionally predisposed toward a small state and against policies that restrict individual freedom. Proponents of social regulation therefore must blunt the Lockean liberal assumption by persuading the middle American that social regulation is in his self-interest and consistent with his political-cultural values. Different master frames may resonate in different social, political, and historical contexts.[130] But at least two have proved to be perennially capable of clearing the cultural and institutional hurdles of a classical liberal state: promoting capitalism and protecting children. These frames work because they link a cause to traditional social roles—for men, productive work in the formal economy, and for women, family caretaking. The more prominent is the child-protection frame, which is effective for several reasons. Because children by definition lack maturity, their protection is considered a legitimate state function. As symbols of the nation's future, children make an effective rallying cry, particularly in times of national anxiety over the country's direction. Finally, because innocent children enjoy sentimental affection, bad events always inspire more political passion when they happen to children than to adults. Framing issues in terms of children's welfare is advantageous because most politically active adults are also parents who are concerned about their children and primed to act politically on their behalf.

### Framing: The Movements against Alcohol Abuse

At two points, roughly a century apart, Americans have mobilized against the perils of alcohol consumption. The first movement, which unfolded roughly from the 1870s to the 1910s, culminated in a constitutional amendment prohibiting alcohol sales and possession. The second movement, which unfolded in the 1980s and 1990s, culminated in scores of strict state laws against drunk driving and a revolution in social norms. Even though these movements took place in vastly different eras, in both cases issue entrepreneurs invoked child welfare themes to broaden their appeal and mobilize middle America. In the case of Prohibition, advocates invoked a secondary theme of economic productivity.

The Prohibition movement began in earnest in December 1873, when women in Washington Court House, Ohio, converged on various saloons and demanded that the tavern keepers surrender their alcohol. Over the next year, the women's crusades spread to 911 communities in thirty-one states and the District of Columbia, with somewhere between 56,000 and 150,000 women participating.[131] Their demands were varied: They asked drinkers to take abstinence pledges; they asked saloon keepers to shut down; and they asked local elected officials to enforce antidrinking ordinances and to revoke liquor licenses.[132] The crusades led to the creation of the Woman's Christian Temperance Union (WCTU), which grew to 2,580 local unions in forty-two states over the next decade.[133] One historian notes that the crusades "gave women the lead in temperance, and they held it for two decades."[134]

What enabled this movement of women to emerge? There is little evidence that alcoholism was spiraling out of control during this period. To be sure, beer consumption was increasing, but consumption of hard liquor was waning.[135] Some scholars have suggested that the Prohibition movement was largely an effort by native-born, middle-class, rural and small-town Protestants to maintain their social prestige by suppressing urban, working-class, non-Protestant immigrants.[136] However, feminist historians have reached a very different conclusion: Far from being "symbolic crusades," as Joseph Gusfield termed them, the temperance and Prohibition movements represented cross-class efforts to stop the very real effects that alcohol misuse was having on families and the economy.[137] What made the movements possible was political entrepreneurs who were able to frame private behavior as a public problem in terms that were consonant with widely shared values and capable of mobilizing well-organized groups.

The founder of the women's crusades was Eliza Jane Thompson, a fifty-seven-year-old Ohio woman whose son had died in an asylum for drunkards (as alcoholics were then called). She and the leaders who followed in her footsteps drew on what Ruth Bordin calls the "doctrine of spheres" to legitimize and compel women's involvement.[138] The male sphere was that of economic provision; the female sphere was that of safeguarding the home and protecting family virtue. In an age when women had no independent sources of income and few legal rights, male alcoholism posed a grave threat to the family and thus was a legitimate target for female activism. In connecting private misfortune to public action, the temperance leader Frances Willard argued for a "politics of the mother heart" and later championed female political empowerment under the banner of a "home protection ballot."[139] Such appeals were effective. Tennessee, which had rejected Prohibition through referendum, became effectively dry once the issue was framed in terms of child protection: State lawmakers in 1877 passed legislation barring liquor sales within four miles of a school.

The Anti-Saloon League, a church-based antialcohol organization that worked closely with the WCTU, agreed that the maternal frame was effective and took it to a new level. Decades of temperance agitation had softened up the public, and the league's job was to translate opinion into action by framing liquor interests as an evil force that caused wife beating, divorce, poverty, and child labor.[140] The league's prolific publishing house produced pamphlets with titles such as *The Saloon as the Enemy of the Child*, *Why Babies Die*, and *The Saloon as the Enemy of the Home*.[141] In one pamphlet, the league said, "The saloons of New Jersey are annually sending thousands of our youths to destruction."[142] In another, the league called saloons the club "that empties the workman's bag; And leaves the wife a bone and rag; That takes the schoolbook from the boy."[143] The league urged women and children to go to polling places and beg voters, "for God's sake don't vote for whiskey."[144] In 1916, the league asked each state affiliate to create a Department of Safety, Health and Child Welfare.[145] Introducing a Prohibition amendment in the U.S. Congress, Representative Richmond P. Hobson of Alabama intoned, "What is the object of this resolution? It is to destroy the agency that debauches the youth of the land and thereby perpetuates its hold upon the Nation."[146]

With the repeal of Prohibition in 1933, the antialcohol forces became dormant. Over the next several decades, the "alcohol issue" came to be owned by medical professionals, who developed the disease model of alcohol misuse. Medical professionals argued that alcoholism was a private medical problem that was more amenable to professionally administered treatment regimens than to coercive public policies. Framing alcohol misuse in technical-expert terms helped to drive middle-American antialcohol advocates underground, at least until the 1980s. Then, they seized on a new way of defining the alcohol problem: drunk drivers who kill children.

In May 1980, Cari Lightner, a thirteen-year-old California girl, was hit and killed by an intoxicated driver who was on probation for previous drunk-driving offenses. Cari's mother, Candy, a part-time real-estate agent, was outraged that drunk driving was treated with such lenience. Three months after her daughter's death, frustrated by legislators' refusal to consider her appeals, she founded a voluntary association, Mothers Against Drunk Drivers (MADD). Craig Reinarman notes that the anti-drunk-driving movement was not spurred by a sudden rise in alcohol-related accidents. "On the contrary, all [participants studied] claim that their work arose from the fact that the injustices attributed to drinking-driving have long been a problem and have never been treated seriously by legislatures and courts."[147]

Through skillful framing, MADD quickly became one of the largest and most respected social-movement organizations in America. Within five years, the group had 375 chapters, run mostly by women. Within seven years, a poll found that, more than any other issue, drunk driving was what Americans cared enough about to get personally involved.[148] MADD was instrumental in getting a national law passed in 1984 that raised the drinking age to twenty-one and, perhaps more important, in securing tougher drunk-driving laws in all fifty states in the four years leading up to the national action.[149] Between 1982 and 2002, the number of people killed in alcohol-related accidents dropped by one-third.[150]

The National Highway Traffic Safety Administration, which provided considerable patronage support to MADD, held that the mothers provided the "missing link" in the movement by supplying "a symbolism, an imagery, and a dramatic focus" to the problem.[151] Candy Lightner created a movement by reframing the issue. Instead of accepting drunk driving as a law enforcement issue, MADD made it a mothers' issue. A 1985 survey found that 87% of MADD chapter presidents, and 85% of chapter officers, were women; and most had had at least some college education and held a professional or managerial job.[152] Thus, Lightner had seized on a frame that not only would attract lots of people but would also attract people with civic skills and resources.

In MADD's reframing of the alcohol problem, children once again were the victims of dangerous adults. Although the group was created in response to the death of a child, and dominated by middle-class mothers, MADD's policy goals were implicitly broader than merely saving children. Everyone, young and old alike, stood to benefit from having fewer inebriated drivers on the road. In fact, in Frank Weed's 1985 survey of chapter officers, nearly three-quarters were neither a victim nor related to a victim of a drunk driver; only 10% had lost a child to drunk driving.[153] Yet by appealing to Americans' concern for child welfare, the movement against drunk driving found a mobilizing wedge that allowed it to secure the support of many issue publics for state and national legislation, even when opposed by powerful beer and liquor interests.

To understand why social movements do or do not form, our subjective interpretation of circumstances is as important as the circumstances themselves. How issues are defined and how causal stories are constructed powerfully affect the width, depth, and length of political mobilization. Issue frames that can tap into middle-American values and anxieties are more likely to mobilize masses of people than are frames couched in technical or expert terms. Thus, when issues can be credibly linked to furthering child welfare, they stand an above-average chance of surmounting America's cultural and institutional obstacles to behavioral regulation.

STRATEGY 3: BOOSTING THE PARTICIPATION PAYOFF

Because people are more likely to participate when they have a sense of individual or collective efficacy,[154] movement leaders must persuade sympathizers that their efforts will make a difference. In more formal terms, social-movement leaders must provide a credible case that an individual expenditure of time or money (personal cost) will increase the probability of a socially beneficial outcome (social benefit). Thus, Proposition 3:

> Movements for public goods must move in *incremental* steps, allowing for the accretion of small wins and creating the impression that participation pays off.

Incrementalism refers to small policy steps that might be expected to aggregate toward ever larger political goals. There are two types of policy incrementalism that increase the probability of momentum at the organizational level, and therefore of efficacy at the individual level. I label them *vertical incrementalism* and *horizontal incrementalism*. Vertical incrementalism refers to the process of making policy at lower levels, and allowing those successes to influence policy making at higher levels. Vertical incremenalism is particularly suited to federalist systems, in which policy-making authority is decentralized—vested in neighborhood, municipal, county, and state units, with national units the last resort in most cases. Frank R. Baumgartner and Bryan D. Jones note that issue advocates often move among levels of government—different "policy venues" —to find the most sympathetic decision-making audience.[155] Baumgartner and Jones conclude that "dramatic changes in policy outcomes are often the result of changes in the institutions that exert control."[156] Vertical incrementalism is the concept that underlies calls for "grassroots movements," "state laboratories," and "letting a thousand flowers bloom." Horizontal incrementalism refers to the slow accretion of new regulations onto an existing body of law. To work politically, incremental policies should allow for, even beg for, amendments that are on the path toward advocates' ultimate policy goal. That is, horizontal incrementalism is inherently instrumental, with each mobilizing project representing a logical step in a long-term policy-making process. The regulatory framework can grow along two key dimensions: scope and severity. Scope refers to the number of parties affected; severity refers to the costs imposed on those affected by the policy. Incremental policy making typically involves marginal changes that are portrayed by their partisans as mere corrections to flaws in existing laws. Indeed, John Kingdon found that policy elites viewed incrementalism "not as a description of the way the world is but as a strategy that one might use to manipulate outcomes."[157] Horizontal incrementalism is embodied by phrases such as "plugging loopholes," "small wins," and "the camel's nose under the tent."

Standing in contrast to incremental strategies are what I refer to as "rational national" strategies.[158] Rational strategies promote policies that are strict and comprehensive. National strategies promote laws to be passed by Congress or executive orders to be issued by the president. Both approaches are rooted in unassailable policy logic. The rational strategy assumes that, because bad guys will look for loopholes, laws must be all-encompassing. The national approach recognizes that, because people and products move freely among jurisdictions, only national laws can prevent weak-regulation jurisdictions from undermining the efforts of strong-regulation jurisdictions.

In their hearts, social-movement leaders favor rational-national policies. As Jane Mansbridge notes, movement volunteers often "would rather lose fighting for a cause they believe in than win fighting for a cause they feel is morally compromised."[159] While the preference for policy purity makes sense from a moral and intellectual standpoint, the rational-national strategy is poorly suited to the practical exigencies of the American political system. Consistent with the framers' desire to prevent tyranny, the U.S. system distributes power among local, state, and national governments; divides authority among a legislative, executive, and judicial branch at each level; and contains multiple veto points. By so diluting power, the U.S. system is rigged to stymie bold policy proposals and frustrate social reformers. Thus, they must discover a strategy that can deliver "rational national" policies but in a way that respects political reality.

Incrementalism is that strategy. First, it offers meaningful opportunities for locally rooted collective action and a reasonable chance of political success, thereby generating individual efficacy and organizational momentum. Thus, incrementalism builds movement capacity. Second, incremental policy victories send valuable signals to elected officials about public preferences, thereby reducing legislators' reluctance to act. Third, incrementalism allows policy innovations and political strategies to spread from one jurisdiction to another, broadening participation. Finally, as other movement leaders have learned, incremental policies build political constituencies. Once people are comfortable with some limited amount of regulation, a little bit more doesn't seem so threatening. Elected officials, seeking to consolidate their power and electoral security, do not like to take risks; neither do American citizens, who are socialized to be wary of elite "solutions." Incrementalist policy approaches reduce the perception of risk and create logical precedents for further policy making. Indeed, mustering a well-organized, broad-based social movement dedicated to incremental policy strategies may be the only way to trump the passionate concentrated interests that typically oppose social regulation and public goods.

## Incrementalism: Movements Against Alcohol, 1850–2000

The late-nineteenth- and the late-twentieth-century movements against alcohol, considered together, stand as the quintessentially illustrative case of both horizontal and vertical incrementalism. Temperance leaders, and their anti-drunk-driving counterparts more than a century later, immediately saw the movement-building potential of proceeding step by step. To be sure, there were rational-national strategies unfolding simultaneously—creating a Prohibition party to push for a constitutional amendment banning alcohol, for example—but the most vibrant parts of the antialcohol movement were those seeking to build participation by focusing on achievable local goals. Because of that incremental approach, the antialcohol movements achieved considerable legal and social reforms. They got their constitutional amendment in the early part of the twentieth century, and some sixty years later, they secured a wholesale change in the laws and norms governing drinking and driving. In each case, antialcohol efforts were dominated by movement organizations that were structurally and ideologically geared toward building mass participation through incremental politics.

The first antialcohol movement was the temperance movement of the antebellum period. The early temperance organizations were federated associations, such as the American Temperance Society (founded in 1826), the Order of the Sons of Temperance (1842), and the Independent Order of Good Templars (1851). Jack Blocker estimates that within a decade of its founding, the American Temperance Society had enrolled one in five (free) adults, for a total of 1.5 million members.[160] The society also included a vibrant contingent of female auxiliaries whose membership in many cases outnumbered that of the male affiliate. This movement embraced both forms of incremental politics. Most obviously, its initial goal was to secure voluntary abstinence pledges from alcohol-consuming citizens. Thus, in a nod toward both forms of incrementalism, the temperance reformers sought noncoercive, individual-level interventions first. To the extent that these temperance societies favored more coercive actions, such actions were local. Some early temperance organizers pushed for the removal of local liquor licenses. The organizational form of these associations—a national headquarters in charge of organizing and message development, and local chapters in charge of political action—represented a practical adaptation to the fragmented nature of the U.S. system, as well as an acknowledgement of the mobilizing advantages of viable local projects. Of course, such policy incrementalism made a good deal of sense in an era when the national government was small and, consistent with the founders' intent, more focused on international than on domestic policy.

In the 1870s, middle-class women took ownership of the alcohol problem. They adopted a strategy that was more broadly political than the ones their temperance-association forebears had advanced but that was nonetheless incremental in its strategies. As noted, the women's crusades of 1874–1875 were aimed at closing individual saloons and other purveyors of alcohol. The women's goals were political in that they aimed to alter the social order through coercion and to hobble politically powerful institutions. Ruth Bordin notes that, in the 1880s and 1890s, 80% of local political meetings held in New York City took place in saloons, one-third of the aldermen in Milwaukee and Detroit were saloon keepers, and half of the Democratic precinct workers in Chicago represented liquor interests.[161] The women's initial approach to the alcohol problem did not extend beyond the neighborhood jurisdiction or demand government regulation. The approach was local and voluntary, and it "worked better than anyone at the time expected."[162]

Having shut down local saloons, the women—now under the banner of the Woman's Christian Temperance Union—pursued a more coercive strategy. They lobbied for so-called local-option laws, in which the state would either require or allow individuals within a city or town to vote regularly on whether to ban alcohol sales within their area. An antialcohol leader at the time said, "Public opinion . . . was not sufficiently strong to make national prohibition an early possibility. . . . Local option was the great entering wedge. . . . It also furnished the opportunity for extensive educational campaigns, in which the merits of prohibition were publicly discussed."[163] In other words, these local-option laws allowed for the expansion of mass participation centered on regular ballot questions. Massachusetts alone had more than twelve thousand local-option elections between 1882 and 1916.[164] Having succeeded in building support through grassroots organizing around local-option elections, antialcohol reformers set their sites on state prohibition. The state prohibition campaign was approved by the Republican party, which feared the Prohibition party's ability to drain Republican votes.[165] By 1913, half of the nation's population was subject to either a state or a local prohibition law.[166]

The Anti-Saloon League, which emerged in the 1890s to take the lead in the antialcohol movement, immediately and quite self-consciously embraced a strategy of vertical incrementalism. This was so perhaps because its founders all had extensive experience in coordinated translocal activism, whether through the Woman's Christian Temperance Union, the National Temperance Society, or the Ohio Anti-Saloon League. The strategy, conceived by Ellen Foster of the WCTU and embraced by the Anti-Saloon League, was as follows:

> If ward or precinct local option prevailed, the League sought to dry up localities and pressed state legislators for a county local-option law. In states allowing county option the League sought to make as many counties as possible dry before proceeding to a campaign for statewide prohibition. National prohibition, their ultimate goal, waited upon the spread of dry territory through local option and statewide prohibition.[167]

The Anti-Saloon League had a formal policy of incrementalism. "Do not strive after the impossible," the Ohio state headquarters instructed local organizers in 1900. "Study local conditions and reach after the attainable."[168]

In 1913, the Anti-Saloon League began a concerted and ultimately successful drive for a constitutional amendment barring the manufacture, sale, and transportation of alcohol—the ultimate rational-national approach. But the groundwork had been laid through a horizontally and vertically incremental strategy. I have already noted the vertical dimension. National prohibition emerged after nearly a century of antialcohol organizing, beginning at the individual level with temperance pledges, then proceeding to the neighborhood level with saloon protests, then to the municipal level with local-option elections, then to the state level with prohibition referenda. Beginning in the late 1880s, the antialcohol forces also had an organizing strategy that sought to build policy incrementally at the national level. In 1890, they secured a law that banned interstate shipment into dry states of liquor intended for retail sales.[169] That law was expanded in 1913 with the Webb-Kenyon Act, which barred interstate shipment into dry jurisdictions of alcohol intended for personal consumption.

Thus, by that year, Prohibition forces were ready for a mass mobilization. They had organized antialcohol groups at the local, state, and national levels; they had educated the unorganized populace through grassroots campaigns; and they had demonstrated the appeal of their policy ideas to elected officials. Most important, by building a track record of incremental victories, they had persuaded the mass public that a constitutional amendment—merely the next logical step—was viable, that participation was not a waste of time.

The Anti-Saloon League persuaded churches to announce its Prohibition Proclamation on September 7 and to hold prohibition sermons and educational drives thereafter. "After 1913 the league became less a movement rooted in specific locations, addressing itself to political conditions peculiar to particular states, and more a centrally directed national organization."[170] The league "nationalized" leaders in already dry states and put them to work on the constitutional campaign. For the next five years, the league helped to elect dry members of Congress and blanketed the nation with educational materials about the evils of alcohol. By one estimate, the league's mighty propaganda arm, the American Issue Publishing Company, was producing ten tons of magazines and pamphlets per day.[171] In 1918, the league's Prohibition amendment was submitted to Congress, where it passed easily. The required ratification by three-fourths of the states came within a mere thirteen months.

The antialcohol forces did not win through incrementalism alone. They also benefited from a lack of unity on the opposing side and from America's entry into World War I, which allowed the Prohibitionists to frame their arguments in terms of sacrifice and troop sobriety. But it is inconceivable that the antialcohol forces could have secured a rational-national ban on alcohol without having accumulated decades of small wins. The temperance forces correctly calculated that building a mass movement required not only resources and effective arguments but also tangible mobilizing projects that, to the individual considering whether to expend personal resources, appeared to have a reasonable chance of succeeding.

When Mothers Against Drunk Drivers was formed in 1980, the leaders made a choice not to target nationwide alcohol consumption or abuse per se, but rather to go after a particular subset of the drinking population (the inebriated driver) in a particular setting (the local community).

MADD started in California but quickly established largely autonomous chapters in counties across the country—375 by 1985.[172] A smaller group, Remove Intoxicated Drivers—USA (RID) was founded in 1978, after two teenagers died in a drunk-driving incident in Schenectady, New York. By 1985, RID boasted seventy active chapters in twenty-three states. The anti-drunk-driving movement, led by MADD, was strategically and organizationally primed for an incremental strategy to eliminate drunk driving.

From the start, MADD had national, state, and local policy goals. But the local chapters were the key. The organization grew rapidly in the early 1980s when victims or family members called Candy Lightner to ask, "What can we do?" and the response was invariably, "Organize a local MADD chapter."[173] Within broad guidelines, local chapters decided for themselves what they would do; their projects ranged from charitable activities, such as supporting people whose loved ones had been killed by drunk drivers, to legislative advocacy, such as lowering the blood-alcohol level needed to trigger a charge of driving under the influence and increasing penalties for DUI. In 1985 more than three-quarters of MADD chapters spent at least some time promoting new laws, and more than 40% spent a great deal of time on such efforts.[174] At the same time, the national MADD headquarters worked on incremental national policy goals: urging the White House to create a commission on drunk driving (which President Reagan did in 1982) and introducing legislation that would require the states to raise the drinking age to twenty-one or risk losing federal highway funds (enacted in 1984).

In neither case did MADD come close to advocating a rational-national strategy, even in hidden ways. Wanting to distance itself from the Prohibitionists, whose policy triumph had been less than perfectly effective and ultimately repealed, the anti-drunk-driving movement focused on modest, noncoercive measures that would ensure broad consensus. As Craig Reinarman notes, "it assiduously avoids attention to corporate interests and structural sources of alcohol problems in favor of a rhetoric of *individual* responsibility, the private moral *choice* of drinkers, and solutions based upon *self*-regulation by both drinkers and the alcohol, advertising, and broadcast industries."[175] Put another way, MADD's policy goals did not make it harder for the American adult to drink, just to drive afterward.

Once it was well established, however, MADD did pursue stricter measures. By the early 2000s, having grown to six hundred chapters, MADD was actively advocating laws to raise excise taxes on beer and wine, a burden that would fall on millions of casual drinkers who were not necessarily drunk drivers. Likewise, by the 1990s, MADD was lobbying for national legislation that would withhold federal highway funds from states that did not lower the blood-alcohol threshold for drunk driving to 0.08, effectively criminalizing the behavior of millions of additional drinking drivers; the bill passed in 2000, and the states were given three years to comply. Thus, MADD continues to embrace an incremental strategy well within the limits of consensus politics.

## Costs and Benefits of Movements Formation: A Summary

The three-pronged social-movement theory is summarized as follows. All political participation is costly, but participation in pursuit of social-regulatory public goods is especially so. These policies run contrary to America's libertarian political culture, are difficult to secure in a fragmented state, and face the familiar free-rider problem. Given these obstacles, one would not expect to see many movements for public goods, yet history tells us that such movements crop up every few decades. These movements arose because advocates found ways to turn the individual's cost-benefit calculation on its head. Even as mobilization for public goods imposes concentrated costs in the interests of securing dispersed benefits, advocates have managed to disperse the costs of participation and concentrate the benefits. They have done so by securing patronage resources; framing issues as threats to hearth and home; and pursuing incremental strategies to increase the prospective payoffs to participation. Most social movements have pursued all three strategies simultaneously, though with different emphases at different points in time.

If the theory explains successful reform movements, how well does it explain the gun control nonmovement? The answer is: quite well.

# CHAPTER THREE

# Socializing Costs: Patronage and Political Participation

JUST AS PUBLIC POLICIES IMPOSE COSTS and confer benefits, so does political participation. However, to the individual or group considering political advocacy, the costs and benefits of participation are not everywhere and always equal. Some issues are inherently harder to organize around than are others. Policies that seek to provide public goods pose particular mobilization problems. If most people are rational, and it is rational not to give money or time to a collective cause unless compelled to do so, how do organizations advocating public goods generate the resources needed to accomplish their aims? One obvious way is to secure institutional patronage. By socializing the burden of collective action, institutional patronage reduces the costs to the individual movement sympathizer, thereby making participation easier. Interestingly, gun control has never lacked for institutional supporters: It has had many *potential* patrons. They just have not catalyzed a movement. This chapter will explore why.

The most important patronage goods are money and volunteer labor; but other goods are also important, including expert advice, legitimization, and coordination and leadership services. Institutional patronage has three characteristics: (1) it is guaranteed, or understood to be provided, from one year to the next; (2) its amount does not fluctuate with events or circumstances; and (3) it is generated through a routinized process, such as taxation, regular membership dues, or interest on investments. By providing a steady stream of diverse resources, patrons both catalyze movements and allow them to expand.

Gun control advocates have had difficulty securing patronage resources from each of the three principal sources: government bureaucracies, voluntary associations, and philanthropic foundations. Government patrons are important because they have access to a reliable stream of tax dollars and because their imprimatur conveys credibility to voluntary organizations. Associational patrons are important because they are able to divert proceeds from social-capital building into financial and human capital necessary for movement expansion. Philanthropic patrons are important because they are presumed to have more flexibility than government agencies and to be more likely to take risky or controversial positions.

The argument of this chapter is as follows. Gun rights supporters have benefited from both governmental and privately generated patronage. Recognizing the importance of institutionalized patronage, gun rights supporters have sought to ensure that those benefits did not accrue to gun control organizations. Thus, the NRA and its allies have pursued a "defund, delegitimize, and deprive" strategy to prevent state bureaucracies and private organizations from providing resources to gun control organizations. The NRA and its allies have been aided in this quest by a tax regime that systematically disadvantages voluntary organizations that are trying to secure public goods. This chapter will demonstrate that the battle over gun control has been as much over patronage as over policy. It is a battle that the gun rights side has largely won. Generally speaking, gun control groups have been unable to secure significant institutional patronage from three particularly important sources: the government, women's voluntary associations, and philanthropic foundations. However, as demonstrated in the counterfactual cases below, when patronage has been secured, gun control participation has increased and the "movement" has gained momentum.

## External Patronage: The State

As I argued in chapter 2, government agencies play an important role in solving the collective action problem. Enterprising legislators and bureaucrats have provided direct and indirect assistance to issue entrepreneurs working on causes such as women's rights and smoking reduction. State patronage can take several forms: financial capital, such as grants and contracts; human capital, such as the leadership skills of government employees; and political capital, such as endorsements and authoritative data that lend weight to outside advocates' efforts. Government agencies do not merely receive interest-group pressures; they also adjudicate among them. When a government agency takes sides in a political debate, it provides resources not otherwise available and signals to members of the concerned public which side warrants their support.

In the realm of gun control, advocates faced two tasks. First, they had to remove state patronage from the opposition: The U.S. government for decades provided direct subsidies to the principal gun rights organization, the NRA. Second, gun control supporters sought to secure state patronage for themselves. The effort of gun control advocates to defund the opposition provisionally succeeded, but only after decades of work; the effort to secure state patronage for themselves proved less successful.

## PATRONAGE AND GUN RIGHTS ORGANIZATIONS

From 1903 until 1996, the U.S. government provided patronage support to the National Rifle Association and allied organizations in a form that was tantamount to a selective incentive for membership growth. A 1971 internal NRA report concluded that the association's "phenomenal growth . . . to more than one million members was made possible primarily by the Defense Department."[1] The support came in three forms. The first form of patronage, provided from 1903 to 1967, involved federal sponsorship of a civilian shooting competition. Second, in the early part of the twetieth century, the War Department (as it was then known) organized local gun clubs to prepare young men for military service. And under the third and most important form of patronage, from 1916 through 1979, the federal government required people to join the NRA if they wanted to take advantage of a government program offering surplus military weapons at bargain prices. These types of government patronage constituted financially and politically important resources for gun rights advocates.

The federal government's support for firearms organizations dates to 1903, when Congress empowered the federal government to sponsor civilian rifle competitions.[2] In 1916, Congress passed the National Defense Act, requiring the War Department to distribute guns and ammunition to civilian rifle clubs, providing funds to administer rifle ranges and to transport military instructors, and opening military ranges to civilians. The aim was to improve the marksmanship of men "who would be eligible for service in time of war."[3] An NRA copyrighted book notes: "The immediate effect of this law was to approve and lend the support of the federal government to the principles and program of the National Rifle Association of America."[4] By 1916 Congress had appropriated for civilian marksmanship training roughly $300,000, an amount equal to more than $9.5 million in 2002 dollars.[5] In 1924, the law was amended explicitly to require that civilians join the NRA if they wanted to buy a cut-rate government gun.

The 1903 and 1916 laws created two patronage bureaucracies: the National Board for the Promotion of Rifle Practice and the Office of the Director of Civilian Marksmanship within the Department of the Army.[6] NRA officers served on the board from its founding, and by congressional fiat the NRA was the official liaison between the army and the civilian reserve.[7] The civilian marksmanship program became controversial in the wake of President Kennedy's assassination by mail-order rifle in 1963, when press outlets noted that the federal government itself was in the mail-order rifle business.[8] The Associated Press reported that the gun subsidy totaled $12 million between 1960 and 1964, or $71 million in 2002 dollars.[9] For several years in the mid-1960s, Representative Henry Gonzalez (D-Tex.) publicly campaigned against the program because, he alleged, Ku Klux Klansmen and right-wing paramilitary groups were joining the NRA to get government weapons at bargain rates. In response, the U.S. Army commissioned a $100,000 study by the Arthur D. Little Company to investigate the program. Its 1966 report concluded that the civilian marksmanship program was valuable to the military and law enforcement and that the NRA affiliation of participating clubs was appropriate.[10] The study also concluded that the subsidized gun distribution program "undoubtedly is an inducement for large numbers of individuals to become members of the NRA."[11]

When the National Council for a Responsible Firearms Policy was formed in 1967, it immediately urged the marksmanship program's elimination, noting that members of a New York gun club who were obtaining supplies through the program had been arrested for plotting the assassination of two national civil rights leaders.[12] Senator Edward M. Kennedy (D-Mass.) tried to curtail government support for the rifle matches and the sales of ammunition to gun enthusiasts. Kennedy said that "although we do not know whether the Army gets any benefit from the program, we do know that its primary and substantial beneficiary is the National Rifle Association." He added that "the U.S. Government is a primary and successful booster, subsidizer, and promoter of the NRA."[13] The amendment failed, but the army in late 1967 canceled its sponsorship of all future national rifle matches. The government did continue to provide administrative assistance at the matches, held at an Ohio National Guard installation known as Camp Perry.[14]

In the late 1970s, there were several attempts to end the civilian marksmanship program entirely. Senator Kennedy in 1978 sought to cut all appropriations to the program, but the bill was soundly defeated. The following year, the Defense Department requested no funds for the program; but after NRA lobbying, Congress restored the subsidy. The one partial victory for gun control forces came in 1979, when the National Coalition to Ban Handguns won a federal lawsuit invalidating the sixty-three-year-old requirement that purchasers of army surplus weapons be members of the NRA. NCBH had argued that the "federal law has compelled hundreds of thousands of American citizens to join an increasingly political, hardline pro-gun organization in order to receive governmental benefits that should be available to *all* Americans."[15] Although the NRA membership requirement was eliminated, the government continued to spend generously on the civilian marksmanship program: about $38 million between 1985 and 1995.[16]

Although gun control advocates had been seeking to eliminate the civilian marksmanship program since the mid-1960s, they did not succeed until 1996. Under the Defense Reauthorization Act of that year, the responsibilities of the army's Office of the Director of Civilian Marksmanship were transferred to a nongovernmental, nonprofit entity, the Corporation for the Promotion of Rifle Practice and Firearms Safety. The NRA vigorously fought the move, which had been under way in earnest since the early 1990s. However, even as the federal sponsorship of the program ended, the government subsidies did not. Senator Frank Lautenberg (D-N.J.) noted that the government would bequeath to the new nonprofit corporation 176,000 old war surplus rifles, worth $53.3 million; 146 million rounds of ammunition, worth $9.7 million; and more than $13.2 million in cash and equipment—an endowment worth more than $76 million.[17] He called the new corporation "private in name only." The NRA had quietly had the patronage provision added to the defense spending bill without notice by gun control advocates. An effort by Senator Lautenberg and several cosponsors in June 1996 to block the transfer, which they called "outrageous" and "a boondoggle," failed by a lopsided vote of seventy-one to twenty-nine. It took gun control advocates more than thirty years to break the government's close patronage relationship with the NRA, but in the end, the subsidies continued. As one gun control advocate told a network news program, "It is pork. NRA pork."[18]

## Patronage and Gun Control Organizations

In some ways, gun control advocates have never lacked for state sponsors. Some of the most ardent advocates of gun control were government officials championing the cause in the absence of citizen pressure. Attorneys general, big-city mayors, police chiefs, lawmakers from all levels of government, even presidents have testified in favor of tighter firearms restrictions and sponsored such measures. And yet, for the most part, these efforts have involved solitary, expressive actions by true believers, rather than collective intergovernmental lobbying efforts or the marshaling of bureaucratic resources for the gun control cause. Typically, state patronage has involved the vocal sponsorship of gun control restrictions by individuals: U.S. attorney general Homer Cummings in the 1930s, Senator Thomas Dodd in the 1960s, Representative John Conyers in the 1970s, Mayor Dianne Feinstein in the 1980s, and Massachusetts attorney general Scott Harshbarger in the 1990s. On the rare occasions when the intergovernmental lobby has teamed with citizen gun control organizations— for example, to restrict "cop-killer bullets" and "assault weapons" and to institute background checks on many handgun buyers—legislators have passed the measures.

Sympathetic government officials and occasional policy victories not-withstanding, gun control organizations have lacked state patronage, and hence the citizen movement has been constrained. This is in large part because the gun rights opposition worked to undermine sympathetic agencies, but it is also because, except occasionally at the state level, gun control advocates did not try to build strong relationships with government agencies. The absence of bureaucratic patronage on the gun control side has confined the political battle to the legislative branch, where gun rights supporters dominate. In addition, the lack of state patronage has prevented gun control advocates from claiming that authoritative experts and evidence are on their side.

Three federal bureaucracies had the potential to serve as a valuable ally to gun control groups: the Consumer Product Safety Commission; the Bureau of Alcohol, Tobacco, and Firearms; and the Centers for Disease Control and Prevention. Each of these agencies began tentatively to associate itself with the gun control cause. And in each case, gun rights forces worked through Congress to block these moves, sometimes with little objection from gun control advocates. Thus, against these bureaucratic threats, gun rights supporters pursued a vigorous "3D" strategy: "defund, delegitimize, and deprive." They sought to defund by pressuring lawmakers to cut the agencies' budget appropriations; to delegitimize by undermining the bureaucracies' reputation or jurisdiction; and to deprive by ensuring that gun control advocates gained no powerful allies. Although most publicized at the national level, similar strategies also occurred at the state level.

### The Consumer Product Safety Commission

The Consumer Product Safety Commission was created in 1972 to protect Americans "against unreasonable risks of injuries associated with consumer products."[19] The commission is an independent regulatory agency headed by three commissioners nominated by the president and confirmed by the Senate. By statute, the commission can require informational or warning labels on consumer products, set minimum safety standards for products, or ban products entirely. As of 2002, the commission had jurisdiction over fifteen thousand types of consumer goods. However, because of gun rights supporters' efforts to deny gun control advocates a foothold in the bureaucracy, firearms and ammunition were not among them. Thus, to the extent that gun control supporters might wish to transform the debate from a crime issue to a consumer issue, they will face considerable challenges in securing relevant bureaucratic patronage.

The Consumer Product Safety Act of 1972, which created the commission, was an early battleground in the struggle over state support for gun control. The Senate version of the bill left open the possibility that firearms and bullets might be regulated, but Representative John Dingell (D-Mich.), a gun rights supporter and NRA board member, quietly inserted a seemingly obscure provision into the House version exempting products covered by Title 26, Section 4181, of the U.S. Code, which pertains to firearms. The commission interpreted the exemption on firearms to extend to bullets, as well. The final bill adopted the Dingell provision, and thus gun control advocates seemingly lost a potential ally in the bureaucracy.

However, in 1974 the newly formed Chicago Committee for Hand Gun Control learned of a potential loophole. The enabling legislation for the Consumer Product Safety Commission granted it authority to administer the Hazardous Substances Act, which had been passed in 1960 to control items that caused personal injury or illness. Unlike the Consumer Product Safety Act, the Hazardous Substances Act did not appear to exempt gun ammunition. Thus, in June 1974 the Chicago Committee for Hand Gun Control petitioned the safety commission to ban the sale, distribution, and manufacture of handgun ammunition, a bid that quickly became known as the "ban the bullets" campaign. In August, the commission agreed that it had jurisdiction under the hazardous-substances law, but soon thereafter rejected the Chicago committee's petition. After an appeal, a federal district court ordered the commission to reverse itself and hold hearings.

The NRA and other gun rights groups alerted their members to the commission's proposed rule making, and within two months more than 100,000 letters had reached the commission. After counting roughly 37,000 letters, the commission staff found only 123 that supported stricter regulation of bullets.[20] At least fourteen bills in the House and three in the Senate were introduced to deny the safety commission jurisdiction.[21] Before the hearings could be held, Congress passed legislation explicitly barring the safety commission from regulating ammunition.

The bid for an ammunition ban was an important skirmish in the struggle for gun control. Gun control advocates saw it as an opportunity, at the very most, to enact handgun regulation without the consent of a reluctant Congress and, at the very least, to call attention to the gun control cause. Gun rights supporters immediately saw the threat posed by allowing gun control advocates a bureaucratic beachhead. In pressing special legislation in Congress, gun rights supporters delegitimized the commission and by extension the consumer-protection approach to gun control. They also deprived the nascent gun control campaign of a potentially important ally. Twenty years later, gun control advocates would begin trying to reframe gun violence as a consumer protection issue. Senator Howard Metzenbaum (D-Ohio), for example, introduced a bill to allow the safety commission to regulate guns and ammunition. But the bill did not pass, and the commission continued to be prevented from taking a patronage interest in the gun control cause.

### The Bureau of Alcohol, Tobacco, and Firearms

In the iron-triangle model of policy making, a close relationship exists among congressional committees, executive-branch agencies, and the interest groups in their policy sphere. This relationship tends to be mutually supportive when the executive agency is charged with distributing federal largesse. On the other hand, when the agency is charged with oversight and regulation, interest groups tend to try to co-opt the agency. Scholars have labeled this phenomenon bureaucratic or regulatory "capture."

In the area of firearms control, the "capture" model has traditionally applied. Beginning in 1968, the principal bureaucracy charged with regulating guns was the Bureau of Alcohol, Tobacco, and Firearms (BATF). BATF was part of the Treasury Department until 2003, when it was renamed the Bureau of Alcohol, Tobacco, Firearms and Explosives and its law enforcement functions were transferred to the Justice Department. Throughout BATF's existence its relationship with gun rights interests has been marked by hostility. Its relationship with gun control organizations has been less hostile but no less distant. BATF has not been available as a patron for gun control groups in the same way that, for example, the Department of Health and Human Services assisted the antismoking movement and the Department of Transportation supported the anti-drunk-driving movement. Indeed, the role of BATF is a classic case study of the NRA's "defund, delegitimize, and deprive" approach to patronage politics.

Throughout its history, BATF has steered clear of gun control primarily because gun rights organizations have credibly threatened reprisals, creating a chilling effect within the agency. In his study of bureaucracies, James Q. Wilson notes that "an agency created as the result of entrepreneurial politics is in a precarious position: since it was born out of an attack on the interests it is now supposed to regulate, its employees must worry that the social movements that created their tasks may desert the fledgling agency because of shifting interests or waning passions, leaving it to confront a hostile interest group alone and unprotected."[22] That account fits the story well. The modern BATF had its origins in the campaign for gun control after Robert Kennedy's assassination, and almost immediately the NRA began a public relations and lobbying effort to discredit and weaken the bureaucratic apparatus.

Under the 1968 Gun Control Act, Congress gave the Internal Revenue Service's Alcohol and Tobacco Tax Division the responsibility for enforcing federal firearms laws. In recognition of that expanded responsibility for gun control, the division in 1969 was renamed the Alcohol, Tobacco, and Firearms (ATF) Division. In 1972, Congress gave the division full bureau status outside the purview of the IRS. Even before gun control had its full complement of interest groups, gun rights organizations sought to ensure that ATF could not further the cause of firearms regulation. In 1971, ATF agents raided the home of Kenyon Ballew, a suburban Washington gun collector and NRA member. When his wife screamed, he drew a pistol, and the agents shot him in the head. Gun rights supporters invoked the incident as the perfect symbol of state tyranny, precisely the sort of abuses that gun ownership was necessary to prevent. Representative John Dingell (D-Mich.), an NRA board member, demanded that the Treasury Department investigate the shooting and take steps to prevent another such incident;[23] and the *American Rifleman* turned it into a cause célèbre.[24] William Vizzard argues that the incident provided a political opportunity for the hard-line faction within the NRA to gain ground and eventually take control of the organization six years later.[25]

The NRA's efforts to undermine first AFT, then BATF as a political agent of gun control intensified in the late 1970s. Once again, the NRA worked its will by mobilizing its membership and enlisting support from congressional allies. The shot over the bow came in May 1977, when the three-year-old National Coalition to Ban Handguns, in conjunction with local gun control groups, launched a "Survival Days" project in four cities. Project leaders asked citizens to turn in their handguns at houses of worship; BATF agents would then collect the guns, and they would eventually be destroyed. The day the turn-in began, the Treasury Department abruptly ordered BATF to bar its agents from participating, catching local BATF agents off guard.[26]

Although the reasons for Treasury's decision never became public, observers concluded that the NRA had been behind the effort. Neal Knox, a leader within the hard-line faction and head of the NRA's lobbying division, wrote in the *American Rifleman*, "Why would an agency of the federal government get involved in a voluntary gun roundup run by an anti-gun private group? Why indeed?" The answer, he said, was that BATF was increasingly coming under the sway of a "new breed" of young BATF agents who were "vehemently anti-gun"; these agents were "zealots" who believed their role was "to seize firearms—to take guns from citizens—to disarm you and me."[27] Knox asserted that BATF was "engaged in an apparently deliberate policy of systematically denying the civil rights and freedoms of America's gun owners and firearms dealers" and argued that the Ballew incident had taken on "even greater significance in 1978 because the power of the federal gun agents has increased."[28]

Ten months after the Survival Days episode, BATF again ignited gun rights groups by proposing new regulations under the 1968 Gun Control

Act. The agency had begun a pilot project of firearms tracing, and the new regulations would have aided that effort by requiring gun manufacturers to imprint serial numbers on all new weapons and requiring federally licensed dealers to report stolen guns and to file quarterly reports on gun sales to other dealers. Although the regulations would not have affected individual gun owners or retail sales, gun rights supporters saw the law as "the first step toward reporting purchasers, which they considered tantamount to registration" of personally owned firearms.[29]

The NRA alerted its members. Within two months, more than 140,000 letters had arrived at BATF headquarters, nearly all of them critical of the proposal. Eventually, the total reached 337,300—or one-third of the NRA's membership.[30] Only 7,800 letters supported the proposed regulations. One antiregulation letter was addressed to "Gestapo headquarters" in Washington.[31] In response, a House subcommittee cut the BATF's budget by $4.2 million, the estimated cost of implementing the proposals, and added language to a bill that would have barred the agency from spending any money implementing the rules.[32] Those proposals passed the House by a lopsided vote of 314 to 80 and the Senate by a similarly decisive vote of 61 to 31. Amid the firestorm, BATF director Rex Davis decided to retire, and the NRA suggested that the backlash against his proposals had hastened his departure.[33] One journalist called the demise of the proposed BATF rules "a nadir for the gun control movement in a year of once-soaring ambitions."[34] Treasury quietly withdrew the proposed regulations in February 1979, eleven months after they had been offered.

Even so, the NRA continued its war on BATF. With support from congressional allies, the rifle association in January 1979 called for hearings into allegations of "rampant civil rights and other abuses" by BATF.[35] The same month that the Treasury regulations were withdrawn, the NRA's chief lobbyist, Neal Knox, announced that the NRA was "declaring war" on the Gun Control Act of 1968 and noted that the forthcoming BATF oversight hearings would represent the first attack in that offensive. Knox promised a "long and costly battle" that would end up being a "war of attrition."[36] In 1979 and 1980, the Senate appropriations subcommittee responsible for the Treasury Department held the hearings, which afforded the NRA an opportunity to showcase everyday Americans and their allegations of abuse by the BATF.[37] Senator Dennis DeConcini (D-Ariz.), the subcommittee's chairman, declared: "If the behavior of BATF agents described yesterday is typical and accurate, it raises a fundamental question about the organization and operation of BATF."[38] He called BATF "an agency that needs to be saved from itself."[39]

On the eve of the 1980 presidential election, the NRA noted, "Much of the assaults against us have come from the Federal bureaucracies. . . ."[40] At that time, Senator James McClure (R-Idaho) introduced legislation to repeal the 1968 Gun Control Act, the foundation of national gun laws in America. With the election of Ronald Reagan in 1980 and the shift to Republican control of the Senate, the NRA and its allies saw a political opportunity to eliminate BATF. However, outgoing and incoming bureaucrats hatched a compromise that would have merged BATF with the Secret Service, a move that was expected to save the imperiled BATF in some form.[41] The NRA opposed the proposal because it feared that the Secret Service would be a more formidable regulator[42] and because BATF served as an effective "villain" around which to rally grassroots opposition to gun control.[43] The proposal died, but efforts to weaken BATF did not. That same year, the House voted 279 to 141 for an NRA-backed amendment to cut $5 million from BATF's appropriation and reduce its staff after Congress members protested "that the BATF had overstepped its mandate and harassed private gun owners."[44]

Between 1970 and 1998, BATF's budget posted the smallest increase of any federal law enforcement agency.[45] William Vizzard, a criminologist and former BATF agent who has written important political histories of the agency and of the gun control issue, argues that "ATF has learned from long years of experience that gun control opponents will capitalize on every opportunity to characterize the agency as 'gun grabbers.' Unlike many other federal agencies, ATF does not even offer routine cleanup bills for fear they will invoke the wrath of gun control opponents."[46] In short, the agency has pursued an "avoidance of any association with gun legislation" and "assiduously avoided contact with the gun-control organizations."[47] Even as early as 1977, the relationship between BATF and gun control organizations was described as "wary."[48]

The NRA's attempts to undermine BATF and chill its association with gun control are only part of the reason why gun control advocates lack this source of bureaucratic patronage. There are at least two other reasons. First, like many law enforcement officers who rely on guns for personal protection, BATF agents and officials differ widely in their views of gun control measures.[49] Although BATF might support measures that would ease enforcement, it would not necessarily support the entire agenda of the gun control lobby. Second, for reasons of culture and choice, gun control groups have never established close ties with BATF.

To be sure, in 1977, gun control groups lobbied against congressional proposals to cut BATF's budget, and the following year gun control advocates testified in favor of BATF's proposals to require serial numbers and dealer-to-dealer transaction records. But in 1981, the National Coalition to Ban Handguns and several state gun control groups sued BATF, alleging it was not regulating gun dealers. Aimed at reducing the number of licensed gun dealers in America, the lawsuit cooled relations between the agency and gun control advocates.

However, by the late 1990s, with a pro-control president in the White House, BATF was poised to become a quiet ally to gun control organizations. The agency began a program to build a statistical case for tighter gun regulations, the very sort of patronage support that gun control groups needed. Specifically, under its Youth Crime Gun Interdiction Initiative, BATF decided to trace every gun used in a criminal act in major American cities. The agency also produced authoritative reports on gun shows, modified assault weapons, illegal firearms markets, and young people's use of firearms. To avoid arousing the gun lobby, the agency justified its research projects in terms of "enforcement" of existing laws, which gun rights organizations were on record as supporting. Likewise, the agency assiduously avoided terms that might inflame the opposition, such as "data," "research," "policy," or "technology." One insider summarized the bureaucracy's strategy as follows: "We had a plan to move from enforcement to policy to politics without anybody noticing, and that's what we did."[50]

And yet, even as the Treasury Department was creating a quantitative foundation for additional firearms measures, gun control advocates were relatively uninvolved in the political battles that enabled this work to continue. To advance policy, bureaucracies require money; thus, policy outcomes depend on battles over appropriations bills. Frequently, Congress uses these bills to restrict agencies' jurisdiction through provisions that bar expenditures for certain purposes. During the Clinton administration, gun control organizations did not rush to BATF's defense, leaving it politically vulnerable and cautious. Thus, although gun rights supporters have lobbied appropriations committees to undermine the gun control cause, gun control advocates have not countered by aggressively lobbying to defend agency budgets.

With the dawn of the pro–gun rights Bush administration, the NRA and its allies were able to undercut the utility of firearms-trace data. Beginning in 2003, bills appropriating funds for the Bureau of Alcohol, Tobacco, Firearms and Explosives (BATFE) contained a provision barring the Justice Department from spending any money to disclose gun-trace records to the public.[51] The provision was inserted to undercut lawsuits brought by cities and individuals, with the help of gun control organizations, against firearms manufacturers. The core claim of these lawsuits was that firearms manufacturers were negligent in distributing guns to scofflaw dealers, and the best evidence for that claim would be that a small number of dealers supplied a disproportionate share of guns used in crimes. By filing a Freedom of Information Act request and obtaining gun-trace records, gun control organizations could show that a small number of dealers received a disproportionate number of inquiries about guns they had sold that had later been used in crimes. The trace records are also important to independent scholars who wish to evaluate the effect of gun control laws. For example, access to trace data would help to assess whether one-gun-a-month laws, on the books in Virginia and Maryland, reduce gun trafficking from those states.[52] Under the law, BATFE can still produce reports revealing the names of questionable dealers, but gun control groups doubt the bureau's political will. "They are intimidated by the NRA."[53]

As this history makes clear, BATF (now BATFE) is a bureaucracy that appears particularly susceptible to political winds, even as its mission—reducing violent crime—enjoys bipartisan support. Even in pro-control administrations, the bureau has had to be careful not to incite the NRA. Thus, it has done what political appointees asked, but no more. Political pressures, coupled with a cultural distance from liberal advocates in the gun control community, have made BATF(E) an unlikely ally. Gun control organizations figured that, given constraints on their resources, cultivating a patronage relationship with BATF was not worth their while. Instead they assumed a sometime-watchdog role. In March 2004, for example, the Brady Campaign filed a lawsuit against the bureau charging that it had failed to enforce the 1994 Assault Weapons Ban (the suit was dismissed in September 2004). After decades of such hostility and estrangement, the development of a supportive, patronage relationship between BATFE and gun control groups appears highly unlikely. Indeed, confrontation appears to be the order of the day.

## The Centers for Disease Control and Prevention

Throughout American history, social problems traditionally presumed to be the product of individual decisions or economic conditions have been redefined as public health problems caused by factors beyond individual choice. Peter Conrad calls this process the "medicalization of deviance," a reflection of the increased prestige of doctors relative to religious authorities in safeguarding human welfare.[54] Beginning in the 1970s, medical and public health professionals began to embrace gun violence as a professional concern, and their efforts started to gain a bureaucratic foothold in the 1980s. Not surprisingly, this attempt to claim gun violence as a public health concern provoked a vigorous response from gun rights organizations. Again, with respect to public health patrons, the aim was to defund, delegitimize, and deprive.

In the first half of the 1970s, a handful of medical professionals moved to claim "ownership" of the gun violence issue. In professional journals and other venues, they began to reframe gun violence as a public health issue, as well as a crime-and-justice issue. The March 1972 issue of the *Medical Annals of the District of Columbia* characterized firearms violence as "a modern plague" that had reached "epidemic proportions," and the April issue reported on a survey finding that most members of the D.C. Medical Society favored licensing of handgun owners and registration of handguns.[55] In 1973, doctors in the Cuyahoga County (Ohio) coroner's office began to publish detailed studies of homicide and suicide in the Cleveland area and, based on those findings, promoted the idea that bullets were "pathogens."[56] A 1974 article in the *Medical Tribune* called on medical professionals to contribute to the gun control debate. A 1976 article in the *Journal of the American Medical Association* argued that handgun violence was "a significant public health problem" and suggested that physicians might play a valuable role in policy debates about gun control.[57] By 1977, physicians were attempting to estimate the costs of treating gunshot wounds and to frame gun violence as a preventable disease;[58] and the American Medical Association was polling its members on handgun control. In 1979 the U.S. surgeon general's annual report noted that firearms were second only to motor vehicles as a cause of fatal injuries and hinted that banning handguns or removing them from the home would reduce deaths and injuries.[59]

These scattered attempts to frame gun violence as a medical problem came together in the early 1980s, when the federal public health bureaucracy began to claim ownership of the gun violence issue. As with tobacco, the surgeon general was the issue entrepreneur. In this case, he was C. Everett Koop, a conservative country doctor who embraced gun control in an administration that had courted gun rights organizations. In 1983, the Centers for Disease Control and Prevention (CDC) established a Violence Epidemiology Branch. Dr. Koop said, "Violence is every bit a public health issue for me and my successors in this century as smallpox, tuberculosis and syphilis were for my predecessors in the last two centuries."[60]

The branch set out to reframe firearms violence as a preventable disease. To promote that view, it became a patron to an emerging group of medical doctors and public health researchers who were interested in what they called a gun violence "epidemic." In 1992, the gun violence research program was folded into the CDC's newly created National Center for Injury Prevention and Control.[61] The following year, the American Academy of Pediatrics and the American Medical Association (AMA) entered the debate. The AMA in particular published scores of influential articles that framed homicide as a threat to the public's health and to schoolchildren in particular. Former surgeon general Koop and George Lundberg, editor of the *Journal of the American Medical Association*, called for strict new gun control measures on the grounds that gun violence had become a "public health emergency."[62]

As doctors and public health officials increasingly claimed ownership of the firearms issue, the CDC's Injury Center "proved to be the only consistent source of federal support for firearms research."[63] The program also provided money for newsletters and other forums by which public health researchers could become a unified force. The NRA was slow to recognize the threat posed by the CDC and for the first decade of the violence program's existence chose to challenge it solely on scientific grounds—by criticizing its research—rather than on political grounds. That changed in the early 1990s as the public health approach to gun control began gaining credibility and attracting new allies to the cause.

The NRA began its defund, deligitimize, and deprive campaign by lobbying the Department of Health and Human Services to close the CDC's violence program. The NRA also began pushing the National Institutes of Health (NIH) to investigate a CDC-funded researcher for scientific fraud; NIH declined.[64] In 1995, the NRA created a physicians' group, Doctors for Integrity in Policy Research, to lobby for the elimination of the CDC's firearms program, then estimated at roughly $2.5 million per year, or less than 5% of the Injury Center's budget and about 0.1% of the CDC's budget. "Taxpayer dollars are supporting unadulterated anti-gun advocacy," the NRA's top lobbyist told a newspaper.[65] As evidence, the rifle association pointed to a 1994 statement by Dr. Mark Rosenberg, who had started the CDC's violence program in the early 1980s and was its director. Dr. Rosenberg had said: "We need to revolutionize the way we look at guns, like what we did with cigarettes. It used to be that smoking was a glamour symbol—cool, sexy, macho. Now it is dirty, deadly—and banned."[66]

In 1995, the NRA secured the help of nine senators, including presidential candidate Bob Dole, to eliminate the firearms program on the grounds that it was promoting a "clearly political campaign against gun ownership."[67] The program survived the elimination attempt, but the message was clear, and in 1996 the CDC for the first time in a decade declined to request research proposals explicitly in the area of firearms.

Later that year anti–gun control members of Congress tried again to cut the Injury Center's budget by the amount equivalent to its spending on firearms research, or $2.6 million. In a House budget hearing, Representative Jay Dickey (R-Ark.) emphasized that CDC epidemiologists had attended conferences sponsored by gun control organizations.[68] A House appropriations subcommittee voted down the budget cuts. "This is the National Rifle Association's amendment," said the subcommittee chairman, Representative John Porter (R-Ill.), who had been an outspoken advocate of gun control since an unstable woman opened fire in an elementary school in his suburban Chicago district in 1988.[69] Porter's objections notwithstanding, the full Appropriations Committee, as well as the

House, passed the measure, which redirected the $2.6 million to another CDC division for research on traumatic brain injury. Beginning in 1996, all CDC appropriations bills stipulated that "none of the funds made available for injury prevention and control . . . may be used to advocate or promote gun control."[70] Dr. Rosenberg made two efforts to secure philanthropic patronage to compensate for the loss of federal funds. One effort failed because a gun rights supporter on the private foundation's board vetoed the $2 million proposal; the other failed because the CDC, concerned about further political problems should it continue pushing the firearms issue, refused to accept the $3 million grant.[71]

In 1998, the firearms program lost an important champion in CDC director Dr. David Satcher, who was appointed surgeon general. That same year, under less supportive leadership at CDC, as well as political and budgetary constraints, the Injury Center let expire a program that had given money to states to track firearms injuries. In 1999, Dr. Rosenberg, the center's founding director, was forced to resign. The center's budget was further reduced, and the CDC's investigations of mass shootings stopped.[72] By 2001, the CDC was spending about $400,000 on firearms-related research, or about 15% of the 1996 level. The gun rights groups' campaign had had a profound chilling effect on the agency. Epidemiologists kept their distance from gun control organizations, stopped speaking openly about guns as a public health problem, and collected firearms-injury data only as part of broader injury-surveillance programs.

The CDC was not a patron in the traditional sense: It did not give money directly to gun control organizations, though if the issue had been less contentious, the agency might well have found a way to do so. However, even if it did not fund political advocacy groups, the CDC provided other kinds of patronage resources that are equally important to emerging social-movement leaders. First, the CDC funded research by "critical communities" of doctors and public health experts who were reframing the gun control debate in a way that would expand the scope of conflict, facilitating the mobilizing efforts of gun control organizations. The dynamics of that reframing process are covered in the next chapter, but it is important to note that the CDC and its individual grantees played an important role in transforming gun control from an issue for criminal-justice authorities into an issue for doctors, nurses, and parents. The CDC findings, for example, provided important data to a group of mothers who organized a large gun control march in 2000, as I describe in chapter 6.

As a prestigious government agency with impeccable scientific credentials, the CDC also lent credibility to interest-group efforts to transform gun control from a conflictual issue to a consensual one. "We're trying to depoliticize the subject," Injury Center director Rosenberg told a reporter in 1995. "A scientific inquiry stands a very good chance of yielding some solutions that can save lives. We're trying to transform it from politics to science."[73] Indeed, in all likelihood Representative Dickey called attention to the CDC's presence at gun control conferences to cast doubt on the assertion that the scientists were apolitical.

Finally, and perhaps most important, the CDC had begun to assemble authoritative data on firearms violence in America, including mattters, such as accidental injuries in gun-owning households, that criminological work had not emphasized. As John Kingdon's seminal study of agenda setting demonstrates, sudden shifts in routine indicators (i.e., gun deaths) tend to push a problem onto the policy-making agenda.[74] Many movements for social regulation—notably those against smoking, drunk driving, and abortion—have arisen after authoritative scientific studies presented new assessments of the scope and nature of threats posed by the behavior. In two of those cases, the authoritative data came from a government agency: the U.S. surgeon general in the case of smoking and the National Highway Traffic Safety Administration in the case of drunk driving. Because shifts in indicators can demand policy responses, interest groups that wish to block such policy making are wise to first block the assembly of such indicators. From this perspective, lobbying to defund government data-collection agencies is a profitable investment of political resources.

However, as was the case with BATF, the attacks by gun rights organizations were not the only reason why gun control supporters lacked institutional patronage. A perception existed within the CDC that gun control advocates were not especially interested in research, the CDC's stock in trade. In that way, gun control groups differed from the health voluntary associations involved in the antismoking movement, which saw government-sponsored studies as important movement-building resources.

## State Patronage: A Summary

Gun rights organizations aimed their "defund, delegitimize, and deprive" strategy at the Consumer Product Safety Commission, the BATF, and the CDC. But they worked to undermine bureaucratic patronage in other areas, as well. For example, in 1983 Senator Steve Symms (R-Idaho) and Representative Larry McDonald (D-Ga.) introduced legislation that would have eliminated federal criminal-justice or law enforcement funds to local governments that banned civilian handgun possession. The bill never made it out of committee in either chamber, but it demonstrated once again that gun rights supporters would use their electoral advantage to deny governmental resources to gun control advocates. A similar pattern of attacks on potential bureaucratic allies has played out at the state level, as well. Though not as well documented, or perhaps as dramatic, these attacks have clearly affected state gun control groups in meaningful ways. In Michigan, for example, the State Department of Community Health, one of the founding members of the Michigan Partnership to Prevent Gun Violence, had to withdraw from the partnership eighteen months later under political pressure. All told, the NRA's defund, delegitimize, and deprive strategy has kept gun control organizations from establishing a patronage relationship with resourceful bureaucracies at the national level and to some extent at the state level, as well.

## INTERNAL PATRONAGE: VOLUNTARY ASSOCIATIONS

The government's important role in empowering social movements is a relatively new phenomenon, occasioned by the growth of government and the professionalization of the civil service. Before the state had the capacity or inclination to facilitate social movements, these movements were led by federated voluntary associations and churches.[75] Even in the modern era, having access to voluntary-association resources is vital to social movements; indeed, social movements cannot survive without them. As chapter 2 noted, voluntary associations attract members by providing material and solidary benefits and in turn deploy members' resources toward purposive ends. Put another way, the dues and volunteer time that members contribute to acquire one type of benefit (material or solidary) end up subsidizing another benefit (political expression). Political activity is, in effect, a by-product of the pursuit of individual interest and social capital.

There is perhaps no better example of a by-product phenomenon than the National Rifle Association and its allied organizations. Many gun owners join the association to secure material benefits, such as a monthly magazine and discounts on insurance and rental cars, as well as to enjoy the solidary benefits of target shooting with fellow hobbyists. In 2002, the NRA had more than 4 million members, who paid $35 a year or $100 for a lifetime membership. Its annual budget for 2001 was roughly $200 million.[76] Members' dues, which constitute nearly 60% of the NRA's budget, finance both professional lobbying of elected officials and efforts to generate grassroots lobbying by individual members. The NRA's lobbying arm, the Institute for Legislative Action, had a budget of $13.2 million in 2001; the association's publications, which include regular updates on political matters, cost $29.5 million; and the association's member services, including messages about threats from gun control advocates, totaled $71 million.[77] Consistent with Olson's by-product theory of political advocacy, the NRA has been able to translate more than $113 million in membership dues into communications that encourage political action by elites and everyday citizens.

On the gun control side, however, this by-product option has been severely constrained. Like many other purposive groups operating at the national level, gun control organizations have no obvious way to provide material or solidary benefits to members, and thus these groups face a free-rider problem. But history tells us that groups have found ways around that problem. One way is to build local chapters that in turn subsidize the national headquarters; another is to enlist as allies organizations that can divert resources generated through solidary and material incentives toward issue advocacy. Gun control leaders have lacked such an opportunity, partly because they chose not to pursue it and partly because the type of movement allies in question were being depleted and diverted just as the gun control campaign was about to consolidate. I will consider these arguments in turn.

To anyone looking at gun violence in America, an obvious question arises: Why no MADD for gun control? Mothers Against Drunk Driving showed that it was possible, even in the late twentieth century, to create a victim-based, federated movement for social regulation that was largely self-financing. Gun control leaders have traditionally shied away from this strategy. As discussed further in chapter 5, they made a conscious decision not to build chapters, in which victims and other gun control sympathizers might have united around locally rooted advocacy projects. Thus, groups that were trying to organize gun control supporters at the local and state levels could not turn to national gun control organizations for patronage support. Indeed, records indicate that the relationship between the state and national groups largely broke down over who was to subsidize whom. During the 1970s, for example, the handful of fledgling state groups wanted Handgun Control, Inc., to share the proceeds from its direct-mail campaign with grassroots advocates, while Handgun Control wanted the mailing lists of state organizations to identify individuals who would write letters to their congressional representatives. Eventually, Handgun Control, Inc., began to provide money for state and local campaigns, a move that has led to demonstrable results, as detailed in chapter 6.

The other constraint on voluntary-association patronage of the gun control campaign is linked to the century-long decline of federated voluntary associations. Social movements are composed not only of single-issue organizations but also of sympathetic multi-issue organizations. These organizations provide movement leaders with preexisting networks of like-minded people who possess politically relevant resources, as well as with money generated through membership dues. Thus, for example, the Anti-Saloon League relied heavily on church collections, and the anti-smoking movement relied on health charities to finance an advocacy organization in Washington. The cross-subsidy form of patronage is best defined as the leveraging of solidary networks of individuals, with financial means and volunteer time, toward purposive policy goals. Movements need lots of committed individuals united in mobilizable organizations.

In the realm of gun control, perhaps the most obvious potential partners for single-issue groups were women's organizations. Not only have women consistently and solidly supported firearms control, but they also have been at the forefront of virtually every movement for social regulation in American history. In other work, I have argued that, while women have been individually and institutionally involved in gun control, they did not embrace it as a "women's issue," at least until the late 1990s.[78] The reluctance of women's organizations to emerge as full partners in the gun control cause has deprived it of valuable institutional patronage and hindered its development. More succinctly, the cross-subsidy form of patronage was unavailable because women's groups for the most part did not provide it.

There are two historical-institutional reasons why women's groups were unavailable as leaders in the gun control campaign. One has to do with a transformation in the structure of women's voluntaries, and the other concerns a reorientation of their policy interests. These explanations are intimately connected. I first consider the shift in policy interests.

As gun control was emerging as a full-fledged issue in the mid-1970s, women were in the midst of a movement of their own, for equal rights and economic advancement. The so-called women's liberation movement produced a boomlet of organizational creation and innovation, particularly in the areas of reproductive rights, equal pay, and the repeal of discriminatory laws. The transformation of women's organizational agenda is clearly documented in a comparison of women's groups in 1963, before the gun control campaign got under way in earnest, and 1993, when it was into its third decade.[79] In 1963, fully half of women's groups (50%) were focused on improving conditions in society at large, but that fraction had shrunk to less than one-quarter of groups (23%) in 1993. Conversely, the fraction of groups focused on women (their political rights, economic advancement, social status, etc.) nearly doubled in the 1963–1993 period, from 24% to 47%.[80] Perhaps the most noteworthy finding is the sharp turn toward a concern with reproductive rights and reproductive health. In 1993, roughly one in six women's groups was devoted to reproductive rights (either pro or con) or to reproductive health. There were 144 groups in that category in 1993, compared with just 1 group in 1963. Thus, over the past three decades, women's organizations have narrowed the definition of "women's issues" to those specifically furthering women's rights. With women's move to a narrower and more specialized focus, it has proved harder to leverage their networks for other social concerns. Put another way, American women have all but abandoned the traditional, more expansive claim to be the authoritative voice of policy reform and protector of social welfare. Feminism has replaced what might be termed "maternalism" as women's central organizing principle.

These new feminist organizations competed with traditional women's groups for members, money, and control of the issue agenda. Thus, feminist groups' arrival on the scene posed a quandary for traditional women's groups, those interested in broad social reform. These groups could either lose market share in the battle for members and dues, or adapt by embracing feminist causes. As it turns out, traditional women's groups did both.

First, with very few exceptions, traditional multipurpose women's groups have steadily lost ground in terms of market penetration. That is, they attract many fewer joiners from their respective membership pool than they used to. Data assembled by Robert Putnam show that eight out of ten large, traditional women's groups suffered significant membership losses—generally from 60% to 90% in population-adjusted terms—between 1966 and 1996.[81] The fraction of adult women who belong to the League of Women Voters, for example, soared by 113% between 1945 and 1965, and then declined by 63% between 1966 and 1996. The fraction of female college graduates who belong to the American Association of University Women dropped by 4% between 1945 and 1965, and then plunged by 80% in the 1966–1996 period.

As their membership base was shrinking, traditional women's groups began to shift their priorities toward more "modern" feminist concerns. Anne Costain argues that such campaigns enabled the struggling traditional groups "to attract women from the younger generation through their successful lobbying on feminist issues—women who, otherwise, would have likely not joined" either the traditional groups or the new, more radical feminist groups.[82] Indeed, she reports, "a structure of cooperative effort to foster women's interests was established that linked older organizations such as the National Federation of Business and Professional Women's Clubs and the American Association of University Women to the newer groups . . . it was evidence that the older organizations played a major role in helping the newer women's movement groups organize to start lobbying." In the process, the older women's groups went through a period of "consciousness raising" and were "energized" by their work for women's rights.[83] Thus, traditional women's groups came to look more like feminist groups as the political tides shifted. The traditional voluntaries may have passed resolutions on the "old issues," but their money and organizational energies were directed toward the "new issues."

The women's movement diverted women's attention to several high-profile issues, all of which involved direct benefits to women, as opposed to more generalized benefits for society at large. First on the agenda was the Equal Rights Amendment (ERA), which passed the U.S. House of Representatives in 1971 and the U.S. Senate in early 1972, and then was subject to an ultimately unsuccessful ratification campaign in the fifty states over the next decade.[84] To become law, an amendment to the U.S. Constitution must be ratified by three-quarters of the states after its passage by Congress. The state campaigns for the ERA typically were led by a state chapter of the National Organization for Women and local coalitions of religious, professional, civic, and labor groups that were united under the banner of ERAmerica.[85] Ethel Klein notes that "feminist efforts to secure congressional passage of the ERA illustrate the importance of the coalition between traditional women's groups and new feminist organizations in working to change women's political status. The ERA provided a rallying point for feminist activism because it served as a symbol of women's rights, but getting the amendment passed by Congress was no small feat. It took an enormous two-year effort involving over fifty organizations," including the Business and Professional Women's Clubs, the American Association of University Women, and the YWCA.[86] These traditional groups joined the ERA cause, sometimes reluctantly, after the newer feminist groups (such as the National Organization for Women, the Women's Equity Action League, and the National Women's Political Caucus) "demonstrated public support for changing women's status."[87] The traditional groups had key assets—money, members, expertise, and networks—and the feminist groups "were dependent on the resources of the traditional women's organizations to launch and sustain their movement."[88]

The other major issue of the 1970s, 1980s, and even the 1990s was abortion. In 1973, the U.S. Supreme Court issued its landmark *Roe v. Wade* decision, which found a constitutional right for a woman to terminate her pregnancy under most conditions. The ruling diverted women's organizational energies in two respects. First, women began establishing health clinics and other services to meet the demand for the newly legalized procedure. And, second, the *Roe* ruling galvanized the antiabortion forces, particularly the well-organized Catholic Church, which in turn spurred women's groups to organize against what they saw as a formidable threat to their gains. In sum, the mid-1970s was a busy time for women. Just as the nation's first-ever "handgun control movement" was on the cusp of forming, a potentially pivotal segment of that force—organized womanhood—was undergoing a dramatic shift in its priorities. Women's reorientation from broad social reform to feminist activism helped take the steam out of the gun control movement. This move ensured that gun control would remain, at least for the time being, a narrowly defined issue spearheaded by elite interest-group spokesmen, rather than propelled by a broad citizens' movement. That is, gun control would be largely confined to an "inside the Beltway" policy debate.

Finally, as traditional women's groups sought to revive themselves by embracing feminism, the interest-group universe was becoming increasingly specialized. Issues that were once the province of multipurpose organizations led by women volunteers were now the province of single-issue interest groups based in Washington.[89] Thus, issues such as gun control now had their "own groups," and it was assumed that those groups were "taking care of" the problem. Single-issue advocacy groups took ownership of the social-reform agenda, including gun control. Thus, although traditional women's associations still had millions of members, their changing focus undermined their ability to lead mass movements for nongendered social reforms.

### External Patronage: Private Philanthropy

In his important study of interest groups, Jack Walker argues, "A comprehensive explanation of unconventional political movements must reach beyond the motives and inclinations of individuals who lead or join the movement to include a description of changes in the larger political environment and the intervention of sympathetic patrons who provide fresh resources and crucial assistance for entrepreneurial leaders at critical times."[90] Walker is right to identify external patronage as crucial to the formation and maintenance of interest groups and social movements. However, the role of foundation patronage in particular should not be exaggerated. It is not true that any issue entrepreneur with a compelling case can rely on private philanthropy to finance his cause. There are three formidable obstacles to philanthropic patronage of social movements in general and the gun control cause in particular. First and most important, under federal tax laws, foundations cannot make grants that earmark money for legislative advocacy, either direct lobbying of lawmakers or grassroots lobbying by their constituents. Second, because of historical experience and dependence on public and elite goodwill, charitable organizations tend to be risk averse, shying away from projects that will attract controversy. Third, leaders of the largest private foundations tend to consider themselves professional philanthropists who generally have adopted a "root cause" approach to their grant making, and the root-cause paradigm calls attention to changing underlying social conditions rather than reforming regulatory regimes. These three considerations are mostly unrelated but mutually reinforcing. They combine to make widespread, sustained foundation funding of any gun control "movement" virtually impossible. By extension, these norms and laws encourage social-movement organizations to depoliticize their approach in order to secure philanthropic support. As a result, the activities of the anti–gun violence "movement" were channeled into soft politics (namely, public education and research) and away from hard politics (namely, grassroots mobilization, lobbying, and electioneering).

### Tax Laws and the Depoliticization of Political Issues

Institutions structure political behavior, and laws are one of the principal institutions in political life.[91] In the United States, one set of laws is particularly important to collective political behavior: the Internal Revenue Code. One cannot understand collective behavior in America without considering the fundamental and absolutely critical role of tax laws. The Internal Revenue Code affects political behavior in two ways. First, it governs what social-movement organizations and other voluntary associations may, and may not, do with their time and money. Second, the code creates an incentive structure that channels financial contributions toward certain types of collective activities and not others.

One of the first decisions that an issue entrepreneur faces is what kind of social-movement organization to create. Typically, the choice is between creating a public charity under section 501(c)(3) of the Internal Revenue Code or a social-welfare advocacy group under section 501(c)(4). Unlike profit-making corporations, charities and advocacy groups are exempt from taxation. Public charities are defined as "corporations, and any community chest, fund, or foundation, organized and operated exclusively for religious, charitable, scientific, testing for public safety, literary, or educational purposes, or to foster national or international amateur sports competition . . . or for the prevention of cruelty to children or animals." Advocacy organizations are defined as "civic leagues or organizations . . . operated exclusively for the promotion of social welfare."[92] Both types of groups may engage in issue politics, but they operate under different rules.

Since 1934, public charities have been limited in the amount of advocacy they may perform. They are barred either from devoting "a substantial part" of their activities, or from spending more than roughly 20% of their budget, on efforts to influence legislation currently before lawmakers, as well as ballot initiatives and referenda.[93] Efforts to influence include lobbying lawmakers or generating public pressure on them. Charities also must stay out of electoral-advocacy activities entirely. The trade-off is that they are eligible to receive grants from foundations and tax-deductible donations from individuals and corporations. Likewise, the federal government subsidizes the costs of charities' educational mailings by providing charities with a 40% discount off the commercial postal rate.

In short, under section 501(c)(3) of the tax code, Congress has provided a partial solution to the collective action problem by (1) creating a mechanism for foundation patronage; (2) subsidizing the costs of recruiting members and money through direct mailings; and (3) providing income tax breaks for individuals who contribute to the commonweal. Foundations are in effect a tax shelter for individuals, so there are strong incentives to channel charitable contributions through such entities. Likewise, for people who itemize their deductions, the tax code subsidizes altruism. Under the code the cost of a gift to charity is discounted by the marginal tax rate. Thus, for people in the 35% tax bracket, the effective cost of a $100 contribution is $65.

The alternative to a public charity is a social-welfare organization. These groups may lobby without restriction, and they may engage in some types of election-related activities. However, the extra latitude to engage in politics comes with a price. Foundations, which are public charities, may not support social-welfare groups' electoral or issue-advocacy activities, and the groups are not allowed to receive government grants and contracts. Likewise, individual donors cannot deduct contributions to 501(c)(4) organizations. If given to a (c)(4), the hypothetical $100 contribution cited above would cost the donor the full $100, or $35 more than the after-tax cost of the gift to a charity. Finally, 501(c)(4) groups whose primary purpose is legislative advocacy do not enjoy postal subsidies.

Because it is easier to raise money for a charity than for an advocacy group, issue entrepreneurs, particularly those trying to organize around public goods, have a powerful incentive to incorporate as a public charity, even if that means curbing their involvement in the political sphere. In this way, federal tax laws shift inherently political activity into the nonpolitical sphere. Although nonpolitical activities, such as public education, are an important part of social movements, their main goals are clearly political. If history is any guide, social movements want first and foremost to influence legislation and elections.

In the case of the firearms issue, the effect of the tax laws at least at the state level has been to shift the organizational focus away from gun control (a political option) and toward violence prevention (a nonpolitical concern). Gun control advocates have solved the organizational dilemma in much the same way that other issue entrepreneurs have: by creating a public charity through which most activities are financed, as well as a poorly funded sister group that can cover minimal amounts of political activity. A sampling of some of the most active state gun control organizations illustrates this choice. The Illinois Council Against Handgun Violence, a public charity, had a budget of $470,000, nearly all of it coming from foundations; its sister advocacy group, Illinois Citizens for Handgun Control, had a budget of $2,000.[94] The Ohio Coalition Against Gun Violence, a public charity, had a budget of about $150,000, again mostly from foundations, while its advocacy group, Safe Ohio, had less than

$1,000 on hand.[95] North Carolinians for Gun Control began as a 501(c)(4) advocacy organization in 1993, but five years later leaders folded that operation into a 501(c)(3) charity, North Carolinians Against Gun Violence, because the groups' leaders concluded that the group needed foundation support to sustain itself.[96] In cases where the advocacy group is larger than the public charity, such as with the gun control groups in New York and Michigan, this is because the advocacy group was in the unusual position of receiving a large gift from a wealthy individual willing to forgo the tax deduction.

At the national level, the pattern holds to a lesser extent. The Educational Fund to Stop Gun Violence, a public charity, received contributions totaling $749,000, about 40% more than the amount raised by its sister advocacy group, the Coalition to Stop Gun Violence ($535,000). By contrast, the Brady Center to Prevent Gun Violence, the public charity, had $4.7 million in contributions in 2001, compared with $7.1 million in contributions to the advocacy arm, the Brady Campaign to Prevent Gun Violence.[97] Brady's success in raising advocacy dollars stems from its long-standing direct-mail program. In the universe of gun control organizations, this success is an anomaly—and potentially an important one. However, although the Brady Campaign does funnel some revenue to nationally significant gun control efforts at the state level, the vast majority of the income is directed toward "educational" direct-mail solicitations and lobbying to secure national legislation, rather than to grassroots movement building.

The attention to tax policy has figured into issue entrepreneurs' choices throughout the history of the gun control campaign. In 1969, the National Council for a Responsible Firearms Policy sought public charity status because it wanted to "qualify for government and private foundation grants."[98] In 1976, the Maryland Handgun Control Committee likewise sought charity status, but the Internal Revenue Service gave it advocacy group status instead. The founder called that a "defining moment" and one of the two factors that most inhibited the group's ability to grow, because of the difficulty in attracting contributions.[99] (The other factor was Maryland's preemption law, which is covered in chapter 5).

Even if it does inhibit political work, charity status is valuable to social-movement organizations. For that reason, gun rights organizations have sought to undermine their opponents by attacking their charity status. In 1977, under pressure from the Citizens Committee for the Right to Keep and Bear Arms, a Seattle-based gun rights organization, Congress asked the Internal Revenue Service to investigate the National Coalition to Ban Handguns. As a result, the coalition lost its charity status and reorganized as a 501(c)(4) advocacy group. In the early 1980s, the NRA filed suit to revoke the postal discounts that the coalition as well as Handgun Control, Inc. (HCI), enjoyed. HCI retained the privilege after organizing a 501(c)(3) educational affiliate. The NRA also filed a complaint with the Federal Elections Commission (FEC) charging that HCI had improperly used its advocacy group to solicit contributions for its political action committee; in 1984 the FEC forced HCI to pay a $15,000 fine.[100]

To summarize, tax laws are institutions that structure political activity. They work to the advantage of groups such as the NRA that can generate membership by providing selective incentives. Groups that are advocating public goods have a more difficult time attracting members. Through tax deductibility, the tax code does offer these groups a means of providing a selective incentive to would-be members, but in exchange these groups must bypass political engagement and instead focus on less overtly political activities, such as research and public education. A senior political strategist at a national gun control organization noted: "People try to view [gun violence] as not a political issue—it's about 'education' or whatever. No. This *is* a political issue. On our side, we tend to do a little dance and pretend it's not political."[101] He refers to the depoliticizing effects of the tax laws as the "great untold story" behind the weakness of the gun control movement.

### Chilling Foundation Patronage

A second obstacle to philanthropic patronage is that foundations and other charitable organizations tend to be risk averse and therefore likely to steer clear of controversial political issues, even when the particular activity would be permissible under the tax laws. Much of this risk aversion can be traced to the late 1960s, when politically tainted grants made by the Ford Foundation drew the wrath of Congress.[102] In 1969, Congress passed the Tax Reform Act, which created new penalties for foundations that engage in or fund political advocacy. The Tax Reform Act, together with the lengthy and quite adversarial hearings that had led up to it, created a chilling effect for decades to come. Most foundations are fearful of inciting elected officials and potentially drawing stricter regulation, and so they tend to avoid even the appearance of involvement in highly charged issues. Thus, the more politicized gun rights supporters can make the gun violence issue, the less likely organized philanthropy will be to support gun control advocates.

As was the case with public bureaucracies, charitable organizations that have sought to support gun control endeavors have been subject to political pressures to stop. Typically, these pressures have come at politically pivotal times in the effort to foment a national gun control movement. For example, in 1971 the Sportsmen's Alliance of Michigan began a campaign asking its members to withhold contributions to the United Fund, which raised money through workplace payroll deductions and distributed grants to community charities, on the grounds that the United

Fund was supporting state and national Councils on Crime and Delinquency, which advocated gun control legislation.[103] After that, the national council withdrew its endorsement of gun control.

Two years later, the Michigan sportsmen's group again sought to deprive a charitable organization of United Fund support. This time, the target was the Young Women's Christian Association (YWCA), which had adopted a resolution supporting owner licensing and registration for all guns and a ban on the domestic production, sale, and possession of handguns. Even before the resolution passed, the sportsmen persuaded the Michigan United Funds (also known as United Ways) to threaten to withhold money from Ys in that state, and after passage the sportsmen called on gun owners to withdraw their support from their local United Way. The Michigan effort was widely reported in the gun press and spilled over into other states. In Minnesota, gun rights advocates suggested they would scrutinize the Minneapolis United Way, as well. The Citizens Committee for the Right to Keep and Bear Arms engaged in a self-described "all out national campaign to expose" the YWCA and urged gun rights supporters to deluge the association's headquarters with postcards pledging to stop supporting the charity. In response to these various attacks, some YWCAs "suffered severe harassment" and "a loss of funds";[104] and some distanced themselves from the national YWCA's gun control position.

In 1975, the Gun Owners Action League of Massachusetts urged a boycott of Gillette products because the company had given money to the Crime and Justice Foundation (formerly the Massachusetts Council on Crime and Correction), which supported gun control. The gun owners' group also instigated an Internal Revenue Service investigation of the foundation, leading it to disengage from the gun control issue entirely.[105]

To be sure, these are old examples. But organizations tend to have long memories, and charitable organizations in particular seek to avoid controversy. Not only do they fear increased government regulation, which excessive political engagement may provoke, but they also rely on public goodwill to support their causes. Thus, they tend to avoid divisive issues that could provoke a backlash. For example, in 1999 the board of the United Way in Kansas City voted unanimously not to take a side in a gun control–related referendum and urged one of its grantees, the Partnership for Children, to stay out of the campaign, as well. The partnership severed ties with the United Way instead.[106]

### Foundations' Root-Cause Paradigm

At least since the early twentieth century, private foundations have defined their role as seeking out and reducing the "root causes" of problems.[107] Grant makers view human problems as products of deeply embedded social conditions and large structural forces. By extension, ameliorating human difficulties requires comprehensive programs that fundamentally alter the way society and its institutions are organized. In this view, it would be less effective to pass laws that regulate individual behavior than to work toward changing the structural conditions that cause individuals to act as they do. This perspective has led grant makers to work toward reducing violence by eliminating its social and cultural underpinnings rather than by controlling guns.

In principle, a foundation could support the gun control "movement" by making grants for research and analysis, for litigation, for the creation of gun control groups, and for policy advocacy in general. However, an analysis of grants provided by major foundations from 1988 to 1992, the worst years of the gun violence epidemic, revealed that only 1% of violence-related grants and grant dollars went to projects related to gun control.[108] Instead, major donors focused on programs that addressed violence in other ways: by preserving and strengthening families, by providing young people with alternatives to gang life, by instituting conflict-resolution programs, and by providing education and training programs. Supporting such efforts allows foundations to pursue their root-cause ideology while simultaneously avoiding political controversy. As one national gun control advocate recalled, "Foundations were timid. They didn't feel like going out on a limb and supporting the partner organization to a legislative lobbying group."[109]

## WHAT HAPPENS WHEN PATRONAGE ARRIVES?

Patronage does not by itself increase citizen mobilization. What patronage does is to build sustainable institutions and propagate credible ideas. Even as the gun control "movement" has lacked institutional patronage on a broad scale, evidence clearly suggests that those patron resources that have been available have been critical in building the modern gun control campaign. Two cases illustrate the argument.

The first case is the Joyce Foundation, a major private grant maker based in Chicago. The foundation began making grants in the area of violence prevention in 1993. Between 1996 and 2004, it distributed nearly $30 million through nearly 120 grants.[110] The foundation's patronage was explicitly intended to reframe violence as a public health problem and to support policy approaches consistent with that conceptualization. Specifically, the foundation sought to support "policy-relevant research," "efforts that lead to the treatment and regulation of guns as a consumer product," "effective Midwest-based coalitions and national coalitions with a strong Midwest presence," efforts aimed at "encouraging and strengthening the activity of medical professionals in addressing gun violence as a public health issue," and projects "communicating public-health policy and research to Midwestern and national policymakers."[111] The foundation provided start-up funds and/or operating support to state gun control organizations in California, Illinois, Indiana, Iowa, Michigan, Minnesota, and Ohio, as well as financing academic research and policy centers that provide intellectual and strategic resources to gun control organizers. Other foundations, including the California Wellness Foundation and the Aaron Diamond Foundation, also committed substantial sums to gun control–related grants, but their grant making did not begin in earnest until the mid-1990s.

The second case is that of Colorado and Oregon, sites of high-profile school shootings in the late 1990s. In the wake of these events, Andrew McKelvey, who had made a fortune through an Internet venture, decided to create a national gun control organization, Americans for Gun Safety (AGS). One of the group's first acts was to finance an extensive grassroots and media campaign to pass ballot initiatives in Colorado and Oregon requiring all sales of firearms at gun shows to be subject to a background check on the would-be buyer. AGS spent $2.8 million on the initiatives, including $200,000 to support state gun control groups, $1.85 million for television ads featuring Senator John McCain (R-Ariz.), and $800,000 for radio ads, mailings, and calls to get out the vote.[112] Handgun Control, Inc., contributed at least $115,000 to the Colorado initiative and $55,000 to the Oregon measure.[113] Both measures passed, Colorado's with 70% of the vote and Oregon's with more than 60%. While it did not build a movement, the AGS patronage allowed state activists to secure symbolic victories in two western states and to establish gun control as a winning issue outside liberal urban areas on the two coasts.

## WHY THE LACK OF PATRONAGE MATTERS

Gun control is an issue that has a resourceful base of supporters, yet its patronage resources have been scarce. One reason is that gun rights groups have pursued an aggressive strategy to deprive gun control groups of patrons in the federal bureaucracy. Working through allies in Congress, the NRA and its coalition partners have secured legislation barring the Consumer Product Safety Commission (CPSC) from regulating guns or ammunition and have secured retaliatory cuts in the budgets of the Bureau of Alcohol, Tobacco, and Firearms and the Centers for Disease Control and Prevention. One reason why these actions were so important was that in two cases—the CPSC and the CDC—a full-fledged partnership with gun control groups might have not only strengthened the "movement" but also enabled issue entrepreneurs to reframe their message in terms of consumer protection and public health, frames that are friendlier to movement building. The next chapter considers the impact that reframing the debate has on the scope of political engagement around gun control.

Gun control advocates have also lacked the alternative to government patronage: private support. This is in part because of the actions of gun rights supporters, but it is mostly the product of institutional factors having nothing to do with gun control per se. I have suggested that one form of patronage—financial and volunteer support from multi-issue membership groups—was limited because the most logical patron, organized middle-class women, were narrowing their focus to women's rights at the very time that gun control advocates most needed them to fulfill their traditional role as stewards of community security. In addition, gun control advocates have lacked patronage support because tax laws and foundation norms make it very difficult to sustain political organizations geared toward public goods. The laws provide a powerful incentive for issue advocates to organize as public charities to secure financial support and government subsidies. However, in the process they must agree in essence to focus on education rather than legislative or electoral change.

When institutional patronage is scarce—when government agencies, voluntary associations, and foundations are not forthcoming—nonprofit organizations must rely on individual patronage. Wealthy individuals, who can supply large contributions at little fund-raising cost, are preferred, and the leading national gun control groups have relied heavily on these generous patrons. However, even wealthy donors have an incentive to free ride, allowing others to support nonprofit organizations that supply or lobby for collective goods. Intensity is one solution to this free-rider problem. People who feel passionately about a cause are more likely to give, and in the case of gun control, passionate donors tend also to hold extreme policy positions. These donors are more likely than the typical gun control supporter to support, for example, a total ban on handgun possession; they are what political scientists term "preference outliers." Thus, gun control leaders are caught in a bind: To raise the money to stay in operation, they must appeal to preference outliers, who are unlikely to respond to tepid appeals touting modest policy proposals. But, as chapter 5 illustrates, the decision to support bolder, more extreme policy proposals tends to constrain movement formation. Ironically, even though liberal private foundations have a reputation for supporting radical social engineering, in fact they tend to be quite politically pragmatic. National gun control leaders note that it is far easier to raise money for incremental policy programs from foundations than from individual donors. A grant proposal submitted to a private foundation will tend to be far more moderate than a direct-mail appeal to an individual donor. If foundations were more forthcoming with ongoing support, gun control groups' policy strategies might be friendlier to movement building.

Thus, patronage (or lack thereof) has played at least two roles in suppressing the gun control movement. First, key sources of patronage have been unavailable, either for political, legal, or organizational reasons. And, second, the patronage resources that have been available have made it difficult for gun control leaders to pursue strategies that would encourage broad participation around gun regulation.

# CHAPTER FOUR

# Personalizing Benefits:
# Issue Frames and Political Participation

> The Americans . . . are fond of explaining almost all the
> actions of their lives by the principle of self-interest rightly
> understood; they show with complacency how an enlightened
> regard for themselves constantly prompts them to assist one
> another and inclines them willingly to sacrifice a portion of
> their time and property to the welfare of the state.
> —Alexis de Tocqueville, *Democracy in America*[1]

I HAVE ARGUED THAT ISSUE entrepreneurs seeking to build movements around public goods must find ways to socialize the costs of participation. But costs are only one side of the equation. To expand the scope of political conflict—to involve the audience, as E. E. Schattschneider put it[2]—issue entrepreneurs also must find ways to individualize the benefits of participation. In this chapter, I show how they do so: by redefining the issues at stake in a way that passive sympathizers see it in their immediate self-interest to become actively involved in the political fray. For most of its history, the gun control issue has been cast in terms that do the opposite. Gun control has been framed in a way that constrains rather than widens the scope of conflict.

This chapter accomplishes four tasks. First, it briefly reviews theories and assertions of scholars who study different aspects of issue framing. Second, it analyzes the history of the gun control debate, which has centered on crime control against individual liberty. Third, the chapter discusses the effort in the 1990s to reconceptualize gun control as a public, rather than an "expert," problem. And, finally, the chapter demonstrates empirically that these attempts to reframe the debate indeed did expand the scope of participation. Reframing the gun control issue got more people involved, over a longer period of time, in more intense ways than they had been before. These findings suggest, then, that the absence of an accessible, compelling issue frame was one of the key factors constraining the gun control movement.

## WHAT'S THE ISSUE?

Scholars in a variety of traditions have long asserted that how we think and talk about an issue profoundly influences the politics surrounding it. As noted in chapter 2, scholars have used many terms to capture this core construct: issue definition, framing processes, causal stories, narratives, and so forth. For the sake of consistency, I will use these terms interchangeably, even though there may be subtle differences among them. Mayer Zald defines frames as "the specific metaphors, symbolic representations, and cognitive cues used to render or cast behavior and events in an evaluative mode and to suggest alternative modes of action."[3] As Zald and others have aptly noted, framing processes are critical parts of the larger political process. "Movements and countermovements not only are involved in mobilization contests to demonstrate who has the most support and resources at their command, they are involved in framing contests attempting to persuade authorities and bystanders of the rightness of their cause."[4] Writing about the notion of public ideas, Mark Moore argues likewise that "the intellectual properties that matter are those that qualify the idea in political and institutional terms, not scientific and intellectual terms."[5]

The empirical literature on issue framing has focused on how differences in the way issues are cast affect political attitudes. Thus, new frames may activate different dimensions of an issue[6] and in so doing affect the salience of the issue for individuals and perhaps alter their opinions about how political leaders should address it.

In altering cognition, framing processes also have the potential to alter an arguably more important construct: political *behavior*. On one hand, reframing an issue may transfer issue ownership from one group to another group. Deborah Stone notes that different causal stories empower different people with different tools, skills, and resources to solve a given problem.[7] Reframing is partly strategic: "People choose causal stories not only to shift the blame but to enable themselves to appear to be able to remedy the problem."[8] That is, "people with pet solutions often march around looking for problems that need their solutions."[9] Concerned individuals need mobilizing frameworks. Those frameworks arrive when skillful advocates interpret events or indicators in resonant ways. If the newly empowered group is large, well organized, and politically potent, the reframing process may expand the scope of conflict in fairly dramatic ways.

Besides transferring ownership, new frames can activate behavior by altering individuals' subjective assessments of their interests. Frames do not in and of themselves manufacture interests. A well-reasoned argument will not normally inspire action absent an underlying reason to get involved. What frames do is legitimize the involvement of interested individuals by creating a "we." Thus, effective frames expand the scope of conflict by linking personal identity to collective action. As William Gamson and David Meyer note, "Changes in the scope of conflict involve new definitions about who is or should be involved as well as changing the alliance possibilities and the resources involved."[10] Although reframing may have little impact on the actions of those already involved, it will have an impact on the actions of what E. E. Schattschneider termed the "audience," whose participation is at the root of conflict expansion.[11]

The hypothesized link between framing processes and actual political behavior is widely supposed but rarely tested. Scholars of political behavior are far more likely to model behavior as a function of measurable factors at the individual level, such as socioeconomic status, age, exposure to recruitment messages, and so forth. As Mark Moore notes, "It is one thing to observe that public actions are consistent with particular public ideas articulated by specific participants in the policy process. It is quite another to prove that the ideas are producing an independent effect on the public actions one observes."[12] And yet, we know that elites try to change the definition of issues, presumably to alter either public or decision makers' behavior. Adam Berinsky and Donald Kinder allow that individuals can "construct their own understanding of political realities. But most often, the hard work of defining what an issue is 'about' will most likely be done by those who have the largest stake—political or commercial—in getting the public to view an issue *their* way. This means that the interpretations that prevail among elites may substantially affect how issues are understood by ordinary citizens."[13]

Building on the insights and assertions of agenda-setting and social-movement scholars, this chapter demonstrates that reframing processes are a critical element in conflict expansion. In the case of gun control, I show how elites interpret "objective" events and indicators and how those interpretations affect the scope and nature of political activity around the issue at hand. From a movement-building perspective, an effective frame will construct self-interest by casting negative indicators as a direct threat that is easily understood by, and legitimizes the involvement of, the median American. In short, issue entrepreneurs identify self-interest by spelling it out.

This observation is at once obvious and deeply counterintuitive. In scholars' understanding, "problem definition" is the process by which issue entrepreneurs transform thousands or even millions of seemingly unconnected individual woes into a collective "public problem." The personal becomes political. To be sure, social-movement leaders must accomplish exactly that. But they must also accomplish the flip side: They must turn a "public problem" into a personal threat. They must persuade sympathizers —would-be movement participants—that the problem might affect them in a direct way. They must make the political become personal.

Thus, the social-movement leader's task is twofold: to construct group interest by bringing a collective-action frame to individuals who already know they have an individual stake in policy reform; and to construct individual interest by bringing a collective-action frame to individuals who may not know they have a stake. In other words, not only must issue entrepreneurs collectivize the benefits of individual goods, they also must *individualize* the benefits of collective goods. When that happens, individuals can see a benefit to participating in social reform and recognize the cost of doing nothing. When issues are so personalized, intensity rises. Even though free-rider problems are still present, they are greatly reduced. Emotion, especially fear, is a partial solution to the free-rider problem. In a strict sense, passion can trump cognition.

In the rest of the chapter, I trace the framing of gun control from 1960 onward. The analysis is based on thousands of documents, including gun control advocates' public speeches, direct-mail solicitations, media interviews, and strategy documents, among other materials. I argue that the dominant "crime frame" was ineffective in expanding the scope of conflict because it played into heuristics about who is victimized by, and in charge of controlling, gun violence. These heuristics were conflict limiting rather than conflict expanding. However, after three decades of stalemate, a small cadre of issue entrepreneurs, using newly available indicators, made a conscious attempt to reframe the debate in a way that the theory predicts would expand the scope of conflict. Their efforts provide an opportunity to test the theoretical connection between frames and behavior, and the results indicate that the connection is indeed significant, both statistically and substantively.

## Gun Control as Crime Control, 1960–1990

Throughout the twentieth century, gun control has been advanced as a method of crime control. This argument is embodied in what I term the "crime frame." The equation of gun control with crime control is almost tautological. After all, with limited exceptions, using a gun to shoot another person is a crime, so controlling guns would by definition be aimed at limiting the scope and/or effects of criminal activity. Thus, the crime frame is quite logical.

However, as an organizing tool, the crime frame has been movement constraining. It puts the violent stranger and his gun at the center of the debate and conveys issue ownership to law enforcement officials charged with maintaining social order and to experts in firearms and criminal behavior. Focusing on the gun and the offender has allowed opponents of gun control to force gun control advocates to fight their battle on technical and scientific grounds, which are inherently movement limiting. The other constraint imposed by the crime frame is a function of human psychology. While people are perennially concerned about crime, they typically discount the probability that a bad event will happen to them. This proclivity is captured by the refrain, "We always thought that this kind of thing happened to other people. We never thought it could happen here." For example, surveys going back to the 1970s indicate that 20% of Americans have been threatened at gunpoint or shot at, but according to one survey only 8% think they are very likely to be a victim of handgun violence in their lifetime.[14] Thus, unless the threat is direct and imminent, and the arguments for mainstream mobilization compellingly clear, rational citizens are unlikely to personalize the benefits of preventive policy measures. They may see the utility of such measures but not the immediacy.

Such is the story with gun control. Even though most individuals who are killed by guns die by their own hand, or at the hands of someone they know, firearms regulation has long been framed in terms of controlling unpredictable criminal attacks by armed strangers. There has been almost no effort to construct group identity among victims and potential victims and to legitimize their ownership of the gun violence issue. Thus, gun control remained an experts' issue. Concerned individuals remained disconnected from one another; outrage remained unorganized. The crime frame has emphasized different elements at different times, as shown below, but the same basic narrative controlled until at least the early 1990s.

The crime frame has featured two distinct yet related concepts: bad hands[15] and bad guns. Most gun control campaigns throughout history have spotlighted criminal use of nonsporting weapons to inflict death or injury. When gun control was first on the national political agenda, from the late 1920s through the late 1930s, the debate centered on gangsters and machine guns. As *Literary Digest* noted in 1927: "Law-abiding citizens in crime centers, we are told, are weary of a condition under which thugs and hold-up men have free access to every sort of firearm, not excepting the machine-gun."[16] In 1934, the General Federation of Women's Clubs sounded a similar theme in its campaign for gun control: "The intent of the campaign that the Federation is waging against the crime wave in this country is to make it more difficult for the gangster to have access to firearms. . . . Its slogan is to 'disarm the gangster, not arm the citizenry.'"[17] The leading gun control advocate of the day, Attorney General Homer Cummings, concluded in 1935 that armed criminals had brought America "close to a serious crisis" and that handgun registration and other measures were necessary.

When the issue next appeared, in the early 1960s, it was prompted by a postwar rise in juvenile delinquency. However, the debate was structured around adult criminals, rather than youths, and again, the "bad hands, bad guns" frame dominated. On one hand, advocates argued that guns were reaching particularly high-risk individuals: "thugs, psychopaths, drug addicts, and teen-agers," in the words of an early gun control advocate.[18] These advocates argued that, because of America's lax gun laws, dangerous persons could buy a firearm through a mail-order outfit.[19] At the same time, advocates focused on the nature and quality of weapons used in crime. For example, FBI director J. Edgar Hoover argued that handguns had become a public menace and needed to be regulated because they were far more lethal than knives and other nonfirearm weapons.[20] Yet, in the early 1960s, gun control was not a term that was broadly used. Only a few elites, in Congress and law enforcement, viewed firearms accessibility as a "problem"; it was not an issue on the mass public agenda, except insofar as gun rights organizations were able to stir up opposition to regulation. In short, "gun control" was owned by a select few criminal justice experts, and the framing of the issue reflected that fact.

In the late 1960s, with the assassinations of Martin Luther King Jr. and Robert Kennedy, and the urban riots of 1968, the major themes remained the same: bad hands, bad guns, lax laws. A *New York Times* story summarized the tone: "The Senate began today what is expected to be a long debate on legislation designed to curb crime and control the sale of guns."[21]

As citizens and professional groups began to get involved in advocating gun control, they, too, adopted the crime frame. For example, the first national gun control organization, the National Council for a Responsible Firearms Policy, noted in its 1967 founding document that the American public's safety "has been threatened by the easy availability of firearms to irresponsible persons. The seriousness of the problem is demonstrated by the large and rising numbers of robberies, riots, murders, suicides and assaults in which guns are used."[22] Although the council rejected the "bad gun versus good gun" distinction and advocated controls on rifles and shotguns as well as on handguns, its fundamental orientation was toward the armed criminal. Likewise, the U.S. Conference of Mayors, which passed a firearms control resolution in 1968, justified its involvement on the grounds that crimes committed with firearms had substantially increased and that "the mail order sale of firearms and ammunition has placed deadly weapons in the hands of juveniles, individuals with criminal records, drug addicts, and others."[23] Testifying before the Senate's Subcommittee to Investigate Juvenile Delinquency in 1968, Colonel John Glenn of the Emergency Committee for Gun Control, a short-lived citizens' group formed after Robert Kennedy's assassination, urged Congress to "respond to this deep feeling expressed by the public and by public figures who want an end to the uncontrolled trafficking in guns; who want an end to the 7,700 murders caused by guns last year; who want an end to the horror and grief that struck nearly 18,000 families last year whose loved ones fell victim to the gun."[24]

Quite coincidentally, and helpfully for the purposes at hand, Roger Cobb and Charles Elder's seminal work on agenda building, written in 1972, addresses the framing of gun control in the late 1960s and the efforts by advocates to use framing to alter the political dynamics. Cobb and Elder write,

> The gun control controversy illustrates attempts both to enlarge and to limit (or privatize) the scope of conflict. The issue initially centered on whether or not more restrictive gun legislation would reduce the incidence of homicide and other violent crimes. The issue was quickly redefined by both sides. The supporters of gun control legislation argued that such legislation would be almost a sure cure to many of the major problems of crime control, overlooking the easily availability of illegal weapons to those bent on crime. Rather than focusing on whether or not the control of firearms would mean fewer violent deaths, opponents of such legislation concentrated on what owning a gun meant to certain people (for example, sportsmen) and insisted that the Constitution guaranteed the right to "keep and bear arms," neglecting to mention that the courts have not upheld this interpretation of the Second Amendment.[25]

Ironically, of course, the reframing process that Cobb and Elder document was really just a minor adjustment to the crime control narrative, not a wholesale change in the paradigm. In sum, in the 1960s the gun control debate and the pro-control groups taking part in it were dominated by policy experts who crafted arguments designed to persuade legislators and their staffs, rather than mobilize the general public.

In the 1970s, gun control became a truly public issue, even if it had not inspired a social movement. As of 1974, there were three national interest groups working to secure stricter firearms legislation in Congress, as well as small lobbying groups in a handful of states. Although not affiliated with one another, these state and national advocates began to focus their message. But again, the message revolved around criminal violence by strangers. One way that advocates honed their message was by identifying the "Saturday night special" as the policy target. The term was not new; media accounts had used it in the late 1960s, and the 1968 Omnibus Crime Control and Safe Streets Act had acknowledged the problem these cheap handguns posed by banning their importation. The precise technical definition of what did or did not constitute a Saturday night special had always been vague, but the term was rich in political symbolism, evoking images of cheap, poorly made firearms that had no purpose other than as instruments of crime. Gun control advocates focused on handguns, especially cheap handguns, as the target of regulation.

Gun control advocates in the 1970s focused their message in another way, as well. Instead of calling attention to all victims of gun violence, advocates focused on one small but sympathetic subset—law enforcement officers shot in the line of duty. These victims represented only about 1 in 100 people killed by guns: 121 police officers were felled in 1971, compared to 10,500 civilians. This frame was rooted in strategy: gun control advocates' desire to expand the scope of conflict by drawing law enforcement to their side. But, as sympathetic as police officers may be, the frame was not one that could draw in the typical American.

Framing gun control as a means of protecting police officers continued through the early 1980s, when "cop-killer bullets" came to dominate the gun control debate. These were sharp-tipped, Teflon-coated bullets that allegedly could pierce the protective vests worn by police officers, and although there were no reports of any officers' having been killed by such bullets, gun control advocates seized on the ammunition to turn the law enforcement community against the NRA. The strategy was effective in making the NRA, which rejected bullet bans of any sort, appear extreme at best and heartless at worst. The strategy was also effective in bringing once-leery police organizations over to the gun control side, which played an important role in the passage of the Brady Bill a decade later. However, once again the focus on cop-killer bullets gave rise to a highly technical debate, particularly as the NRA attempted to rebut the gun control case on scientific grounds.

In the late 1980s and into the mid-1990s, the framing of the gun control debate continued to revolve mainly around criminal justice. But this time, the "bad hands" and "bad guns" had changed. The target of gun control efforts became the urban gang and the "assault weapons" that gang members used. The new focus on assault weapons gained clarity after Patrick Purdy used an AK-47 to kill five children at a Stockton, California, elementary school playground in January 1989. In that year, the National Coalition to Ban Handguns changed its name to the Coalition to Stop Gun Violence to reflect its view that assault rifles, as well as handguns, should be outlawed.[26] Handgun Control, Inc., added assault weapons to its list of bad guns, as well, arguing in a fund-raising letter that the NRA was spending millions of dollars to protect guns "increasingly favored by drug peddlers and gang members" and imploring citizens to care enough "to keep handguns out of the wrong hands and ban assault weapons."[27] By 1992 the Coalition had enlisted a teacher wounded in the Stockton shooting, Janet Geng, to lobby Congress and sign direct-mail solicitations. In one such letter, she warned, "the next Patrick Purdy could be prowling through your neighborhood right now—after purchasing an AK47 or Uzi with the NRA's blessing."[28]

## GUN RIGHTS SUPPORTERS: A DEBATE ON THEIR TERMS

Even as the crime frame continued to dominate into the early 1990s, there was a growing movement to change the debate in ways that might favor the pro-control side. I describe that effort below. But first, we must consider the vital role of gun rights forces in shaping the debate. As gun control forces were trying out different aspects of the crime-control frame, their opponents offered a consistent message: gun control would not work, probably would backfire, and certainly would infringe the rights of law-abiding citizens. As Philip Cook and James Leitzel have noted, these arguments support Albert Hirschman's theory that all antireform arguments revolve around futility, perversity, and/or jeopardy.[29] These arguments accomplished two major tasks for the gun lobby. They softened gun control support by creating questions about the wisdom of firearms regulations. And more important for present purposes, they dissuaded would-be gun control advocates from active participation by portraying the issue as highly complicated and technical, the natural province of firearms experts rather than laypeople. In essence, the crime frame allowed gun rights advocates to transform what might have been an easy "valence" issue[30] into a difficult "expert" issue. Using the three core arguments—futility, perversity, jeopardy—gun rights forces turned the gun controllers' issue frame against them.

### "Futility"

Gun rights supporters' belief in the futility of gun control is captured in their best-known axiom, "If guns are outlawed, only outlaws will have guns." This was the pro-gun advocates' self-evident narrative to counter the anti-gun advocates' self-evident narrative that guns should be outlawed because otherwise outlaws can obtain guns. The NRA used the futility argument as early as 1934, during Senate hearings on the National Firearms Act. When it comes to suppressing crime, said NRA chief Karl T. Frederick, "the mere enactment of a law is, in itself, useless. Laws against murder have not stopped murder, and I don't suppose that laws against committing murder with pistols will be any more effective. I think that it is . . . almost impossible to accomplish very much in the way of disarming the crook."[31] By 1999, when gun control was once again atop the political agenda, the NRA's chief, Wayne LaPierre, rejected new laws because, "Crazy people and criminals don't care what the gun laws are. . . . The countries that have bans, you can still get guns."[32] The futility argument also has been championed by gun rights supporters within academic circles, notably Daniel Polsby, whose widely cited essay, "The False Promise of Gun Control," argued flatly, "Gun-control laws don't work."[33]

## "Perversity"

The gun rights forces have consistently argued that increased regulation of gun ownership would actually increase rather than decrease criminal violence. In his 1934 Senate testimony, the NRA's Karl Frederick likened criminal violence to a disease that is fought in part through the power of human resistance: "We oppose crime partly through the organized forces of the police and law enforcement agencies, but we also oppose crime by the resistance of the victims of crime, and in my opinion, anything which appreciably decreases those forces which are opposed to crime, will inevitably produce an increase in crime."[34] To bolster its perversity arguments, beginning in 1959 the NRA's flagship magazine, the *American Rifleman*, began running a column called "The Armed Citizen," which recounted stories of regular folks successfully using guns in defense of themselves and others.[35] The perversity argument gained ground in the 1960s, as gun rights supporters began framing handgun ownership as a means of deterring urban lawlessness. By the late 1990s, the perversity argument had emerged as perhaps the most central part of the NRA's case against gun control. Polsby's 1994 essay used the logic of economics to argue that gun control laws "act perversely" by making it easier for criminals, who disobey laws, to prey on law-abiding people, who obey them. Three years later, gun control opponents were able to point to quantitative evidence of this proposition. In an academic article and a trade book, *More Guns, Less Crime,* John R. Lott and his colleagues purported to demonstrate statistically that allowing honest citizens to carry concealed guns deterred criminal violence and, by implication, that laws restricting concealed carrying would increase violence.[36] Although other scholars called this finding into serious question, the Lott logic added a scientific veneer to gun rights advocates' long-standing attempt to frame gun control in terms of policy perversity.[37]

## "Jeopardy"

Perhaps the best-known and most common frame for gun rights supporters is the "jeopardy" argument. This argument portrays gun control as a violation of sacred American values, including the constitutional right to bear arms. The "jeopardy" argument holds that even modest gun control measures are one step down the "slippery slope" to Nazi- or Soviet-style tyranny in the United States, as embodied in the NRA mantra "registration leads to confiscation." A 1974 editorial in the *American Rifleman* associated gun control supporters directly with totalitarianism: "Nearly all of the clamor for more gun control or gun bans comes from those who take a soft attitude toward communism." By 1999, NRA chief Wayne

LaPierre told a newsmagazine: "People believe they have a constitutional right and freedom to own guns in this country. And they don't want their names on government lists. They know what the next step is. It's a knock on the door confiscating their guns."[38]

Indeed, at least since the 1960s, the NRA and others have made the case that gun ownership is integral to citizenship and patriotism. Harking back to the citizen militias of the Revolutionary War, the NRA has portrayed gun owners as a "traditionalist" bulwark against a misguided "thrust in sociopolitical thinking . . . in the direction of increased governmental authority and decreased individual liberty."[39] At the NRA's 1991 annual meeting, a celebration of the bicentennial of the Bill of Rights, LaPierre told the crowd, "What a night for patriots. As I listened to our stirring anthem, and watched all those glorious flags streaming by, words you all know by heart came to mind, a simple yet powerful little slogan so many Americans display with pride, These colors don't run. Now I'd like to take that same slogan, and change it with a word or two. . . . The NRA doesn't run."[40]

Observers of the gun control debate have long recognized the effectiveness of the futility, perversity, and jeopardy frames. Three days after the 1972 assassination attempt on Governor Wallace, the *New York Times* editorialized that "the depressing aspect of recurrent flurries of public interest and Congressional response is that these all quickly evaporate in surrender to the gun lobby's powerful propaganda machine."[41]

## How the Crime Frame Limited the Movement

To summarize this section, from the 1920s through the early 1990s, gun control was framed as a method of crime control. In this frame, the criminal perpetrator and his firearm were at the center of the policy debate. Gun control advocates relied on a self-evident narrative: bad hands plus bad guns spells bad news. However, the American public did not need to be persuaded of those facts, nor did it need to be converted to the logic of firearms restrictions. What citizens needed was an accessible narrative that told them why they, and not law enforcement experts, had legitimate ownership over the gun issue and why it was in their immediate self-interest to act. Instead, what they received was a consistent, unyielding message from the NRA that the case for gun control was both technically and morally flawed. Although Americans fear crime, to be sure, the crime frame bogged down in expert debates that left little room for involvement by laypeople.

The chief architect of Handgun Control, Inc., Nelson "Pete" Shields, recognized the power of issue frames to inspire political behavior: "People who are willing to vote for or against candidates on the basis of a single issue are people who are personally affected by that issue. People to whom the issue is only intellectual tend not to be dominated by it. As a result, on the issue of gun control, the anti-control side, being made up mostly of gun owners who are personally and emotionally affected by the issue, is more politically potent—even though in a minority—than the pro-control side which for the most part is not personally and emotionally affected."[42] While crime affects people in personal and emotional ways, crime victims, their loved ones, and those who live in fear do not necessarily know one another or have a group identity. Group identity, as a subset of culture change, is constructed by critical communities and carried through social-movement organizations.[43] Rather than trying to create group identity among victims or potential victims, gun control advocates focused on the other two elements of the crime equation: the perpetrator and the weapon. This framing process constrained the movement for gun control in three ways.

First, the crime frame narrowed the range of victims, and therefore narrowed the scope of potential conflict. Because stranger-on-stranger violence is more common in cities than in nonurban areas, only urban dwellers are likely to be concerned about crime. And once framed as a measure for reducing urban violence, gun control had to compete with many other policy proposals to reform a deviant urban subculture.

Second, by framing gun control as crime control, advocates inadvertently bolstered arguments by the opposition that firearms regulations were futile and that only self-defensive measures stood a chance of being effective. The paradox of gun control is that demand for it increases at precisely those moments when crime is highest and faith in government to prevent crime is, by extension, weakest. Blaming government for not enforcing existing laws is something everyone can agree on. James Q. Wilson and Mark H. Moore argued in 1981 that comprehensive national gun control was unlikely to be adopted, because the "average legislator simply cannot afford to come before his or her constituents with the following proposal: 'Your government, having failed to protect you against crime, now proposes to strip from you what you regard as an effective means of self-defense as well as an enjoyable hobby.' "[44]

Third, by focusing on weaponry, the crime paradigm limited public involvement by conveying issue ownership to criminal-justice experts who themselves were divided on the wisdom of gun control. Gun control advocates were cognizant of the movement-limiting nature of the focus on weaponry. But rather than changing the frame, they adjusted it by constructing the notion of "bad guns" as opposed to other guns whose purposes were not so malevolent. From the start, the two largest advocacy groups—the Brady Campaign and the Coalition to Stop Gun Violence—

focused on handguns and military-style "assault weapons," while leaving mainstream long guns alone. This was a strategic choice: By focusing on weapons not normally associated with sport shooting, gun control advocates hoped to avoid inflaming hunters, plinkers, and rural people who used guns to repel wildlife. Gun control advocates also reasoned that mainstream rifles and shotguns were seldom used in stranger-on-stranger crime in cities, where control advocates were concentrated. Hence, to them handguns and assault rifles were the problem, and regulating access to these weapons was the solution. Of course, the NRA effectively neutralized the "bad gun" frame with its jeopardy argument: that regulation of handguns would inevitably lead to confiscation of long guns from law-abiding hunters and sportsmen.

## CHANGING THE FRAME: PERSONALIZING GUN CONTROL

The crime frame dominated the gun control debate from the 1930s at least through the mid-1990s. However, even as early as 1983, a prominent state gun control advocate was questioning its efficacy. "We are allowing our opponents to put us in a box," he complained. "Can we form a new vocabulary, a more enlightened response to the old arguments and raise the level of the dialogue?"[45] Beginning in the mid-1980s and accelerating in the 1990s, a small "critical community"[46] set about to do just that by recasting gun control as a measure to safeguard public health. Amid increases in teenage violence, first in urban gangs then in suburban schools, the public health message was narrowed to focus on safeguarding children. Although the crime frame remained prominent, the "child frame" dominated the debate from the mid-1990s to the 2000s. Increasingly, advocates talked in terms of "gun safety" rather than "gun control." This attempt to change the terms of debate offers an opportunity to test empirically the theory that issue frames have the power to constrain or expand the scope of political conflict, particularly citizen participation.

The child frame was made possible by a combination of circumstance and choice. By circumstance, I mean the availability of events and indicators that would provide raw material to support new issue frames. By choice, I mean the willful actions of issue entrepreneurs to locate and package these indicators so as to perpetuate a new way of thinking about firearms policy in America. In the case of gun control, these strategic choices narrowly preceded changes in circumstance, but changing circumstances clearly allowed these new understandings to take root beyond elite circles.

As noted in chapter 3, the reframing process began in earnest in the mid-1980s, when the surgeon general and public health experts in the

U.S. Centers for Disease Control and Prevention, together with a small community of physicians, began to argue that gun violence was a health problem as opposed to a crime problem. They likened guns to germs, capable of inflicting damage without regard to the characteristics of the afflicted individual. By extension, public health advocates argued that the policy debate should revolve around making guns and gun ownership safer rather than punishing perpetrators. This reconceptualization of gun control shifted the focus from aberrant individuals and aberrant weapons to mainstream victims and mainstream products.

As public health experts were beginning to claim issue ownership of gun violence, the nation began to witness what would become an unprecedented, seven-year increase in youth-on-youth violence. Between 1985 and 1994, the arrest rate for youths aged thirteen to seventeen nearly doubled.[47] The rate at which teens committed homicide tripled, and the rate at which they were murdered doubled in that time frame.[48] Indeed, teens and young adults were responsible for *all* the dramatic rise in violent crime in the late 1980s and early 1990s. Public health officials, swayed by exhortations to claim gun violence as a professional concern, labeled the 1987–1994 surge in violence an "epidemic."

Initially, the epidemic was concentrated among members of urban gangs, principally young African-American and Latino males. In this period neighborhood-based gangs began to compete with one another over market share in the new and profitable trade in crack cocaine. However, as territorial battles were settled, youthful gun violence spread outward, compelled by a logic of self-defense and a cultural norm associating firearms with status. By the early 1990s, violence by and against young people appeared to be less connected to the drug underworld and increasingly like a new feature of urban youth culture. The pivotal event that allowed for the credible reframing of gun violence as a child-protection issue occurred in January 1989. That was when an unemployed welder armed with a semiautomatic AK-47 rifle opened fire on a Stockton, California, elementary school playground filled with children, killing five of them. The event not only galvanized a successful campaign to ban the importation and, in some states, the possession of "assault weapons"; it also provided a vivid reference point in the mainstreaming of gun control. In the early 1990s, government-sponsored surveys documented an increase in the numbers of students carrying guns to school, findings that brought widespread coverage in the media and associated guns with something other than urban street crime.

Parental fears that the epidemic would spread to "safe schools" were borne out in the late 1990s, with a series of shootings of students by other students in small-town and suburban schools. The most famous of these was the shooting at Columbine High School in Littleton, Colorado, in

April 1999. In that incident, two students, armed with a cache of weapons, killed twelve of their classmates, a teacher, and themselves, and wounded twenty-one others. All told, between February 1996 and May 2000, there were sixteen high-profile shootings in schools. Forty people died, and eighty-seven were wounded, most of them schoolchildren. The median age of the shooter was fourteen.

The rise in youthful violence was actually two epidemics. The first, confined to minority teens in urban areas, was sustained over a longer period of time and was far more deadly in terms of the number of victims. The second, confined to largely white nonurban schools, garnered far more news coverage, largely because most of these incidents entailed multiple deaths in circumstances where gun violence was unexpected. Even as they were different in nature and scope, these epidemics provided the raw material by which gun control advocates could credibly reframe their issue to broaden, deepen, and lengthen public engagement. The new frame would portray gun control not as crime control but as a method of protecting innocent children.

To illustrate how dramatically the crime frame yielded to the child-protection frame, I have compiled a data set that charts the number of mentions of "children" or "kids" within five words of "gun" or "guns" in the *New York Times* over the period January 1980 through December 2000.[49] Figure 4.1 shows the increase in such mentions. In the 1980s, there were fewer than five stories per year; in the first part of the 1990s, there were typically ten to twenty stories per year. By the late 1990s, the number of stories per year jumped to the range of thirty to sixty.

The trend line in figure 4.1 is a crude indicator. But it does provide suggestive evidence that there was a growing problem, either real or perceived, with kids and guns, and that elites (including media elites) were paying attention to the problem.

A second, more refined approach to the question of how gun control was being reframed is to analyze letters to the editor.[50] They provide a reasonably good proxy of what citizen opinion leaders think, and it is these attentive laypeople who shape everyday discourse. I examined the way gun control was framed in letters to the editor of three important national newspapers—*USA Today,* the *Washington Post,* and the *New York Times*—in 1991 and in 1999 through 2000. The analysis provides strong evidence that, indeed, the school shootings reframed gun control from a criminal-justice issue into a child-protection issue. In 1991, 8% of pro-control letters (3 of 36) discussed gun control policy in terms of protecting children. In 1999, by contrast, that figure had increased six-fold, to 48% (68 of 143).

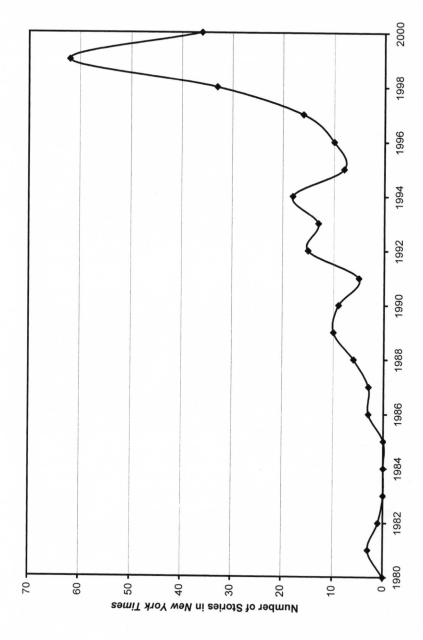

Figure 4.1. Newspaper Stories about Kids and Guns. Source: Nexis search of *New York Times* headlines and lead paragraphs.

A sample of text from the letters will clarify the point. In 1991, the typical letter was similar to the following, published in the *New York Times* on April 10:

> To the editor: In television interviews on PBS and ABC last week, Attorney General Dick Thornburgh said that one of his reasons for not supporting the bill requiring a seven-day waiting period for gun purchase is that only one-sixth of all murders committed with firearms involve guns legally purchased from an established dealer. He did not say that more than 12,000 murders are committed annually with firearms, and that one-sixth is equivalent to no fewer than 2,000 murders a year, or six every day. To this must be added the larger number of people injured by legally purchased firearms, with President Reagan and James Brady only the most prominent. Maybe if Mr. Thornburgh received every day a list of the six human beings killed with legally purchased guns, he would stop saying "only one-sixth."[51]

This letter and others like it portray gun control as an element of crime control. Placing tighter restrictions on legal gun markets, the author contends, would reduce the murder and injury rate. Another letter from 1991 responds to the drive-by murders of two Washington, D.C., women: "The tragic shootings of Marcia Williams and Patricia Lexie as they drove along public thoroughfares in Washington are ample testimony to the scourge of gun proliferation. . . . If we can muster the political will to face down a powerful lobby in order to ban smoking in public places due to the dangers of 'secondary smoke,' I suggest we now give some thought to the dangers of 'secondary bullets.'"[52]

By 1999, after two years of school shootings, the crime-control message had been eclipsed by another issue frame. In that year, nearly half of all letters sounded child-related themes. The following portions of the letters—all published in major newspapers in 1999 or 2000—provide a general sense of the way pro-control arguments had been reframed:

> Now that the Virginia lawmakers have blocked a move to ban guns in schools, let's thank them for proposing a minute of silent prayer in the classrooms. The kids can use it to pray they don't get shot.[53]

> In an April 4 letter, Robey Newsom, New York City region director of the New York State Rifle and Pistol Association, asks why law-abiding citizens should be forced to use trigger locks if police departments are resisting such a change. Sadly, all too many citizens are allowing their unlocked guns to fall into the hands of children, with tragic consequences.[54]

> We must not too quickly forget the larger and much more disturbing issue of our increasingly violent culture. We have no choice in this country but to remove the easy tools of violence from the reach of small and unbalanced hands. We should

all take grim note of the fact that the gun control debate once focused on disarm-ing criminals, and that we are now disarming our children.[55]

The unmitigated gall of the Republican Party of Carroll County Maryland! Raffling off a 9 mm Baretta handgun as a way to raise money for the Republican Party shows just how little they care about the consequences of the easy avail-ability of guns in this country. Republicans thumb their noses at the anguished parents of the Columbine High students and other victims of our national love of guns. . . . With adults setting the example with this sort of crass behavior, it is no wonder that children are turning out selfish and dangerous![56]

We mothers cringe, cry and curse every time we see another child fall victim to an act of gun violence, and in a year marked by scene after bloody scene of children slaughtered by firearms, we've cried a lot. It's time that we mothers exerted pressure on our representatives to pass serious gun laws.[57]

How much longer can this avoidable loss of life be justified by the constitutional "right to bear arms"? The right of American children to attend school freely and without fear seems to have somehow been forgotten.[58]

Together, these letters contain all three of the elements of a collective-action frame that William Gamson identifies as inspiring broad-based po-litical action. They sound emotionally charged themes of injustice (chil-dren dying or living in fear); of agency (we must pressure legislators); and of identity (regular citizens and everyday parents versus a local political party, gun manufacturers, and Second Amendment supporters).[59]

These frames were occasioned by events but crafted and disseminated by issue entrepreneurs working through advocacy groups. In the early 1990s, the established gun control groups began to use statistics devel-oped by the federal Centers for Disease Control and Prevention and other government agencies to frame gun control as a means of advancing child safety. The former leader of a national gun control organization recalls:

That's what impacted people, because people like to think they can always pro-tect their children, and when the children go to school they suddenly realize, "Oh my God, I've lost control, I can no longer protect my child, and to think there's a gun in that school that could injure or kill my child is a very disturbing thought." So certainly in terms of its emotional appeal, that was absolutely the strongest appeal out there, and so we were making the issue of children and guns very pointedly an issue before the Jonesboro [middle school] shooting [in 1998] or any that followed.[60]

Beginning in 1997, the child frame was adopted by President Clinton, who began using the term "child safety locks" to describe what up to then had been commonly known as "gun locks" or "trigger locks." The child frame was pioneered by policy entrepreneurs and political elites, but its most ardent purveyors were regular citizens: the organizers of the Million Mom March, a national protest for gun control organized after a shooting at a Jewish day care center in Granada Hills, California. The march, held in May 2000, drew hundreds of thousands of people to the National Mall in Washington and to statehouses and other public venues in seventy-three cities and towns nationwide. It was by far the largest demonstration ever in favor of tighter firearms laws. The march received extensive local and national press attention: fully 535 stories and letters in the nation's fifty highest-circulation newspapers between September 1999, when the march was conceived, until mid-June 2000, a month after it took place.[61]

As its name would suggest, the Million Mom March was primarily aimed at mobilizing women, who had been largely absent from gun control debates and activism but who were presumed to have an interest in the issue, particularly following the school shootings of the late 1990s. Thus, the event's publicity materials were suffused with maternal rhetoric and symbolism. For example, the march's slogan was "sensible gun laws, safe kids," and the principal organizer argued that if a woman could create a child in nine months, surely Congress could pass gun control legislation in that time frame. After the march, the organizers adopted the slogan "from a march to a movement" and set about creating chapters to advocate gun control as a child-safety measure. In short, the Million Mom March was a natural experiment in expanding, and sustaining, issue-oriented political participation. Or, in Joseph Gusfield's terms, it was an exercise in transferring issue ownership to women.[62]

Thus, after decades as a criminal-justice issue, gun control had by the late 1990s acquired a more accessible frame, one that would in principle appeal to a broad swath of the population and a politically potent one, at that: middle-class parents, especially mothers. If my cost-benefit theory is correct—that issue frames have the power to personalize benefits and in turn legitimize and compel political action—then the events of the late 1990s should provide empirical evidence of these effects. Below, I use a variety of data sources to illustrate that, indeed, the reframing of gun control has enhanced citizen mobilization in favor of tighter restrictions.

## How Frames Mobilize People

When gun control advocates started portraying their policy as a child-protection measure, more people participated more intensely over a longer period of time. In terms of the theory, conflict expanded along all three dimensions: breadth, depth, and length. Recasting gun control as a measure to safeguard children's health and safety (1) spurred broader individual involvement and issue ownership by new demographic groups;

(2) intensified engagement and involvement around the gun issue; and (3) inspired the creation of institutions to promulgate these new understandings and mobilize action around them. The evidence for these effects is consistent and shows up in a variety of ways, including histories of advocacy-group foundings, major national surveys of public opinion, and an original survey of participants in the Million Mom March. For information on that survey, which I oversaw, see appendix C. The evidence for lengthening, broadening, and deepening citizen engagement around the issue is considered in turn.

## Lengthening Political Conflict: Group Formation

Even before the school shootings of the late 1990s, gun violence involving youths proved a powerful spur to the creation of social-movement organizations and advocacy coalitions. The first gun control group in America, the Committee to Ban Teen-Age Weapons, active in the 1940s, was created in response to a postwar increase in gun violence among youths.[63] The National Council for a Responsible Firearms Policy, created in 1967, grew out of one man's concern over a highly publicized shooting of one teenager by another in Falls Church, Virginia, in 1962. In 1981, trustees and residents of Morton Grove, Illinois, pushed for the town's famous handgun ban after a gun shop sought permission to open near a junior high school and concerned adults "didn't want the kids looking in the window, dreaming of guns."[64] Sarah Brady, the nation's best-known gun control advocate, became involved not because her husband was shot during the Reagan assassination attempt but because her young son found a loaded gun in a car.

Although child-related incidents have long inspired collective action around gun control, this was never truer than in the 1990s. Indeed, for 60% of the forty-six gun control organizations created during that time, the impetus was citizens' concern about gun violence by and against youths. As table 4.1 shows, the founders of these groups were motivated either by the increase in youth-on-youth violence or by a particular incident involving a young person and a gun. Seven of the groups were founded by parents whose child had been shot.

For movement-building purposes, the most important of these groups is the Million Mom March. There are no reliable estimates of total Million Mom March membership nationwide. However, thirty months after the march, there were 107 chapters in thirty-four states and the District of Columbia.[65] Several electorally pivotal states, such as New York and Illinois, had multiple chapters. California alone had 19 chapters as of November 2002. Not all of these chapters were equally vibrant and ac-

TABLE 4.1
Gun Control Organizations Founded 1990–2002

| Group (State) | Est'd | Circumstances of Founding | Child Link? |
|---|---|---|---|
| Hawaii Firearms Control Coalition | 1990 | Founded by state Department of Health official as a coalition of mothers of victims, lawmakers, law enforcement, and antidomestic violence leaders | |
| Oregonians Against Gun Violence/Ceasefire Oregon | 1990 | Founded by parents of Rebecca Schaeffer, a young actress killed by a stalker | X |
| Citizens for a Safer Minnesota | 1990 | Grew out of a woman's efforts to secure a state assault weapons ban in wake of Stockton, Cal., playground massacre in 1989 | X |
| Zero Accidental Killings (TX) | 1991 | Group of mothers founded by Diane Clements, whose 13-year-old was accidentally shot by friend during game of hide-and-seek | X |
| Coalition to Reduce Gun Violence (MI) | 1991 | Founded by a state legislator; brought together 64 organizations interested in reducing violence | |
| Iowans for the Prevention of Gun Violence | 1991 | Founded after a graduate student killed four students and a faculty member at University of Iowa in 1991 | X |
| Virginians Against Handgun Violence | 1992 | Formed by mothers upset about a gang-related shooting outside a Norfolk middle school | X |
| Enough Is Enough—Women Against Gun Violence (MI) | 1992 | Started by a woman concerned about the level of gun violence, to help push the Brady Bill | |
| New Mexico Ceasefire | 1992 | Formed in response to high gun-suicide rate among young people | X |
| Mothers Against Violence (AL) | 1992/3 | Founded by nurse Carmen McCain after her 16-year-old son was killed in drive-by shooting | X |

TABLE 4.1 (*cont.*)
Gun Control Organizations Founded 1990–2002

| Group (State) | Est'd | Circumstances of Founding | Child Link? |
|---|---|---|---|
| Coalition Against Concealed Guns (MO) | 1992 | Women's, religious, and law enforcement groups that united to fight effort to loosen restrictions on obtaining concealed-carry permit | |
| Connecticut Coalition Against Gun Violence | 1992 | Founded by women activists concerned about gang violence in Bridgeport and New Haven | X |
| Parents United to Rally for Gun Elimination (NY) | 1993 | Founded by a Brooklyn mother after her son was shot and killed | X |
| Citizens Against Handgun Violence (WI) | 1993 | Formed to push for Madison mayor's proposed handgun ban | |
| Utahans Against Gun Violence | 1993 | Founded by Ron and Norma Molen after shooting death of their 22-year-old son, who was protecting a friend from her ex-boyfriend in her college dorm at Indiana U in 1992 | X |
| New Yorkers Against Gun Violence | 1993 | Founded by Brooklyn mothers after a schoolteacher was shot in Prospect Park | X |
| Legal Community Against Violence (CA) | 1993 | Founded by lawyers after a mass shooting at a San Francisco law firm | |
| North Carolinians Against Gun Violence | 1993 | Founded by Chapel Hill political activists after a teenager with a gun killed a jogger | X |
| HELP for Survivors (IL) | 1994 | Founded by a medical doctor and a child welfare executive whose 15-year-old son had been shot and killed | X |
| Mothers Against Violence in America (WA) | 1994 | Founded by advertising executive concerned about violence by and against children; sought to follow MADD model to bring mothers' perspective to the issue of violence | X |

TABLE 4.1 (cont.)
Gun Control Organizations Founded 1990–2002

| Group (State) | Est'd | Circumstances of Founding | Child Link? |
|---|---|---|---|
| Californians for Responsible Gun Laws | 1994 | Founded by veterans of Mothers Against Drunk Driving | X |
| Women Against Gun Violence (CA) | 1994 | Founded with help from American Jewish Congress during height of youth-violence epidemic to reframe gun violence as a mothers' issue | X |
| (Committee for the) Silent March | 1994 | Founded by a Brooklyn woman after the shooting of a teacher in a park near her home | X |
| Michigan Citizens for Handgun Control | 1994 | Founded by a newspaper reporter who "had to read about all the murders, suicides, etc.," and, when she retired, "felt the most important contribution I could make" was to elect pro-control lawmakers | |
| Texans Against Gun Violence | 1994 | Formed to fight loosening of restrictions on concealed carry permits | |
| Ceasefire Inc. | 1995 | Founded by punk singer Courtney Love after suicide of husband Curt Kobain, to promote handgun-free homes | |
| Stop Handgun Violence (MA) | 1995 | Founded by business leaders in response to growth in gun death and injury among youths | X |
| Citizens (Hoosiers) Concerned About Gun Violence (IN) | 1995 (2000) | Grew out of a "healthy city" initiative in Indianapolis, and was spurred by a young people's protest outside a firearms store that had sold a gun to a boy who then killed his adopted father | X |
| Wisconsin Anti-Violence Effort | 1995 | Started by peace and justice activists to reduce gun violence | |
| Ohio Coalition Against Gun Violence | 1995 | Founded by Interracial Religious Coalition of Toledo after the killing of a recent high school graduate in a parking lot | X |

TABLE 4.1 (*cont.*)
Gun Control Organizations Founded 1990–2002

| Group (State) | Est'd | Circumstances of Founding | Child Link? |
|---|---|---|---|
| Michigan Partnership to Prevent Gun Violence | 1995 | Founded by public health officials concerned about attempts to loosen gun laws | |
| Stop Gun Violence—Orange County Citizens for the Prevention of Gun Violence (CA) | 1995 | Founded by Mary Leigh and Charles Blek, whose son was killed in an armed robbery | X |
| Louisiana Ceasefire | 1996 | Founded by a university professor after the Japanese exchange student he was hosting was shot on Halloween by a neighbor who mistook the teenager for a burglar | X |
| Citizens of Arizona to Prevent Gun Violence | 1998 | Founded by 30 people representing public health, law enforcement, and religious groups, victims, parents, and government agencies concerned about the high gun violence rate in Arizona | |
| Colorado Coalition Against Gun Violence | 1998 | Founded by Physicians for Social Responsibility | |
| Safe State Kansas | 1998 | Founded to counter NRA attempts to relax concealed-carry laws in Kansas | |
| PAX | 1998 | Founded by two advertising executives, including one whose brother was shot in Empire State Building in 1997, to change the "gun culture" | |
| Bell Campaign (merged with Million Mom March, 2000) | 1999 | Founded by a group of foundation and public health activists to build a victims' movement for gun control based on the Mothers Against Drunk Driving model | |
| Safe Schools and Workplaces Campaign Committee (MO) | 1999 | Founded to fight concealed-carry referendum; framed issue in terms of protecting schoolchildren and workers | X |

TABLE 4.1 (cont.)
Gun Control Organizations Founded 1990–2002

| Group (State) | Est'd | Circumstances of Founding | Child Link? |
|---|---|---|---|
| Indiana Partnership to Prevent Firearm Violence | 1999 | Founded by public health and medical professionals, with law enforcement and community leaders, to reduce the rate of gun violence in the state | |
| SAFE Colorado | 1999 | Created after Columbine High School shootings | X |
| Maine Citizens Against Handgun Violence | 1999 | Founded in response to school shootings, domestic violence, and concern over child access to firearms | X |
| Common Sense About Kids and Guns | 1999 | Founded by wife of Sen. Edward Kennedy to encourage safe storage of firearms to prevent accidents and suicide among youths | X |
| Million Mom March (and MMM Foundation) | 2000 | Founded by mothers after California day care shooting and related incidents at schools | X |
| Americans for Gun Safety | 2000 | Founded by Internet entrepreneur to find a middle ground in the gun control debate | |
| CeaseFire Pennsylvania | 2002 | Grew out of Million Mom March organizations in the state | X |

*Note:* This table was assembled from lists compiled by national gun control organizations, interviews, and newspaper stories. Information could not be obtained for Contra Costa Coalition to Prevent Gun Violence, Georgians Against Gun Violence, Florida Coalition to Stop Gun Violence, GRIEF of Indiana, Kansans for Handgun Control, New Hampshire Ceasefire, Pennsylvanians Against Handgun Violence (1992), or San Diego Committee Against Violence.

tive, obviously, but they were at the very least a latent force of like-minded women who were motivated to push for tighter gun regulations and who knew how to contact one another when necessary. Million Mom March organizations provided the local face-to-face organizational base for state and national gun control groups and in many places worked in tandem with them.

In line with William Gamson's argument that challenger groups succeed in part when they become accepted as a legitimate representative for their side of an issue,[66] the Million Mom March chapters received extensive and sympathetic coverage from local media outlets; were routinely contacted by reporters seeking to balance comments from gun rights groups; and inspired a concerted drive by gun rights supporters to create and build a parallel organization of women, the Second Amendment Sisters, to undermine women's "ownership" of the gun control issue. The Million Mom March lengthened the scope of conflict by institutionalizing not only its chapters but also women's ownership of gun control, now recast as a "moms' issue." In effect, a grassroots uprising gave birth to an elite, opinion-shaping organization that locked in the new child-centered issue frame that was evolving out of the school shootings.

## *Broadening Political Conflict: Individual Participation*

In continuing the process of redefining gun control as a citizens' issue, rather than an experts' issue, the Million Mom March organization made a strategic calculation that the framing of an issue influences participation. The claim is that issues defined as the proper province of parents are likely to produce broader and more sustained participation than are issues that are defined as the proper province of experts, such as law enforcement officials or policy analysts. Even before the march, the evidence lent credence to this assumption.

In the introduction, I argued that gun control was perennially on the elite agenda but seldom the focus of mass mobilization. However, that pattern began to change in 1998, when the number of stories mentioning gun control activism began to rise. (See figure 1.2.) In 1997, the *New York Times* had sixteen such mentions; by 2000 the number had quadrupled, to sixty-four. Indeed, when examined across the entire forty-three years documented, the graph shows a clear and unusually steady rise in gun control activism in the late 1990s, precisely when the issue was reframed in terms of child protection.

Such aggregate evidence may be spurious. Perhaps the advent of the child frame and the rise in citizen activism are merely coincidental, rather than causally related. To lend credence to the framing-behavior connection, one ideally would want evidence at the individual level, rather than

TABLE 4.2
Gun Control Activity, by Gender (1996 and 1999)

| Activity | Women | | | Men | | |
|---|---|---|---|---|---|---|
| | 1996 (%) | 1999 (%) | % CHANGE | 1996 (%) | 1999 (%) | % CHANGE |
| Joined org. | 2.9 | 3.4 | +17 | 6.4 | 4.4 | –31 |
| Gave money | 5.8 | 5.9 | +2 | 7.2 | 6.9 | –4 |
| Wrote public official | 2.1 | 5.0 | +138 | 3.1 | 4.4 | +42 |
| At least one of these acts | 7.9 | 10.3 | +30 | 12.7 | 10.6 | –16 |

Source: National Gun Policy Surveys.

the aggregate level. Fortunately, a national survey conducted during the early phase of the reframing process, and again four years later, permits us to examine whether individual engagement indeed broadened.

In 1996, when the newly formed gun control groups were still finding their voice, and before the spate of mass shootings in public schools, the National Opinion Research Center at the University of Chicago conducted the first National Gun Policy Survey (NGPS). The 1996 survey asked respondents whether, in the past five years, they had (1) joined an organization that supports gun control; (2) given money to an organization that supports gun control; or (3) written a letter to, or e-mailed, a public official supporting gun control. At my request the 1999 NGPS, conducted five months after the Columbine shootings, repeated those three participation questions.

Table 4.2 shows the fraction of respondents reporting engagement in such activities and the change in the participation rate between the two survey years. As gun control was being recast as a child-protection measure, we should expect to see an increase in political activity among the demographic group with socially recognized moral authority over children: women and mothers. And, indeed, the surveys document such an effect. While male participation shows no clear pattern, female participation was unambiguously on the rise.

As the table shows, all three forms of participation increased among women. Among men, group-based participation actually declined, while letter writing rose. Overall, the fraction of women who were involved in some way rose substantially (by 30%), while the fraction of involved men dropped (by 16%).

Another way to look at the survey data is from the perspective of a "rational prospector" —that is, an interest-group leader seeking members or donors.[67] In 1996, a rational prospector would have targeted men; they were simply more likely to be involved in all three types of activity than were women. By 1999, however, women were catching up. Their participation rate overall (having done any of the three activities) was nearly identical to that of men, and their propensity to write letters to public officials actually surpassed that of men. This finding is particularly surprising insofar as decades of political-science studies have found that women are significantly less involved in civic and political activities than are men.[68]

The 1999 gun policy survey also asked respondents about whether they *had been contacted* to participate in any gun control–related activity. Research on everything from charitable giving to political-party volunteering has long found that one of the best predictors of involvement is recruitment, or "being asked." Because the question was not asked in any of the earlier gun policy surveys, we unfortunately cannot gauge whether there was more mobilization or recruitment in the wake of the school shootings. However, the recruitment questions in the 1999 survey can give us some insight into the receptivity of different groups to those messages. Consistent with the findings above, these questions suggest that women were more easily mobilized than were men.[69] While women were less likely than were men to be contacted to do something for gun control, women who were contacted were more likely to do what was asked. For example, 5% of women were contacted to join a pro-control organization, compared with 8% of men. But, among those contacted, 17% of women joined, compared with only 7% of men. A similar pattern emerges for contacting a public official. Fully 26% of women who were asked to write said they did so, compared with 19% of men.

Taken as a whole, the survey evidence strongly suggests that, after the Columbine shootings, the gun control issue was "feminized." There is ample circumstantial evidence that Columbine helped to close the participation gap between men and women. Because the 1999 survey took place before organizing for the Million Mom March had begun in earnest, the survey did not capture the activities that were related to the march or inspired by it. If the survey had been conducted after the march, women's participation in gun control activities likely would have registered larger gains.

Of course, the most visible measure of broadened participation was the Million Mom March itself. The march drew hundreds of thousands of women to the Washington Mall and to more than seventy cities and towns nationwide on Mother's Day 2000. The march was a calculated attempt to broaden the scope of political conflict by incorporating middle-class women into the advocacy ranks.

Did the march actually broaden involvement, or did it merely bring together in one place people who had previously been involved in gun control activism? My survey of nearly eight hundred participants at the main event, in Washington, suggests that most of the participants were indeed new to the gun control cause; they were first-time activists. Fully 72% had never taken any action to further firearms regulation, such as writing a letter to an elected official or giving money to a gun control group.

Not only did the march draw new people to the cause; it also reached a politically potent demographic group that had been sympathetic toward gun control but largely uninvolved in advocacy for it. That key demographic group was educated, middle-class, civically skilled women experienced in political organizing and engagement. According to my survey, more than half of the marchers (51%) had at least some graduate school experience. This is sharply higher than the 7% of adult women (age twenty-five or older) that the Census Bureau estimates hold a graduate degree. The marchers were also wealthier than is the typical American: 40% of the sample had a household income over $100,000, compared with just 10% of American households.[70] Not surprisingly, more than half of the participants came from suburban areas. Thus, it appears that the march was skewed toward the middle- and upper-income brackets.

Moreover, as expected, the marchers were far more civically active than is the typical American. Fully 71% of all respondents had been actively involved in a sociopolitical cause at some time in the past. The most common category of involvement was "civil, women's, or gay rights," cited by 43% of the total sample, followed by abortion rights, cited by 34%. Fully 45% had been involved in multiple causes. The marchers were far more likely to have been involved in liberal causes than in conservative or middle-of-the road causes. Respondents were also far more active in standard civic pursuits than is the typical American. Respondents were asked a question off the Roper Social and Political Trends Survey about whether, in the past year, they had carried out any of eight civic activities, such as writing a letter to Congress or serving on a local organization board. Fully 77% had done at least one of the eight activities—compared with just 35% in Roper's national sample.[71] Roughly speaking, the marchers were more than twice as civically inclined as is the average American.

To summarize, the reframing of gun control as a family issue widened the scope of conflict by conveying issue ownership to American women. Evidence from newspaper coverage, a survey of a nationally representative sample of the American population, and a study of Million Mom March participants all points toward a greater socialization of political conflict in light of the new, more accessible understandings.

### Deepening the Political Conflict: Intensity

Finally, changing the issue frame intensified political engagement: Sympathizers cared more and did more than they might have otherwise. The intensification took three forms. First, the gun control issue became more important to those who were already gun control sympathizers. Second, these sympathizers took a harder line against the acceptability of guns. Third, gun control sympathizers took part in gun control activism to a greater extent than they would have otherwise. Survey evidence documents each of these three measures of deepened engagement.

First, studies suggest that gun control has grown in importance, particularly among women, the group expected to be most susceptible to the new issue frame. Approximately once a decade, a representative national sample of Americans has been asked how important the gun control issue is to them. The question was asked as part of the General Social Survey in 1976 and 1984, and at my request the identical question was placed on the 1999 NGPS. In 1999, the fraction of Americans who rated gun control as important, or one of the most important issues, was 26%, compared with 17% in 1984 and 13% in 1976. However, among women, the jump was even larger—29% in 1999, compared with 16% in 1984 and 11% in 1976. Of course, this measure is imprecise: The observed increase occurred during a fifteen-year span (1984–1999) and cannot conclusively be pegged to the school shootings in the late 1990s. However, in light of the other surveys, it seems reasonable that at least part of the 1999 increase stemmed from the school shootings.

Second, in support of that interpretation, a separate longitudinal survey of Americans has documented an increased uneasiness about guns in the home, and again the shift is particularly noticeable among women. Since 1974, the DDB Needham Life Style surveys have asked a representative sample of Americans how much they agree, or disagree, that "there should be a gun in every home."[72] A solid majority of women has consistently rejected such a notion, but women's disagreement significantly intensified in the 1990s. For fifteen years, the surveys found growing aversion to keeping a gun in the home, and an analysis of the data shows that the trend has been driven exclusively by women who "definitely" do not think guns belong in the home. This suggests that women experienced an intense backlash against guns throughout the 1980s and 1990s.[73] The fraction of women who "definitely disagree" that there should be a gun in every home rose from about 40% in the 1970s and early 1980s to 53% by 1998. The increase in men's strong disagreement was far less pronounced.

I have offered two measures of intensity that have increased as the gun control debate has been reframed. In the first case, I showed that, after the school shootings, more women considered gun control to be a very important issue to them. I also showed that women grew more hostile to guns. The third measure, from my panel study of Million Mom March participants, links cognitive intensity and political behavioral more explicitly.

In the original survey, I asked respondents to rank the top three reasons for attending the march. Two "child-centered" reasons were listed among the eight possible choices. (See appendix C for the method of coding frames.) In the follow-up survey, I asked respondents to indicate what sorts of pro-control activities they had undertaken since the march. If maternal frames motivate women's action, we would expect that, other things being equal, those who attended the march out of concern for children would be more intensely involved in pro-control activity after the march than would participants who saw the issue differently.

The surveys find limited support for that proposition. To evaluate the association between conceptual frame and political behavior, I created four measures of "follow-up activity": unilateral acts (e.g., writing a letter to Congress), intense acts (e.g., organizing a local gun control committee); recruitment acts (e.g., asking someone to sign a petition), and total acts. (These variables and the observed frequency of each follow-up act are summarized in appendix C.) I then segmented the respondents into two groups: those who reported being at the march out of concern for children—that is, those who saw the gun control issue through a "child frame" —and those who were at the march because of other motivations, such as to reduce violent crime or to address a long-standing concern about gun availability. Respondents were coded as having a "child frame" if, among their top three motivations, they checked either or both of the two child-centered rationales ("fear for the safety of my children" or "protect the safety of children") and *did not* check either of the two criminal-justice rationales ("reduce our nation's high crime rate" or "fear for my own safety") among the top three or "speak out on behalf of . . . a victim" as the number one reason.

Table 4.3 compares the average number of follow-up acts performed by the two groups of respondents: those who conceived of gun control through a child-centered frame and those who did not. As the table shows, the maternally motivated respondents were consistently more involved in follow-up activities, however measured, than were other respondents.

Although the difference between the means is not significant at the conventional .05 level, in two cases the difference is significant at the .10 level. Finding statistically significant differences is especially difficult in small samples, such as this one. I cautiously interpret the consistency of the findings—that maternally motivated respondents were more involved—as evidence that frames have consequences for political action.

These findings are upheld in regression analysis. To test for a causal connection between framing and sustained activism, I ran four multivariate regression models, corresponding to each of the four dependent variables. The analyses adapt and build on Sidney Verba, Kay Lehman Schlozman, and Henry Brady's civic participation model, the gold standard for

TABLE 4.3
Million Mom March: Mean Number of Follow-up Acts by Issue Frame

| | RS with Child Frame | RS with Other Frame | "Child Frame" Effect | P Value for Difference |
|---|---|---|---|---|
| Unilateral Acts | 4.36 | 3.63 | +0.73 | 0.062* |
| Intense Acts | 0.93 | 0.65 | +0.28 | 0.161 |
| Ask Acts | 0.75 | 0.68 | +0.07 | 0.708 |
| Total Acts | 5.05 | 4.21 | +0.84 | 0.069[a] |

Note: Data for adult women (21+) only (N = 180).
[a] Significant at the .10 level.

predicting what drives people to get involved in public affairs.[74] The independent variables in my model include ten standard predictors of participation, capturing demographic and political propensities. I also include a block of three emotional and cognitive variables that I term the "commitment" block. These variables capture how important the gun control issue was to the respondent; what kind of experience, if any, the respondent had had with gun violence; and whether the respondent saw the issue through a child-centered frame. If framing processes do inspire action, we should expect to see a more intense involvement by participants who viewed gun control as a child-safety issue. Intense involvement is measured in two ways: degree of effort, as captured by the number of follow-up activities; and the likelihood of having engaged in intense activities, those that are more difficult or time-consuming to pursue.

As table 4.4 shows, the "child frame" variable is highly significant in three of the four models, and is of the proper sign in the fourth. It is important to note that the magnitude of this variable is modest but meaningful. On average, an individual who conceived of gun control as a child-safety issue would carry out 18% more follow-up acts than would someone who conceived of the issue in other terms, all else being equal. More substantively, for the average respondent, conceiving of gun control in child-protection terms increased the number of "intense acts" by one.[75] This does not seem like much of an increase until one considers that the average number of intense acts performed was well under one, and the median respondent performed no intense follow-up acts. The statistical and practical significance of the "child frame" variable is not a simple artifact of motherhood (which is controlled for), or of issue importance (also controlled). Instead, ideas and emotions connected to maternal roles appear to matter.

For purposes of the theory of issue frames that I have laid out, the findings above lend support to the proposition that personalizing the gun control issue, and by extension the benefits of political engagement, leads to greater mass engagement. Indeed, regression models that account for cognitive and emotional variables perform considerably better than those that include only the textbook predictors of civic engagement (demographic variables, recruitment, etc.). Table 4.5 shows the improvement in goodness-of-fit statistics for the four models analyzed in table 4.4 as cognitive and emotional variables are entered. The models that incorporate emotions and cognitions are substantially more powerful than those that do not, adding 4–5 percentage points to the goodness-of-fit statistics. While that may seem like a modest boost, it is important to remember that the "best" models of civic participation explain only about 33–45% of the variance.[76] By that benchmark, an improvement of 4–5 percentage points is important and meaningful. All told, capturing intensity and

Table 4.4
Four Models of Sustained Involvement in Gun Control Activity

| Dependent Variable | All Acts[a] (OLS) | Unilateral Acts[a] (OLS) | Intense Acts (logistic) | Recruit Acts (logistic) |
|---|---|---|---|---|
| Civic voluntarism model (Verba et al.) | | | | |
| *Education* | | | | |
|   Highest level of education | −0.112*** | −0.086** | −0.980*** | −0.200 |
| *Income and time* | | | | |
|   Pretax income (2000) | 0.010 | 0.011 | 0.128 | −0.109 |
|   # of children at home | −0.005 | −0.009 | −0.232 | −0.014 |
| *Institutional affiliation* | | | | |
|   Work or student | −0.201** | −0.187** | −0.999** | −0.283 |
| *Civic skills* | | | | |
|   Total civic acts (Roper) | 0.037** | 0.036** | 0.242*** | 0.155* |
| *Political engagement* | | | | |
|   Political ideology | 0.024 | 0.019 | −0.071 | 0.065 |
|   # of causes active in previously | −0.002 | −0.015 | 0.148 | 0.221 |
|   Active in gun control previously | 0.282*** | 0.221*** | 0.444 | 0.509 |
| *Recruitment* | | | | |
|   Contacted by Million Mom March since march | 0.372**** | 0.336**** | 1.436*** | 0.786** |
|   Recruited through media only | 0.093 | 0.106* | −0.038 | 0.326 |
| Civic voluntarism + commitment | | | | |
| *Intensity* | | | | |
|   Gun Control most important issue | 0.258** | 0.170 | 0.679 | 1.054* |
|   Experiences with gun violence | 0.083 | 0.049 | −0.390 | 0.514 |
| *Issue frame* | | | | |
|   See gun control as child protection issue | 0.160** | 0.160** | 1.005** | 0.423 |
| *Constant* | 1.556**** | 1.422**** | 2.549* | −1.369 |
| R-square/pseudo R-square | 0.353 | 0.330 | 0.403 | 0.229 |

[a] I used the natural log of these dependent variables to reduce their skewed distribution.

\* $p < .10$; \*\* $p < .05$; \*\*\* $p < .01$; \*\*\*\* $p < .001$; numbers are unstandardized coefficients (B).

framing effects increases the goodness-of-fit statistics by 13–26%, depending on the measure of follow-up involvement. To have an accurate understanding of why people participate, this study suggests, scholars should not overlook how people think and feel about issues. The maternal frame caused the gun control issue to hit home and gave women a language to legitimize their engagement.

## An Alternate Explanation?

This chapter has argued that reframing the gun control issue has lengthened, widened, and deepened political participation around firearms regulation. Before reaching that conclusion, however, it is important to examine an alternate possibility: that people got more involved in gun control activity because gun violence was escalating. That is, perhaps it was underlying trends that induced activism.

TABLE 4.5
Including Emotion and Cognition Improves Models of Sustained Participation

|  | All Acts ($R^2$) | Unilateral Acts ($R^2$) | Intense Acts (Pseudo $R^2$) | Recruit Acts (Pseudo $R^2$) |
|---|---|---|---|---|
| Civic voluntarism model | 0.311 | 0.293 | 0.348 | 0.181 |
| Civic voluntarism + commitment | 0.353 | 0.330 | 0.403 | 0.229 |

*Note*: R-squares (used for OLS models) are unadjusted; pseudo R-squares (used for logistic models) are Nagerkerke statistics.
*Source*: Analysis of Million Mom March data.

There is no evidence for this conclusion. In fact, the increase in gun control activism came at a time when gun violence was dropping precipitously—and had been for a half-dozen years. Firearms crimes per 100,000 skyrocketed between 1985 and 1993, and then they fell as quickly as they had risen. By 1999, when Columbine occurred, the firearms crime rate was down 45% relative to the 1993 level. The gun murder rate likewise had dropped by 44%, reaching lows not seen since the 1960s. The same pattern is in evidence when we look at the subpopulation of youths. Young people were dramatically less likely to be involved in firearms offenses, either as victims or perpetrators, in the late 1990s than they were in the late 1980s and early 1990s. Figure 4.2 shows the run-up in homicides, by and against, juveniles in that period, and the concomitant decline after the mid-1990s. Even allowing for a normal lag between trends and reactive engagement, it seems unlikely that the lag would be six years or more.

Nor was school violence—a subset of crimes by and against youths— on the increase. According to the Justice Department, the violent victimization rate fell from 48 crimes per 1,000 students in 1992 to 43 per 1,000 students in 1998.[77] Finally, accidental shootings involving children, which had always been rare, had become even more rare over the decade.

In sum, the evidence strongly suggests that it was the framing of the issue, rather than the underlying trends, that spurred activism. The "child frame" resonated in the wake of the rare but highly publicized school shootings, which changed the face of gun violence in America. The gun violence epidemic of the 1980s and early 1990s was concentrated among one group: young African-American and Latino men who lived in inner cities and were often involved in gangs and/or the illegal-drug trade. The gun violence epidemic of the late 1990s was concentrated among another group: white teenage boys who lived in rural areas and suburbs and had not typically been involved in significant illegal activity. The school shootings made violence a (white) mainstream problem, even though these shootings were responsible for only a tiny fraction—0.08%—of gun murders in the United States. Even as the crime rate goes down, the "gun

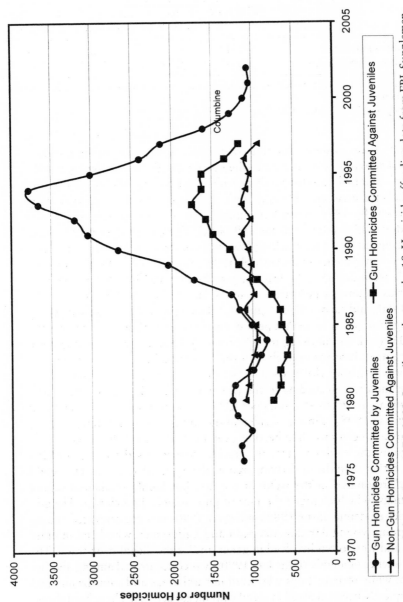

Figure 4.2. Kids and Guns, 1976–2002. Juveniles are those under 18. Homicide offending data from FBI, Supplementary Homicide Reports, analyzed in *Homicide Trends in the United States* (http://www.ojp.usdoj.gov/bjs/homicide/tables/weapagetab.htm). Homicide victimization data adapted from Snyder and Sickmund, *Juvenile Offenders and Victims: 1999 National Report*, 19 (http://ojjdp.ncjrs.org/ojstatbb/html/qa128.html).

problem" in the United States remains an "adult crime problem," although it has been reframed as a "child-protection problem." The reframing of the issue was driven not by statistics so much as by events.

## WHY DID REFRAMING WORK?

Until the late 1990s, arguments for gun control revolved around what for gun control advocates was a self-evident truth: Guns are easily accessible; bad people use bad guns to hurt and kill; thus, restricting access to firearms will improve social welfare. In fact, the third prong of the syllogism was highly contestable. Framing gun control as a means of reducing crime or lethal violence opened the door to technical arguments about the effectiveness of policy instruments, the characteristics of different makes and models of firearms, the motivations of the criminal mind, and so forth. In essence, the crime frame brought the gun control debate to a stalemate in which experts on both sides debated questions in terms not easily accessible to the typical American concerned about violence.

Gun control leaders always recognized the need for consensus-building frames. That is why the major organizations focused exclusively on handguns (and later, so-called assault weapons) while steering clear of polices governing rifles and shotguns. With each defeat, gun control advocates crafted ever more consensual frames to expand their political appeal. The reconceptualization of gun control as a way to protect children was the apotheosis of this desire. The child frame was consensual in two senses: It used depoliticizing language, and it constructed universally sympathetic victim narratives. The child frame allowed women to be altruistic, while also being political.

The child frame was the product of its time, and it resonated because it tapped into parental anxieties about cultural violence. John Kingdon has suggested that a focusing event is more likely to move an issue onto the political agenda when the event "reinforce[s] some preexisting perception of a problem."[78] When a focusing event such as a school shooting occurs, people begin a collective search for the proper way to categorize the event—its proper conceptual box. The focusing event is likely to be put into whatever conceptual box is most salient, to be reconciled with emerging understandings and trends. In laymen's terms, the event will be translated, rightly or wrongly, into "the best evidence yet" for some emerging claim about "the way things are these days."

Indeed, this is the key to understanding why the school shootings had such power over the redefinition of the gun control issue. The shootings took place against a backdrop of public concern about declining values, civility, and community in America. Gallup polls asking about "the most

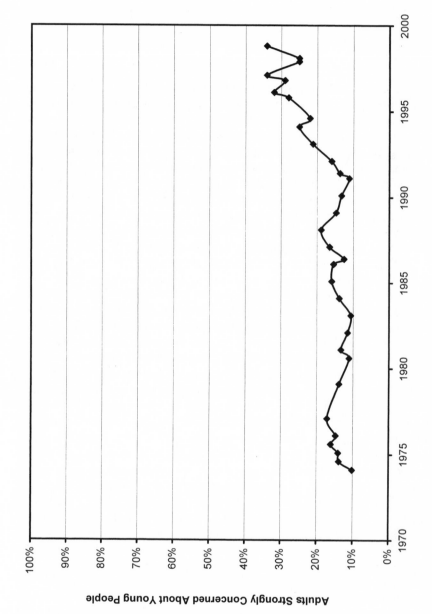

Figure 4.3. Rising Concern about American Youths, 1974–1998. Source: Roper Social and Political Trends surveys.

important problem facing this country" show an unmistakable and steady increase in American concern over "ethics, morals, family decline, children not being raised right." This trend, which began in the early 1990s, preceded the school shootings, and was accelerated by them. The sharpest increase occurred in 1997 and early 1998, when the first of the school shootings were taking place. It is difficult to say definitively that the shootings caused the spikes. But there is a clear correlation between the two. For example, one major spike registered in a survey taken one month after a March 1998 school shooting in Jonesboro, Arkansas, in which fifteen were killed or injured; another major spike registered in a survey taken a month after the Columbine massacre. Nonetheless, the important finding from these surveys is that concern about declining social values was clearly intensifying before the shootings.

Further evidence along the same lines comes from the Roper Social and Political Trends surveys, which have asked a nationally representative sample of American adults to name the two or three issues that they are personally most concerned about. The surveys, conducted thirty-two times over the 1974–1998 period, show a sharp increase beginning around 1990 in adults' concern about "the way young people think and act."[79] As figure 4.3 shows, throughout the 1970s and 1980s, about 15–20% of adults cited youth misbehavior as among their top concerns; this rate might be thought of as the normal level of grown-ups' fretting about the younger generation. But in 1991, the level of concern began to spread, reaching 35% of adults by the late 1990s—a level two to three times that seen in the turbulent 1970s.

It is worth noting that the increase in media discourse about youths and guns, as discussed earlier, very closely tracks the trend in public concern about children and values more generally. Both trend lines began going up in the early 1990s and peaked in 1999, the year of the Columbine shooting.

The reframing of gun control as child protection widened the gulf that already existed within advocacy circles. For example, the Violence Policy Center's Josh Sugarmann argues that with the reframing, "It became a defensive battle. The gun control movement in the 1980s moved from gun control to stopping gun violence."[80] That said, the new frame also allowed the gun control campaign to go on the offensive by encouraging broader, more intense, and more sustained citizen participation around the issue. The child frame was effective both because it activated current anxieties about child welfare and because it linked a policy proposal (gun regulation) to a deeply embedded moral principle (the protection of children) that is not bounded by space or time. The child frame is not necessarily the only frame that might expand popular mobilization in favor of gun control or other social-regulatory proposals, but over the centuries it has proved to be a particularly effective one. The quantitative evidence presented here—that when kids' welfare is perceived to be at stake, average Americans turn out in meaningful ways for gun control—is not particularly surprising in light of other social-regulatory movements' experience throughout history. If the child frame is a hearty perennial, the present case has added yet one more bulb to the garden. The only surprise, perhaps, is that it took so long for the gun control campaign to find a way to articulate the family-centered frame that had worked so well for so many movements before.

# CHAPTER FIVE

# Changing the Calculation: Policy Incrementalism and Political Participation

> It is difficult to draw a man out of his own circle to interest
> him in the destiny of the state. . . . But if it is proposed to
> make a road cross the end of his estate, he will see at a glance
> that there is a connection between this small public affair
> and his greatest private affairs. . . . Thus far more may be
> done by entrusting to the citizens the administration of minor
> affairs than by surrendering to them in the control of
> important ones.
>
> —Alexis de Tocqueville, *Democracy in America*[1]

SOCIALIZING THE COSTS OF PARTICIPATION, and personalizing the benefits, are two ways by which issue advocates can expand political conflict to their advantage. This chapter considers a third mechanism: increasing the expected value of social benefits relative to the expected value of personal costs. The individual's cost-benefit assessment improves when he calculates that a minor investment of political resources (individual costs) will produce the desired policy outcome (social benefits). This is what I have termed the participation payoff. In a decentralized, fragmented democracy, an expected participation payoff is increased when social-movement organizations pursue *policy incrementalism*: small policy steps that might be expected to aggregate toward ever larger political goals. In the United States, all bona fide social movements have proceeded incrementally.

Perhaps the most important reason that gun control has never generated a mass movement is that gun control advocates spurned incrementalism in favor of a "rational national" strategy of policy change. The rational-national strategy favored bold, comprehensive, nation-spanning gun control laws that offered little opportunity for broad-based participation. The alternative—incrementalism—is significantly more conducive to movement building. Vertical incrementalism—the process of making policy at lower levels of government and allowing those successes to influence policy making at higher levels—is particularly important in federalist systems, in which policy-making authority is decentralized. Horizontal incrementalism—expanding the scope or severity of an existing body of law—is particularly suited to democracies characterized by inter-est-group pluralism, porous and fragmented institutional structures, highly competitive parties, and classical liberal political cultures. The Founding Fathers designed the U.S. system, with its separation of powers and checks and balances, precisely to stymie swift, bold policy change. In short, incrementalism may be the only strategy that has a chance of succeeding in the United States, at least in normal times.

Strictly speaking, incrementalism refers to policy making, not participa-tion. However, the gun control case shows that there is a clear link be-tween the policy-making strategies that advocates embrace and the scope and duration of popular participation they might expect. Incrementalism encourages participation by bolstering individuals' sense of collective ef-ficacy. People participate when they are reasonably hopeful that their par-ticipation will contribute to a desired outcome. To calculate that probabil-ity, rational individuals not only assess the (prospective) probability of the activity's success should they join, but also the (retrospective) record of success when others have been involved. To attract participants, then, advocates need to demonstrate that their efforts have momentum: past successes snowballing into probable future successes. In other words, to gain strength, movements need already to be moving. Incrementalism en-courages conflict expansion by favorably altering the perception of orga-nizational momentum, both past and future, thereby increasing the esti-mated benefit/cost ratio of individual participation. In sum, policy incrementalism encourages popular political participation; rational-na-tional policy agendas discourage it. They are movement constraining.

The gun control case elucidates an important dynamic in contemporary America: "the policy-politics paradox." Advocates for sociopolitical re-form often face an agonizing trade-off between pursuing legislation that would work ("good policy") and political strategies that would be effec-tive in securing that legislation ("good politics"). Although sensible policy and smart politics should go hand in hand, in fragmented democracies these goals are more typically at odds. Good policy makes for bad politics; good politics makes for bad policy.[2] In the face of this policy-politics para-dox, gun control supporters opted for sound policy, in effect forgoing a movement-building strategy in the interest of moral and ideological pu-rity. Gun rights supporters, on the other hand, put politics above policy ideals. They systematically chipped away at gun regulations to achieve the comprehensive result they ultimately desired. Thus, gun rights advocates pursued a politics-driven strategy that has largely succeeded in mobilizing supporters; gun control advocates pursued a policy-driven strategy that has largely failed to deliver the legislative results they desired.

American social movements often divide over the question of whether to pursue a slow, laborious, incremental approach that involves seemingly inconsequential local victories and unsavory compromises, or whether to stick to principle and hope for that serendipitous yet rare political opportunity in which bold, national action is possible. The gun control "movement" eventually splintered over this very issue, contributing to sometimes bitter clashes within the national gun control leadership that have undermined cooperative efforts. Although they came to dominate the policy debates, the go-slow forces remain, at best, ambivalent about incrementalism. In a sense, the reason there was no gun control movement in America was because national gun control leaders unwittingly chose not to have one.

Whether that choice is changing—and there is evidence that it is—will be considered in the next chapter. This chapter will offer a brief history of gun control leaders' efforts to pass rational-national firearms regulation; explain why they pursued that strategy; and discuss the myriad ways that it backfired, with grave implications not only for passing stricter gun control laws but also for broadening and deepening public involvement in that cause.

## The Rational Strategy

From the start, gun control advocates have been deeply divided over specific policy proposals, but they have been united over the ultimate need for comprehensive gun control laws. This section reviews the historical evolution of the policy proposals offered by gun control advocates. First, I show that gun control advocates, particularly but not exclusively at the national level, have pursued gun policies that would be both broad and severe—that is, not incremental by any definition. In terms of breadth, the policies would have imposed direct costs on tens of millions of gun owners, as opposed to burdening the far smaller universe of dealers and manufacturers. During the gun control campaign's formative years, and to some extent in the years since, advocates also picked policies that were severe: banning handguns and, in some cases, retroactively registering hunting weapons, as well.

Gun control leaders' public promotion of sweeping policy reforms depressed, in indirect and unforeseen ways, public participation in the gun control cause. The gun control groups began by pushing policy proposals that most people did not support and a well-organized minority vehemently opposed. I argue that the handgun-ban gambits of the 1970s and early 1980s created a political legacy that undermined any chance of mass participation around gun control for years to come. After Handgun Control, Inc., embraced an incremental strategy, epitomized in the Brady Bill, participation began to rise.

My argument about the political utility of incrementalism runs contrary to that of scholar William Vizzard and many gun control leaders. Their arguments are worth considering here. In a compelling book, Vizzard argues that the gun control "movement" has been doomed precisely because it has chosen an "incrementalist model" of policy making.[3] He concedes that institutional fragmentation and checks and balances, coupled with a cultural aversion to elites and big government, "have left little choice but to embrace an incrementalist model."[4] However, he argues, policy incrementalism may strengthen gun rights supporters in three ways: "by raising legitimacy issues regarding the policy area, by generating incoherent and fragmented policy with significant implementation problems, and by providing politicians with future excuses for not revisiting a controversial or risky policy issue."[5] Indeed, contemporaneous accounts reveal that gun control advocates feared that modest measures, if passed, would provide symbolic reassurance that the problem had been addressed, thereby taking the steam out of the movement and precluding effective policy change.[6]

Vizzard takes to task Handgun Control, Inc. (now the Brady Campaign) for having embraced an incremental strategy in the mid-1980s. "The strategy of pursing limited initiatives, selected more for their political acceptability and symbolic appeal than for their utility continued" in the 1990s. "HCI, the most powerful of the gun control advocates, barely makes a pretense of advancing comprehensive policy, and most control advocates in Congress seem never to have actually considered the concept."[7] Vizzard's arguments are echoed by the Violence Policy Center, which has staked out the left flank of the Washington-based gun control forces. After a series of sniper shootings in the Washington area in 2002, the center's director told a newspaper, "We're in a precarious position. When something truly horrible like this happens and the gun control movement offers limited responses, it reinforces the idea that gun control can't solve anything."[8]

Opponents of incrementalism are concerned with effective gun control policy, and their arguments make a good deal of sense from a policy-analysis standpoint. And there may be a link between the dynamics Vizzard identifies and a weakening of the gun control cause. For example, if incremental policies are ineffective, then that might deprive gun control advocates of a policy case around which to rally public support. Likewise, if elected officials pass symbolic incremental measures, that might interrupt momentum for meaningful policy change.

On balance, however, incrementalism serves a valuable purpose with respect to political mobilization. Incrementalism builds organizational capacity by providing winnable goals; sends valuable signals to legislators about public sentiment and thereby reduces uncertainties about how a policy stance might affect their electoral fortunes; allows for issue advocates in one area to emulate the successful strategies of advocates in other areas; and builds constituencies to protect incremental gains. In sum, incrementalism is aligned with the institutional and cultural realities of American democracy, which is friendlier to modest or locally rooted actions than to bold, national projects.

## THE CAMPAIGN TO BAN HANDGUNS

In the 1970s and 1980s, most leading gun control advocates at the state and national levels advocated a boldly nonincremental strategy: a swift ban on the civilian possession of handguns, including those already owned. Some national organizations continued to embrace that policy goal into the 1990s, and even the 2000s. Their position was based on three arguments. The first was that handguns have no place in a civilized society. Because most of the early activists were either religious leaders or victims of gun violence, moral objections took center stage. A popular slogan at the time was, "We need handguns like we need a hole in the head."[9] Second, gun control advocates argued that handguns do more harm than good: They are ineffective in warding off criminal activity and in fact make violence and criminality easier to pursue. Third, the gun control advocates argued that only a complete ban would be effective. As the National Coalition to Ban Handguns contended in a 1975 statement:

> Severe penalties won't work because c[ri]minals will not oblige by registering their guns or leaving them behind at the scene of a crime. Banning Saturday Night Specials won't work because only 25 percent of handguns extant are in that category. Licensing won't work because it would not screen out 'crimes of passion' ordinarily committed by persons without a previous conviction record. That leaves banning handguns. We believe that eliminating handguns will work.[10]

Thus, for gun control advocates there were moral as well as rational policy justifications for removing handguns from civilian hands. There were also sound organizational reasons for pursuing a ban. By definition, nonprofit advocacy groups rely on voluntary contributions of time and labor, and those volunteers and donors tend to feel passionately about the cause and to support dramatic policy remedies. To survive, advocacy groups must cater to these preference-outlier constituencies, whether they be individual donors, volunteers, or staff members, who are paid less than they could receive in a for-profit enterprise.

However, even as a handgun ban may have satisfied policy logic and organizational imperatives, gun control supporters fell into a "principle-implementation" trap. Buoyed by decades of polls showing a consistent and pronounced gun control consensus among the American public, advocates pursued a specific policy objective that most Americans by the 1970s did not support and that was sure to inflame the well-organized minority of gun rights sympathizers. In places where the ban sentiment appeared stronger, gun control supporters understandably assumed that the support was firm, rather than vulnerable to doubt-raising pressure from the gun rights side. In both cases, gun control advocates overestimated their ability to use a political campaign to persuade gun control sympathizers to become gun ban voters. Conversely, they underestimated the ease with which the other side could raise doubts that would resonate with Americans' political predispositions to distrust government. Studies have shown that such "principle-implementation" problems are common in social-reform initiatives. In the classic statement of the problem, Anthony Downs argued that public support for reform is cyclical: Initial outrage over a problem and the clamor to solve it inevitably fade as people come to understand how costly the solution will be and how much they or others will have to sacrifice.[11]

The story of how gun control leaders shunned horizontal incrementalism, and then belatedly embraced it, unfolds in several key periods: the mid-1970s, the early 1980s, and the late 1980s. In the 1990s, the would-be movement divided again over the question of incremental strategies, suggesting that the gun control effort is weak in part because its leaders are at war with themselves. In the following section, I chronologically review the key battles over horizontal incrementalism and suggest how these battles have hindered a full-fledged, sustained gun control movement from developing.

### The Mid-1970s: Banning Handguns

In the 1970s, four national gun control organizations came into existence. Two of them quickly established themselves as the leaders of the pack: the National Coalition to Ban Handguns (NCBH) and the National Council to Control Handguns (NCCH). Formed in 1974 as a consortium of women's, civic, labor, and religious associations, NCBH sought national legislation to prohibit importation, manufacture, sale, transfer, ownership, possession, and use of pistols among the general public. (NCBH was later renamed the Coalition to Stop Gun Violence.) NCCH, formed in January 1974, had the same goal. Upon its founding, this organization quickly became the wealthiest and most politically important gun control group in America—the de facto chief of the gun control "movement." (NCCH later was renamed Handgun Control, Inc., and then the Brady Campaign to Prevent Gun Violence.) NCCH estimated that a national handgun ban could be enacted within eight years.[12]

The opening salvos for the nascent gun control campaign were moves to prohibit, directly or indirectly, private citizens from possessing or using handguns. Two of these efforts contemplated national action; two sought a change of state law; and one sought a change in local law. The only one that passed was the local law, enacted by the Washington, D.C., city council, which required the existing stock of handguns to be registered, prohibited handgun sales, and barred anyone not already possessing a handgun from legally owning one.[13] The NRA filed suit to reverse the council's action, but the law was upheld. The other four efforts failed.

The first of the failed proposals to ban handguns came in the form of a bill in Congress introduced by Representative John Conyers (D-Mich.) following extensive hearings around the country in 1975. Conyers was an articulate patron of the rational-national cause. "Short of an outright ban on the possession of handguns," he stated at the time, "there appears to be no way to legally or effectively prevent the acquisition of these weapons by criminals and by generally law-abiding persons who may be driven to use them in an assault, which too often results in unintended homicide."[14] Gun control advocates fixed their hopes on the Conyers bill, refusing to accept anything less. Representative Abner Mikva (D-Ill.), a ban proponent, pulled together an advocacy coalition of interest groups and lawmakers to push for a "strong bill," but he was quick to add that legislation requiring national gun registration would clearly not be strong enough.[15] When the Ford administration forwarded a bill that would have banned the domestic manufacture of Saturday night specials, cheap and poorly made handguns, the National Council to Control Handguns and other advocates publicly opposed the proposal, calling it "a disaster" that "is the illusion of control, not the reality."[16] The ban bill sponsored by Conyers and backed by gun control elites did not even make it out of the subcommittee; in fact, Conyers was the only subcommittee member who voted for it.

The remaining three initiatives were probably the most significant, from the standpoint of movement building, because they represented attempts by gun control organizations to circumvent elected officials. These efforts garnered widespread media attention and had long-term repercussions for the politics of gun control in America.

The first was the attempt in 1974 to petition the federal government to ban handgun ammunition under the consumer product and hazardous substance laws. The Chicago Committee for Hand Gun Control initiated the campaign in response to a rapid increase in handgun crime in that city, but the committee aspired to effect policy change at the national level.[17] As noted in chapter 3, the gun lobby organized a massive letter-writing campaign that led Congress to pass special emergency legislation exempting bullets from the Consumer Product Safety Commission's purview. Organizers had conceded that theirs was a long shot from the outset and that, if anything, they simply wanted to influence public opinion and "arouse commitment" to handgun control.[18]

As the Chicago committee was organizing to ban bullets, gun control advocates in at least three other states were organizing to ban handguns altogether. One of these efforts, in California, was legislative. But the more nationally visible ban efforts were in Michigan and Massachusetts, where gun control supporters organized to place a handgun ban initiative on their respective state ballots in 1976.[19]

Although the Michigan group did not succeed in gaining access to the ballot, the Massachusetts group did. Organized in a politically liberal and gun control–friendly state, the initiative quickly became a political litmus test. Pro-control supporters had long argued that most Americans wanted stricter gun laws and that elected officials, beholden to the gun lobby, were standing in the way of the public will and the common good. The Massachusetts initiative tested this theory by taking the vote directly to the people, bypassing the ostensibly compromised lawmakers.

Sponsored by a citizens' group, People vs. Handguns, the proposal garnered significantly more momentum than had Conyers's bill. Indeed, because more than 100,000 Massachusetts voters (almost 3% of the state's adult population) signed petitions to get the initiative on the ballot, and because the initiative's sponsors were able to beat back myriad attempts to derail their campaign, the Massachusetts effort quickly took on tremendous symbolic meaning for the burgeoning gun control movement.[20]

The National Council to Control Handguns recognized what it termed "the national importance" of the Massachusetts drive and gave People vs. Handguns $16,000 to run television ads in the final days of the campaign.[21] A strategy document from the mid-1970s stated NCCH's intention to use the Massachusetts experience to guide a program of handgun ban initiatives from 1977 to 1982.[22] But the Massachusetts initiative failed: Voters rejected the proposed handgun ban by a margin of two to one.[23] This loss profoundly influenced gun politics nationwide.

Soundly defeated at the polls, the gun control group People vs. Handguns disbanded in 1978. It did so because, by law, another initiative bid could not be tried until six years after the defeat and because the ban gambit had frozen supporters' momentum. As a result of the plebiscite, the Massachusetts group's leaders realized that legislators would not support gun control legislation, "especially after the magnitude of the handgun ban defeat," and, they acknowledged, it is "next to impossible to keep a one-issue group financially solvent and active when there is no reasonable chance of success in the foreseeable future."[24]

## After Massachusetts: Banning under a Different Guise

Before the Massachusetts defeat, leaders of the National Council to Control Handguns had speculated that an incremental strategy might be necessary: "the law may come in stages and each piece may be imperfect, but it will come," reads an organization-building document produced in late 1975 or early 1976.[25] After the Massachusetts defeat, the question of incrementalism broke the emerging gun control movement into two camps: those who believed on principle that handguns had no place in civilized society, and those who agreed but thought that the nation was not ready for a ban on handgun possession. The "incrementalism" camp was led by the National Council to Control Handguns, under the leadership of Pete Shields. The ban camp was led by the National Coalition to Ban Handguns, under the direction of Michael K. Beard, a young former legislative aide who had worked on handgun-ban legislation sponsored by Washington D.C.'s congressional delegate in the early 1970s.

In his 1981 book, *Guns Don't Die—People Do*, Shields articulated the reasons behind NCCH's strategic shift toward horizontal incrementalism.

> [I]f we continue to allow the debate to proceed along idealistic, i.e., extreme, lines, I don't believe we will ever achieve effective handgun control nationally. What's more, I think that's why the pistol lobby encourages this all-or-nothing kind of debate. They agree with me that such debates only serve to polarize the issue and end up turning off and even alienating the public. Consequently they achieve exactly what the pistol lobby wants—nothing.[26]

Shields went on to argue that ban proposals would go nowhere as long as people continued to believe in the principle of self-defense and to disregard the risks of handgun ownership. "The polls have consistently shown that the people do not want an absolute ban on handguns," he wrote. "What they do want, however, is a set of strict laws to control the easy access to handguns by the criminal and the violence-prone—*as long as those controls don't jeopardize the perceived right of law-abiding citizens to buy and own handguns for self-defense.*"[27]

Shields's analysis was correct. In fact, the NRA immediately recognized the political danger that an incremental strategy would pose. The political threat of incrementalism—that small steps are more politically effective than large ones—is the driving force behind the NRA's "slippery slope" argument. The fear was well articulated in 1976, when the NRA's chief lobbyist, Harlon B. Carter, wrote in the *American Rifleman*:

> When political leaders can obtain social and political goals by increment, they are doing to the American people what can be done to a frog: Toss him into boiling water, and he will promptly jump out. But put him in a pan of cold

water and turn on the heat beneath him gradually, by increments, and soon, having never sensed the time when he can jump, the frog will be cooked. This leads the people inevitably to a benign dictatorship.[28]

### California's Bid for a Handgun Freeze, 1982

Six years after the Massachusetts defeat, gun control supporters once again tried a comprehensive policy strategy to be pursued through a voter initiative, this time in California. And, as in Massachusetts, the vote assumed national significance.[29] Advocates of Proposition 15, the so-called handgun-freeze initiative, declared that it represented "our breakthrough opportunity . . . our chance to pierce the myth of the gun lobby's invincibility."[30] In its publications, the NRA called millions of gun owners' attention to the opposition's grand ambitions.[31]

The California organizers were bound to avoid the mistakes that their colleagues in Massachusetts had made. There were several differences between the two initiatives, but the most important was that the California proposal would not require existing handgun owners to surrender their weapons. There would be no "confiscation." Instead, the proposed law would require only that existing handgun owners register their weapons and would ban future handgun sales. In addition, to blunt the NRA's "slippery slope" argument, the measure specified that the legislature could not consider any ban on existing handgun ownership without voter approval.[32] In sum, the proposal did not reduce the stock of privately possessed handguns; it merely sought to bring it under tighter government control and keep handgun ownership from expanding.

As in the Massachusetts case, the California initiative started off ahead in the polls. A June 1982 poll showed the handgun freeze winning by a margin of 60–40%.[33] Five months later, it ended up losing by the same margin.[34] What happened in these intervening months? First, San Francisco supervisors adopted a ban on handgun possession within city limits, raising questions about the credibility of the state campaign to stop short of confiscation. Second, gun rights supporters such as the Gun Owners of California spent millions of dollars stoking precisely those fears. A Field Poll taken after the vote indeed found that that initiative went down because of its ban on handgun sales; an initiative proposing handgun registration alone might have passed.[35] The poll suggested that the prospect of a statewide handgun freeze caused enough suburbanites to join with their rural pro-gun counterparts to defeat the initiative.

Even more ominously for gun control supporters, the California initiative, coupled with other ban efforts that were then taking root, had contributed to a doubling of the NRA's membership, to 2.4 million, over a three-year period.[36] At the same time, as emotion over the shootings of

John Lennon and Ronald Reagan receded, gun control groups were failing to sustain the membership gains they had experienced a year or two
before.[37] The *Washington Post* concluded that the "nationwide handgun
control movement" had been "thrown back on the defensive."[38] William
Vizzard argues that "morale in gun control organizations waned and the
remaining political momentum for control evaporated."[39] Once again, a
ban gambit had boomeranged.

## The National Strategy

From its start in the late 1960s, the gun control "movement" was going
to be oriented toward elite politics at the national level, rather than mass
political or social change at the grass roots. No matter their differences,
elite gun control advocates agreed that their primary goal was to push a
comprehensive gun control bill through Congress.[40] The movement was
not going to focus on nonlegislative goals such as changing social norms,
nor was it going to build policy from localities upward. Particularly after
the failed Massachusetts initiative, the gun control campaign was going
to be a centralized, top-down gambit.

The national approach was rooted in a confluence of policy logic, organizational imperatives, and political context. The policy logic was
straightforward: Given that guns and violent people were mobile, local
(or even state) regulations would be ineffective. Only comprehensive, national regulations would keep weak laws in gun-friendly jurisdictions
from undermining strong laws in control-friendly areas.[41] The organizational logic was that the subnational units would siphon resources from
the national organization and, at best, produce laws that would be only
minimally effective. In the eyes of handgun control elites, the policy and
organizational logics were inextricably linked: If only national laws
would be effective, why organize chapters oriented around state or local
campaigns? Finally, the early leaders were influenced by political context.
Many were inspired by the successful, if historically anomalous, citizen
movements for civil rights, women's rights, and consumer protection, and
thought that another outsiders' campaign, for gun control, could be
next.[42]

Even as the national-policy approach was clearly dominant, at regular
intervals over the gun control campaign's first three decades, news reports
suggested that gun control leaders, at last, were going to embrace federalism and adopt a vertically incremental approach. In 1980, for example,
the *Christian Science Monitor* reported that gun control advocates, "convinced that a national handgun law is unlikely to be enacted in the 97th
congress," are "marshalling forces at the state level to attack handgun

abuse."[43] In 1984, the *Monitor* noted that gun control advocates had moved another step down: "Instead of concentrating on passage of federal and state laws banning possession of concealable firearms, they are setting their sights on local controls."[44] A year later, the *American Rifleman* warned that "Anti-gun activity is heating up on the state and local levels across the country."[45] And a 1989 *American Rifleman* article warned in a headline, "Anti-Gun Fight Heats Up at State and Local Levels."[46] As late as 2004, a California gun control advocate argued, "Given the bleak forecast at the federal level, it is more critical than ever for state and local governments to act to stem our nation's epidemic of gun violence. . . . There is no reason to wait for Congress and the president to take the first steps; we can make significant progress for state and local reform."[47]

These nods toward subnational action notwithstanding, national leaders of the gun control "movement" never fully embraced a bottom-up strategy for policy change. Elite leaders cheered on state and local initiatives, typically when the national landscape appeared particularly inhospitable; and in some cases national groups contributed money. But they did not fully commit themselves to a grassroots-movement model over the long term. Once again, this decision was ultimately rooted in gun control leaders' assessment of what was sound gun control policy. And that assessment was powerfully rooted in history. This section analyzes the logic behind the "national" part of the "rational national" approach. It demonstrates that this was a choice made by gun control advocates— and later, made *for* them.

## A Preference for National Action

In the early 1960s, police officials began expressing concern about the number of firearms used in urban crimes that had originated in states with weak gun laws.[48] That President Kennedy was assassinated by a mail-order firearm only reinforced the argument that, to be effective, gun legislation would have to regulate interstate transfers—in other words, gun control would have to come from Congress. As Mayor Maynard Jackson of Atlanta put it in 1975, "Strong national legislation is really what is needed if local efforts are to succeed."[49] The policy logic dovetailed nicely with the jurisdictional constraints on Congress, which has clear Constitutional authority over *interstate* commerce but much less involvement in *intrastate* matters, particularly in the early 1960s.

The national strategy was well articulated from the start and was reflected in organizations' names. The first modern gun control organization, the National Committee for the Control of Weapons, formed by

New York political leaders in December 1963, was primarily interested in federal legislation that would crack down on interstate shipments of guns and importation of firearms.[50] It advocated tighter state laws as an afterthought. The National Council for a Responsible Firearms Policy, established in early 1967, likewise supported firearms laws at all levels of government but focused its energies on getting legislation through Congress. The council's founding brochure explained the logic: "The complete freedom of movement from one state to another—one of the features and strengths of our federal system—makes it possible . . . for the relatively less restrictive policies of some states to seriously impair, or even nullify, the more restrictive policies which other states regard as essential to public order and safety."[51] The focus on national legislation also reflected the limitations of the council, which had little money, no paid staff members beyond a part-time executive director, and little capacity to start and nurture affiliates around the country.

Although the National Council to Ban Handguns supported laws at all levels, its focus was national. As state gun control groups formed, NCBH provided background support—for example, by providing educational materials and advice. But it never pursued local or state policy change as its core political strategy. Its goal was to be a "gun control Common Cause," but NCBH's approach was significantly different from that of its organizational role model.[52]

The National Council to Control Handguns quickly came to dominate the field.[53] For that reason NCCH's decision to pursue a national strategy is particularly important to the argument of this study. Fortunately, internal memos from the organization's early years have found their way into a publicly accessible archive, and so it is possible to document how, during its formative years, the gun control campaign turned away from vertical incrementalism.[54]

After its first year, and for the pivotal decade to come, NCCH was led by Nelson T. "Pete" Shields, whose twenty-three-year-old son had been shot to death in 1974, a victim of the notorious "zebra killings" in San Francisco. Mr. Shields, who became NCCH's executive director in September 1975 and its board chair in 1978, was a Fortune 500 executive who had a hierarchical management style and a top-down approach to political change. He was largely responsible for charting the organization's course until the mid-1980s.[55]

Early strategy papers reveal the logic that would drive NCCH (later Handgun Control, Inc.) for the next twenty-five years. A "proposal for support" produced in late 1975 or early 1976 declared, "The American people are ready for the passage of laws to control handguns, if their political leaders are not."[56] What had prevented such a law, the paper argued, was "the absence heretofore of an effective, adequately funded, national movement for handgun control law."[57] The proposal then suggested what sounded like a grassroots, bottom-up political strategy: "the effort for handgun control law must come from throughout the nation to Washington and not the other way around."[58] NCCH set out to become a "citizens' lobby," modeled on Common Cause, which had been founded five years earlier.[59] Under Pete Shields's leadership, the proposal stated, "the NCCH has rethought its basic assumptions and set upon a vigorous development program designed to transform a modest effort at Washington lobbying into a national citizens' organization with specific goals, a timetable for their achievement and a means of measuring progress."[60]

The early rhetoric conveyed an organization set to lead a grassroots movement. However, the strategies that NCCH actually pursued were far closer to a national interest-group model of political pressure than to a grassroots-movement model. This shift, from a grassroots to a national orientation, reflected an abrupt change in strategic thinking within the organization. Initially, Washington-based advocates set out to forge a movement involving both state and national organizations. During the first half of 1976, the two-year-old council held a series of discussions with state gun control leaders over what was called a "plan of coalescence."[61] At a meeting in June 1976, the state groups voted to "coalesce" under the NCCH umbrella. The plan called for the local and state organizations, which numbered only about a half dozen at the time, to retain their independent incorporation and governing boards. However, NCCH would run the fund-raising and membership-solicitation operations and distribute some unspecified fraction of the proceeds back to the state groups. Each state or local group would have a seat on the NCCH board.[62]

NCCH abandoned its coalescence plan shortly after the November 1976 elections. It laid out the logic in a nine-page memo.[63] First, NCCH believed that with the election of Jimmy Carter, who had endorsed handgun control during his presidential campaign, the prospects for a national gun control bill were good.[64] Second, the memo implied that the overwhelming defeat of the Massachusetts handgun-ban referendum, to which NCCH had provided financial support, had contributed to the decision.[65] Although the Massachusetts experience is not outlined in the memo, other sources have made clear that the defeat had stunned and demoralized gun control advocates.[66] Third, NCCH argued that two other operations—NCBH and the U.S. Conference of Mayors Handgun Control Project—were better suited to take care of state and local groups.[67] Finally—and this is the key reason—NCCH had national legislative ambitions and did not want resources diverted to what it saw as basically ineffective state and local gun control initiatives.[68]

In that vein the memo outlined various policy, organizational, and political barriers to a decentralized, state-local approach. First, on the policy front, it argued that "[l]ocal and state handgun control laws have proven to be ineffective in the absence of a comprehensive national law."[69] Second, on the organizational front, the memo noted that decentralized membership drives are ineffectual and that mobilizing individual members for political activism had "proved to be the most difficult, time consuming, expensive and controversial undertaking of most national lobbies we're familiar with," including Common Cause.[70] The memo went on to detail how state or local affiliates typically drain resources from the national headquarters. Local members have a "driving need for activity"; because national efforts come in "fits and starts," local organizations generate projects to maintain media visibility; these activities use up resources, creating the need for more fund-raising; and local activists become more focused on their own survival, causing a split with national activists.[71] Third, on the political front, the memo argued that efforts for state and local initiatives would represent a pointless and inopportune diversion of resources, appropriate perhaps for a movement model of social change but not for the top-down model that gun control leaders had embraced. As the memo stated, "Where the emphasis of the national organization is to build law from the local level up to the national, it can work. Where the primary and immediate goal is for national law, as it is with NCCH, local organization becomes very difficult."[72]

The memo laid out, in explicit terms, NCCH's commitment to a national legislative strategy to the exclusion of all else:

Recognizing that:

- NCCH's sole priority for the next two years will be a base national law in the 95th Congress (which subsequently can be supplemented by stronger state or local law);
- NCCH's major immediate need is membership and up-front funding (both of which can be accomplished nationally);
- Formal affiliate organization building is both extremely difficult and potentially diluting to the national effort;

NCCH will *not* propose a formal affiliate relationship with state and local groups but rather will seek to recruit a network of activists [sic] individuals within each key State and or Congressional District. . . . The primary criteria for inclusion of any individual or organization in the NCCH network will be 100% commitment to the national cause first and foremost.[73]

NCCH's strategy of identifying gun control sympathizers in each congressional district, and mobilizing them by telegram from Washington, had preceded the 1976 elections.[74] But afterward, this sort of "Astroturf campaign" became the sole approach. "With the most receptive national political leadership in years now coming into office, NCCH must concentrate its entire limited resources on acquiring as big and as broad a constituency as it can as fast as it can—with obvious emphasis on the swing Congressional districts."[75]

This approach did not go over well at the state level. For example, at the second annual forum on handgun control, held in Boston in January 1976, a participant challenged an NCCH representative: "I guess what I am hearing from you . . . is that you in Washington are going to keep your finger on the interests of people located in California and through all the states. I disagree wholeheartedly. All the national organizations that are successful—Common Cause and the ACLU—have local chapters, state associations, and a national board."[76] Another unidentified participant added, "It seems to me whatever it might be, an initiative petition in three states or an educational group in Colorado, all are very important when it comes to the big push for national gun control legislation."[77] By late 1979, state gun control organizations issued a joint letter to the national groups calling them a "four masted schooner with no rudder" and complaining that a "lack of communication" had created a "lack of understanding," leading to "confusion and a form of competition which can be destructive."[78]

State gun control groups continued to seek aid from the national organization. In 1981, the president of Chicago's Committee for Handgun Control sent Mr. Shields and Mr. Beard a formal request for affiliation. She argued, "The prospect for success in the movement is far greater at the state level than at the federal level right now—and success at the state level is imperative psychologically and politically if strength in congress is to grow."[79] However, an anonymous assessment of the national groups that same year criticized the groups for their failure to assemble and lead a movement for gun control. The U.S. Conference of Mayors was faulted for "lack of long range planning ability" and "lack of urgency or drive." NCCH was chided for "alienation of supporters through overuse of direct mail" and blamed for "autocratic leadership" and "resistance to cooperative efforts."[80] NCBH, while praised for supporting local organizations financially, was criticized for failing to provide the "kind of structure and staff" to "embrace and unify supporters around the country."[81] By 1983, the president of the National Alliance of Handgun Control Organizations (NAHCO) asked, "What is required to convince the nationals that greater interaction between them (closer cooperation or unification) and a new, imaginative relationship with NAHCO may produce the results that they are working for?"[82] He added, referring to two influential federated voluntary associations, "Do we need a complete restructuring along the lines of Common Cause or the League of Women Voters?"[83]

The national organizations decided to pursue a centralized approach to gun policy largely for policy reasons: They believed that only national legislation would work and that an inside lobbying strategy was the way to achieve it. This was particularly true of the National Council to Control Handguns (later Handgun Control, Inc., or HCI), the larger of the two national groups. Recalls one state leader from the 1970s and 1980s:

> I always felt the people of HCI, though paying lip service to our great successes, had a different vision of the road to success. And their vision was that we [state groups] were going to keep them from winning by bleeding off the money and the support and volunteers—although they didn't use volunteers—but the money and the support for local issues, which were doomed to failure by their standards. [HCI believed] that you had to have a big national push, and that you couldn't make a difference on guns at the local level because of the interstate [mobility].[84]

Although policy considerations were paramount, organizational constraints were also an important factor in the decision to concentrate resources on national legislative strategies. The National Coalition to Ban Handguns, which state leaders praised for its willingness to provide tangible support, "did not want the administrative or financial burden of caring for chapters," nor did it want to risk the conflicts that frequently arise between national organizations and their chapters over finances and governance.[85] At Handgun Control, Inc., the rationale was similar: "Once you form a chapter, what do you do with a chapter? . . . The problem with chapters is that they are a very heavy lift. They require a lot of maintenance, a lot of care and feeding."[86] HCI felt that chapters were useful only insofar as they could mobilize members to influence their congressional representatives to support gun control bills. By this logic, chapters in solidly control-friendly states, and probably in gun rights states, would be a waste of resources. Building chapters seemed like a luxury to the national organizations, which were never particularly wealthy to start with and whose financial fortunes tended to rise and fall with events. "We never have enough money to support ourselves, forget about supporting affiliates. . . . [And] without a financial benefit to states, why would they give up control?"[87]

Although their exclusively national focus would soften as Congress repeatedly killed gun control bills, national gun control groups continued to resist throughout the 1980s and 1990s the establishment of formal chapters or affiliate groups. Interestingly, where the national organizations have decided to provide meaningful support to state and local activist groups, political participation around gun control has increased, as detailed in the next chapter. But first, there is another side to the centralization story. The gun control forces' focus on national legislation was not only a strategy they chose; it was also a strategy that was thrust upon them. The role of the gun rights side in centralizing the struggle—that is, undermining whatever grassroots movement might have been in the offing—is equally important to the account at hand.

## A MOVEMENT PREEMPTED

In 1981, as the national gun control groups were struggling unsuccessfully to make progress in Congress, the suburban Chicago hamlet of Morton Grove made a decision that would land it at the center of a national firestorm. On June 8, finding no authority under zoning laws to prohibit the opening of a gun shop near a school, the village's six trustees voted to ban the sale and possession of handguns within town limits. One of the trustees told a reporter at the time, "We felt gun control would have to be a grass-roots effort, as with child labor and pollution laws, and wanted to send a message to other villages and towns that they could enact such ordinances."[88] The Morton Grove ban came just three months after the assassination attempt on President Reagan and the Chicago City Council's decision to freeze the number of handguns in civilian possession.

Interestingly, the gun rights forces appeared to take the political potential of the Chicago-area developments far more seriously than did the gun control side. Although gun control supporters were encouraged by the Chicago and Morton Grove examples, they did not seriously attempt to create momentum out of them. Instead, national gun control groups remained focused on national legislation, and state groups on state legislation. In addition, none of the existing organizations had at its disposal a local network of supporters who could push their respective municipal governing bodies for gun control ordinances. For example, although the National Coalition to Ban Handguns helped finance Morton Grove's legal fight against a gun rights challenge, NCBH did not try to spearhead a nationwide local-ordinance movement to build on the Morton Grove victory.

To the gun rights side, however, Morton Grove posed a grave political threat. When the U.S. Court of Appeals for the Seventh Circuit rejected a Second Amendment challenge and upheld the ordinance, the NRA's top lobbyist likened the development to Pearl Harbor, declaring the ruling day one that "will live in infamy" and "a day of darkness for our United States Constitution."[89] But Morton Grove also presented an important political opportunity to gun rights organizations. Said an NRA spokesman at the time, "The nice thing about Morton Grove is that the people who have been beating their breasts about moderate controls have been exposed for the frauds they are."[90]

After the handgun-ban ordinance passed in Morton Grove, similar ordinances were enacted in the Chicago suburbs of Evanston and Oak Park.[91] An NRA mailing proclaimed, "What was once the unthinkable has now become reality. . . . We must stop a possible domino effect . . . these fanatics must be stopped—NOW!"[92] An NRA spokesman told the *New York Times*, "We are focusing our attention on Morton Grove because their actions exemplify what we believe is the first step toward banning all gun possession."[93] The NRA's concerns about a snowball effect were probably exaggerated, but they made a degree of sense in the sociopolitical context. By the early 1980s, national gun control organizations had become institutionalized, the public was dismayed by the killing of John Lennon and the near-assassination of President Reagan, and local ordinances were passing while scores of national bills had not.

Asking ominously, "Will Your Hometown Be Next?" the *American Rifleman* urged readers to take action: get to know local officials, establish a committee to monitor local legislation, and contact the NRA immediately upon hearing of proposed gun control ordinances in their city or town.[94] However, the NRA had no intention of fighting ordinance battles one by one, because it had a far more efficient strategy: secure legislation in state legislatures to deprive localities of their right to regulate firearms.[95] The "preemption" strategy[96] was deeply rooted in Dillon's rule, the century-old principle that cities and towns are not autonomous entities but rather creatures of the state, with their lawmaking powers ultimately subject to nullification by this higher authority. The NRA used this principle against gun control supporters.

Officially, gun rights advocates argued that preemption was necessary to eliminate a hodgepodge of local laws that would create confusion, and potential criminal liability, on the part of honest gun owners. However, before Morton Grove banned handguns, scores of cities and towns had enacted gun control ordinances, many of which were stricter than state and federal laws. Yet the record contains no evidence that these established ordinances were of much ongoing concern to the NRA and its allies. The vehement reaction to Morton Grove suggests that gun rights supporters were motivated primarily by a political concern that the new ordinance would create momentum for a gun control movement. It was a reasonable fear. Gun control sentiment has always been strongest in urban areas. Likewise, local elected officials are considered more immediately responsive to constituent sentiment than are officials at higher levels of government. The threat that the Morton Grove precedent would spread to other control-friendly jurisdictions was one that the gun lobby was not willing to accept.

Almost immediately, beginning in gun control–friendly Illinois, supporters of gun rights undertook efforts to ensure that no other locality would follow Morton Grove. The same month that the Morton Grove ordinance passed, the Illinois House of Representatives, under pressure from gun rights groups, voted to bar municipalities from passing gun regulations.[97] Although the bill died before it could reach the state Senate or the governor,[98] gun rights supporters pressed on in other states. Indeed, passing such "preemption" bills became the all-consuming goal of the NRA and other gun rights supporters in the 1980s and into the 1990s. A 1986 NRA brief noted that enacting preemption laws "remains the top legislative priority."[99]

The NRA's preemption strategy was largely successful. In 1979, two states (Maryland and Pennsylvania) had full preemption, and five states had partial preemption—for example, barring localities from keeping records of gun transfers (Indiana) or prohibiting localities from enacting owner-licensing or gun registration ordinances (California).[100] By 1984, the number of full-preemption states had risen to nine, and partial-preemption states numbered six.[101] By 1989, full-preemption states had doubled to eighteen, and partial-preemption states numbered three.[102] By early 2005, forty-five states had full or partial preemption.[103] Thus, in the course of twenty-five years, the fraction of states in which localities were fully free to regulate guns dropped from 86% to 10%. In sum, as gun control advocates sought to shift to more amenable, local venues, gun rights supporters used federalism—and legislative dominance—to deprive gun control advocates of those opportunities.

Did the NRA's preemption campaign quash any possibility that a vigorous gun control movement would take hold in America? The answer is necessarily speculative, but the evidence suggests that the preemption laws were far more politically significant than most observers have realized.

Although national gun control leaders certainly did not support this wave of gun rights lawmaking, there is no indication that—at the time—they considered preemption to be the death knell of their ability to reach their policy goals. After all, they were focused on national legislation and thought local ordinances were ineffective in reducing gun violence. A former leader of a national gun control organization recalls the preemption campaign this way:

> There's no question that the NRA's effort to pass preemption laws was a serious setback, and there's no question that whatever the implications in terms of policy, what you do lose at the local level is the ability to rally people around a local issue. . . . I think the reason why the gun control movement sat back and "let it happen" was because the gun control movement was subsumed with other battles. We were trying to pass the Brady Bill, trying to pass the assault weapon ban, and we were trying to work in certain states, like Virginia, for one-gun-a-month and other battles like that, and you always have to pick and

choose your battles. And the problem with preemption is that—long before 1993 and 1994, when some of these laws were going through, or even before that—the NRA was so far ahead of us in state legislatures, and they still are so far ahead of us in state legislatures, that it would have taken a huge diversion of resources to try to beat them on preemption. . . . This is a case of the NRA having a much better grassroots network, . . . having funded a lot of state candidates, recruited state candidates, having so many different inroads into the state legislatures—more than we did. We were hopelessly outgunned in that battle and there was nothing we could do about it.[104]

In short, from the perspective of national gun control groups, preemption was something of a side battle that they were unable and possibly unwilling to fight. And yet, to state gun control activists, preemption was considerably more important. Like their national counterparts, most state gun control leaders placed limited faith in the policy effectiveness of local ordinances. But they did see the political potential, via the snowball effect, of organizing around local projects. A founder of the Maryland Handgun Control Committee, established in 1976, argued that preemption was one of the two factors[105] that most inhibited his group's ability to expand: "With gun control you pretty much have to do something national, you can't try it anywhere because of all these preemption laws. You can't start small; you've got to start big. It's too hard, it's just too hard."[106] A 1982 report of state organizations' efforts noted that the Indiana group was having trouble devising an approach because of the state's preemption law and requested ideas as to how any gun control effort might get off the ground there.[107] Preemption also raised the costs of participation in direct ways, by forcing advocates who wanted to make a visible contribution to travel to the state capital. Without preemption, gun control sympathizers could have acted politically at far less cost. A state gun control official who became a national gun organizer noted in 1999, "Without-pre-emption, the whole movement would be completely different. The gun-control movement would be working on 50 to 100 different actions around the country."[108]

## Why Rational National Made Sense at the Time

Gun control advocates are not dumb or naive, nor have they ever been. Like all issue advocates, and all human beings for that matter, they operate within an environment of constraints and opportunities. They do the best they can to make their way in a world of scarcity and uncertainty. People are the product of their historical experience. Some points in history are better than others to pursue policy reforms, and some strategies work better than others at different times. Reformers analyze their options based on a combination of scientific reasoning, wishful thinking, and heuristic "rules of thumb" about how the world works. Some ideas are more likely to succeed than others. Finally, advocates must work with what they have—money, staff members, volunteers, and allies—or the lack thereof. Thus, three factors drove gun control advocates toward a rational-national approach: (1) organizational imperatives, (2) policy logic, and (3) political-historic models.

The organizational imperatives involved financial constraints facing nonprofit organizations that rely heavily on voluntary contributions from individuals. People who contribute to advocacy groups tend to have more intense and extreme preferences than those who free ride, and people with strong beliefs do not necessarily respond to tepid appeals for modest measures. The need to keep such donors contributing can play a role in nonprofit groups' decisions about the types of policy proposals to pursue. A longtime national gun control leader captured this reality when he complained that mainstream gun control proposals are "so reasonable, so milquetoast" that "it's hard to energize people unless they think that America will be a very different place as a result."[109] Or, as one national gun control leader told me succinctly, "Our members want a handgun ban." To sustain themselves financially, membership organizations need to appeal to policy preferences of their core donors. For some gun control groups, that made it harder to embrace incremental strategies.

The policy logic was straightforward and rooted in credible assumptions about human nature. In the quest for firearms, bad guys will find a way to evade state and local laws and will find loopholes in weak national laws. Therefore, gun control leaders reasoned that any effective gun control regime would have to be big and bold. Gun control leaders adopted this reasoning in part because they lacked systematic data about how firearms got into the hands of criminals. Not until federal authorities began tracing guns used in crime did advocates realize how many such guns are supplied by the "secondary" market, rather than by federally licensed firearms dealers. Gun-trace data allowed gun control advocates to construct more narrowly tailored (i.e., incremental) policy proposals aimed at suppressing the secondary market and pushing firearms transactions into the primary market. "Yes, things like 'ban handguns' get people fired up, but it wasn't clear what else would have been effective at the time. Now we have a whole other group of things that would be, as far as saving lives, maybe even more effective."[110]

Finally, gun control leaders were deeply influenced by historical models. Many early gun control leaders were inspired by the citizen movements for civil rights, women's rights, and consumer protection that unfolded in the 1950s, 1960s, and 1970s. They thought that a national victory for gun control could be next. Yet the gun control campaign was beginning to institutionalize nationally at a time when the power and moral authority of the federal government were waning. By 1974, the War on Poverty and the premises that inspired it were under attack, and President Nixon was deeply embroiled in the Watergate scandal that would bring him down shortly after the national gun control lobby had announced its presence.

Many early leaders were products of their time. They had been schooled in the religious and secular movements for civil rights and against the Vietnam War, and as a result they were "dedicated to doing things on the cheap and *outside* the existing power structures," as a pioneer in the early handgun-ban effort recalled. He noted that those early advocates, including some of the most prominent organizers at both the state and national levels, were "true believers" who "assumed that people would 'do the right thing' if only they were shown the need. Money, being the root of all evil, was something that we should exist without. Politics was the enemy of progress. Most of our state organizers never got much beyond the manual typewriter and mimeograph stage of organizing. Politics was the enemy of progress, not a tool for reaching a goal."[111] The legacy of vigorous outsider movements, coupled with the antipolitics backlash that Watergate inspired, left mid-1970s organizers with a certain innocence about how the American political process actually works. "Most of the early organizers were the type of people who wrote letters to the editor about what politicians were doing wrong, without ever getting to know the politicians themselves, or the editors," the gun control leader said. "I can't count the number of times I heard that we didn't want to be tainted with politics like the NRA. We should be 'pure.' Organization is something for the bad guys."[112] Thus, paradoxically, the spirit of the times was that bold policy reforms not only could be accomplished but could be accomplished by circumventing conventional political processes. Good, bold people with good, bold ideas would carry the day, without having to mess with politics.

These three factors—policy logic, organizational imperatives, and political-historical context—converged and reinforced one another, pushing gun control leaders to far more extreme lengths than was politically wise. The gun controllers' early extremism, in turn, allowed their formidable opponent, the "gun lobby," to use the anti-gun leaders' grand ambitions against them. When a few local gun control sympathizers began experimenting with incrementalism, the national gun lobby began working systematically and largely successfully to shut down the mobilizing opportunities that incrementalism provides.

The rational-national strategy was pursued for the right reasons—but in the wrong nation at the wrong time. The national gun control campaign began organizing at a transition in American history, one that is obvious only in retrospect. The United States was founded by leaders who feared the concentration of power in ambitious men's hands. Thus, they designed the national government to be small—and to stay that way. The Constitution takes pains to disperse authority: through federalism, which assigns certain tasks to the national government and leaves the rest to the states; and through the separation of powers and a system of checks and balances, which together limit any individual branch's ability to amass power. James Madison summarized the Constitution framers' plot to undermine bold reformers: "Ambition must be made to counteract ambition."[113] Several political developments since the founding have further fragmented American politics, namely the development of political parties, the growth of the public presidency, the institution of a committee and subcommittee system in Congress, and the proliferation of interest groups and media voices in the policy-making process.

Paradoxically, even as the framers' vision of a fragmented state continued to be realized, the twentieth century witnessed a clear growth in national authority. This came in the form of the unprecedented regulatory and welfare-state regimes ushered in under President Franklin Roosevelt's New Deal and expanded under President Johnson's Great Society and War on Poverty programs; the landmark civil rights laws of the mid-1960s; and the wave of Supreme Court rulings, under the Fourteenth Amendment, that have restricted state autonomy in favor of nationwide civil rights and liberties standards. And yet, as the national government was getting bigger, American society seemed to be getting smaller. The development of railroads, automobiles, interstate highways, airlines, and modern communications media allowed people, products, information, norms, and so forth to move at lightning speed across state lines. And the move from an agrarian to an industrial economy encouraged mass migration from the South to the North and, recently, back to the South, blurring long-standing cultural allegiances. These developments undercut the rationale for diverse state laws and helped to justify the development of nation-spanning standards.

Thus, the twentieth century witnessed the collision of two competing forces: political fragmentation and social integration. Political fragmentation, rooted in the Constitution and exacerbated by modern developments, powerfully constrains enactment of bold, rationally comprehensive, and nation-spanning policy interventions. Social integration, rooted in the industrial and technological revolutions, would seem to require precisely such bold policies. Gun control advocates experienced these countervailing pressures: constraints imposed by the Constitution and modern political fragmentation, on the one hand, and the call of national power and homogenization, on the other. In fact, these competing conditions were coming to a head in the mid-1970s, precisely as gun control advocates were first attempting to form a national movement. Thus, gun control advocates found themselves at a historic moment in which fundamental institutions and modern exigencies came into conflict—the politics that the framers had locked in two centuries earlier versus the politics that modern reformers were trying to make in the here and now.

For cultural and policy reasons, gun control advocates chose the politics of the here and now. They sought a model of policy change, the rational-national strategy, that was anathema to the framers' design but seemed reasonable in light of the times. In doing so, gun control leaders failed to appreciate the extent to which the long arm of history embodied in the U.S. Constitution structures politics and political outcomes. In particular, they failed to understand that, as a general rule, there are no shortcuts to policy reform in the United States. Policy reform is slow, arduous, frustrating, and long—and major policy reform often involves mass mobilization.

## How "Good Policy" Became "Bad Politics"

In 1986, gun rights supporters secured the Firearm Owners' Protection Act,[114] which repealed significant parts of the Gun Control Act of 1968, the landmark legislation that had greatly expanded federal regulation of firearms.[115] Afterward, realizing that comprehensive gun control laws would not be forthcoming from Congress anytime soon, gun control supporters began to embrace incrementalism—in part, but not in full. The implications of that decision for mass participation are explored in chapter 6. But first I describe how the rational-national strategy hindered, in both the short term and the long term, the emergence of a vigorous national gun control movement in America. Early decisions left a profound legacy that inhibited later reformers.

The gun control entrepreneurs of the 1970s chose the rational-national strategy because it made sense from a policy perspective and because, at that unique historical moment, it made sense from their political perspective, as well. But the rational-national approach boomeranged. It undercut the gun control cause not only at the critical moment of its emergence but also in the three decades to follow. By embracing the rational-national strategy, gun control leaders foreclosed the possibility of creating a broad-based gun control movement, making their cause appear far less mainstream than it actually was. At the same time, gun control leaders emboldened gun rights leaders by providing legitimacy to the latter's cultural and political appeals. These effects are considered in turn.

First, let us consider how the rational-national strategy—the decision to elevate policy analysis over political strategy—narrowed gun control's appeal and discouraged sustained mass participation. Most obviously, the decision to push for an outright national ban on handguns eliminated the majority of Americans from the pool of potential movement activists. In the mid-1970s (and afterward), most people rejected a ban on the private possession of handguns, even as they supported every gun control proposal up to the point of a ban. Thus, gun control groups were dedicating themselves to a policy approach that had only minimal support among the mass public, while failing to press for restrictions that enjoyed popular endorsement. This made gun control advocates look like extremists, even in the eyes of their sympathizers. To make matters worse for ban advocates, opinion polls on these sorts of questions are unreliable. As studies have shown, public support for policies *in theory* is always higher than support for policies in *actual practice*; this is the "principle-implementation gap."[116] Thus, while people support abstractions like "free speech" or "gun control," that support invariably drops once opponents begin to emphasize the practical trade-offs, such as costs and other implementation challenges. Thus, whatever nonmajority support there was for a handgun ban in the abstract was itself an exaggeration of the support that would actually have been available to gun control advocates in the political battle itself. To be sure, no movement has ever required majority support for its positions. However, expanding the scope of conflict is vastly easier if most people agree with an advocate's policy goals than if most disagree.

Second, the rational-national strategy provided few opportunities for citizen participation. Beyond writing a letter to one's senator or congressperson in Washington, there was little for the ordinary gun control supporter to do. There were no locally rooted projects in which grassroots supporters of gun control could get involved. Instead, by design, gun control became an expert issue in the hands of a small group of policy professionals at Washington-based interest groups. This elite orientation had an indirect ripple effect on participation, as well. With opportunities for mass participation limited and out of view, it was inevitable that the public face of gun control would be that of the preference-outlier activist, not the "typical citizen" next door. Thus, gun rights supporters could easily brand control leaders as out-of-touch tyrants whose ideas posed a grave danger to American values.[117] This image further dissuaded mainstream gun control sympathizers from joining the cause.

By pursuing a policy strategy that did not enjoy majority support and afforded few opportunities for participation in any case, gun control advocates set themselves up for failure. As their efforts to secure bold policy reforms came to naught time and time again, gun control's mainstream supporters and advocates found themselves beset with a pervasive sense of futility. This sense of futility drove many potential activists away; after all, why would one get involved if one knew ahead of time that it would be a waste of time? As E. E. Schattschneider noted, "people are not apt to fight if they are sure to lose."[118]

The repeated failure to secure a handgun ban at the state or national level also helped to fracture the emerging gun control movement. In the wake of the Massachusetts defeat, NCCH abandoned its public push for a handgun ban and adopted a step-by-step program of more moderate measures. On the other hand, NCBH stuck to its desire for the swift elimination of handguns from society. This fundamental difference in philosophy would structure the gun control campaign for years to come. Over the next two decades or more, the two leading gun control organizations remained estranged from each other, competing far more than they cooperated. Thus, even though the groups had complementary assets—NCCH had money and prominent leadership, while NCBH had a vast network of voluntary associations—their strategic differences (and, at times, personality conflicts) kept them from taking advantage of this opportunity for synergy. Their philosophical differences kept gun control organizations from working effectively together to widen the scope of conflict.

The failures to secure ban laws also created the belief, so pervasive today, that the so-called gun lobby was invincible. In this way, gun control advocates' initial embrace of the rational-national strategy boomeranged. In dedicating themselves to politically unrealistic goals, gun control advocates drove away the mainstream base and compounded mainstream supporters' alienation with repeated failures in high-profile policy battles. For institutional and perhaps cultural reasons, policy is made incrementally in America.[119] As the gun control case demonstrates, issue advocates who ignore that reality risk becoming—or at least appearing to be—a fringe movement, easily branded a threat to democracy.

The rational-national strategy empowered gun rights groups to do exactly that: to wage cultural warfare by likening gun control advocates to Nazis and communists.[120] Threatened by what they saw as an attempt to deprive them of their guns and their rights, organized gun owners launched a no-holds-barred effort to defund and demobilize gun control organizations. A handgun ban would have imposed direct, visible, and immediate costs on gun owners. Policies that impose costs in this way tend to inspire countermobilizations that stop reform efforts in their tracks.[121] In this case, gun control advocates' rational-national strategy strengthened gun rights supporters in at least two ways.

First and foremost, the policy gambits of the 1970s and early 1980s provided credible threats around which gun rights supporters could mobilize. The repeated attempts to ban handguns at the national and subnational levels allowed the NRA to make a persuasive case that gun control advocates would stop at nothing, that confiscation of all firearms was their ultimate aim. William Vizzard traces this argument to New York City's

Sullivan Law, a 1911 ordinance that required a police permit to possess a handgun.[122] He argues that, even many decades later, "the New York precedent was a constant reminder of 'what they want to do.' . . . A reading of Congressional hearings or discussions with opponents of firearms legislation regularly reveals that the Sullivan Law was an example of its opponents' ultimate fear."[123] Although the Sullivan Law severely restricted civilian access to handguns, the efforts in the early 1970s went even further, breathing new life into the NRA's "slippery slope" argument. For example, in a May 1975 fund-raising appeal that invoked George Orwell's *1984*, NRA executive vice president Maxwell Rich stated,

> Let me tell you exactly what the anti-gun lobby is doing right this very minute to confiscate our firearms and ammunition. The 'Committee for Handgun Control, Inc.' has won a court order which requires the federal Consumer Product Safety Commission to decide if handgun ammunition is a 'hazardous subject' [*sic*] and should be made illegal. . . . Maybe you don't own a handgun, but this is only the beginning. . . . Next the anti-gun lobby will go after large bore ammunition. And then shotgun shells.[124]

He concluded, "I have never before in my life had to write such a significant letter asking for money. But the day of total, complete and absolute gun confiscation is so close that I have no choice."[125]

With that argument in its arsenal, the NRA was able to knit together two distinct American gun cultures: the small-town and rural long-gun owners, who had never been especially supportive of handgun proliferation, and the gun aficionados for whom firearms are powerful cultural icons. When gun control advocates pushed a handgun ban, they handed the NRA a golden opportunity to arouse the politically important rural interests, who are heavily represented in most state legislatures and overrepresented in the U.S. Congress. The newly credible slippery-slope argument also made many Americans suspect that gun control advocates really were extremists, thereby making moderate gun control sympathizers less likely to become active participants in the cause.

The ban gambit also played a key role in encouraging the gun rights forces' turn to hard-line politics in the mid-1970s. To "be able to counter effectively one of the most powerful anti-gun campaigns yet mounted,"[126] the NRA in 1974 created, and began aggressively raising money for, its Office of Legislative Affairs.[127] By September 1975, it had raised nearly $2 million.[128] The NRA also registered its top officials as lobbyists.[129] At the same time, advocates dissatisfied with what they saw as the NRA's insufficiently hard-line stance created Gun Owners of America, which pulled the NRA in the direction of protecting its right flank. Shortly thereafter, in 1977, hard-liners within the NRA board of directors staged a coup d'état, known as the Cincinnati Revolt, at the organization's annual meeting. The hard-liners, led by chief lobbyist Harlon Carter and his lieutenant Neal Knox, vowed that the NRA would never again compromise on gun control legislation.[130] As late as 1975, the NRA had officially issued its "qualified" support for a waiting period to buy handguns in hopes of reducing crimes of passion and weeding out "undesirables."[131] But after the revolt, any gun bill, no matter how seemingly innocuous or commonsensical, would be resisted at all costs because any legislative victory would provide momentum to the other side, which the NRA branded "the gun grabbers." Gun control advocates would not be able to secure a national handgun waiting period until 1993. Osha Gray Davidson argues that 1977 marked the pivotal moment when the 106-year-old sportsmen's club became "the Gun Lobby."[132]

Thus, even as the NRA's policy positions were veering more and more toward a libertarian extreme, the gun controllers' ban gambits allowed the gun lobby to claim that it represented the median American. It could do so in part because the ban battles helped the NRA to hone its message to appeal to mainstream voters. According to a 1975 survey that the NRA commissioned to help it fight the Massachusetts battle, the winning message was this: The public does not care much about gun control (low salience) or feel very committed to a pro-control position (softness); does not think it would reduce crime (ineffectiveness); and believes people should and do have a right to defend themselves with firearms (protection and civil liberties).[133] David Bordua argues that the NRA fought the Massachusetts initiative in part because gun rights advocates knew they would win with a message that tapped into those vulnerabilities in pro-control sentiment.[134] After the Massachusetts vote was in, gun rights advocates could credibly assert that gun control activists were hopelessly out of touch with public sentiment, even in relatively liberal states. As Davidson argues, the "NRA's reputation for legislative invincibility received a tremendous boost from this victory."[135]

The perception of invincibility deprived individual gun control sympathizers of political efficacy. In terms of the theory, the ban gambit increased gun control sympathizers' prospective calculation of the costs of participation, relative to the benefits. Fighting the gun lobby appeared to be a lost cause and a waste of resources. Of course, this perception derived in part from the fact that gun rights supporters were numerous, intense, and well organized. But the perception of their invincibility stemmed as much from the risky "go for broke" strategies of the gun control side as from the strengths of the gun rights side.

Thus, in several key ways, the handgun-ban approach boomeranged, ultimately undermining gun control advocates' ability to organize and mobilize their troops. Some gun control leaders foresaw these problems. For example, the leader of the National Council for a Responsible Firearms Policy, a small Washington-based organization created in 1967, repeatedly inveighed against the ban strategy, calling it unworkable and inequitable. In pursuing a handgun ban and then pulling back, out of political expediency, the gun control "movement" created for itself "a credibility problem as to its real, ultimate objective, causing apprehension among large numbers of law-abiding gun owners concerning its real motive."[136] The leader of the Chicago Committee for Handgun Control urged her Delaware counterpart to change the organization's name to something other than "Ban Handguns" because the name "automatically eliminates from your membership more than 50% of the population [and] will be a stumbling block in your efforts to create a significant group with enough political influence to effect change."[137] Even the National Coalition to Ban Handguns was cautious in the wake of poll findings that a handgun ban did not have majority support: "We know that there is work to do."[138] On the other hand, some gun control leaders figured that, if the NRA was going to object to any measures proposed, then there was little point in assuming a posture of compromise.

I have argued that the ban gambit helped to derail an emerging gun control movement. But it did not depress political participation in the short term. Indeed, the handgun-ban referenda at the state level energized hundreds of citizens, who gathered signatures on petitions, wrote letters to the editor, and urged their friends and neighbors to support the proposals. This is consistent with the conventional wisdom that the people most likely to participate in a political cause have more extreme positions than the median voter and that only dramatic proposals will energize these preference outliers. Indeed, as noted in chapter 3, gun control groups' attachment to the gun ban position was driven in part by their need to attract sustained contributions.

Thus, one might argue that, even if it is a more practical approach to policy making, incrementalism may actually depress rather than encourage mass participation because those who support modest measures are unlikely to feel intensely enough to shift from free rider to activist. As the gun control case makes clear, these two interpretations are not necessarily at odds. While dramatic proposals may galvanize an activist core in the short term, they are inherently self-limiting in the long term, both because they have narrow appeal and because they are likely to fail. Nonincremental policy proposals are useful for generating public and media attention but form a poor foundation for movements

## BELATEDLY . . .

The core argument of this chapter is that decisions made in the 1970s and 1980s structured—and constrained—the gun control "movement" for decades to come. Recognizing the limitations of the rational-national approach, the national gun control leadership slowly, often imperceptibly, shifted toward an incremental strategy. For the most part, gun control groups have learned from their mistakes and become more sophisticated in their politics.

First to go was the insistence on a gun ban. Today, of the four major national gun control groups, only one—the Violence Policy Center, which has no mass membership base—endorses a ban on civilian possession of handguns.[139] The center argues that a handgun ban is a matter of rational policy, but its stance fuels ancient flames, allowing the NRA to argue, credibly, that gun control leaders *still* want to confiscate guns from law-abiding citizens. However, even beyond the leaders of the Violence Policy Center, the turn toward incremental policy proposals continues to be controversial among activists. A former board member of Handgun Control, Inc., captured many activists' sentiments when he said, with reference to the group's incremental strategy, "HCI is counter-productive for the cause of gun control in America."[140] A leading researcher-activist concurred: "HCI is willing to accept small victories. Those victories are smaller than the ones I am willing to see."[141]

The path toward vertical incrementalism has been even rockier. Both Handgun Control, Inc. (now the Brady Campaign) and the Coalition to Stop Gun Violence have provided support to state gun control efforts over the years. They have sent high-profile spokespeople to campaign, provided financial contributions to select local and state campaigns, offered tactical advice, hired lobbyists to press state legislatures, and so forth. Although present in the 1970s and 1980s, such activities greatly accelerated in the late 1990s and early 2000s, as national leaders began to understand the political power of "trickle up" policy making. For example, in the mid-1990s HCI established a regional office in California as an experiment in grassroots organizing; four other field representatives were hired later. Similarly, the Coalition to Stop Gun Violence in the early 2000s obtained foundation grants to allow it to work with, and financially support, gun control groups in a handful of states. The Coalition began to think of itself as "a little trade association for the groups we were working with."[142]

Whether the shift toward state and local organizing will result in a movement will depend on a host of factors. My concluding chapter will explore this question. The next chapter explores a more immediate question: Have the belated, halting, often isolated efforts at incrementalism expanded citizen participation around gun control? Based on three case studies of incremental strategizing, the answer is yes.

# CHAPTER SIX

# Mobilizing around Modest Measures: Three Cases

FOR THE FIRST TWO DECADES OR MORE of its organized life, the campaign for gun control was characterized by a smattering of small, resource-poor, and often short-lived associations of concerned citizens, a larger universe of national religious, civic, and labor groups willing to lend their moral support to the cause, and two or three advocacy organizations in Washington, D.C., whose strategic decisions along the way affected the development (or not) of the gun control "movement." The decision to pursue a national handgun ban—a position that one national gun control group still holds and another held until the early 1990s—constrained the movement by alienating supporters and strengthening opponents. The decision to focus on national efforts and provide only sporadic, ad hoc support to local and state efforts made it difficult for the "movement" to gain momentum. By the late 1990s, however, the "rational national" strategy was no longer the clearly dominant approach. Indeed, bottom-up incrementalism had begun to take root.

If my theory is correct, that both horizontal and vertical incrementalism are movement enhancing, we should have seen popular participation rise in the places and at the times when incremental approaches were attempted. Below, I examine such relevant counterfactuals,[1] cases in which gun control advocates tried incrementalism, if only in limited ways. These cases are (1) the effort to pass the loophole-plugging Brady Bill in the early 1990s; (2) the effort to pass local gun control ordinances in California in the second half of the 1990s; and (3) the effort to build a grassroots movement of women gun control advocates in the early 2000s. Although constrained from developing into a full-fledged, broad movement for gun control, these cases suggest that incremental strategies in fact do lead to a sustained expansion and intensification of citizen participation.

## THE BRADY BILL

When gun control organizations finally did unite around an incremental policy, they managed both to drum up political participation and to secure a new gun control law. Many factors affected the Brady Bill's passage, including the fact that pro-control Democrats controlled the presidency and both branches of Congress in the wake of the 1992 election. However, political opportunities do not guarantee policy outcomes. Gun control advocates won passage of the Brady Bill in large part because they built a broad coalition to agitate for it, and that coalition was possible because the bill proposed—and built on—incremental, rather than comprehensive, change.

Passed in 1993, and effective the following year, the Brady Bill was designed to plug a loophole created twenty-five years before with the passage of the Gun Control Act. The 1968 act had barred certain classes of presumably high-risk people, such as drug addicts and minors, from purchasing handguns. However, the law contained no mechanism by which gun sellers could verify that the would-be purchaser was not in one of these restricted groups. The Brady Law created that enforcement mechanism. The law required people buying handguns from federally licensed sellers to undergo a federal background check to determine whether they were eligible to own a weapon. The law then imposed a five-day waiting period during which the background check was to be conducted.

Thus, the Brady Law was a horizontally incremental step in two respects. It represented a modification of one piece of existing law, rather than imposing an entirely new regulatory regime. And, while making it harder for ineligible individuals to buy a handgun, the law did not extend ownership restrictions to anybody not already covered by the law. Besides representing a strategy of horizontal incrementalism, the Brady Bill was also, and less obviously, an example of vertical incrementalism. Its major provisions were modeled on laws that at least eighteen states had passed, mostly since the mid-1960s. Thus, scores of members of Congress had experience with these laws and had confidence, if not in the laws' effectiveness, at least in their ability to be implemented without seriously infringing the rights of gun owners.

With the twin virtues of being modest and road tested in the states, the policy prescriptions embodied in the Brady Bill galvanized participation in the short term and set the gun control campaign on a trajectory of expansion. In the short term, the Brady Bill ignited a broad array of interest groups that had been sympathetic but quiescent during the handgun-ban days. For example, during the 1988 House debate, 120 uniformed police officers paraded through the U.S. Capitol handing out buttons supporting the waiting period provision.[2] In 1991, the commanding officer of New York's Seventy-fifth Precinct sent twelve busloads of citizens to Washington to lobby for the Brady Bill.[3] In Massachusetts, a partially paralyzed armed-robbery survivor and the sister of a murder victim formed Citizens to Prevent Handgun Violence specifically to lobby for the Brady Bill.[4] The most significant participant of all was President Reagan. Even after being shot, he had vocally opposed gun control proposals; but at Sarah Brady's request, he emerged in 1991 to endorse the Brady Bill. "It's just plain common sense that there be a waiting period to allow local law enforcement officials to conduct background checks on those who wish to buy a handgun," Reagan said.[5]

As figures 1.1 and 1.2 showed, there was a spike around the time of the Brady Bill's passage in both gun control advocacy efforts and in media adoption of the term "gun control movement." For example, the number of articles citing gun control advocacy doubled in 1993 relative to 1992 and the two prior years. Signing the bill, President Clinton said it had passed "because grass-roots America changed its mind and demanded that this Congress not leave here without doing something about this."[6]

The campaign for the Brady Bill also helped to persuade Handgun Control, Inc., that true grassroots organization, as opposed to mere identification of local sympathizers, was necessary to change national policy. As one longtime state gun control leader notes:

> Handgun Control initially felt that state groups weren't that essential, that they could do what they wanted to do from national. And [with] the Brady Bill finally—near the end—they began to realize they can't be everywhere, cannot reach everyone, and that's when they started really laying on the state groups of what can we do to help you. They really started corresponding with us, and [there was] a lot of contact, and [they] bent over backward. And after the Brady Bill was passed, there was immediately on the e-mail, this great message: Thank you, thank you so much, we could not have done it without you. So they're much more sensitive to the fact that it's a big country, [and] you need to have your local groups functioning and be in touch with them.[7]

Equally important, the incremental nature of the Brady Bill made it more difficult for the gun rights side to mobilize a broad constituency in opposition. Members of Congress who were normally fearful of arousing the "latent public" of gun owners sensed little cause for alarm with the Brady Bill.[8] One member of Congress, a California Republican and outspoken gun rights supporter, voted for the Brady Bill because "to oppose this would be to oppose law enforcement" and because "a lot of folks called me that have been life members of the National Rifle Assn. to say that just because they are life members" they don't necessarily oppose the idea of background checks.[9]

The Brady Bill victory enabled gun control advocates to claim the mainstream mantle that had eluded them during their handgun-banning days. A 1991 *Washington Post* story reported that, after a victory in the House, Handgun Control, Inc., had acquired a "newfound reputation as one of Washington's most formidable lobbying operations—a remarkable transformation for a group that only a few years ago was routinely dismissed as an inept public interest group."[10] Although the rhetoric was perhaps overblown, the conclusion was not. In embracing an incremental policy goal, Handgun Control, Inc., and its state and local supporters at least for the time being had created a sense of efficacy among the pro-control majority. While there were costs to participation, there were also—for the first time in years—potential benefits as well.

## The Local Ordinance Campaign in California

I have argued that gun control advocates have pursued a national strategy in part because they wanted to and in part because they had to. The danger in such an explanation is that it is close to being nonfalsifiable: "They don't go local because they can't, but if they could go local, they wouldn't." Thus, to test the theory that going local would expand participation, one has to find a case in which gun control advocates both *wanted* to pursue a local ordinance strategy and *could* do so. Illinois, where it all began, could go local but has chosen not to do so. However, another prominent state, California, has found both the political will and the legal authority to pursue a local strategy.

Because of its status as a political bellwether, California makes a particularly interesting case study in gun control organizing. Beginning in the mid-1990s, California gun control advocates began to challenge the limits of the state's partial-preemption law by passing scores of local gun control ordinances. The ordinance campaign is widely credited with having laid the groundwork for a raft of state gun control laws passed in the 1999–2002 period that made California's one of the strictest and most comprehensive gun control regimes in the nation.

California's preemption law was passed in 1969 in response to a San Francisco ordinance that required most guns within the city to be registered.[11] Signed by then-governor Ronald Reagan, the law stated: "It is the intention of the Legislature to occupy the whole field of regulation of the registration and licensing of commercially manufactured firearms."[12] This was the state's prerogative under Dillon's rule, the principle that cities are creatures of the state. For twenty-five years, the standing assumption among gun control advocates was that this statute prohibited local action across the board, that state gun control laws were the controlling authority. Frustrated over the state's unwillingness to impose real gun control, one activist asked in 1969, "Can nothing pre-empt something?"[13]

The politics of preemption began to change in California in 1993, when a disgruntled former client of the Pettit and Martin law firm entered the firm's San Francisco office armed with two assault weapons and began shooting. He killed nine people, including himself, and injured six others.

Thereafter, Bay Area lawyers formed the Legal Community Against Violence (LCAV).

The lawyers' group first set out to secure a national ban on the type of weapon used to kill their colleagues. They had ample precedent for their ban gambit: California had banned assault weapons (including those used in the Pettit and Martin shootings) after the Stockton playground massacre in 1989, and the George H. W. Bush administration had followed by barring imports of 43 makes and models of foreign-made assault weapons.[14] By 1994, with the Democrats in charge of both houses of Congress and a pro-control president in the White House, the lawyers' organization and others successfully secured a federal ban on the possession or transfer of 175 types of assault weapons manufactured after September 13, 1994. Its name notwithstanding, the assault weapons ban was incremental in at least four respects: It followed action at the state level; it built on existing federal policy; it affected a narrow category of guns that were of interest primarily to fringe elements within society; and it was a *prospective* ban that did not affect assault weapons already in private hands.

But LCAV's signature strategy was the one that it embraced next: vertical incrementalism. Against the rational-national school, the volunteer lawyers' group in 1995 launched a campaign to pass local gun control ordinances across California, seemingly in defiance of the state preemption law. "In the mid '90s, gun violence levels had reached their peak, and nothing was happening at the federal level and nothing was happening at the state level," a longtime LCAV activist recalled, "and people were just becoming fed up. And local officials began to think, If our leaders aren't going to do anything on this subject, maybe we will because our communities are suffering terribly."[15]

The local-ordinance campaign grew out of a law passed by the City of Lafayette in 1994 requiring gun dealers to obtain a police permit; barring gun sales near residential neighborhoods, schools, parks, and houses of worship; and requiring gun dealers to provide trigger-locking devices with all guns. In response to the ordinance, gun rights activists and firearms dealers sued the city, and the city asked the lawyers' group for help. A California trial court in 1996 dismissed the lawsuit, and the following year a state appellate court agreed, in essence ruling that the state's preemption law was not as broad as many had thought. Another local ordinance, involving a West Hollywood ban on the sale of cheap handguns, also was upheld around that time. In the wake of the cities' actions, and the court rulings upholding them, the local-ordinance "movement just swept across the state. We saw it as a great opportunity, a great niche for our organization," a longtime LCAV activist recalled.[16]

The lawyers' group had used its expertise to open a new pathway for local gun control activism. Local action had ground to a halt after the

1969 preemption law. The futility of local entrepreneurship had been reinforced by a 1982 state court of appeal decision invalidating the handgun ban that San Francisco had passed that year on the grounds that the ban violated the 1969 law. Against a background so unfavorable to gun control advocates, the volunteer lawyers persuaded the California courts that they could interpret the preemption law narrowly, thereby paving the way for a range of restrictive policies that would be nonetheless consistent with state law.

Moreover, the lawyers' group expanded its civic engagement beyond pro bono legal assistance. The lawyers decided to create a "local ordinance project" that would venture into grassroots organizing, pulling together local gun control advocates and sympathizers in various cities and towns around California and providing them with a legal blueprint for political mobilization. Under the project, begun in 1995, LCAV would contact sympathetic parties—such as city attorneys and local elected officials, physicians and public health authorities, law enforcement leaders, and women's and civic groups—and hold workshops to educate them about the policy rationale and political advantages of local ordinances. As a leader in the ordinance campaign noted: "When we go into communities, we think ideally to get a local ordinance passed, you have a cross section of the community. You have activists, but not only the activists. Because it's easy for a politician to say, those are the extreme gun control people and those are the extreme gun nuts on that side. So [we looked] for somebody a little more mainstream we can trust, so you have physicians, League of Women Voters, the PTA, those groups."[17] Also instrumental was Women Against Gun Violence, which was formed in 1994. That group pushed local ordinances outlawing Saturday night specials in southern California and showcased those directly affected by gun violence.[18]

Between 1996 and 2000, the number of California cities and counties that had firearms regulation quadrupled (to 111), and the number of firearms regulations grew nearly sevenfold, to 300.[19] These laws included banning the sale of "Saturday Night Specials" (56 ordinances by 2000); requiring firearms dealers to obtain a local license or permit (32 ordinances); explicitly or indirectly prohibiting firearms dealers in residential areas (72 ordinances); and requiring dealers to keep records of ammunition sales (15 ordinances).[20] It is important to note that, besides being local, these measures were also modest. With the exception of the Saturday-night-special ban, they targeted gun *dealers* rather than gun *owners*. Thus, with respect to gun owners, the costs of these policies were indirect, and therefore less likely to provoke a broad countermobilization.

For gun control organizers, the local ordinances were politically useful in many ways. First, consistent with my cost-benefit theory of incrementalism, local ordinances are easier to pass than state laws. Because local elected officials have a comparatively small, homogeneous constituency, they tend to be more responsive than state or federal legislators, and local gun control supporters are more likely to know each other, making collective political action feasible. Second, and also consistent with the theory, local ordinances can produce a policy snowball effect at the state level. In 1999 alone, California enacted three major laws predicated on local ordinances: banning Saturday night specials, limiting handgun purchasers to one gun per month, and requiring a locking device to be sold with every gun.[21] Third, the local approach created a cohort of elected officials who had voted for gun control, survived politically, and gone on to higher elected office, where they would spearhead state laws modeled on local ordinances. In a sense, the local campaigns provided political information to elected officials that allowed them to be less risk averse in higher office.

Fourth, and most important, the local-ordinance approach "provides a natural opportunity for the formation of grassroots coalitions and the mobilization of activists."[22] The lawyers worked closely with California chapters of the Million Mom March because both were interested in local action, but at the same time they offered different, yet complementary, movement resources.[23] An LCAV leader argues that the political utility of the local-ordinance strategy stemmed from the fact that it "gives people something to do, some tangible goal, something to achieve." She reasons that, "when you start talking about federal policies and Congress and Washington, D.C., and even the state level, it's really beyond most people. They don't feel like they have access to those elected officials and any power, but when you're talking locally, people have a lot more power."[24]

If there has ever been a movement for gun control in America, it unfolded in California in the 1990s. Perhaps not coincidentally, California had an infrastructure to support local and statewide efforts. In terms of patronage resources, several California philanthropies had made "violence prevention" a priority, including the California Wellness Foundation, which had allocated $40 million over the 1993–2003 period. Because of a loophole in the tax laws, LCAV was eligible to receive foundation grants; and indeed, most of its $900,000 budget came from charitable sources.[25] California also was the site of the original regional office of Handgun Control, Inc. (now the Brady Campaign), which worked closely with local gun control coalitions in pushing for state legislation. The Coalition to Stop Gun Violence, the other long-established national gun control organization, also established a local presence by hiring a lobbyist to work with California groups in pushing state laws.

These factors were critical. But the key to California's gun control movement was the availability of local projects around which issue entrepreneurs could rally everyday citizens, together with the support structure to ensure that those local victories could snowball into state legislative campaigns. Interestingly, the California gun control movement was not dominated by any single group. LCAV was central, but so were a host of other players—university-based public health experts, grassroots antiviolence groups, research organizations and foundations, women's groups, and representatives of national gun control lobbies. California funders and gun control advocates "built this infrastructure such that, if you go in, you can get work done," recalled a national gun control leader. "If you go to California and work, people are very optimistic about the future. They're used to success."[26]

## The Million Mom March

My final case of incrementalism in action is the Million Mom March. As noted in chapter 4, the March, as a continuing organization, attempted to channel women's moral and material resources toward the gun control cause. The March was organized around a list of policy proposals developed by Handgun Control, Inc., to build on the Brady Law. These proposals included modest measures, such as expanding background-check requirements to private sales at gun shows and limiting handgun purchases to one per month, as well as more comprehensive measures, such as the licensing of all handgun owners and the registration of all handguns—the bête noire of the gun rights forces. Although the March's demands included incremental policy steps, such as closing the "gun show loophole," Congress adjourned without having passed any new gun laws. Meanwhile, in the months after the massive demonstration, the Million Mom March organization ran out of money, lost its office space, and laid off its staff.

In policy circles, the Million Mom March was cited as a failure because it did not result in immediate, nationally comprehensive gun regulations. Many observers saw the March as yet another fleeting outburst of pro-control sentiment that was doomed by election-year politics. However, even as the event itself did not produce immediate legislative change, it left in its wake thousands of gun control advocates organized in scores of state and local committees in virtually every state. Indeed, in some states—Alaska, Idaho, Nebraska, and Mississippi, to name a few—the Million Mom March provided women who had been quietly supportive of gun control with their first opportunity to organize collectively. In other words, the Million Mom March became the first-ever association of gun control advocates in those states.

The March's federated organizational structure positioned it well to spearhead gun control advocates' first truly national grassroots campaign. After the march (the event itself), 230 chapters began to organize, and at least 100 institutionalized. Then, in a revolutionary move, the Brady Campaign in October 2001 formally adopted the Million Mom March and its chapters. The nation's dominant gun control organization, which for twenty-five years had rejected the political utility of chapters, at last had a grassroots base. The merger expanded the number of ways that everyday gun control supporters could participate at the local, state, and national levels, and it provided that grassroots base with a seat on the national organization's board of directors. While Handgun Control, Inc., had a history of swooping down to the state or local level to take advantage of a fortuitous moment, and then exiting the field once the moment had passed, the Brady Campaign's adoption of the Million Mom March signaled a change in philosophy. After the merger, the Brady organization created an eleven-person state and local outreach division at the national office, and staff members internally lobbied their leaders for a long-term commitment to state and local efforts. Although the merger was rocky, and relations between national and local leaders sometimes strained, the march clearly left the gun control forces poised for a nationwide movement based on the principles of horizontal and vertical incrementalism.

In the first two and one-half years after the march, the nation's newspapers carried at least 2,300 stories mentioning the local activities of the Million Mom March organization and its individual members.[27] These activities included staging a protest in Washington, D.C., over President Bush's appointment of gun rights supporter John Ashcroft to be attorney general; running for elected office in Rhode Island and Michigan; helping organize around a ballot initiative to close the gun show loophole in Colorado; distributing candidate questionnaires in Minnesota; speaking out against a gun raffle and barring gun shows at state-funded facilities in Maryland; lobbying state legislators in Florida; distributing information on gun control in Washington State; endorsing candidates in New Mexico; financing "family gun safety" public service advertisements in Oregon; and staging scores of anniversary marches on Mother's Day 2001 and 2002. To summarize, even after the March's national office collapsed, local Million Mom March groups and activists were involved in electoral politics, direct and grassroots lobbying, public opinion formation, agenda setting, and protest politics. In each case, the mothers' organizations focused on modest, winnable goals, rather than comprehensive proposals that stood little chance of success.

As noted in chapter 4, by late 2002 there were 107 active chapters in thirty-four states and the District of Columbia. By early 2005, the number had shrunk to roughly 40 to 60 active chapters in about twenty states.[28] The reduction in numbers is to be expected: A gun-friendly presidential administration, coupled with a reduction in gun violence in the early 2000s, posed a challenge to movement building. However, the staying power of the Million Mom March is historically noteworthy. The gun control effort has never managed to sustain such an expansive, locally rooted infrastructure. Equally noteworthy is that the mothers' intensity remains. At a January 2005 "Lobby Day" in Richmond, Virginia, for example, a member of the Northern Virginia Million Mom March chapter upbraided her state delegate when he sheepishly spoke of his fear of the NRA. "You don't represent the NRA," she said angrily. "You represent us, your constituents."[29] In essence "the Moms," as they are called, embraced vertical incrementalism and invigorated the stalled gun control "movement." A longtime gun control advocate who lost a family member to gun violence remarked: "If you're going to change social [practices], and that's what you have to do if you're ever going to change public policy, you've got to do it at the local level because you have to do it between people who know one another, and the moms have available to them to be in every school in this country, every PTA, every church and every neighborhood. And they have an opportunity to change people's outlook on this issue on a daily basis. And when all that happens, those people will finally tell their legislators, 'You are also going to change public policy.' " Although the sudden arrival of Million Mom chapters posed some inevitable tensions—particularly with existing state gun control groups, which were for the most part less than a decade old—news accounts made clear that the mothers' groups lent a new voice and a unique form of local organization to the emerging gun control coalitions in many states. By focusing primarily on local projects and grassroots organizing—and by selecting modest policy goals—the Moms used vertical and horizontal incrementalism to expand political participation by everyday citizens in pro-control states.

## How Incremental Policy Encourages Participation

As noted in chapter 5, gun control neatly illustrates the proposition that policy and politics are often at loggerheads. Gun control advocates saw comprehensive legislation from Congress as the only logical course, and they embraced the rational-national policy strategy without regard to its political feasibility. Consistent with that strategy, gun control advocates for decades eschewed local, and to some extent state, policy approaches— which may have been more politically feasible—on the grounds that such campaigns would be ineffective at best and counterproductive at worst, in terms of policy outcomes. In a sense, gun control advocates sought to maximize policy effectiveness, which in their view required sacrificing opportunities for mass mobilization.

As a result, instead of increasing the benefit-to-cost ratio of political participation, the gun control groups did the opposite, enhancing the perceived invincibility of the gun rights side and contributing to a pervasive sense of futility among gun control sympathizers. On those occasions when gun control advocates attempted to go local, their opponents used their advantage in state legislatures, and the prerogatives of Dillon's rule, to deny gun control supporters the opportunity to work in these friendlier venues.

From the perspective of objective policy analysis, gun control leaders' approach makes a certain degree of sense. The inescapable laws of economics and human nature suggest that, to have a chance at being effective in reducing gun violence, firearms laws must be comprehensive and national. As Daniel Polsby and others have noted, demand for firearms among determined offenders is inelastic, meaning that they will seek every avenue to circumvent any law standing in their way; and local and/or weak gun regulations are by definition easier to circumvent than are national and/or comprehensive statutes.[30] Local and modest policies are ineffectual when the targets of the policy (people, products) have a high degree of mobility and when loopholes are obvious. Thus, to gun control advocates there seemed to be little reason to pursue incrementalism when rational-national approaches would work better. But in choosing the rational-national approach, gun control advocates sacrificed political feasibility and engendered a passionate countermobilization among gun owners who felt morally stigmatized.

As political scientists recognize, policy in the United States almost always is made incrementally, through the gradual accretion of modest measures that often originate at the local and state levels before "going national." These were the lessons of the anti-abortion, anti-alcohol, and anti-smoking movements a century or more ago, as well as in the contemporary period. This is also the lesson of the gun rights "movement." Pro-gun organizations have pursued incremental strategies to remove restrictions on firearms. During the 1980s, they worked to pass statewide preemption laws, and during the 1990s, they sought to relax the licensing system for people wishing to carry concealed weapons. In neither case did they immediately push for total deregulation, even if that may have been their preferred outcome. Both campaigns, for preemption and less restrictive carry laws, were largely successful, with all but a handful of states adopting the NRA's proposals.

Scholars of mass movements have long recognized that political opportunities are critical to movement formation. In these accounts, opportunities can take two forms: the porousness of state institutions and/or periodic openings in the "political opportunity structure." But, as this study has shown, another form of opportunity is equally important: the opportunity to participate in activities whose goals are local and/or winnable. In a fragmented, liberty-minded democracy, mass participation is a key route to political advancement, and policy incrementalism is a key mechanism for widening, deepening, and lengthening organized citizen engagement.

As the gun control case suggests, incrementalism is conducive to movement building in at least five ways. First, it builds *organizational capacity*. Because incremental strategies are more likely to succeed than are rational-national strategies, individuals calculate that their participation in modest efforts is likely to pay off. And because incremental strategies by definition are less extreme than rational-national strategies, incremental strategies will appeal to a broader segment of the population. Thus, organizations that adopt incrementalism have a larger pool of actual and potential donors and volunteers. Organizations that pursue incrementalism also are in a better position than are more doctrinaire organizations to deliver small wins and provide organizational momentum. Like gamblers at the track, donors, volunteers, and politicians like to back a perceived winner. Incrementalism may produce a snowball effect that is difficult to stop. In addition, incrementalism provides opportunities for solidarity-building expressive action at the local level. It is easier to build a movement when individuals have opportunities to meet, organize, and recruit in a face-to-face manner because interpersonal suasion comes into play. These conditions are difficult to create when the object of participatory action is formidable or remote.

The second way that incrementalism boosts participation is by sending reliable information to elected officials about public demands. I refer to this as *preference signaling*. Particularly in the modern age of the "permanent campaign,"[31] elected officials tend to be risk averse, unwilling to act without a clear showing of public backing. In this regard, visible political activism and concrete policy outcomes, which incremental strategies can deliver, are more influential than are passive responses to opinion polls. To politicians, actions speak louder than words.

Third, incremental politics allows for creative (or competitive) *emulation* across different jurisdictions. If citizens in one jurisdiction mobilize around a policy proposal, they provide a tactical example that others may follow. During the 1911 debates over New York's seminal gun registration bill, state senator Timothy Sullivan captured this dynamic succinctly, arguing that "the [gun] manufacturers oppose my bill because they know that if we pass it other States will follow suit."[32] At the same time, a regulatory movement in one jurisdiction may put pressure on people in another jurisdiction to prevent whatever undesirable behavior was "regulated out" of the first area from moving over to the second. In their study of state welfare policy, Paul Peterson and Mark Rom labeled this dynamic a "race to the bottom" in which public assistance benefits and eligibility rules became ever more restrictive as states competed with one another to keep poor people away.[33] Although Peterson and Rom focused on redistributive policy, a similar dynamic plays out in regulatory policy. Thus, actions by one jurisdiction have the power to mobilize citizens in another.

Fourth, incremental policies are enactable and thus *create constituencies* that are easily mobilized to protect their gains and, potentially, to seek more. As prospect theorists have demonstrated, people react more intensely to the threat of loss than to the promise of gain.[34] The same is true of interest groups, which have a great deal at stake monetarily and ideologically in protecting favorable laws and programs. Because social movements must go on the defensive as well as the offensive, incremental policy victories provide convenient rallying points. Related to that, incremental policies can create logical precedents for future action around which movement actors can organize. Once a policy is in place to cover one category (of people, products, etc.), then it becomes easier to make the case that the policy should be expanded to cover others, as well. Policies in essence serve as political resources for movement actors by providing a focal point for mobilization and a rationale for doing something. This is the essence of the slippery-slope theory.

Finally, incrementalism encourages the gradual *cultural change* that is necessary to ensure popular support for new laws. The women who protested outside the corner saloon in the late nineteenth century laid the groundwork for local prohibition laws in the early twentieth century; the "Yes, I mind if you smoke" campaigns of the 1970s laid the groundwork for smoking bans in offices and restaurants in the 1990s. Elite legislative proposals that fundamentally challenge common behaviors or values tend to meet with popular resistance; on the other hand, popularly championed laws that codify emerging norms tend to enjoy broad public assent. Thus, changing laws often means first changing culture—in effect, creating grassroots demand. In the case of gun control, pro-regulation forces sought a legislative harvest without first tilling the cultural field. This allowed the gun rights forces to continue to dominate the cultural realm by equating gun possession with core American values, such as individual self-determination, liberty, and anti-statism, and likening gun control proponents to Nazis and communists.[35] By promoting comprehensive national legislative proposals for which the nation was not culturally ready, gun control leaders simultaneously legitimized that image and undermined their ability to expand their movement base by changing the culture over the long term.

The gun control case illustrates two types of federalism colliding with each other: policy federalism and political federalism. Political federalism refers to the idea that lawmaking occurs at multiple levels of government (national, state, county, local), and that issue advocates thereby shop for the friendliest venue. Policy federalism refers to the idea that policy outputs in one jurisdiction are affected by laws in another jurisdiction.[36] In general, advocacy at the local level is more expedient than at higher levels, but national policies in certain issue areas may be more effective. Hence, political federalism sometimes is at odds with policy federalism, and rational politics sometimes is at odds with rational policy. Issue entrepreneurs must decide which view of federalism to emphasize. One form, policy federalism, is movement constraining; the other form, political federalism, is movement expanding. For most of their organizational history, gun control advocates chose strategies that would constrain their movement rather than expand it.

# CHAPTER SEVEN

# Conclusion: Politics, Participation, and Public Goods

THE MODERN CAMPAIGN FOR GUN CONTROL began in the early 1960s, when the U.S. Senate's Juvenile Delinquency subcommittee began assembling the case for tighter regulation of the domestic firearms market. Over the next four decades, as state and national interest groups were established to further the cause, and hundreds of gun control bills were introduced in Congress and state legislatures, a sustained, nationwide citizens' movement for gun control failed to coalesce. Meanwhile, one president was killed, another one badly wounded, and a third nearly shot by two different perpetrators within two weeks. Other highly publicized casualties of gun violence included singers, civil rights leaders, senators, and schoolchildren. In addition, at least two serious waves of gun violence claimed hundreds of thousands of citizens as victims.

In 1972, the *Wall Street Journal* famously editorialized that the battle over gun control was emblematic of a fundamental cultural rift between "cosmopolitan" America, which sees gun control as commonsense policy, and "bedrock" America, which views gun control as a threat to the existing moral universe.[1] The political divide grew deeper after that, and the debate more sustained and shrill. The divide identified in 1972 later acquired a name—the "culture war"—and gun control became one of the war's central battlefronts. In the 1990s and early 2000s, political candidates ran on—and away from—gun control to a greater extent than at any time before. Likewise, a national gun control movement began to come together and yet failed to do so fully. This study has offered an explanation for that failure.

## MAJOR FINDINGS

Based on studies of other movements for social reform, this work began by laying out a theory of mobilizing for public goods. I argued that just as public policies impose costs and benefits,[2] so does political mobilization. The cost-to-benefit ratio is particularly high in the case of public goods because nonparticipating individuals can free ride on the efforts of others. The challenge, then, is for issue entrepreneurs to alter that ratio. Historically, movement leaders have done so in three ways: (1) by socializing the costs of participation through state or private patronage; (2) by personalizing the benefits through issue frames that invoke individuals' conceptions of their self-interest and proper social role; and (3) by altering the prospective calculation of the benefits-to-costs ratio by selecting incremental, winnable battles that will inspire a sense of political efficacy in movement activists. To the extent that social-movement organizations can meet these three challenges they are more likely to expand the scope of conflict by broadening the number of people involved, by deepening their commitment, and by lengthening the time over which the public is engaged.

Meeting these three challenges may not be sufficient for a movement to arise. Political opportunities, resources, and collective efficacy—the workhorse predictors in standard social-movement models—are also necessary. I simply argue that movement leaders, especially those pursuing social-regulatory policies, will have difficulty succeeding in the absence of institutional patrons, culturally resonant frames that speak to the moral identities of civically resourceful people, and a strategy of incremental gains. Must all three of these movement "plus factors" be in place for a social-regulatory movement to arise, or will just one or two suffice? Historical case studies suggest that all three must be present simultaneously. But mine is a probabilistic model necessarily derived from a small number of cases. Probabilistic models hold no guarantees, except that, under a certain set of conditions, outcome A is more likely than outcome B. There are always exceptions. That said, one general conclusion emerges from this study: The more ways that movement entrepreneurs can find to socialize the costs of political engagement, and to personalize the benefits to individual sympathizers, the more likely these leaders are to turn their "movement" from rhetoric to reality.

The gun control campaign has always had many assets that are important to movement building, including sympathetic elected officials willing to champion the cause, shootings and crime waves that dramatized the problem, majority support among the public for tighter firearms restrictions, and single- and multi-issue organizations capable of mobilizing the masses. But these critical movement ingredients—opportunities, organizations, and opinion—were not enough. Unlike other movements, such as those against tobacco, smoking, and abortion, the gun control campaign struggled to obtain patronage, to craft a resonant issue frame, and to settle on a strategy that could deliver movement-building victories. As a result, even as Americans were bombarded every day by reports of violence, and even as one-third of Americans reported that someone close to them had been shot, gun control remained remote—difficult to relate to, difficult to rally around. Somewhat counterintuitively, gun control did not inspire a true social movement, in part because its elite leaders for decades did not think one necessary and in part because their opponents, rightly sensing what a gun control movement could accomplish if it did coalesce, used their political advantages to keep that movement from arising.

In the first instance, that of securing patronage, gun control organizations never were able to secure the same strong government patronage that other movements counted on to move their agendas. This was largely because gun rights organizations pursued a "defund, delegitimize, and deprive" strategy to ensure that gun control advocacy would remain a fringe campaign, rather than one that could establish a beachhead in the apparatus of the state. The emerging gun control movement also suffered because one of its most resourceful and best-organized constituencies—middleclass women—was shifting its focus away from all-encompassing public goods and toward a narrower set of issues revolving around women and their status. Thus, gun control leaders lacked a set of institutional patrons capable of delivering volunteers, money, and moral authority to the cause. The structure of federal tax laws also played an important role. Obscure and hopelessly complex, the tax code nonetheless has a profound impact on the nature of American pluralism and politics more generally. Through provisions governing private foundations and individual donations, the tax code provides selective incentives for groups pursuing public goods, but only if they do so in a way that is charitable, rather than political. The effect of these laws is to channel collective action into efforts to change social norms, rather than to change laws or influence the elections that decide who gets to make those laws. Adding to the suppressive effects of the tax laws was foundations' historically grounded fear of political controversy and their ideologically motivated desire to attack the "root causes" of social problems. These factors together made philanthropic foundations the unlikeliest of patrons for the gun control cause.

Building a sustainable gun control movement was also hobbled by the way the issue came to be framed. For understandable reasons, gun control became synonymous with crime control. More specifically, the political debate revolved around anonymous perpetrators (bad hands) and their firearms (bad guns). In principle, such a frame would be movement enhancing on the grounds that the image taps into individual fears and anxieties, which would be expected to motivate involvement. But in reality, the crime frame was movement constraining because it invited debate about the nature of the criminal mind and the technical specifications of different firearms. Emphasizing these themes turned gun control into an issue for experts, including law enforcement personnel and the National Rifle Association. In short, for most of its first four decades, the modern battle over gun control centered on arguments that gun rights organizations could dominate. However, as I demonstrated, when gun control was framed as a means of protecting children, public engagement increased along the three relevant dimensions of breadth, depth, and length. More people joined the gun control campaign, they felt and acted more intensely, and new social-movement organizations formed.

Finally, gun control advocates pursued political strategies that were not conducive to movement building. Taking the polling numbers and violence statistics as self-evident support for their cause, and relying on the backing of prominent lawmakers and other government officials, gun control advocates advanced a "rational national" approach to policy making, eschewing vertical and horizontal incrementalism in favor of bold steps. Thus, rather than organizing around local projects that stood a chance of advancing, they organized around efforts to pass comprehensive legislation in Congress. Rather than organizing around modest measures and allowing policy regimes to expand by accretion, leading gun control advocates started out by seeking bans on handguns. Thus, gun control advocates pursued a political campaign, emphasizing elite-driven policy change, without a social movement, which might have tilled the field. They pursued an inside game without an outside game. And they pursued "rational" policy over efficacious politics.

The rational-national model failed politically because it was inherently self-limiting: Gun control became an issue for and by elites. Arguments were distant and intellectual, and opportunities for consequential involvement were scarce. To the individual gun control supporter, the costs of participation were high and the perceived benefits low. At the same time, the rational-national gambit hardened the well-organized and politically powerful gun rights organizations and made them stronger. Ironically, gun rights advocates were far more attuned to the movement-building potential of incremental action than were gun control advocates. Indeed, small victories for gun control, no matter how modest or symbolic in terms of policy impact, served as dramatic focusing events on the gun rights side. These gun control victories inspired the gun rights forces to ply their advantage in the national legislature and in state legislatures to ensure that more sympathetic venues were closed to their opponents.

Gun control advocates were seeking sweeping top-down policy change at precisely the time that such change was becoming increasingly unlikely. The contemporary gun control campaign, which began to coalesce in the early 1970s, coincided with the beginning of a decades-long decline in popular trust in the federal government, the discrediting of the government-led social policies of the 1960s, and the erosion of key allies such as federated women's organizations and mainline Protestant churches. David Meyer documents similar issues within the nuclear-freeze movement, which turned to professionalism and interest-group advocacy on the grounds that "grassroots activism and decentralized democracy . . . represented old and archaic notions of political action."[3]

The traditionalists, on the other hand, were ascending politically, aided ironically by policy purists seeking to end gun violence in America. Bedrock America, for whom the NRA is a standard-bearer, understood the historical moment and exploited it by playing up traditional themes: distrust of government, belief in rugged individualism, reverence for constitutional literalism. The NRA and other traditionalists were also organized in such a way as to maximize policy success. The NRA is a mass-membership association with a federated structure that mirrors the structure of the American system of government. Organized at the national, state, local, and sometimes sublocal level, the association is well equipped both to block gun control proposals wherever they arise and to funnel resources up or down when needed.[4] For example, locally organized grassroots volunteers can be mobilized to contact Congress, while the NRA's national legislative office can provide money, policy information, and advertising to state and local campaigns. In sum, the traditionalists elevated politics over policy analysis: They correctly identified and exploited the historical and institutional opportunities afforded them.

On the gun control side, the turn toward an expert-led, inside-the-Beltway strategy proved shortsighted. In an effort to secure a quick victory that they believed would save lives, gun control advocates used a new, more expedient model of social change—a Washington-based interest-group model—against an adversary that was using an older, more effective model. That older model involved working through mass-membership voluntary associations to mobilize legislative and electoral participation at the local, state, and national levels. Gun control opponents understood the challenges inherent in the American system—its federal structure and divided powers—and used these institutions to their advantage. Gun control supporters tried, ultimately in vain, to circumvent these structures and the difficulties that they presented.

Thus, up until the late 1990s, strategic decisions by elites on both sides ensured that the gun control battle would be fought on the terms and terrain that provided an advantage to the anti-control side and kept the gun control forces from developing a vigorous, sustained social movement. By choice and circumstance, gun control was a top-down political campaign without a bottom-up social movement. Pro-control sympathizers were marginalized, lacking the resources, collective identity, and prospectively winnable opportunities that inspire civic participation. They were left to get mad and write futile letters to their Congress members or send a contribution to a lobbying organization in Washington.

## What These Findings Mean

The gun control case brings into focus two very different models of collective action: a policy-driven model and a politics-driven model. Gun control organizers pursued a policy-driven model, while gun rights supporters pursued a politics-driven model. In the interests of producing what they saw as the best policy, gun control supporters sought to win purely by the force of their ideas, rather than by mobilizing a constituency. Gun control politics became an inside policy game, accessible only to an elite cadre of experts who either didn't seek, or were precluded from forging, bonds with potential political patrons and allies.

In many ways, the story of gun control is much like the story of the failed effort to pass the Equal Rights Amendment. In her authoritative account, Jane Mansbridge notes that feminist true believers in the pro-ERA camp, motivated by purist ideals of gender equality, failed to frame a political vision that would appeal to the majority of Americans who supported women's advancement but rejected a radical reordering of social roles. The ERA debate got bogged down in arcane constitutional debates, with the pro-ERA camp forthrightly exaggerating the likely impact of the amendment on gender roles and the ERA's opposition successfully framing the amendment as a threat to mothers and families.[5]

The gun control case illustrates in stark terms several stubborn realities of American politics. The first is that the system is designed to block radical departures from existing policy and thus is bound to frustrate passionate reformers with bold ideas. Quick fixes are likely to boomerang, while methodical incrementalism is likely to succeed. David A. Stockman, President Reagan's crusading budget director who left the administration after becoming disillusioned by the failures of the Reagan Revolution, wrote in his memoir: "Our Madisonian government . . . is conservative, not radical. It hugs powerfully to the history behind it. It shuffles into the future one step at a time."[6] In the American political system, as in Aesop's fables, the tortoise usually beats the hare. The second lesson is that movements for public goods face an inevitable tension between passion and pragmatism. This was true in the case of the ERA, and it is true in the case of gun control, whose evolution has been powerfully influenced by early efforts to ban handguns. The third lesson is that political culture matters as much as institutions in structuring at least one outcome: the scope of public participation. Social scientists lately have tended to view political culture as a meaningless construct, but this study suggests that culturally resonant issue frames have the power to expand political participation in a way that technically compelling policy arguments cannot.

## THE MORE THINGS CHANGE, AND THE MORE THEY DON'T

A cable news program reported in May 2002 that gun control advocates, realizing that they stood little chance of securing national legislation under President George W. Bush, were turning their attention to local and state activity.[7] But such headlines have appeared regularly in newspapers and magazines for at least twenty years. By the early 2000s, as in earlier eras, some local activity was in the offing, but a full-fledged movement was not on the horizon.

To be sure, there was more gun control activism in the 1999–2001 period than at perhaps any other time in American history. Beginning in 1993, the campaign for gun control began to change. This was in part because a gun control supporter, Bill Clinton, was in the White House and in part because the nation had endured a dramatic six-year increase in gun violence. Those factors were important and worked in conjunction with other forces to encourage gun control activism. But favorable changes at the national level were not the only impetus.

I have provided brief counterfactual case studies from the 1990s: examples when patronage resources *were* available, when issue frames *were* accessible, and when incremental approaches *were* pursued. In each of those cases, I documented that social-movement organizations were born or strengthened, and individual participation became broader and more intense. These trends had their beginnings in 1993, but they escalated after 1999.

What happened? In the period between 1993 and 2002, three important developments combined to provide gun control advocates the assets they had been lacking. First, government agencies, especially the BATF, and private foundations stepped out of the shadows—at least temporarily—and discovered a way to advance gun control without explicitly doing so. The BATF, under the direction of Clinton appointees, dedicated itself to enforcement and occasionally defied the NRA. At the same time, private foundations adopted a "public health" agenda that was sympathetic to building organizations dedicated to violence prevention, including gun regulation. Second, beginning with the Stockton playground shooting in 1989 and escalating after the spate of school shootings from 1997 to 1999, gun control advocates seized on a new way of portraying gun control: as a measure to protect children. In retrospect, the groundwork for this framing mechanism had been laid in the 1980s, as public health professionals and the Centers for Disease Control set out to transform and depoliticize the discourse. The shootings of children, and the organizations these events inspired, carried that message in a way that would resonate with middle-American parents.

Finally, gun control organizers in the 1990s began to embrace incremental policy making. To be sure, there remain deep divisions within their ranks over whether local and moderate measures help or harm the cause. But there is little question that the dominant strategy is to embrace such efforts. The Brady Bill, passed in 1993, showed that modest gun control measures could win the approval of a majority in both houses of Congress. The Million Mom March left in its wake chapters of local gun control organizers for the first time in American history. The Legal Community Against Violence provided an example of a local-ordinance strategy that can produce dramatic statewide change in a relatively short period of time.

At the same time, an assessment of the quest for gun control in the early twenty-first century must account for what has not happened, as well as what has. Even after the Million Mom March brought hundreds of thousands of women to Washington and other protest sites around the country, Congress tabled the modest gun control bill before it. In 2004, Congress declined to renew the decade-old ban on the manufacture, importation, and sale of certain semiautomatic "assault weapons." In the 2004 presidential campaign, as in 2000, the major-party candidates suppressed the gun issue, and in both cases the candidate favored by the NRA, George W. Bush, went to the White House. Several of the major philanthropic patrons of gun control groups began pulling out. With violent crime at historic lows, and mass shootings seemingly abating, the movement that appeared to some to be emerging in the late 1990s had lost its catalyst. One national gun control leader said privately in early 2005 that the movement was dead, at least for the time being.

Although the national gun control campaign had a grassroots presence for the first time in its history, in the form of the Million Mom March, relations between the Brady Campaign and independent state gun control groups remained distant. Ironically, the bad feelings stemmed in part from the Brady Campaign's decision to adopt the Million Mom March chapters and build a gun control movement. Officials at Brady's national office talked privately about an "ugly three or four years" in their relations with the state activists and expressed hope that they could "knit the movement back together." Confronted by perennial resource constraints, national gun control organizations faced internal tensions about how much to devote to state and local organizing as opposed to the traditional national strategy. Amid these debates, even advocates for the grassroots approach admitted that there was no clear strategy for building a nationwide movement around state-policy proposals, as the NRA had done so successfully with its preemption, concealed-carry liberalization, and immunity campaigns during the 1980s, 1990s, and beyond.

Throughout the 1990s—and particularly in the inhospitable 2000s— the leading national gun control organizations turned increasing attention to litigation as a strategy for achieving policy reform. In 1989, both the Brady Campaign and the Coalition to Stop Gun Violence (as they are now known) had hired lawyers to spearhead these efforts. The litigation strategy was intended to be a complement to, not a substitute for, legislative advocacy. But as legislative victories became difficult to achieve, it was clear that the organizations were willing to shift resources toward court battles on the grounds that lawsuits were more likely to succeed.

The focus on litigation gained momentum in the late 1990s, when nearly three dozen cities and other government entities, in addition to several gun victims, filed suit against gun manufacturers alleging that their distribution practices were negligent and posed an illegal "public nuisance." Both gun control organizations employed lawyers to lend support to the lawsuits—everything from providing expert advice to filing friend-of-the-court briefs to serving as full-fledged cocounsel on the cases. As of early 2005, none of these suits had resulted in a jury verdict that was upheld on appeal. But at least three cases had resulted in generous settlements for the victims, and the legal theories being pioneered by the gun control lawyers had gained acceptance in some appellate courts.[8] "This is our one avenue right now that's actually producing results," one national gun control leader told me in early 2005.

Meanwhile, the NRA sought to wipe out the lawsuits through legislation providing immunity to firearms manufacturers. By early 2005, the NRA and its affiliates had persuaded thirty-three state legislatures to enact such immunity laws, and in late 2005 Congress passed a bill that would apply nationwide. If lawsuits had continued to be allowed in some states, the litigation strategy may have proved effective in reducing gun trafficking while educating the public about systemic problems in the gun distribution system. But lawsuits were unlikely to serve as a foundation for building a national gun control movement; they are not mechanisms of mass mobilization, at least not directly. After all, only victims and city governments had standing to sue, and then only in one-third of the states. What is more, national gun control groups had trouble energizing their local and state activists to fight the NRA's national immunity legislation. Facing a tepid response, national gun control officials reframed the anti-immunity fight as "justice for gun victims" in hopes of lighting a spark. Finally, while the lawsuits temporarily brought gun control groups together with government entities, those entities were clients, not patrons. Thus, for a host of reasons, the litigation strategy was unlikely to contribute significantly to a broad-based national gun control movement in America.

This study began by suggesting that the gun control paradox was misspecified. While observers have traditionally asked, Why no gun control in America? the true question is a prior one, Why no gun control *movement* in America. This book has advanced a set of arguments about social movements, and mobilization around public goods, that has attempted to resolve the participation paradox. The challenge ahead is to test that theory against other issues that inspire motivation without movement. In the meantime, the question remains: Is the history of gun control politics doomed to repeat itself? Will an assassination or mass shooting—and there will be one—evoke nothing more than a momentary burst of out-rage from concerned citizens? Or will the groundwork laid in the Colum-bine era produce the nation's first movement for gun control? Ultimately, the answer may depend on the willingness of the gun control leadership to give the people the opportunity to make the difference that they desire.

# Gun-Related Trends

THE MOST RELIABLE LONGITUDINAL SERIES on gun possession in the modern era is contained in the General Social Survey (GSS), conducted by the National Opinion Research Center at the University of Chicago. Since 1973, in most years, the GSS has asked a representative national sample of Americans, "Do you happen to have in your home [if HOUSE: or garage] any guns or revolvers?" Cross-tabulations of the results are available at http://webapp.icpsr.umich.edu/GSS/rnd1998/merged/cdbk-trn/owngun .htm. Figure A-1 is derived from those cross-tabs.

Figure A-2 was constructed from tables compiled by Jon S. Vernick and Lisa M. Hepburn and presented in their chapter, "State and Federal Gun Laws," in Jens Ludwig and Philip J. Cook, eds., *Evaluating Gun Policy* (Washington, D.C.: Brookings Institution Press, 2003). The chart counts the following gun control laws: handgun bans, handgun permits, long-gun permits, handgun registration, long-gun registration, Saturday night special bans, assault weapon bans, background checks on handgun sales by federally licensed firearms dealers (FFLs), background checks on long-gun sales by FFLs, background checks for non-FFL sales of handguns, background checks for non-FFL sales of long guns, waiting periods for handgun purchases, waiting periods for long-gun purchases (included only for completeness—there are no such laws), minimum-age restrictions for firearm purchases, laws limiting handgun buyers to one purchase per month, gun dealer licensing and inspection, minimum-age restrictions for handgun possession, and child access protection laws (providing criminal penalties to adults who store guns where children can easily reach them). I do not include laws governing concealed carrying of guns, because the so-called CCW laws enacted in the study period were actually gun *de*-control laws, aimed at providing easier access to these permits. Nor do I include laws that provided for stiffer sentences for gun-related crimes, given that these laws do not control guns before the fact but merely punish offenders after they have committed a crime.

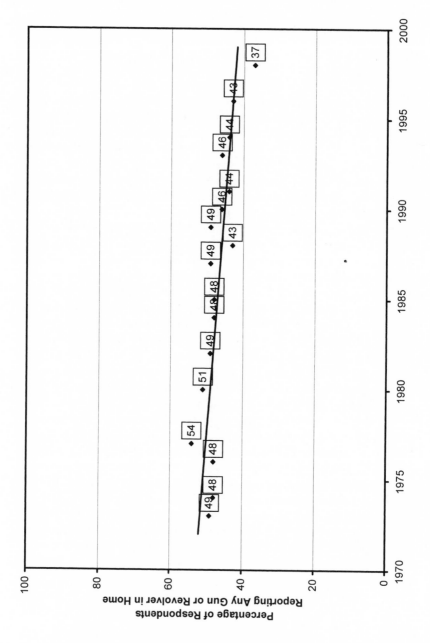

Figure A.1. Declining Household Gun Ownership, 1973–1998. Source: General Social Survey, National Opinion Research Center.

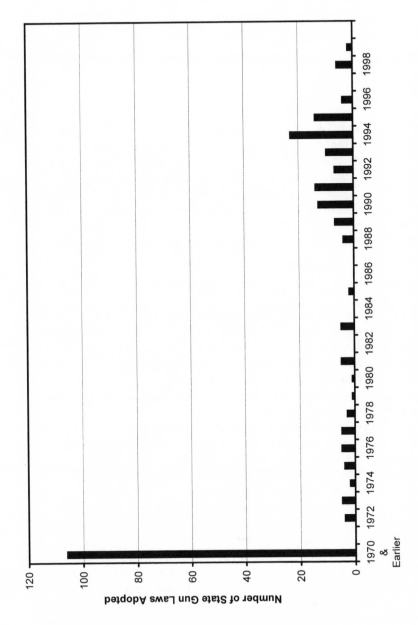

Figure A.2. Adoption of State Gun Laws. Source: Adapted from counts in Vernick and Hepburn (2003). Note: Often one state will pass multiple provisions in a given year. For example, all laws passed in 1981 were in Missouri, and all laws in 1988, Hawaii.

# Brief Case Studies of Other Social-Reform Movements

THIS SECTION BUILDS on the major case studies presented in chapter 2 by demonstrating that the theoretical propositions about movement formation are robust across issues. To provide positive cases with which the negative gun control case legitimately could be compared, chapter 2 examined three social-regulatory issues: antialcohol, antismoking, and antiabortion. In the interests of space and simplicity, each proposition in the theory was illustrated with a case study of just one of those three issues. Below, I show that other issues also illustrate the theory.

## SOCIALIZING THE COSTS: STATE PATRONAGE

The antismoking movement is an important example of the pivotal role that state patronage can play in encouraging the formation and expansion of social movements. But it was not alone. Scholars of the women's temperance movement of the nineteenth century note that one of the first actions was to organize a petition campaign to persuade Congress to create a commission that would investigate and provide authoritative information on the alcohol menace,[1] and of course other antialcohol activists were busy building the Prohibition Party, which they hoped would assume national office and harness the power of government to eradicate alcohol. Nearly a century later, the federal government played a critical role in spurring the women's liberation movement. In her authoritative account, Anne Costain puts particular emphasis on President Kennedy's decision to create the first ever Presidential Commission on the Status of Women, which was led by a top Labor Department official and gathered authoritative evidence about women's discontent. The commission played "a major role in creating the early agenda of the women's movement."[2] Affiliated commissions in all fifty states performed a similar function at the subnational level. What is more, sympathetic government officials, concerned about the limits of state-sponsored action, helped enable the creation of the National Organization for Women, the principal social-movement organization for women's rights.[3] Finally, the modern antialcohol movement, embodied by Mothers Against Drunk Drivers (later Mothers

Against Drunk Driving), was launched with patronage support from the National Highway Traffic Safety Administration, which provided a seed grant of $65,000 to help MADD's founders establish a national network of chapters.[4] Perhaps more important than providing money, the federal safety administration churned out research as early as 1968 showing the link between alcohol consumption and traffic accidents and deaths. John D. McCarthy argues that the agency "became the major institutional advocate of the drunk-driving frame, and, through its state and local programs, created a vast interlinked constituency of supporters for it."[5]

## Socializing the Costs: Associational Patronage

Again, the antiabortion movement is just one of many social-regulatory movements that have sought institutional patronage from voluntary associations. The temperance and Prohibition movements of the nineteenth century, for example, worked through Protestant churches. As head of the Woman's Christian Temperance Union, Frances Willard wrote some two thousand letters in the summer of 1875 alone to church leaders in every state asking them for names and addresses of women who might be interested in organizing movement organizations in their areas.[6] Later, the Anti-Saloon League, which emerged in the early 1890s and became the most important Prohibition-movement organization, persuaded thousands of churches to join as affiliates and to set aside one Sunday per year in which the league could present its work and raise money by passing the altar plate to a captive audience. Indeed, some 60% of the league's leaders were clergy members, and the league called itself "the church in action against the saloon."[7]

## Personalizing the Benefits: Framing

Besides the antialcohol movements, other social-regulation advocates have also used the child-protection frame to good effect. The antiabortion movement, of course, frames its goals in terms of protecting children. Demonstrators use photographs of aborted fetuses with infant features, as well as films such as *Silent Scream*, to dramatize their case. "It's a child, not a choice," is one of the movement's popular slogans. The Progressive-era antitobacco movement was led by Lucy Page Gaston's female-dominated Anti-Cigarette League, which saw cigarette smoking as leading to the moral corruption of American youth and the eventual decline of society. The reformers considered cigarettes to be what we now call a gateway drug, in which youthful smoking inevitably led to alcohol abuse and moral dissolution in adulthood. As John Burnham notes, "The 'cigarette-smoking boy,' typically an urban urchin and rowdy and probably identified at least part of the time with the Victorian underworld, became a symbol of danger for moral reformers."[8] The contemporary antismoking movement was losing steam until it seized on the child-protection frame in the 1990s. By spotlighting the tobacco companies' efforts to market to children, as symbolized by Joe Camel, the antismoking movement could construct a causal story that pitted Big Tobacco against innocent children and virtually demanded a political reaction from anxious parents.

## Altering the Prospective Cost-Benefit Calculation: Incrementalism

Once again, although the antialcohol movement provides a clear case of horizontal and vertical incrementalism at work, other movements have also embraced these strategies. The antismoking movement, which has severely circumscribed a practice that was once widespread, began with simple warning labels on packs of cigarettes and a court ruling that television stations must run one antismoking public service announcement in prime time for every four cigarette commercials.[9] Generally speaking, as Ronald Troyer and Gerald Markle demonstrate, the antismoking movement began with "assimilative" strategies, such as trying to persuade individuals to quit or educating the public about the health hazards of smoking. By the mid-1970s, however, the movement switched to "coercive" approaches, consisting of laws and regulations governing behavior.[10] In other words, the movement pursued a strategy of horizontal incrementalism. Although the particular tactics were not inherently given to mass mobilization, they did harness the power of the state to create a latent public that could be mobilized later. By pursuing education, rather than coercion, the early antismoking advocates avoided the popular backlash that might have stymied any future movement.

Later, as it was gathering steam, the antismoking movement pursued a vertically incremental strategy. By 1979, there were about a thousand local antismoking groups focused on legislation to protect "nonsmokers' rights."[11] At least a hundred of these groups by 1983 were affiliated with GASP, the Group Against Smokers' Pollution, which had formed in California in the 1970s.[12] Also arising at that time was Californians for Non-smokers' Rights, which was formed in 1980 "to focus the limited resources of the nonsmokers' rights advocates on one community at a time."[13] In its first three years, the organization worked with local activists and helped to secure twenty-one city or county clean-air ordinances in California.[14] By 1984, the California group became Americans for Nonsmokers' Rights, dedicated to enacting local ordinances in cities and towns around the country.

The tobacco industry took notice of the political mobilizing power of this development: "Over time we can lose the battle over smoking restrictions as decisively in bits and pieces—at the local level—as with state or federal measures."[15] As the National Cancer Institute asserted, "Local ordinance development puts in motion an educational process of letters to the editor, press coverage, town hall meetings, and public hearings"—in short, opportunities for meaningful mobilization.[16] By 2000, there were an estimated 642 local ordinances limiting smoking in workplaces and 753 ordinances that limited smoking in restaurants.[17] In 1996, nearly two-thirds of all workers were covered by a smoke-free policy, up from only 3% in 1986.[18] These ordinances were passed before the tobacco industry sought statewide preemption laws; thus, for political reasons, state laws typically set standards that would not undermine those already in force in local jurisdictions.

The antiabortion movement also has employed an incremental strategy, perhaps born of necessity. After the Supreme Court's 1973 *Roe v. Wade* ruling, which found a fundamental right to abortion under most conditions, the antiabortion movement sought to restrict access to abortion locally and to carve out modest exceptions to *Roe* at the state and national levels. Thus, in a pattern reminiscent of the temperance strategies of the 1870s, antiabortion forces sought to drive local abortion providers out of business by staging protests outside their doors and by creating parallel institutions that would counsel women not to have abortions. At the state level, the antiabortion forces mobilized around winnable restrictions, such as parental-consent laws and preprocedure counseling requirements. At the national level, they sought and secured laws eliminating government funds for abortion services. Facing considerable hurdles, including a Supreme Court ruling that upheld the "right to choose" and a populace that generally supported that perspective, the antiabortion movement could have been doomed. Instead, it sustained itself in large part because it pursued a combination of tangible local projects and policy proposals that stood a chance of being enacted.

# Survey of Million Mom March Participants

## SURVEY 1: PARTICIPANTS IN THE MILLION MOM MARCH

The first survey was distributed throughout the day by a team of seventeen people. The two-page survey took anywhere from four to fifteen minutes to complete. Respondents were assured anonymity and confidentiality, instructed to skip any questions they felt uncomfortable answering, and provided with the principal investigator's contact information. We obtained 793 completed surveys, a 90% response rate.

The nature of the event—an all-day "march," or gathering, on the Mall in Washington, D.C.—made it difficult to obtain a perfectly random sample. However, we took numerous steps to make the sample as random as possible, and we are confident that the sample was representative of the larger population of marchers. To maximize randomness, we collected surveys throughout the day and at all areas of the Mall (e.g., the front, the sidelines, the back); we surveyed only one representative in groups of people attending together; we attempted to survey everyone coming through one of the main points of entry; we surveyed everyone in line for refreshments at different points in the day; we distributed the surveys to every third "picnic blanket" at different places on the Mall; and in cases of two-gender couples, we alternated between the male and female partner. We detected no obvious patterns among the nonresponders that would give us cause for concern about nonresponse bias (that is, the nonresponders were diverse by gender, race, and age). Contrary to the image of the "oversurveyed American," most respondents appeared to take the survey very seriously, taking time to answer the questions accurately and thoughtfully.

## SURVEY 2: THE FOLLOW-UP

Although the initial survey was anonymous, respondents were asked whether they would be willing to be contacted over the summer to discuss their experiences. Fully 64% of them provided contact information (a first name, plus a phone number or e-mail address or both). This yielded a potential panel of 505 respondents (out of 793 total). Of those 505,

428 (85%) have been successfully contacted, either by e-mail, phone, or mail. Completed surveys have been received from 220 respondents (51% of those successfully reached; 44% of those who provided contact information; and 28% of all marchers surveyed). The survey was conducted in September 2000, with follow-up surveys sent in November and December 2000; there is no systematic difference in terms of number of follow-up activities between those who responded in September and those who responded two to three months later. Table C-1 summarizes the results.

## VARIABLES OF INTEREST IN THIS STUDY

The cognitive-frame variables were constructed from answers to the following question on the original survey:

*Following is a list of statements that we often hear from people who advocate gun control. Please read all eight, then indicate the TOP 3 reasons you are at the march today. Rank your reasons by putting 1, 2, and 3 in the space provided.*

RANK (1, 2, AND 3)

___I am here because I think gun control is necessary to *reduce our nation's high crime rate*

___I am here to *speak out on behalf of someone close to me* who was a victim of gun violence

___I am here because I *fear for the safety of my children* and/or other children close to me

___I am here because I *fear for my own safety* and/or the safety of my neighborhood

___I am here because I think it's time to *send Congress and the gun lobby a message*

___I am here because gun control is an important *part of my religious belief* that all life is sacred

___I am here because I want to do something to *protect the safety of children* at home or school

___I am here to express my *long-standing concern about the easy availability of guns* in this country

The following five frame variables were created from the combination of answers to that question. In all cases, respondents were coded as 1 if the frame applied, and 0 if it did not.

*Child Frame:* Respondents were coded as having a "child frame" if they mentioned either "fear for the safety of my children" or "protect the safety of children" (or both) among their top three and *did not* mention "reduce our

TABLE C.1
Summary of Million Mom March Survey Questions

| Variable Category | Survey 1: MAY 2000 (N = 793) | Survey 2: SEP–NOV 2000 (N = 220) |
|---|---|---|
| *Demographic information* | —State of residence, gender, children at home (ages), education, age, type of community (suburb, city, etc.), income, marital status, race<br>—Employment status | Kids at home |
| *Prior civic and movement activity* | —In past year: contacted elected official, attended public meeting, served on committee, served as officer of org., attended rally or speech, wrote letter to editor, signed petition, worked for polit. party?<br>—Ever involved in: civil/women/gay rights, peace/antinuclear, antitobacco/drunk driving, abortion (choice or life), environment/animal protection, other? | |
| *Political orientation/interest* | —Party ID<br>—Ideology (7-point scale) | Planned presidential vote choice |
| *March-related information* | Who at march with?<br>How heard about march (media, vol. assn., etc.)? | What have done since march (17 possible items)<br>Heard from MMM since march?<br>Visited MMM Web site past mo.?<br>Tried to persuade someone to get involved in gun control issue? (How? How successful?)<br>Asked kid's parents if they have gun in home? |
| *Prior gun-related experiences* | Involvement in gun control issue?<br>Self or loved one victim of gun violence?<br>Gun in home? | |

TABLE C.1 (*cont.*)
Summary of Million Mom March Survey Questions

| Variable Category | Survey 1: MAY 2000 (N = 793) | Survey 2: SEP–NOV 2000 (N = 220) |
|---|---|---|
| *Gun-related opinions and interest* | Should be a handgun ban? | Should be a handgun ban? |
| | | How important is gun control? |
| | | Abortion or gun control more important in pres. vote choice? |
| | | Education or gun control more important in pres. vote choice? |
| | | How closely following candidates' positions on gun issue? |
| | | How would pro-gun position affect your vote for congressional candidate? |
| | | Degree of attention to votes in Congress? |
| | | Degree of attention to gun-related news stories |
| *Motivations* | Why at the march? | |
| *Reflections* | | If not involved before the march, why not? How, if at all, did experience affect you or your views . . . any thoughts that this survey has not addressed? |

nation's high crime rate" or "fear for my own safety" among the top three or "speak out on behalf of . . . a victim" as the number one reason.

*Crime Frame:* People were coded as having a "crime frame" if they included "reduce our nation's high crime rate" or "fear for my own safety" (or both), but did not include either of the child-related answers.

*Mixed Frame:* People were coded as having a "mixed frame" if they included one of the "crime-related" statements and one of the "child protection" statements among their top three.

*Moral Frame:* Respondents were coded as having a "moral frame" if they said gun control was part of their "religious belief that all life is sacred" and did not check either of the child-protection or crime-related statements.

*Bear Witness Frame:* Respondents were coded as having a "bear witness" frame if speaking for a gunshot victim was the top motive, or if it was second only to sending congress a message or concern over gun availability.

On the dependent variable side of the equation, I created four measures of follow-up activity. They are described below, along with the regression models in which they were used.

*Unilateral Acts:* These are acts that a marcher carries out by herself, as opposed to asking someone else to do them. Unilateral acts include talking to friends about the march, making a contribution to a gun control organization, signing a petition, or volunteering for a local gun control group. The survey provided a list of seventeen such activities, including an "other" category that could accommodate multiple responses. Respondents' observed level of activity ranged from 0 acts to 18 acts. Because the distribution of this variable was not normal, I created a trichotomous variable for regression purposes. Thus, the "unilateral acts" variable takes on three values: 1 (for 0–3 acts); 2 (for 4–5 acts); and 3 (for 6+ acts).

*Intense Acts:* This is a subset of "unilateral acts" that is designed to capture a respondent's commitment to the gun control cause. I coded as "intense" all acts that required more than a trivial expenditure of time, effort, or risk. Included in this variable were volunteering, organizing, writing letters, and persuading someone to get rid of a gun. In the data set, the observed range was 0–12 such acts. However, because more than half the sample had done no intense acts, I created a dichotomous variable for regression purposes. Thus, the "intense acts" variable takes on two values: 0 (no intense acts) and 1 (at least one intense act).

*Recruitment Acts:* This category was created from a question that asked respondents what they had done (if anything) to get others involved in gun control activity. The survey provided eight possible answers, including an "other" category that could take on multiple responses. The observed range of "recruitment acts" performed was 0–6. Again, because more than 60% of the sample had not done any recruitment acts, I created a dichotomous variable for regression purposes. Hence, the "recruitment acts" variable takes on two values: 0 (no acts) and 1 (at least 1 act).

*Total Acts:* The fourth dependent variable is the summation of "unilateral acts" (which includes "intense acts") and "recruitment acts." It has an observed range of 0–24. Because the variable was not normally distributed, I took the natural log of ("total acts" + 1) to pull in the right tail and satisfy ordinary least squares regression conditions. Thus, the actual dependent variable is in natural log form.

The prevalence of each of the possible follow-up activities is summarized in the table C-2.

TABLE C.2

Gun Control Activities after the March (listed in order of prevalence, N=220)

| Activity | % YES |
|---|---|
| *Unilateral Acts* | |
| Talked to friends or family members about my experience at the march | 94 |
| Wore a Million Mom March button or T-shirt | 62 |
| Visited the Million Mom March Web site | 37 |
| Signed a petition in favor of gun control | 36 |
| Contacted an elected official to support gun control | 30 |
| Displayed a Million Mom March bumper sticker | 23 |
| Contributed to the new Million Mom March organization | 22 |
| Contributed to or joined a gun control group (other than MMM) | 20 |
| Did something else ("other") | 16 |
| Tried to persuade someone to get rid of a gun or not to buy a gun | 12 |
| Got together with someone I met through the Million Mom March | 11 |
| Attended a local meeting where gun control was on the agenda | 9 |
| Wrote a letter to the editor in favor of gun control | 5 |
| Volunteered for a local gun control or antiviolence group | 4 |
| Helped form a local or state chapter of the Million Mom March | 3 |
| Organized a local committee on guns or violence (not MMM chapter) | 2 |
| Attended the first Million Mom March conference (Denver, Sept. 2000) | 1 |
| At least one of the above | 97 |
| *Recruitment Acts* | |
| Asked someone to consider a candidate's position on gun control when voting | 29 |
| Asked someone to contact an elected official to support gun control/safety | 11 |
| Asked someone to sign a petition in favor of gun control | 10 |
| Asked someone to put a bumper sticker on his/her car | 8 |
| Asked someone to do something else | 5 |
| Asked someone to write a letter to the editor in support of gun control/safety | 4 |
| Asked someone to make a contribution to a gun control group | 3 |
| Asked someone to volunteer for a local gun control group | 2 |
| At least one of the above | 42 |

# Notes

1. Mitchell Zuckoff, "Subdued NRA Shifts Gears as Calls for Gun Control Grow," *Boston Globe*, 30 April 1999, A1.

2. Sara Kugler, "Gun-Control Group Gains," *Denver Post*, 16 July 1999, A7.

3. Robert J. Spitzer has argued that gun politics follows a "cycle of outrage, action, and reaction," in which an event triggers a public demand for new gun laws, which in turn provokes a backlash by gun rights supporters. See *The Politics of Gun Control* (New York: Chatham House, 1998), 13.

4. *New York Times*, 11 March 2001, sec. 4, 1.

5. *Washington Post*, 7 March 2001, A10.

6. *San Francisco Chronicle*, 24 March 2001, A1.

7. The figure was 31% in 1999 and 36% in 1993. Interestingly, the fraction is roughly comparable to the fraction of respondents in a 1993 Gallup poll who said they "personally know someone who has been injured or killed by a drunk driver." Note that the gun question is more restrictive, referring to "close" relatives or friends, as opposed to someone who is merely personally known to the respondent. The Gallup poll on drunk driving is archived at the Roper Center and accessible via the Lexis-Nexis database.

8. There were approximately 202 million adults over eighteen in 1999; 63 million is 31% of 202 million.

9. Hazel Erskine, "The Polls: Gun Control," *Public Opinion Quarterly* 36, no. 3 (1972): 456.

10. It is important to be clear about what is meant by key terms that reappear throughout this book. I use the term "gun control" as a catchall phrase to refer to a constellation of proposals to regulate the importation, manufacture, transfer, and possession of firearms. I am principally concerned with policies that seek to regulate or restrict access to individuals before they have committed any offense, rather than policies that seek either to enforce existing laws or to punish gun violence offenders after the fact. Throughout this book I use the terms "gun control," "firearms regulation," "firearms restrictions," and "gun laws" interchangeably. On the participation side, I use the term "gun control advocates" or "gun control supporters" to refer to the universe of political actors operating through or on behalf of voluntary associations favoring tighter firearms restrictions. Unless specified, the term "advocates" does not refer to elites (i.e., members of Congress) or to sympathizers within the mass public. The term "gun control groups" refers to organizations that are exclusively devoted to restricting firearms availability, or that have a division that does the same. To describe actors on the other side of the political fence, I use the terms "gun rights supporters," "gun rights activists," or "gun rights organizations." Rather than taking a position that firearms posses-

sion is a right (a question on which there is a great deal of debate), my use of these terms acknowledges the prerogative of political actors to be called what they prefer to be called. Finally, occasionally it is semantically necessary to refer to the collective efforts of gun control groups over a certain period of time; typically, I use the term "campaign" or "push," rather than "movement."

11. Sherry L. Murphy, *National Vital Statistics Reports* 48, no. 11 (24 July 2000): 71; Elizabeth Arias et al., *National Vital Statistics Reports* 52, no. 3 (18 September 2003): 74.

12. U.S. Department of Justice, Bureau of Justice Statistics, "Crimes Committed with Firearms, 1973–2003 (2003), http://www.ojp.usdoj.gov/bjs/glance/guncrime.htm (accessed 24 January 2005). That 5.4 million figure does not include injuries from accidental discharge of a firearm or from attempted suicide.

13. Data are for 1989 to 1998. The rates reached a high of 15 per 100,000 in 1993 and a low of 11 per 100,000 in 1998. Data from U.S. Department of Health and Human Services, Centers for Disease Control and Prevention, *National Vital Statistics Reports* 48, no. 11 (24 July 2000), table 18, http://www.cdc.gov/nchs/data/nvsr/nvsr48/nvs48_11.pdf (accessed 11 January 2003).

14. The U.S. rate was 13.7 firearms deaths per 100,000 people; the rate for England and Wales was 0.4; for Norway, 3.1; for Australia, 2.9. See Lois A. Fingerhut, Christine S. Cox, and Margaret Warner, "International Comparative Analysis of Injury Mortality: Findings from the ICE on Injury Statistics," *Advance Data*, no. 303 (7 October 1998): 15.

15. I define mass shootings to be those in which at least three people were killed or wounded.

16. February 1997 through January 2002.

17. Richard Hofstadter, "America as a Gun Culture," *American Heritage*, October 1970, 4.

18. Tom W. Smith, "The 75% Solution: An Analysis of the Structure of Attitudes on Gun Control, 1959–1977," *Journal of Criminal Law & Criminology* 71, no. 3 (1980): 300.

19. John T. Young, David Hemenway, Robert J. Blendon, and John M. Benson, "Trends: Guns," *Public Opinion Quarterly* 60, no. 4 (1996): 642–643.

20. Young et al. 1996, 642.

21. Author's analysis of National Gun Policy Surveys, conducted by the National Opinion Research Center, 1996–1999.

22. Young et al. 1996, 645; National Gun Policy Surveys, 1996–1999.

23. Author's analysis of DDB Needham Life Style data. The Life Style surveys were commissioned by the advertising agency DDB-Needham and were conducted yearly after 1975 by the commercial polling company Market Facts. I am grateful to Robert Putnam for use of these data sets.

24. National Gun Policy Surveys, 1996–1999.

25. This conclusion is derived from the results of the authoritative General Social Survey, conducted by the National Opinion Research Center. The GSS has asked a representative national sample of Americans nearly every year since 1973, "Do you happen to have in your home [if HOUSE: or garage] any guns or revolvers?" Cross-tabulations of the results are available at http://webapp.icpsr.umich.edu/GSS/rnd1998/merged/cdbk-trn/owngun.htm (accessed 2 February 2005).

26. See, for example, Erskine 1972, 464; Stephen P. Teret et al., "Support for New Policies to Regulate Firearms: Results of Two National Surveys," *New England Journal of Medicine* 339, no. 12 (17 September 1998): 816.

27. Osha Gray Davidson, *Under Fire: The NRA and the Battle for Gun Control* (Iowa City: University of Iowa Press, 1998); Josh Sugarmann, *National Rifle Association: Money, Firepower & Fear* (Washington, D.C.: National Press Books, 1992).

28. William J. Vizzard, *Shots in the Dark: The Policy, Politics, and Symbolism of Gun Control* (Lanham, Md.: Rowman & Littlefield Publishers, 2000); Spitzer 1998; Philip E. Converse, "Changing Conceptions of Public Opinion in the Political Process," *Public Opinion Quarterly* 51, pt. 2: supplement (1987): S12–S24; Howard Schuman and Stanley Presser, "Attitude Measurement and the Gun Control Paradox," *Public Opinion Quarterly* 41, no. 4 (1977–1978): 427–438.

29. Spitzer 1998, 134.

30. See, for example, Alexander DeConde, *Gun Violence in America: The Struggle for Control* (Boston: Northeastern University Press, 2001); and Gregg Lee Carter, *The Gun Control Movement* (New York: Twayne Publishers, 1997). These are both fine works, and I do not disparage either. I mention them only to underscore the argument that the shorthand "movement" label has been adopted without full consideration of whether it is empirically justified.

31. B. Bruce-Briggs, "The Great American Gun War," *Public Interest* 45 (Fall 1976): 37–62.

32. Their count did not include laws that restrict certain categories of persons from owning a gun; criminal laws restricting the use of guns (e.g., laws banning armed robbery); or some gun decontrol laws, such as preemption measures that prohibit localities from regulating firearms or firearm immunity laws that bar lawsuits against gun manufacturers. See Jon S. Vernick and Lisa M. Hepburn, "State and Federal Gun Laws: Trends for 1970–99," in *Evaluating Gun Policy: Effects on Crime and Violence*, ed. Jens Ludwig and Philip J. Cook (Washington, D.C.: Brookings Institution Press, 2003), 348.

33. Anne Garner and Michael Clancy, *Firearms Statutes in the United States* (Washington, D.C.: U.S. Conference of Mayors, 1979).

34. The headline is at http://www.theonion.com/news/index.php?issue= 4104&n=2 (accessed 27 January 2005).

35. I am of course paraphrasing Supreme Court justice Potter Stewart's assessment of pornography. See *Jacobellis v. Ohio*, 378 U.S. 184, 197 (1964).

36. William A. Gamson and David S. Meyer, "Framing Political Opportunity," in *Comparative Perspectives on Social Movements*, ed. Doug McAdam, John D. McCarthy, and Mayer N. Zald (New York: Cambridge University Press, 1996), 283.

37. E. E. Schattschneider, *The Semi-sovereign People: A Realist's View of Democracy in America* (New York: Holt, Rinehart and Winston, 1960).

38. In Sarah and Jim Brady's honor, Handgun Control, Inc., in 2001 was renamed the Brady Campaign to Prevent Gun Violence.

39. I thank an anonymous reviewer for this insight.

40. To obtain a count of these references, I used the Lexis-Nexis database. I counted "movement" references only when the word was used by journalists

(reporters and editorial writers) or other nonparticipating observers. Thus, if an advocacy group wrote a letter or an opinion piece and referred to pro-control forces as a "movement," that reference did not count. I excluded such references made by advocacy groups because I wanted to capture the assessment of outside observers (journalists) as to whether gun control advocacy merited the "movement" mantle. It is worth noting that "movement" references by advocates were also quite rare. Even including these references in my count would not alter the basic finding.

41. Doug McAdam, *Political Process and the Development of Black Insurgency, 1930–1970* (Chicago: University of Chicago Press, 1982); Aldon D. Morris, *The Origins of the Civil Rights Movement: Black Communities Organizing for Change* (New York: Free Press, 1984); David J. Garrow, *Bearing the Cross: Martin Luther King, Jr., and the Southern Christian Leadership Conference* (New York: William Morrow & Co., 1986); Jo Freeman, *The Politics of Women's Liberation* (New York: David McKay Co., 1975); Anne N. Costain, *Inviting Women's Rebellion: A Political Process Interpretation of the Women's Movement* (Baltimore: The Johns Hopkins University Press, 1992).

42. The data set contains 3,247 stories for the forty-three years surveyed. The *New York Times Index* contains thumbnail summaries of each story (not just the headline or the lead paragraph), so in stories about citizens' debates, for example, the summary mentions both sides. Use of this metric is justified on several grounds. First, the *Times* has long been editorially supportive of gun control measures, so it would be expected to cover citizen mobilization for them. Second, the *Times'* main daily circulation area is three states (New York, New Jersey, and Connecticut) where public support for gun control is comparatively strong; thus, stories about gun control advocacy would presumably be of interest to *Times* readers. Third, the *Times* is a national newspaper covering stories in states outside the Northeast; thus, more than other big-city dailies, it could be expected to cover gun control advocacy outside its home region. Although this metric captures only "public" actions (those observable to reporters), such actions are good measures of "movement-ness," given that advocates for changing the status quo in the direction of expanded public goods typically rely on activating the public and the media. See James Q. Wilson, *Political Organizations* (Princeton, N.J.: Princeton University Press, 1995).

43. The other major national gun control groups, the Violence Policy Center and Americans for Gun Safety, are not membership-based organizations.

44. Among the groups that released membership figures, the average was 1,700 members apiece. However, that figure is biased by the fact that many small groups were not counted in the sample while the largest groups were. The median membership figure was 1,150. The ten groups for which I have numbers had a combined membership of nearly 17,000 people. If the twenty-six groups for which I do not have membership figures had 1,150 members each (surely an inflated figure), that would put the total state gun control membership at roughly 47,000.

45. Carl Bakal, "The Traffic in Guns: A Forgotten Lesson of the Assassination," *Harper's*, December 1964, 68.

46. U.S. Congress, House, Committee on the Judiciary, Subcommittee on Crime, *Firearms Legislation*, 94th Cong., 1st sess., pt. 1, 18 February–9 April

1975, 4. Conyers went on to threaten that the silent majority could be awakened to vote against gun control opponents.

47. Peter C. Stuart, "A Failure of Nerve; Shooting Down Gun Control," *New Leader*, 11 September 1978, reprinted in *The Issue of Gun Control*, ed. Thomas Draper (New York: H. W. Wilson, 1981), 109.

48. "Pistols and Politics," *Washington Star*, 7 May 1981.

49. Davidson 1998, 169, quoting Harlon Carter, the NRA's chief lobbyist, after a speech to the New York State Conservation Council in September 1981.

50. Katherine Zartman, "Statement of Katherine Zartman, President, Illinois Citizens for Handgun Control, at Third Annual Walk against Handgun Violence, October 23, 1983" (on file with author).

51. Robert Dreyfuss, "Dark Days for Gun Control," *Rolling Stone*, 2 September 1999, 43.

52. Andrew McGuire of the now-defunct Bell Campaign, quoted in Dreyfuss 1999, 44.

53. Andrew Cuomo, speech before Handgun Control, Inc., May 2000, quoted in Peter Harry Brown and Daniel G. Abel, *Outgunned: Up Against the NRA* (New York: Free Press, 2003), 239.

54. Andrew Cuomo, speech before Handgun Control, Inc., May 2000, quoted in Brown and Abel 2003, 240.

55. John Wildermuth, "Rampages Elicit Little Outcry for Gun Control," *San Francisco Chronicle*, 24 March 2001, A1.

56. Telephone interview with an eastern gun control advocate, 9 June 2002 (on condition of anonymity). The advocate has been involved in the gun control cause for two decades.

57. I thank Robert Putnam for this example.

58. John Stuart Mill, *A System of Logic Ratiocinative and Inductive* (London: Longmans, Green, 1930).

59. Barbara Geddes, "How the Cases You Choose Affect the Answers You Get: Selection Bias in Comparative Politics," in *Political Analysis 2*, ed. James A. Stimson (Ann Arbor: University of Michigan Press, 1990), 149.

60. Maurice Jackson, Eleanora Petersen, James Bull, Sverre Monsen, and Patricia Richmond, "The Failure of an Incipient Social Movement," *Pacific Sociological Review* 3, no. 1 (1960): 35.

61. See, for example, Peter Bachrach and Morton S. Baratz, "Two Faces of Power," *American Political Science Review* 56, no. 4 (1962): 947–952; Matthew A. Crenson, *The Un-politics of Air Pollution: A Study of Non-decisionmaking in the Cities* (Baltimore: The Johns Hopkins University Press, 1971); John Gaventa, *Power and Powerlessness: Quiescence and Rebellion in an Appalachian Valley* (Urbana: University of Illinois Press, 1980); Jane J. Mansbridge, *Why We Lost the ERA* (Chicago: University of Chicago Press, 1986); Theda Skocpol, *Boomerang: Clinton's Health Security Effort and the Turn against Government in U.S. Politics* (New York: W. W. Norton & Co., 1996); Seymour Martin Lipset and Gary Marks, *It Didn't Happen Here: Why Socialism Failed in the United States* (New York: W. W. Norton & Co., 2001).

62. The larger archive, which covers both state and national gun control issues, was amassed by David J. Steinberg and is in his possession in Alexandria, Virginia.

He graciously lent it to me for more than a year. The smaller archive, primarily concerning the Committee for Handgun Control (Chicago), was preserved by Katherine Zartman. It is stored at the University of Illinois at Chicago.

63. D. Kahneman and A. Tversky, "Prospect Theory: An Analysis of Decision under Risk," *Econometrica* 47, no. 2 (1979): 263–291.

64. Howard Schuman and Stanley Presser, "The Attitude-Action Connection and the Issue of Gun Control," *Annals of the American Academy of Political and Social Science* 455 (1981): 40–47. Those counted as "passionate" were respondents who said their feelings about gun permits were "extremely strong" relative to their feelings about other public issues.

65. Author's analysis of the General Social Survey, National Opinion Research Center, 1984. Although the data are old, they were collected during a time in which gun violence was relatively low and gun control was not on the national agenda. Thus, if anything these data *understate* the importance of the gun control issue in a typical year.

66. Schuman and Presser 1981.

67. Philip J. Cook and John H. Laub, "The Unprecedented Epidemic in Youth Violence," in *Youth Violence: Crime and Justice: A Review of Research* 24, ed. Michael Tonry and Mark H. Moore (Chicago: University of Chicago Press, 1998), 27–64.

68. Cook and Laub 1998.

69. The poll is archived at the Roper Center for Public Opinion Research and available through Lexis-Nexis.

70. Going back to 1973, polls have asked a representative sample of Americans this question. The question has appeared on the General Social Survey, the National Gun Policy Survey, and ABC/Washington Post polls. The racial breakdown is available for 1991, 1993, and 1994 only. The remarkable consistency of the findings from those three years suggests that the 20% figure is probably robust over time.

71. K. Austin Kerr, *Organized for Prohibition: A New History of the Anti-Saloon League* (New Haven, Conn.: Yale University Press, 1985); Gary A. Giovino et al., "Surveillance for Selected Tobacco-Use Behaviors—United States, 1900–1994," *Morbidity and Mortality Weekly Report* 43, no. SS-3 (18 November 1994).

72. The effectiveness question is one of a few gun control questions for which results are sensitive to question wording.

73. Yankelovich Partners Inc., August 1993. Sample size = 500. The poll results are available through the Lexis-Nexis survey database.

74. National Gun Policy Survey, conducted by the National Opinion Research Center at the University of Chicago. The survey, sponsored by the pro-control Joyce Foundation, comprised a nationally representative sample of 1,200 respondents.

75. Although there is as yet no reliable way to measure gun control sentiment by state, there is a reliable way to measure anticontrol sentiment: by measuring the fraction of the state's population that belongs to the National Rifle Association. These are gun owners who have spent money to join an organization in exchange for both immediate material incentives—such as magazines and insurance discounts—and expressive goods such as collective political advocacy on

behalf of gun rights. In short, NRA membership is a reasonable proxy of "gun culture," or anticontrol sentiment, in a given state. According to the pluralist logic, there should be a strong negative correlation between a state's per capita NRA membership and the strength of the state's gun control laws. To measure NRA membership per state, I obtained the circulation figures for the three NRA magazines for 1999. Every member receives his choice of magazine as part of the membership package, and only a handful of copies are distributed to nonmembers (e.g., libraries). Thus, magazine circulation is a near-perfect proxy for NRA membership. To measure the strength of state gun laws, I used the Open Society Institute's index (2000). The index is a composite of thirty criteria (such as gun registration, owner licensing, state preemption of local ordinances, and so forth); the index ranges from –10 to 100. The higher the score, the stronger the gun laws. The top-scoring state was Massachusetts (76), and the lowest was Maine (–10). The simple correlation between the Open Society Institute Index and per capita NRA membership is strong and highly significant: –.42 (p < .01). However, a closer inspection of the data shows that the correlation is strongly influenced by a dozen or so states that have particularly strong gun laws, or particularly weak ones. Eliminating those outliers cuts the correlation nearly in half. In any case, even when all states are included in the analysis, per capita NRA membership explains less than 18% of the variance in state gun laws (univariate regression conducted by author).

76. Wilson 1995; Theodore Lowi, "American Business, Public Policy, Case-Studies, and Political Theory," *World Politics* 16, no. 4 (1964): 677–715.

77. Louis Hartz, *The Liberal Tradition in America* (San Diego: Harvest, Harcourt Brace & Company, 1955).

78. Anthony King, "Ideas, Institutions and the Policies of Governments: A Comparative Analysis: Part III," *British Journal of Political Science* 3, no. 4 (1973): 418 (emphasis in original).

79. Mancur Olson, *The Logic of Collective Action* (Cambridge, Mass.: Harvard University Press, 1965).

80. Russell Hardin, *Collective Action* (Baltimore: The Johns Hopkins University Press/Resources for the Future, 1982).

81. Olson 1965.

82. Joseph R. Gusfield, *The Culture of Public Problems: Drinking-Driving and the Symbolic Order* (Chicago: University of Chicago Press, 1981).

CHAPTER TWO
A MOVEMENT IN THEORY

1. William A. Gamson, *Talking Politics* (Cambridge, U.K.: Cambridge University Press, 1992).

2. Doug McAdam, *Political Process and the Development of Black Insurgency, 1930–1970* (Chicago: University of Chicago Press, 1982).

3. John D. McCarthy and Mayer N. Zald, "Resource Mobilization and Social Movements: A Partial Theory," *American Journal of Sociology* 82, no. 6 (1977): 1212–1241; McAdam 1982.

4. John D. McCarthy, "Constraints and Opportunities in Adopting, Adapting, and Inventing," in *Comparative Perspectives on Social Movements*, ed. Doug McAdam, John D. McCarthy, and Mayer N. Zald (Cambridge, U.K.: Cambridge University Press, 1996), 141–151.

5. Sidney Tarrow, *Power in Movement*, 2nd ed. (Cambridge, U.K.: Cambridge University Press, 1998).

6. William A. Gamson and David S. Meyer, "Framing Political Opportunity," in *Comparative Perspectives on Social Movements*, ed. Doug McAdam, John D. McCarthy, and Mayer N. Zald (Cambridge, U.K.: Cambridge University Press, 1996), 283.

7. The best articulation of the thesis that institutionalization stifles movements is Frances Fox Piven and Richard A. Cloward, *Poor People's Movements: Why They Succeed, How They Fail* (New York: Vintage Books, 1979).

8. Peter Eisinger, "The Conditions of Protest in American Cities," *American Political Science Review* 67, no. 1 (1973): 11–28; Doug McAdam, John D. McCarthy, and Mayer N. Zald, eds., *Comparative Perspectives on Social Movements* (Cambridge, U.K.: Cambridge University Press, 1996).

9. Doug McAdam, "Conceptual Origins, Current Problems, Future Directions," in *Comparative Perspectives on Social Movements*, ed. Doug McAdam, John D. McCarthy, and Mayer N. Zald (Cambridge, U.K.: Cambridge University Press, 1996), 27.

10. McAdam 1996, 25.

11. McAdam 1982.

12. John Gaventa, *Power and Powerlessness: Quiescence and Rebellion in an Appalachian Valley* (Urbana: University of Illinois Press, 1980).

13. Robert J. Spitzer, *The Politics of Gun Control*, 2nd ed. (New York: Chatham House, 1998), 13.

14. Hazel Erskine, "The Polls: Gun Control," *Public Opinion Quarterly* 36, no. 3 (1972): 460. The poll was conducted by the Gallup Organization.

15. Erskine 1972, 460–461.

16. Tom W. Smith, "The 75% Solution: An Analysis of the Structure of Attitudes on Gun Control, 1959–1977," *Journal of Criminal Law & Criminology* 71, no. 3 (1980): 301, 307.

17. Elizabeth Brenner Drew, "The Gun Law That Didn't Go Off," *Reporter*, 8 October 1964, 35.

18. Carl Bakal, *No Right to Bear Arms* (New York: Paperback Library, 1968).

19. Bakal 1968, 31.

20. Bakal 1968, 85.

21. Bakal 1968, 187.

22. *Congressional Quarterly Almanac*, Vol. XX (Washington, D.C.: CQ Service, 1964), 272.

23. *Congressional Quarterly Almanac* 1964, 272.

24. Drew 1964, 35.

25. John P. MacKenzie, "Dodd Says 'Almost Hysterical' Foes Have Killed Firearms Bill for Year," *Washington Post*, 13 August 1964.

26. Drew 1964, 35.

27. Carl Bakal, "The Traffic in Guns: A Forgotten Lesson of the Assassination," *Harper's*, December 1964, 62.

28. Erskine 1972, 464.

29. Erskine 1972, 469.

30. Alfred Balk, "The Firearms Theater of the Absurd," *Saturday Review*, 22 July 1967, 28.

31. Personal interview with David Steinberg, Arlington, Va., 5 January 2000.

32. *Congressional Quarterly Almanac*, Vol. XXIV (Washington, D.C.: CQ Service, 1968), 565.

33. These included Senate majority leader Mike Mansfield (D-Mont.); Senator Warren G. Magnuson (D-Wash.), who had killed the Dodd legislation after JFK's assassination; Senator Philip A. Hart (D-Mich.); and Senator Birch Bayh (D-Ind.). See *Congressional Quarterly Almanac* 1968, 564.

34. Murray Edelman, *The Symbolic Uses of Politics* (Urbana: University of Illinois Press, 1964).

35. "The Gun Menace," *New York Times*, 18 May 1972, 46.

36. Richard Martin, "New Moves to Control Firearms Won't Go Far If the Past Is a Guide," *Wall Street Journal*, 19 May 1972, 1.

37. United Press International, "Congress to Get Gun Bill in Wake of Ford Attack," *Chicago Tribune*, 24 September 1975.

38. Steven Brill, *Firearms Abuse: A Research and Policy Report* (Washington, D.C.: Police Foundation, 1977), 154, 156.

39. *Congressional Quarterly Almanac*, Vol. XXVIII (Washington, D.C.: Congressional Quarterly, 1972), 520.

40. "G.I.'s in Vietnam Mail 'Flood' of Guns to U.S.," *New York Times*, 8 March 1970, 4.

41. Hazel Erskine, "The Polls: Fear of Violence and Crime." *Public Opinion Quarterly* 38, no. 1 (1974): 143.

42. Harris Survey, cited in "Drawing Line on Handguns," *Chicago Tribune*, 21 December 1975, and in John T. Young et al., "Trends: Guns." *Public Opinion Quarterly* 60, no. 4 (1996): 634–649.

43. General Social Survey, National Opinion Research Center, March 1974 and March 1975. Cited in Young et al. 1996, 643.

44. The other three groups would exist for a relatively short period of time. They were DISARM, the National Handgun Control Center, and the U.S. Conference of Mayors' Handgun Control Project. DISARM, headed by former attorney general Ramsey Clark, never occupied a central role and faded without notice. Within a year of its founding, the National Handgun Control Center had merged with the National Coalition to Ban Handguns. The Conference of Mayors' project lasted six years and played an important role in its short history.

45. The states that had active single-issue gun control groups in 1975 were California (2), Georgia, Illinois (2), Massachusetts, Missouri, Michigan, Ohio, Rhode Island, and Tennessee. In 1973, the states that had such groups were Illinois (2), Michigan, Ohio, and Rhode Island.

46. Ellis Cose, "Gun-Control Coalition Primed: Mikva," *Chicago Sun-Times*, 7 October 1975, 21.

47. It is not clear when NCCH officially abdicated its pro-handgun-ban position. A memo dated July 12, 1976, suggests that the group stopped using the word "ban" to avoid having to articulate all the categories of people to be exempted. Gary Kleck states that the switch occurred between September 1977 and November 1978. (See Gary Kleck, "Absolutist Politics in a Moderate Package," in *Armed*, ed. Gary Kleck and Don B. Kates [Amherst, N.Y.: Prometheus Books, 2001], 138.) In a November 15, 1978, fund-raising letter cited by Kleck, NCCH's chief executive, Pete Shields, said that "while many of us might prefer an outright ban of handguns, we are realistic enough to know that such a goal is unattainable in America today." In his 1981 book, Shields said that that the group articulated a "control" rather than a "ban" position to avoid polarizing the debate and thereby playing into the NRA's hands. He said the control position also stemmed from political pragmatism, NCCH's recognition that Americans would not consent to giving up their right to self-protection through firearms.

48. In October 2001, the Brady Campaign underwent yet another name change when it merged with the remnants of the Million Mom March organization. For a few years it was known as the Brady Campaign united with the Million Mom March. The implications of this merger are explored in chapters that follow.

49. National Coalition to Ban Handguns, "Program for the National Coalition to Ban Handguns," 1975 (on file with author).

50. Felice Michaels Levin, "Evaluation of the Handgun Control Project, U.S. Conference of Mayors," report prepared for the George Gund Foundation, Cleveland, 1977, 8.

51. Levin 1977.

52. "Big New Drive for Gun Controls," *US News & World Report*, 10 February 1975, 26.

53. Richard L. Strout, "Gun Control an 'Idealistic Dream,' Says Saxbe, but Growing Trend Favors It," *Christian Science Monitor*, 18 January 1974.

54. *Congressional Record*, 94th Cong., 1st sess., 23 September 1975, E4924–E4925.

55. Nancy Hicks, "2d Threat against Ford Spurs New Action by House Panel to Curb Handguns," *New York Times*, 24 September 1975, 27.

56. "Big New Drive for Gun Controls" 1975, 25. Other publications echoed that assessment. See, for example, Harry Wilensky, "Gun Control Bill May Be Near," *St. Louis Post-Dispatch*, 30 April 1975; and "Gun Control, 1975," *Christian Science Monitor*, 9 January 1975.

57. Bureau of Justice Statistics data, based on Uniform Crime Reports.

58. General Social Survey, 1979, 1982.

59. Pete Shields, *Guns Don't Die—People Do* (New York: Arbor House, 1981), 161.

60. Paul Taylor, "Rolling Stone Publisher, Police Take Aim at Guns," *Washington Post*, 31 August 1982, A3.

61. National Alliance of Handgun Control Organizations, "Articles Establishing the National Alliance of Handgun Control Organizations," n.d. (on file with author).

62. National Alliance of Handgun Control Organizations, Treasurer's Report, 11 March 1983; National Alliance of Handgun Control Organizations, "Resolutions Approved by the Members, March 13, 1983" (both on file with author).

63. Letter from James S. Lipscomb, Executive Director, George Gund Foundation, to Katherine W. Zartman, National Seminar Project, 21 October 1985 (on file with author).

64. Jim Oliphant, "How the Gun Debate Died," *Legal Times*, 22 October 2002, 14.

65. Robin M. Ikeda et al., *Fatal Firearm Injuries in the United States, 1962–1994* (Atlanta: Centers for Disease Control, National Center for Injury Prevention and Control, 1997), 28.

66. The poll was conducted in December 1993. Results are available through the Lexis-Nexis reference database.

67. Jon S. Vernick et al., "Public Opinion Polling on Gun Policy," *Health Affairs* 12, no. 4 (1993): 198–208.

68. National Rifle Association, "The 1994 Clinton Crime Bill's Firearms Provisions," http://www.nraila.org/Issues/FactSheets/Read.aspx?ID=80 (accessed 7 February 2005).

69. *Congressional Quarterly Almanac*, Vol. XLVII (Washington, D.C.: Congressional Quarterly, 1991), 271; *Congressional Quarterly Almanac*, Vol. XLIX (Washington, D.C.: Congressional Quarterly, 1993), 297.

70. James Q. Wilson, *Political Organizations* (Princeton, N.J.: Princeton University Press, 1995).

71. Jack L. Walker, *Mobilizing Interest Groups in America* (Ann Arbor: University of Michigan Press, 1991), 12. The book was completed by several colleagues after Walker died in a car accident.

72. Walker 1991, 12.

73. Walker 1991, 97.

74. Michael Taylor and Sara Singleton, "The Communal Resource: Transaction Costs and the Solution of Collective Action Problems," *Politics and Society* 21, no. 2 (1993): 195–214.

75. Mark Wolfson, *The Fight against Big Tobacco* (New York: Aldine de Gruyter, 2001).

76. In 1965, an estimated 42% of the population smoked, including 52% of men. By 2000, the fraction of the total population that smoked was 23%. See Gary A. Giovino et al., "Surveillance for Selected Tobacco-Use Behaviors—United States, 1900–1994," *Morbidity and Mortality Weekly Report* 43, no. SS-3 (18 November 1994): 5; and A. Trosclair et al., "Cigarette Smoking among Adults—United States, 2000," *Morbidity and Mortality Weekly Report* 51, no. 29 (29 July 2002): 642–645.

77. Cassandra Tate, *Cigarette Wars* (New York: Oxford University Press, 1999), 4.

78. Tate 1999, 75.

79. Ronald J. Troyer and Gerald E. Markle, *Cigarettes: The Battle over Smoking* (New Brunswick, N.J.: Rutgers University Press, 1983), 40.

80. U.S. Department of Agriculture, "Glickman Announces $340 Million to Aid Tobacco Farmers," Press Release 0245, 20 July 2000.

81. U.S. Department of Health and Human Services, Centers for Disease Control and Prevention, "History of the 1964 Surgeon General's Report on Smoking and Health," http://www.cdc.gov/tobacco/30yrsgen.htm (accessed 7 February 2005).

82. Richard Kluger, *Ashes to Ashes: America's Hundred-Year Cigarette War, the Public Health, and the Unabashed Triumph of Philip Morris* (New York: Alfred A. Knopf, 1996).

83. Kluger 1996, 704.

84. Kluger 1996, 704.

85. Stanton A. Glantz and Edith D. Balbach, *Tobacco War: Inside the California Battles* (Berkeley: University of California Press, 2000), 166.

86. Kluger 1996, 704.

87. Kluger 1996, 704.

88. Wolfson 2001, 123.

89. Wolfson 2001, 123.

90. Wolfson 2001, 134.

91. Wolfson 2001, 144.

92. Wolfson 2001, 145.

93. "States Spend Settlement to Snuff Out a Bad Habit," *USA Today*, 1 August 2000, 10D; more information is available at http://www.healthy-miss.org (accessed 7 February 2005).

94. U.S. Department of Health and Human Services, Centers for Disease Control and Prevention, *Investment in Tobacco Control: State Highlights 2001* (Atlanta: Centers for Disease Control and Prevention, 2001).

95. Wolfson 2001, 188.

96. Wolfson 2001, 188.

97. Wolfson 2001, 187.

98. McCarthy and Zald 1977.

99. Wilson 1995.

100. Wilson 1995, 33–34.

101. Theda Skocpol, *Protecting Soldiers and Mothers* (Cambridge, Mass.: The Belknap Press of Harvard University Press, 1992).

102. Mancur Olson, *The Logic of Collective Action* (Cambridge, Mass.: Harvard University Press, 1965).

103. Kristin Luker, *Abortion and the Politics of Motherhood* (Berkeley: University of California Press, 1984), 126.

104. Ziad Wael Munson, "Becoming an Activist: Believers, Sympathizers, and Mobilization in the American Pro-life Movement" (Ph.D. diss., Harvard University, 2002), 197.

105. Munson 2002, 41.

106. Munson 2002.

107. Munson 2002.

108. Munson 2002, 192.

109. Walker 1991, 49.

110. Loren Renz and Steven Lawrence, *Foundation Growth and Giving Estimates, 2003 Preview* (New York: Foundation Center, 2004), http://fdncenter.org/research/trends_analysis/pdf/fgge04.pdf (accessed 12 February 2005).

111. Ethan Bronner, "With Richer Backers, Rights Groups Cash In," *Boston Globe*, 30 December 1989, 1.

112. Wolfson 2001, 47–48; Kathleen B. McGeady, Robert Wood Johnson Foundation, 21 May 2004 (e-mail to author, on file).

113. K. Austin Kerr, *Organized for Prohibition: A New History of the Anti-Saloon League* (New Haven, Conn.: Yale University Press, 1985), 41.

114. Karen Paget, "The Big Chill," *American Prospect*, May–June 1999, http://www.prospect.org/print/V10/44/paget-k.html (accessed 7 February 2005).

115. Jane J. Mansbridge, *Why We Lost the ERA* (Chicago: University of Chicago Press, 1986), 119.

116. Henry E. Brady, "Political Participation," in *Measures of Political Attitudes*, ed. John P. Robinson, Phillip R. Shaver, and Lawrence S. Wrightsman (San Diego: Academic Press, 1999), 796.

117. Raymond Tatalovich and Byron W. Daynes, eds., *Moral Controversies in American Politics: Cases in Social Regulatory Policy* (Armonk, N.Y.: M. E. Sharpe, 1998); Ronald Inglehart, *Culture Shift in Advanced Industrial Society* (Princeton, N.J.: Princeton University Press. 1990).

118. Joseph R. Gusfield, *Contested Meanings: The Construction of Alcohol Problems* (Madison: University of Wisconsin Press, 1996).

119. Joseph R. Gusfield, *The Culture of Public Problems: Drinking-Driving and the Symbolic Order* (Chicago: University of Chicago Press 1981), 3.

120. Gusfield 1981.

121. Mark H. Moore, "What Sort of Ideas Become Public Ideas?" in *The Power of Public Ideas*, ed. Robert B. Reich (Cambridge, Mass.: Ballinger Publishing Company, 1988), 75.

122. David A. Snow and Robert D. Benford, "Master Frames and Cycles of Protest," in *Frontiers of Social Movement Theory*, ed. Aldon Morris and Carol Mueller (New Haven, Conn.: Yale University Press, 1992), 133–155.

123. Frank R. Baumgartner and Bryan D. Jones, *Agendas and Instability in American Politics* (Chicago: University of Chicago Press, 1993).

124. Robert B. Reich, ed., *The Power of Public Ideas* (Cambridge, Mass.: Ballinger Publishing Company, 1988).

125. Thomas R. Rochon, *Culture Moves: Ideas, Activism, and Changing Values* (Princeton, N.J.: Princeton University Press, 1998).

126. David A. Rochefort and Roger W. Cobb, *The Politics of Problem Definition* (Lawrence: University of Kansas Press, 1994).

127. Deborah A. Stone, "Causal Stories and Policy Agendas," *Political Science Quarterly* 104, no. 2 (1989): 281–300.

128. Roger W. Cobb and Charles D. Elder, *Participation in American Politics: The Dynamics of Agenda-Building* (Baltimore: The Johns Hopkins University Press, 1972), 51.

129. Baumgartner and Jones 1993, 239.

130. Craig Reinarman, "The Social Construction of an Alcohol Problem," *Theory and Society* 17 (1988): 91–120.

131. Jack S. Blocker Jr., *American Temperance Movements: Cycles of Reform* (Boston: Twayne Publishers, 1989), 77.

132. Kerr 1985, 44.

133. Kerr 1985, 50.

134. Blocker 1989, 64.

135. Kerr 1985, 25.

136. Joseph R. Gusfield, *Symbolic Crusade: Status Politics and the American Temperance Movement* (Urbana: University of Illinois Press, 1963).

137. Ruth Bordin, *Woman and Temperance: The Quest for Power and Liberty, 1873–1900* (New Brunswick, N.J.: Rutgers University Press, 1990).

138. Bordin 1990.

139. Mark Edward Lender and James Kirby Martin, *Drinking in America: A History* (New York: Free Press, 1982), 107; Bordin 1990, 58.

140. Peter H. Odegard, *Pressure Politics: The Story of the Anti-Saloon League* (New York: Octagon Books, 1966).

141. Odegard 1966, 39–42.

142. Odegard 1966, 40.

143. Odegard 1966, 46.

144. Odegard 1966, 95.

145. Kerr 1985, 152.

146. Kerr 1985, 1.

147. Reinarman 1988, 91.

148. Survey cross-tabulations available from Roper Center for Public Opinion Research. The poll was conducted by Peter D. Hart Research on behalf of *Rolling Stone* magazine.

149. Reinarman 1988, 100.

150. National Highway Traffic Safety Administration, Fatality Analysis Reporting System (FARS) data, compiled at http://www.infoplease.com/ipa/A0908129.html (accessed 7 February 2005).

151. John D. McCarthy, "Activists, Authorities, and Media Framing of Drunk Driving," in *New Social Movements: From Ideology to Identity*, ed. Enrique Laraña, Hank Johnston, and Joseph R. Gusfield (Philadelphia: Temple University Press, 1994), 146–147.

152. Frank J. Weed, "Grass-Roots Activism and the Drunk Driving Issue: A Survey of MADD Chapters," *Law & Policy* 9, no. 3 (1987): 265.

153. Weed 1987, 266.

154. McAdam 1982; Sidney Verba, Kay Lehman Schlozman, and Henry E. Brady, *Voice and Equality* (Cambridge, Mass.: The Belknap Press of Harvard University Press, 1995).

155. Baumgartner and Jones 1993, 31–35.

156. Baumgartner and Jones 1993, 33.

157. John W. Kingdon, *Agendas, Alternatives, and Public Policies* (Boston: Little, Brown and Company, 1984), 80.

158. John Kingdon (1984) coined the term "rational comprehensive" to refer to strategies that defy horizontal incrementalism. My term, "rational national," is broader, accounting for the defiance of vertical incrementalism, as well.

159. Mansbridge 1986, 3.

160. Blocker 1989, 14.

161. Bordin 1990.

162. Blocker 1989, 77.

163. Ernest H. Cherrington, a leader in the Anti-Saloon League. He is quoted in Carroll H. Woody and Samuel A. Stouffer, "Local Option and Public Opinion," *American Journal of Sociology* 36, no. 2 (1930): 176n.

164. Woody and Stouffer 1930, 178.

165. Bordin 1990.

166. Kerr 1985, 138.

167. Blocker 1989, 104.

168. Kerr 1985, 95.

169. Blocker 1989.

170. Kerr 1985, 148.

171. Kerr 1985, 151.

172. McCarthy 1994.

173. Weed 1987, 262.

174. Weed 1987, 271.

175. Reinarman 1988, 105.

CHAPTER THREE
SOCIALIZING COSTS: PATRONAGE AND POLITICAL PARTICIPATION

1. Aaron Epstein, "How Pentagon Boosted NRA," *Philadelphia Inquirer*, 14 May 1979.

2. James B. Trefethen and James E. Serven, *Americans and Their Guns: The National Rifle Association Story through Nearly a Century of Service to the Nation* (Harrisburg, Penn.: Stackpole Books, 1967), 128.

3. Trefethen and Serven 1967, 128.

4. Trefethen and Serven 1967, 128.

5. The 2002 equivalent was calculated from the Consumer Price Index figures posted on the Bureau of Labor Statistics Web site, www.bls.gov. The series goes back to 1913. If we assume that the inflation rate between 1903 and 1913 is roughly equal to the rate between 1913 and 1924, then the CPI for 1903 would be 5.7, compared to the 2002 figure of 180.7. Hence, one dollar in 1903 would be worth roughly $31.70 in 2002, and the $300,000 appropriation would be worth $9,510,526.

6. Trefethen and Serven 1967, 181.

7. Trefethen and Serven 1967, 307.

8. "Be Strong, Carry a Gun," *New Republic*, 14 December 1963.

9. Associated Press, "Gun Program Costs Millions," *Washington Post*, 16 August 1964.

10. Trefethen and Serven 1967, 310.

11. Quoted in comments of Senator Edward M. Kennedy. *Congressional Record*, 90th Cong., 1st sess., vol. 113, pt. 18, 22 August 1967, 23473.

12. National Council for a Responsible Firearms Policy, "Government Gun Subsidy Assisted Would-Be Assassins," 27 June 1967 (on file with author).

13. *Congressional Record* 1967, S11961.

14. Frank T. Lohman, Director, National Board for the Promotion of Rifle Practice, letter to David J. Steinberg, Executive Director, National Council for a Responsible Firearms Policy, 9 May 1974 (on file with author).

15. "The NCBH vs. the NRA," *Handgun Control News*, March/April 1979, 1.

16. *Congressional Record*, 104th Cong., 2nd sess., 27 June 1996, S7094.

17. *Congressional Record* 1996, S7094.

18. Robert Walker, Handgun Control Inc., quoted on NBC Nightly News, 16 May 1996, reprinted in *Congressional Record* 1996, S7097.

19. Consumer Product Safety Act of 1972, www.cpsc.gov/about/faq.html.

20. Richard A. Ryan, "Ban-the-Bullet Campaign Fizzles," *Detroit News*, 6 April 1975.

21. U.S. Conference of Mayors, "Issues and Alternatives 1975" (Washington, D.C.: U.S. Conference of Mayors, 1975), 57.

22. James Q. Wilson, *Bureaucracy: Why Government Agencies Do What They Do* (New York: Basic Books, 1989), 80.

23. *Congressional Record*, 94th Cong., 1st sess., 23 September 1975, E9395–9396.

24. William J. Vizzard, *Shots in the Dark: The Policy, Politics, and Symbolism of Gun Control* (Lanham, Md.: Rowman & Littlefield Publishers, 2000).

25. Vizzard 2000, 60.

26. Richard Phillips, "U.S. Withdraws Support for Gun Turn-in Drive," *Chicago Tribune*, 22 May 1977.

27. Neal Knox, "ILA Pledges to Fight BATF Firearms Abuses," *American Rifleman*, March 1978, 62.

28. Knox 1978, 59.

29. William J. Vizzard, *In the Crossfire: A Political History of the Bureau of Alcohol, Tobacco and Firearms* (Boulder, Colo.: Lynne Rienner, 1997), 56.

30. Anthony Marro, "Pro-Gun Lobby Opens Fire on Treasury Dept. Official," *Washington Star*, 2 October 1978.

31. Charles R. Babcock, "Firearms Rule Draws a Fusillade," *Washington Post*, 17 May 1978.

32. Babcock 1978.

33. "BATF's Rex Davis Resigns," *American Rifleman*, August 1978, 77.

34. Peter C. Stuart, "A Failure of Nerve; Shooting Down Gun Control," *New Leader*, 11 September 1978, reprinted in *The Issue of Gun Control*, ed. Thomas Draper (New York: H. W. Wilson, 1981), 105–110.

35. "NRA-ILA Calls for BATF Hearings," *American Rifleman*, NRA *Official Journal*, March 1979, 5.

36. "Knox Declares War on GCA '68," *American Rifleman*, April 1979, 7.

37. "BATF Abuses Exposed to Senators" *American Rifleman*, NRA *Official Journal*, September 1979, 7–8; "Senators Told of More BATF Abuses" *American Rifleman*, NRA *Official Journal*, June 1980, 15–16.

38. "BATF Abuses Exposed to Senators" 1979, 8.

39. Phil Gailey and Mary Thornton, "Beleaguered Bureau at Treasury Becomes the Target of the Pro-Pistol Lobby," *Washington Star*, 29 April 1981, A6.

40. "Four Years of the Carter Administration," *American Rifleman*, October 1980, 59.

41. Vizzard 1997, 79.

42. Wendy L. Martinek, Kenneth J. Meier, and Lael R. Keiser, "Jackboots or Lace Panties? The Bureau of Alcohol, Tobacco, and Firearms," *The Changing Politics of Gun Control*, ed. John M. Bruce and Clyde Wilcox (Lanham, Md.: Rowman & Littlefield, 1998), 17–44.

43. Vizzard 1997, 81.

44. *Congressional Quarterly Almanac*, Vol. XXXVII (Washington, D.C.: Congressional Quarterly, 1981), 357.

45. Martinek, Meier, and Keiser 1998, 24.

46. Vizzard 2000, 176.

47. Vizzard 2000, 128, 176. Vizzard's comment about BATF's assiduous avoidance of contact with gun control organizations referred specifically to a handgun-freeze campaign in California in the early 1980s, but the insight has been true over time, well beyond that specific campaign.

48. Felice Michaels Levin, "Evaluation of the Handgun Control Project, U.S. Conference of Mayors," report prepared for the George Gund Foundation, Cleveland, 1977, 25.

49. Personal interview with former Treasury Department official, March 2002 (on condition of anonymity).

50. Personal interview with former Treasury Department official, March 2002.

51. Consolidated Appropriations Act of 2005, H.R. 4808, Division B, "Salaries and Expenses," http://thomas.loc.gov (accessed 28 January 2005). The bill became P.L. 108–447.

52. South Carolina's one-gun-a-month law, passed in 1975, was repealed in 2004.

53. Personal interview with Dennis Henigan, Legal Action Project, Brady Center to Prevent Gun Violence, Washington, D.C., 28 January 2005.

54. Peter Conrad, "Medicalization and Social Control," *Annual Review of Sociology* 18 (1992): 210, 213.

55. *Congressional Record*, 92nd Cong., 2nd sess., 16 August 1972. Reprint of Senator Kennedy's statement "Firearms Control."

56. Charles S. Hirsch et al., "Homicide and Suicide in a Metropolitan County," *Journal of the American Medical Association* 223, no. 8 (19 February 1973): 900–905; Lester Adelson, "The Gun and the Sanctity of Human Life; or the Bullet as Pathogen," *Pharos* 43, no. 93 (1980): 15–25.

57. Charles H. Browning, "Handguns and Homicide: A Public Health Problem," *Journal of the American Medical Association* 236, no. 19 (1976): 2198–2200.

58. Madhira D. Ram, Juan J. Geldres, and Jose B. Bueno, "Health Care Costs of Gunshot Wounds," *Ohio State Medical Association Journal* 73, no. 7 (July 1977): 437–439; Anthony J. Mahler and Jonathan E. Fielding, "Firearms and Gun Control: A Public-Health Concern," *New England Journal of Medicine* 297, no. 10 (8 September 1977): 556–558.

59. U.S. Department of Health, Education, and Welfare, Office of the Surgeon General, *Healthy People: The Surgeon General's Report on Health Promotion and Disease Prevention* (Rockville, Md.: Department of Health, Education, and Welfare, 1979).

60. Nikki Meredith, "Public Health Officials Taking a New Approach to Homicide," *Chicago Tribune*, 30 December 1984.

61. In 1986, the Violence Epidemiology Branch had been folded into a division of injury epidemiology and control, which became the Injury Center in 1992.

62. Leslie Baldacci, "Violence Called 'Emergency'; Medical Experts Push Gun Control as Health Issue," *Chicago Sun-Times*, 10 June 1992.

63. Arthur L. Kellermann, "Obstacles to Firearm and Violence Research," *Health Affairs* 12, no. 4 (1993): 144–145.

64. Gary Taubes, "Violence Epidemiologists Test the Hazards of Gun Ownership," *Science* 258, no. 5080 (9 October 1992): 215.

65. Curt Anderson, "Senators Try to Kill Funds for 'Anti-Gun' Health Group," *Chicago Sun-Times*, 4 November 1995.

66. William Raspberry, "Sick People with Guns," *Washington Post*, 24 October 1994.

67. David Satcher, "Gunning for Research: In the NRA Attack on Firearms Studies, the Scientific Truth Is the Most Important Casualty," *Washington Post*, 5 November 1995.

68. Jeff Nesmith, "CDC and Guns," *Atlanta Journal-Constitution*, 2 May 1996.

69. Jeff Nesmith, "Gun Violence Study Survives Budget Vote," *Atlanta Journal-Constitution*, 14 June 1996.

70. See, for example, H.R.3755, Departments of Labor, Health and Human Services, and Education, and Related Agencies Appropriations Act of 1997, at http://thomas.loc.gov.

71. Interview with Dr. Mark Rosenberg, 10 February 2005. The first grant proposal was to the Robert Wood Johnson Foundation; the second, to George Soros's Open Society Institute. At Dr. Rosenberg's urging, Mr. Soros's foundation instead gave the grant to the Harvard School of Public Health, which then spearheaded the firearms-injury surveillance project.

72. No reason ever came to light for Dr. Rosenberg's resignation, but most observers assumed that it was related at least in part to his pursuit of the firearms program.

73. Doug Levy, "Doctors, NRA Take Aim at CDC's Anti-violence Program," *USA Today*, 25 August 1995.

74. John W. Kingdon, *Agendas, Alternatives, and Public Policies* (Boston: Little, Brown and Company, 1984), 90.

75. Theda Skocpol, *Protecting Soldiers and Mothers* (Cambridge, Mass.: The Belknap Press of Harvard University Press, 1992); K. Austin Kerr, *Organized for Prohibition: A New History of the Anti-Saloon League* (New Haven, Conn.: Yale University Press, 1985); Peter H. Odegard, *Pressure Politics: The Story of the Anti-Saloon League* (New York: Octagon Books, 1966).

76. The membership figure is for 2002 (announced at the 2002 Annual Convention in Reno and widely reported). The budget figure ($198,652,438) is for 2001 and is drawn from National Rifle Association, "Return of Organization Exempt from Income Tax" (Form 990), 2001 (on file with author).

77. National Rifle Association, 2001.

78. Kristin A. Goss, "NOW Is Not the Time: Women & Gun Control in the United States," paper presented at the Annual Meeting of the Midwest Political Science Association, Chicago, 25–28 April 2002; and at the "Alva Myrdal's Questions to Our Time" conference, Uppsala, Sweden, 6–8 March 2002.

79. This analysis is based on my coding of 1,120 national or nationally prominent women's groups listed in one or more of the following directories: *The International Directory of Women's Organizations* (1963), produced by the National Council of Women of the United States; the *Encyclopedia of Associations*, volume 1, National Organizations (1963 ed.), produced by Gale Research, a Detroit company that compiles data on voluntary associations; and the *Encyclopedia of Women's Associations Worldwide* (1993 ed.), also produced by Gale Research. The data from the 1963 Gale addition were compiled by Debra Minkoff, and I used her dataset to supplement my own for the year 1963. These directories provide a reasonably complete inventory of significant women's groups that were active at each point in time. In addition, I have included membership data on 14 large traditional voluntary associations. These data shed light on the changing fortunes of these social-reform organizations. A more complete analysis of these data is contained in Goss 2002.

80. In coding the data, I allowed groups to have more than one focus. For example, they could have focused on members and on women in general. Hence, the percentages do not sum to 100.

81. Two groups gained in per capita terms: the Female Moose (up 47%) and Hadassah (up 2%). The groups that lost were: the PTA (–53%); the Federation of Business and Professional Women (–84%); the American Association of University Women (–80%); the League of Women Voters (–63%); the General Federation of Women's Clubs (–78%); the Women's Bowling Congress (–57%); the Eastern Star (–70%); and the Woman's Christian Temperance Union (–91%). In all cases, the percentages reflect declines in the fraction of the relevant population group who belonged to the organization (not on the actual number of members over time). See Robert D. Putnam, *Bowling Alone: The Collapse and Revival of American Community* (New York: Simon & Schuster, 2000).

82. Anne N. Costain, *Inviting Women's Rebellion: A Political Process Interpretation of the Women's Movement* (Baltimore: The Johns Hopkins University Press, 1992), 51.

83. Costain 1992, 50.

84. Jane J. Mansbridge, *Why We Lost the ERA* (Chicago: University of Chicago Press, 1986).

85. Mansbridge 1986, 120–121.

86. Ethel Klein, *Gender Politics* (Cambridge, Mass.: Harvard University Press, 1984), 25.

87. Klein 1984, 29.

88. Klein 1984, 29.

89. Jeffrey M. Berry, *Lobbying for the People* (Princeton, N.J.: Princeton University Press, 1977); Theda Skocpol, "Advocates without Members: The Recent Transformation of Civic Life," in *Civic Engagement in American Life*, ed. Theda Skocpol and Morris P. Fiorina (Washington, D.C.: Brookings Institution Press, 1999), 461–509.

90. Jack L. Walker Jr., *Mobilizing Interest Groups in America* (Ann Arbor: University of Michigan Press, 1991), 52.

91. Theda Skocpol, "Unravelling from Above," *American Prospect*, March–April 1996, 20–25; Steven J. Rosenstone and John Mark Hansen, *Mobilization, Participation, and Democracy in America* (New York: Macmillan, 1993).

92. U.S. CODE, Title 26, Subtitle A, Chapter 1, Subchapter F, Part 1, Sec. 501.

93. There are two sets of rules: the "substantial part" test and the 501(h) exemption. With the exception of churches, charities may decide which to follow. Most charities follow the substantial part test. Those that take the "h exemption" must limit lobbying on a sliding scale (up to $1 million on total lobbying and up to $250,000 on grassroots lobbying). The scales are based on a percent of the organization's charitable expenditures. See Internal Revenue Service, Letter to Charity Lobbying in the Public Interest, 26 June 2000 (on file with author).

94. Telephone interview with Thom Mannard, Illinois Council Against Handgun Violence, 11 September 2002.

95. Telephone interview with Toby Hoover, Ohio Coalition Against Gun Violence, 4 June 2002.

96. Telephone interview with Lisa Price, North Carolinians Against Handgun Violence, 29 July 1999.

97. IRS Form 990 data supplied by the Brady organizations.

98. The group received 501(c)(4) status instead. David Steinberg, personal letter to Selig Sacks, 23 January 1969 (on file with author).

99. Personal interview with Michael Berkey, cofounder and former president, Maryland Handgun Control Committee, Baltimore, 8 June 2002.

100. "FEC Orders HCI to Pay Penalty and Re-structure Organization," *National Rifle Association Monitor*, 31 July 1984, 1.

101. Telephone interview with a national gun control advocate, 2 September 1999 (on condition of anonymity).

102. The grants went to staff members of the recently assassinated Senator Robert F. Kennedy and to encourage a voter registration effort around the Cleveland mayoral election. These grants and the political firestorm that followed are the stuff of lore in foundation circles.

103. "UF Held Hostage," *Grand Rapids Press*, 22 May 1973.

104. National Board of the YWCA of the U.S.A., "At This Point in Time: Report for the Period April 1, 1973 to August 31, 1974" (on file with author).

105. Judith Vandell Holmberg and Michael Clancy, *People vs. Handguns: The Campaign to Ban Handguns in Massachusetts* (Washington, D.C.: U.S. Conference of Mayors, 1977), 47.

106. Donald Bradley, "Partnership for Children Seeks to Take Political Stands," *Kansas City Star*, 10 February 1999.

107. Peter Frumkin, "More's the Pity: Not Every Victim Ought to Be a Charity Case," *Washington Post*, 17 November 2002.

108. Dianne Metzger and Virginia C. Strand, "Violence Prevention: Trends in Foundation Funding," *Health Affairs*, 12, no. 4 (1993): 212.

109. Anne Lowrey Bailey, "Many Grant Makers Are No Longer Shy about Gun Control," *Chronicle of Philanthropy*, 7 September 1993, 11.

110. The amounts were tallied based on records provided by the Joyce Foundation and posted online at http://www.joycefdn.org/programs/gunviolence/gunviolencemain-fs.html (accessed 31 January 2005).

111. Joyce Foundation, statement of program purposes, http://www.joycefdn.org/programs/gunviolence/gunfs.html (accessed November 2002).

112. Americans for Gun Safety, "Colorado and Oregon Voters Approve Historic Voter Initiatives to Close the Gun Show Loophole," 7 November 2000 (on file with author).

113. Trent Seibert, "Groups Tally Donations in Amendment Contests," *Denver Post*, 19 September 2000; Charles E. Beggs, "Gun Measure Battle Tops $2.5 million," Associated Press, 3 November 2000.

CHAPTER FOUR
PERSONALIZING BENEFITS: ISSUE FRAMES AND POLITICAL PARTICIPATION

1. Alexis de Tocqueville, *Democracy in America*, vol. 2, book 2, chap. 8 (New York: Alfred A. Knopf, 1994), 122.

2. E. E. Schattschneider, *The Semi-sovereign People: A Realist's View of Democracy in America* (New York: Holt, Rinehart and Winston, 1960), 2.

3. Mayer N. Zald, "Culture, Ideology, and Strategic Framing," in *Comparative Perspectives on Social Movements*, ed. Doug McAdam, John D. McCarthy, and Mayer N. Zald (Cambridge, U.K.: Cambridge University Press, 1996), 262.

4. Zald 1996, 262.

5. Mark H. Moore, "What Sort of Ideas Become Public Ideas?" in *The Power of Public Ideas*, ed. Robert B. Reich (Cambridge, Mass.: Ballinger Publishing Company, 1988), 80.

6. Byran D. Jones, *Reconceiving Decision-Making in Democratic Politics* (Chicago: University of Chicago Press, 1994); David O. Sears, "Symbolic Politics: A Socio-psychological Theory," in *Explorations in Political Psychology*, ed. Shanto Iyengar and William J. McGuire (Durham, N.C.: Duke University Press, 1993), 113–149.

7. Deborah Stone, "Causal Stories and the Formation of Policy Agendas," *Political Science Quarterly* 104, no. 2 (1989): 297.

8. Stone 1989, 297.

9. Stone 1989, 298.

10. William A. Gamson and David S. Meyer, "Framing Political Opportunity," in *Comparative Perspectives on Social Movements*, ed. Doug McAdam, John D. McCarthy, and Mayer N. Zald (Cambridge, U.K.: Cambridge University Press, 1996), 282.

11. Schattschneider 1960.

12. Moore 1988, 71.

13. Adam J. Berinsky and Donald R. Kinder, "Making Sense of Issues through Frames: Understanding the Kosovo Crisis," paper presented at the Annual Meeting of the American Political Science Association, Washington, D.C., August 2000, 3.

14. Cambridge Reports poll, conducted in April and May 1978. Summary reprinted in *Congressional Record*, 95th Cong., 2nd sess., 5 June 1978, vol. 124, pt. 12, 16239–16241.

15. Josh Sugarmann of the Violence Policy Center has criticized gun control advocates' reliance on what he terms the "wrong hands" theory. See Josh Sugarmann, *National Rifle Association: Money, Firepower & Fear* (Washington, D.C.: National Press Books, 1992).

16. "The Battle to Disarm the Gunman," *Literary Digest*, 19 February 1927, 9.

17. "Club-Women Mapping War on Gangsters," *Literary Digest*, 16 June 1934, 19.

18. Philip Benjamin, "New Group Urges Laws to Curb Sale of Firearms," *New York Times*, 4 December 1963.

19. Josephine Ripley, "The Right to Bear Arms," *Christian Science Monitor*, 16 December 1963.

20. J. Edgar Hoover stated that guns are "7 times more deadly than all other weapons combined," causing death in 21% of assaults, compared to a 3% rate for other weapons. J. Edgar Hoover, Memo to All Law Enforcement Officials, *FBI Law Enforcement Bulletin*, June 1963 (on file with author).

21. John W. Finney, "Senate Opens Debate on a Bill to Curb Crime and Gun Sales," *New York Times*, 2 May 1968.

22. National Council for a Responsible Firearms Policy, "For Firearms Policies in the *Public* Interest: The Purpose and Program of the National Council for a Responsible Firearms Policy," 1967, 1 (on file with author).

23. U.S. Conference of Mayors, "Resolution 10: Firearms Control," passed at annual meeting, Chicago, 15 June 1968 (on file with author).

24. U.S. Congress, Senate, Committee on the Judiciary, Subcommittee to Investigate Juvenile Delinquency, *Federal Firearms Legislation*, 90th Cong., 2nd sess., 26 June 1968, 114.

25. Roger W. Cobb and Charles D. Elder, *Participation in American Politics: The Dynamics of Agenda-Building* (Baltimore: The Johns Hopkins University Press, 1972), 44–45.

26. "Coalition to Stop Gun Violence Timeline" (Washington, D.C.: Coalition to Stop Gun Violence, 1999).

27. Handgun Control, Inc., undated fund-raising solicitation, circa 1989 (on file with author).

28. Coalition to Stop Gun Violence, undated fund-raising solicitation, circa 1992 (on file with author).

29. Philip J. Cook and James A. Leitzel, "'Perversity, Futility, Jeopardy': An Economic Analysis of the Attack on Gun Control," *Law and Contemporary Problems 59*, no. 1 (1996): 91–118; Albert O. Hirschman, *The Rhetoric of Reaction* (Cambridge, Mass.: The Belknap Press of Harvard University Press, 1991).

30. Barbara J. Nelson, *Making an Issue of Child Abuse* (Chicago: University of Chicago Press, 1984).

31. U.S. Congress, Senate, Committee on Commerce, *To Regulate Commerce in Firearms*, 73rd Cong., 2nd sess., 29 May 1934, 88. The subcommittee is not named in the hearing transcript.

32. Jon Meacham, Howard Fineman, and Matt Bai, "'I Think the Real Target Is the Second Amendment,'" *Newsweek*, 23 August 1999, 31.

33. Daniel D. Polsby, "The False Promise of Gun Control," *Atlantic Monthly*, March 1994. The quotation is on p. 1 of the reprint.

34. Testimony of Karl T. Frederick, before a subcommittee of the Committee on Commerce, U.S. Congress, Senate, 29 May 1934, 87. The subcommittee is not named in the hearing transcript.

35. Alexander DeConde, *Gun Violence in America: The Struggle for Control* (Boston: Northeastern University Press, 2001), 165.

36. John R. Lott Jr., *More Guns, Less Crime: Understanding Crime and Gun Control Laws* (Chicago: University of Chicago Press, 1998); John R. Lott Jr. and David B. Mustard, "Crime, Deterrence and Right-to-Carry Concealed Handguns," *Journal of Legal Studies* 16, no. 1 (1997): 1–68.

37. For a critique of the Lott and Mustard work, see John J. Donohue, "The Impact of Concealed-Carry Laws," in *Evaluating Gun Policy: Effects on Crime and Violence*, ed. Jens Ludwig and Philip J. Cook (Washington, D.C.: Brookings Institution Press, 2003), 287–325; Jens Ludwig, "Concealed-Gun-Carrying Laws and Violent Crime: Evidence from State Panel Data," *International Review of Law and Economics* 18, no. 3 (1998): 239–254; and Dan A. Black and Daniel S. Nagin, "Do 'Right-to-Carry' Laws Deter Violent Crime?" *Journal of Legal Studies* 27, no. 1 (1998): 209–213.

38. Meacham, Fineman, and Bai 1999, 30.

39. John M. Snyder, "NRA Registers as Lobby to Uphold Gun Ownership," *American Rifleman*, April 1974, 16.

40. Sugarmann 1992, 241.

41. "The Gun Menace," *New York Times*, 18 May 1972, 46.

42. Pete Shields, *Guns Don't Die—People Do* (New York: Arbor House, 1981), 133.

43. Thomas R. Rochon, *Culture Moves: Ideas, Activism, and Changing Values* (Princeton, N.J.: Princeton University Press, 1998).

44. James Q. Wilson and Mark H. Moore, "Enforcing the Laws We Have," *Washington Post*, 1 April 1981.

45. D. M. Maillie, Speech before the National Alliance of Handgun Control Organizations conference, Cleveland, 11–13 March 1978 (on file with author).

46. Rochon 1998.

47. Philip J. Cook and John H. Laub, "The Unprecedented Epidemic in Youth Violence," in *Youth Violence: Crime and Justice: A Review of Research* 24, ed. Michael Tonry and Mark H. Moore (Chicago: University of Chicago Press, 1998), 40.

48. Cook and Laub 1998, 45.

49. I then reviewed each article to screen out those about other countries and those where the coincidence of terms was spurious.

50. Letters to the editor have the virtue of being both publicly available and clearly argued. They also have some drawbacks. In general, they are likely to have been written by particularly well-educated and politically attentive citizens, and so they may not reflect the thoughts of a random sample of Americans. In addition, letters to the editor typically come in response to events, and are crafted to

resonate with people's conception of those events. And so letters to the editor reflect irregularly timed, strategic sentiments, rather than documenting the regular evolution of public understanding.

51. Walter A. Strauss, Letter to the Editor, *New York Times*, 10 April 1991, A24.

52. Jeffrey Lubbers, Letter to the Editor, *Washington Post*, 30 November 1991, A22.

53. Theresa McKenna, Letter to the Editor, *Washington Post*, 18 February 2000, A22.

54. Jonathan Pastor, Letter to the Editor, *New York Times*, 10 April 2000, A18.

55. Matthew Garrett, Letter to the Editor, *New York Times*, 17 March 2000, A20.

56. Steven W. Brenna, Letter to the Editor, *Washington Post*, 8 March 2000, A30.

57. Alison Hendrie, Letter to the Editor, *New York Times*, 17 October 1999, sec. 4, 16.

58. Chris Hurts, Letter to the Editor, *USA Today*, 22 April 1999, 14A.

59. William A. Gamson, *Talking Politics* (Cambridge, U.K.: Cambridge University Press, 1992).

60. Personal interview with a national gun control advocate, 8 August 2002 (on condition of anonymity).

61. The counts are derived from a Lexis-Nexis database search.

62. Joseph R. Gusfield, *The Culture of Public Problems: Drinking-Driving and the Symbolic Order* (Chicago: University of Chicago Press, 1981).

63. DeConde 2001, 156.

64. Osha Gray Davidson, *Under Fire: The NRA and the Battle for Gun Control* (Iowa City: University of Iowa Press, 1998), 131.

65. The states without a chapter were, with a few exceptions, rural states in the South and West: Alabama, Arizona, Arkansas, Idaho, Indiana, Mississippi, Montana, Nebraska, Nevada, North Dakota, Oklahoma, South Carolina, South Dakota, Vermont, West Virginia, and Wyoming.

66. William A. Gamson, *The Strategy of Social Protest*, 2nd ed. (Belmont, Cal.: Wadsworth Publishing Co., 1990).

67. Henry E. Brady, Kay Lehman Schlozman, and Sidney Verba, "Prospecting for Participants: Rational Expectations and the Recruitment of Political Activists," *American Political Science Review* 93, no. 1 (1999): 153–168.

68. Nancy Burns, Kay Lehman Schlozman, and Sidney Verba, *The Private Roots of Public Action: Gender, Equality, and Political Participation* (Cambridge, Mass.: Harvard University Press, 2001).

69. The findings need to be presented with a caveat. It is not possible to gauge with precision whether the recruitment led to action. The recruitment questions asked whether people had been contacted to perform the activity *within the past year*, while the activity questions themselves asked whether the person had performed the activity *within the past five years*. Hence, for some unknown fraction of cases, the activity may have preceded the recruitment. I present tentative find-

ings here, on the assumption that people are far more likely to remember—and hence report—activities that have taken place within the past year.

70. I derived that figure based on 1998 household income data available through the Census Bureau's Web site.

71. The Roper figure is from 1994. The 1998 figure should not differ significantly from the 1994 figure.

72. The validity and reliability of this commercial data set of consumer attitudes have been extensively tested by Steven Yonish and Robert Putnam. See Robert D. Putnam, *Bowling Alone: The Collapse and Revival of American Community* (New York: Simon & Schuster, 2000), 420–424.

73. This figure does not bode well for the NRA's marketing push to get women to buy guns for self-protection.

74. See Sidney Verba, Kay Lehman Schlozman, and Henry E. Brady, *Voice and Equality* (Cambridge, Mass.: The Belknap Press of Harvard University Press, 1995), table 13.6.

75. I derived that estimate by holding all independent variables at their means and allowing "child frame" to vary between a value of 0 and a value of 1. This is the standard procedure for interpreting logistic coefficients.

76. Verba, Schlozman, and Brady 1995.

77. "Crimes in the Nation's Schools Declined in the 1990s According to Departments of Justice and Education," Department of Education press release, http://www.ed.gov/PressReleases/10–2000/102600a.html (accessed 13 February 2005).

78. John W. Kingdon, *Agendas, Alternatives, and Public Policies* (Boston: Little, Brown and Company, 1984), 98.

79. I am grateful to Robert Putnam for noticing the relevance of this trend and for providing me with the data.

80. Jim Oliphant, "How the Gun Debate Died," *Legal Times*, 22 October 2002, 14.


CHAPTER FIVE
CHANGING THE CALCULATION: POLICY INCREMENTALISM
AND POLITICAL PARTICIPATION


1.. Alexis de Tocqueville, *Democracy in America*, vol. 2, book 2, chap. 4 (New York: Alfred A. Knopf, 1994), 104.

2. I use "good" and "bad" to refer to the normative assessment of gun control partisans. I do not imply that there is any consensus on what is "good" gun control politics or policy.

3. William J. Vizzard, *Shots in the Dark: The Policy, Politics, and Symbolism of Gun Control* (Lanham, Md.: Rowman & Littlefield Publishers, 2000).

4. Vizzard 2000, 172.

5. Vizzard 2000, xvi.

6. *Congressional Quarterly*, 19 April 1975, 797.

7. Vizzard 2000, 83.

8. Jim Oliphant, "How the Gun Debate Died," *Legal Times*, 22 October 2002, 13.

9. "Ban the Bullet," *Time*, 3 March 1975, 8.

10. National Coalition to Ban Handguns, "Statement by Bishop James Armstrong," 19 June 1975 (on file with author) (emphasis omitted).

11. Anthony Downs, "Up and Down with Ecology: The Issue Attention Cycle," *Public Interest* 28 (Summer 1972): 789–804.

12. National Council to Control Handguns, "A Proposal for Support," (1975), 6 (on file with author).

13. See D.C. Code Ann. §§7–25022.1 to 2502.14 (2000).

14. Nancy Hicks, "2d Threat against Ford Spurs New Action by House Panel to Curb Handguns," *New York Times*, 24 September 1975, 27.

15. Ellis Cose, "Gun-Control Coalition Primed: Mikva," *Chicago Sun-Times*, 7 October 1975, 21.

16. National Council to Control Handguns, *Handgun Control*, 22 October 1975, 1 (on file with author).

17. Personal interview with Florence McMillan and Patricia Koldyke, founders, Chicago Committee for Handgun Control, Chicago, Ill., 19 April 2001.

18. John Lesar, "Gun Opponents Battle Ammo," *Atlanta Journal*, 10 March 1975, 7B.

19. "Act before It Is Too Late," *American Rifleman*, September 1974, 22; Clayton Jones, "Gun-Control Forces Say U.S. Is Ready to Restrict Weapons," *Christian Science Monitor*, 27 December 1974, 1.

20. Judith Vandell Holmberg and Michael Clancy, *People vs. Handguns: The Campaign to Ban Handguns in Massachusetts* (Washington, D.C.: U.S. Conference of Mayors, 1977), 1, 74–75; National Council to Control Handguns, "The NCCH Relationship with Other Handgun Control Groups" (n.d.) (on file with author).

21. Holmberg and Clancy 1977, 70; National Council to Control Handguns, "The NCCH Relationship."

22. At that time, in addition to Massachusetts, twenty-three states allowed ballot initiatives. See National Council to Control Handguns, "A Proposal for Support," 14.

23. Holmberg and Clancy 1977, 1, 74.

24. John J. Buckley and Judy Holmberg, Leaders, People vs. Handguns, letter to David Steinberg, Executive Director, National Council for a Responsible Firearms Policy, Inc., 15 May 1978 (on file with author).

25. National Council to Control Handguns, "A Proposal for Support," 3.

26. Pete Shields, *Guns Don't Die—People Do* (New York: Arbor House, 1981), 145.

27. Shields 1981, 146.

28. Harlon B. Carter, "The Hidden Dangers of Gun Control," *American Rifleman*, September 1976, 49.

29. Peter D. Hart and Doug Bailey, "Gun Control: What Went Wrong in California," *Wall Street Journal*, 1 March 1983, 34; Norman Thorpe, "Gun Proposal Prompts Battle in California," *Wall Street Journal*, 20 October 1982, 35.

30. Paul Taylor, "Powder Burn: As Gun-Control Advocates Hit a Bull's Eye or Two, the NRA Tries to Sharpen Its Aim," *Washington Post*, 6 July 1982, A1.

31. See, for example, "Proposition 15 Campaign in Full Swing," *American Rifleman*, October 1982, 58.

32. Paul Taylor and Jay Mathews, "Gun Control Jammed: Defeat of California Initiative Throws Proponents Back on the Defensive," *Washington Post*, 9 November 1982, A6.

33. Hart and Bailey 1983.

34. Hart and Bailey 1983.

35. Jay Mathews, "Gun Control: What Was California Saying?" *Washington Post*, 14 November 1982, C7.

36. Taylor 1982.

37. Taylor 1982.

38. Taylor and Mathews 1982.

39. Vizzard 2000,128.

40. See National Council to Control Handguns, "The NCCH Relationship" and "A Proposal for Support."

41. National Council for a Responsible Firearms Policy, "For Firearms Policies in the *Public* Interest: The Purpose and Program of the National Council for a Responsible Firearms Policy (1967) (on file with author).

42. National Council to Control Handguns, "The NCCH Relationship," 6. See also Coalition to Stop Gun Violence, "Who We Are," http://www.csgv.org/who_we_are/ (accessed 22 October 2004).

43. George B. Merry, "Battle over Handguns Moves from Washington to State Capitals in 1981," *Christian Science Monitor*, 17 December 1980.

44. George B. Merry, "Massachusetts Handgun Control Advocates Seek Local Regulation," *Christian Science Monitor*, 27 November 1984.

45. "Anti-Gun Groups Step Up Activities at State and Local Levels," *American Rifleman*, January 1985, 53.

46. "Anti-Gun Fight Heats Up at State and Local Levels," *American Rifleman*, February 1989, 43.

47. Juliet Leftwich, "Americans Must Work for State, Local Reform of Firearm Laws," *Daily Journal (Cal.)*, 2 December 2004.

48. See Elizabeth Brenner Drew, "The Gun Law That Didn't Go Off," *Reporter*, 8 October 1964, 33.

49. "Big New Drive for Gun Controls," *US News & World Report*, 10 February 1975, 25.

50. Philip Benjamin, "New Group Urges Laws to Curb Sale of Firearms," *New York Times*, 4 December 1963, 19.

51. National Council for a Responsible Firearms Policy 1967.

52. Jones 1974, 1.

53. See Vizzard 2000, 65, referring to HCI as "[b]y far the most visible of the gun-control advocacy groups"; and Memorandum from Anonymous to United States Organizations Working for Handgun Control, September 1981, 2 (on file with author). The latter was an anonymous report circulated after the 1981 meeting of the National Alliance of Handgun Control Organizations.

54. The archive of papers from Chicago's Committee to Control Handguns is housed at the University of Illinois at Chicago.

55. Mr. Shields stepped down from the chairmanship in 1989. He died in January 1993, at age sixty-nine.

56. National Council to Control Handguns, "A Proposal for Support," 1.

57. National Council to Control Handguns, "A Proposal for Support," 1–2.

58. National Council to Control Handguns, "A Proposal for Support," 4.

59. National Council to Control Handguns, "The NCCH Relationship," 6.

60. National Council to Control Handguns, "The NCCH Relationship," 7.

61. National Council to Control Handguns, "Proposed Plan of Coalescence for the Handgun Control Movement," 9 July 1976 (on file with author).

62. National Council to Control Handguns, *Handgun Control*, 22 October 1975; "Proposed Plan of Coalescence."

63. National Council to Control Handguns, "The NCCH Relationship."

64. National Council to Control Handguns, "The NCCH Relationship," 3.

65. National Council to Control Handguns, "The NCCH Relationship," 3.

66. Alexander DeConde, *Gun Violence in America* (2001), 200; Buckley and Holmberg 1978.

67. National Council to Control Handguns, "The NCCH Relationship," 3–4.

68. National Council to Control Handguns, "The NCCH Relationship," 6–7.

69. National Council to Control Handguns, "The NCCH Relationship," 2.

70. National Council to Control Handguns, "The NCCH Relationship," 6.

71. National Council to Control Handguns, "The NCCH Relationship," 7.

72. National Council to Control Handguns, "The NCCH Relationship," 7.

73. National Council to Control Handguns, "The NCCH Relationship," 7–8.

74. For example, NCCH's "Proposal for Support," dating from late 1975 or early 1976, stated on page 20 that a major goal for the 1977–1980 period would be to use direct mail to "launch a district by district program in the elections of 1978 and 1980 to get pro-handgun control congressmen elected."

75. National Council to Control Handguns, "The NCCH Relationship," 4.

76. U.S. Conference of Mayors, *Second National Forum on Handgun Control: Proceedings* (Washington, D.C.: U.S. Conference of Mayors, 1976), 54.

77. U.S. Conference of Mayors 1976, 54.

78. Memorandum from Representatives of State and Local Handgun Control groups, to the Leadership of the National Coalition to Ban Handguns, the United States Conference of Mayors Handgun Control Project, Handgun Control, Inc., and the National Council for a Responsible Firearms Policy, Inc.," 14 September 1979 (on file with author).

79. Katherine W. Zartman, President, Committee for Handgun Control, Inc., letter to Pete Shields, President, Handgun Control, Inc., 12 October 1981 (on file with author).

80. Memorandum from Anonymous 1981, 2.

81. Memorandum from Anonymous 1981, 2.

82. D. M. Maillie, Speech before the National Alliance of Handgun Control Organizations conference, Cleveland, 11–13 March 1983, 2 (on file with author).

83. Maillie 1983, 5.

84. Interview with state gun control leader, on condition of anonymity, April 2001.

85. E-mail interview with Michael Beard, founding president, National Coalition to Ban Handguns, 2 February 2005.

86. Interview with Anonymous, former national gun control leader, in Washington, D.C., 8 August 2002 (on condition of anonymity).

87. Personal interview with Josh Horwitz, executive director, Coalition to Stop Gun Violence, Washington, D.C., 14 January 2005.

88. Nathaniel Sheppard Jr., "Illinois Town Faces Lawsuit after Limiting Pistol Use," *New York Times*, 4 July 1981, A6.

89. Warren Cassidy, "Morton Grove: The Next Step," *American Rifleman*, April 1983, 54.

90. Taylor 1982.

91. Handgun-Free America, "Precedent for Banning Handguns," http://www.handgunfree.org/HFAMain/about/precedent.htm (accessed 19 January 2005).

92. Osha Gray Davidson, *Under Fire: The NRA and the Battle for Gun Control* (Iowa City: University of Iowa Press, 1998), 133.

93. Sheppard 1981.

94. "Action Alert: Will Your Hometown Be Next?" *American Rifleman*, February 1982, 57.

95. George B. Merry, "Handgun Control: Both Sides Post Losses, Wins in Ongoing Battle," *Christian Science Monitor*, 26 May 1983, 10.

96. Merry 1983, 10.

97. Sheppard 1981.

98. Sheppard 1981.

99. Darwin Farrar, "In Defense of Home Rule: California's Preemption of Local Firearms Regulation," *Stanford Law and Policy Review* 7, no. 1 (1996): 54 (quoting Institute for Legislative Action, National Rifle Association of America, NRA-ILA State Legislative Issue Brief, 1986).

100. Anne Garner and Michael Clancy, *Firearms Statutes in the United States* (Washington, D.C.: U.S. Conference of Mayors, 1979).

101. Counts of preemption laws are derived from U.S. Department of the Treasury, Bureau of Alcohol, Tobacco, and Firearms, *State Laws and Published Ordinances—Firearms*, 16th ed. (Washington, D.C.: Department of the Treasury: Bureau of Alcohol, Tobacco, and Firearms, 1984).

102. See U.S. Department of the Treasury, Bureau of Alcohol, Tobacco, and Firearms, *State Laws and Published Ordinances—Firearms*, 19th ed. (1989).

103. NRA Institute for Legislative Action, "Compendium of State Firearms Laws" http://www.nraila.org/media/misc/compendium.aspx (accessed 6 February 2005).

104. Interview with former national gun control leader, Washington, D.C., 8 August 2002 (on condition of anonymity).

105. The other factor was the Internal Revenue Service's decision to deny the group 501(c)3 status, and instead to classify it as a 501(c)4 advocacy group, not eligible to receive tax-deductible contributions.

106. Interview with Michael Berkey, former president, Maryland Committee for Handgun Control, in Baltimore, Md., 8 June 2002.

107. National Alliance of Handgun Control Organizations, Notes from the President, April 1982 (on file with author).

108. Mark Pertschuk, then of the Coalition to Stop Gun Violence, quoted in Robert Dreyfuss, "Dark Days for Gun Control," *Rolling Stone*, 2 September 1999, 46.

109. Carl Bogus, former board member of Handgun Control, Inc., quoted in Dreyfuss 1999, 44.

110. Personal interview with Joshua Horwitz, 14 January 2005.

111. E-mail interview with Michael Beard, 2 February 2005.

112. E-mail interview with Michael Beard, 2 February 2005.

113. The Federalist No. 51, at 349 (James Madison) (Jacob E. Cooke ed., 1961).

114. Pub.L. No. 99–308, 100 Stat. 449 (1986).

115. 82 Stat. 1213.

116. Morris P. Fiorina and Paul E. Peterson, *The New American Democracy* (Needham Heights, Mass.: Allyn & Bacon, 1999).

117. Kristin A. Goss, "Policy, Politics, and Paradox: The Institutional Origins of the Great American Gun War," *Fordham Law Review* 73, no. 2 (2004): 681–714.

118. E. E. Schattschneider, *The Semi-sovereign People: A Realist's View of Democracy in America* (Hinsdale, Ill.: Dryden Press, 1975), 4.

119. Sven Steinmo, "American Exceptionalism Reconsidered: Culture or Institutions?" in *The Dynamics of American Politics: Approaches and Interpretations*, ed. Lawrence C. Dodd and Calvin Jillson (Boulder, Colo.: Westview Press, 1994); Anthony King, "Ideas, Institutions and the Policies of Governments: A Comparative Analysis: Part III," *British Journal of Political Science* 3, no. 4 (1973).

120. Goss 2004.

121. The ability of senior citizens to mobilize against cuts in Social Security is just one of many illustrations of this dynamic. See Andrea Louise Campbell, *How Policies Make Citizens* (Princeton, N.J.: Princeton University Press, 2003).

122. Vizzard 2000, 88. The Sullivan Law is at 1911 N.Y. Laws 442.

123. Vizzard 2000, 88.

124. Maxwell Rich, Executive Vice President, National Rifle Association, letter to potential supporters, 5 May 1975 (on file with author).

125. Rich 1975.

126. John M. Snyder, "NRA Registers as Lobby to Uphold Gun Ownership," *American Rifleman*, April 1974, 16.

127. The Office of Legislative Affairs became the Institute for Legislative Action in 1975.

128. National Council to Control Handguns, *Handgun Control*, 22 October 1975, 2.

129. Snyder 1974, 16.

130. DeConde 2001, 130; Josh Sugarmann, *National Rifle Association: Money, Firepower & Fear* (Washington, D.C.: National Press Books, 1992), 51.

131. Ashley Halsey Jr., "The President's Stand on Guns," *American Rifleman*, August 1975, 23.

132. Davidson 1998, 36.

133. See David J. Bordua, "Gun Control and Opinion Measurement: Adversary Polling and the Construction of Social Meaning," in *Firearms and Violence: Issues of Public Policy*, ed. Don B. Kates Jr. (San Francisco: Pacific Institute for Public Policy Research, 1984), 51–70. The poll was taken by Decision/Marketing/ Information (DMI) in 1975. Its results even were entered into the *Congressional Record* (Bordua 1984).

134. Bordua 1984.

135. Davidson 1998, 130.

136. National Council for a Responsible Firearms Policy, "Gun-Control Pioneer Lashes President Bush's Response to Gun Crime: Council Being Terminated after 22 Years," Press Release, 28 December 1989 (on file with author).

137. Katherine W. Zartman, President, Committee for Handgun Control, Inc., letter to Barbara Bell, Leader, Ban Handguns, 6 November 1981 (on file with author).

138. National Coalition to Ban Handguns, "Statement by Bishop James Armstrong," 19 June 1975.

139. The Coalition to Stop Gun Violence, formerly the National Coalition to Ban Handguns, "philosophically supports banning new sales of handguns but [is] currently concentrating on policies that close illegal trafficking channels and eliminate unregulated firearms sales" (e-mail to author, 7 February 2005).

140. Carl Bogus, former board member of Handgun Control Inc., quoted in Dreyfuss 1999. 43. Bogus, a professor of law at Roger Williams University, was at the time an adviser to the Violence Policy Center.

141. Stephen Teret, director of the Johns Hopkins Center for Gun Policy and Research, quoted in Dreyfuss 1999, 44.

142. Personal interview with Joshua Horwitz 14 January 2005.


Chapter Six
Mobilizing Around Modest Measures: Three Cases

1. John Gaventa, *Power and Powerlessness: Quiescence and Rebellion in an Appalachian Valley* (Urbana: University of Illinois Press, 1980).

2. Osha Gray Davidson, *Under Fire: The NRA and the Battle for Gun Control* (Iowa City: University of Iowa Press, 1998), 197.

3. Sam Roberts, "In Memory of Those Shot in Civilian Wars," *New York Times*, 28 March 1991, B1.

4. Toni Locy, "Boston Group Launched to Fight for Handgun Control Law," *Boston Globe*, 21 July 1992, 22.

5. Michael Kranish, "Reagan Speaks Up for Handgun Bill," *Boston Globe*, 29 March 1991, 1.

6. "Brady Bill Becomes U.S. Law," *St. Louis Post-Dispatch*, 1 December 1993.

7. Telephone interview with a midwestern gun control advocate, 19 June 2002 (on condition of anonymity).

8. Richard Wolf, "Many Factors Aided Gun Bill," *USA Today*, 10 May 1991.

9. Alan C. Miller, "Gallegly to Again Back Brady Bill," *Los Angeles Times*, 30 April 1991.

10. Michael Isikoff, "The 'Brady Bill': Success and Growing Pains," *Washington Post*, 31 May 1991.

11. Eric Gorovitz, "California Dreamin': The Myth of State Preemption of Local Firearm Regulation," *University of San Francisco Law Review* 30 (1996): 395–426.

12. Gorovitz 1996, 408.

13. National Council for a Responsible Firearms Policy, Bay Area Chapter, "Newsletter," Fall 1969 (on file with author).

14. Paula Yost, "Permanent Import Ban on Assault Rifles: 43 Types Affected by Bush Order," *Washington Post*, 8 July 1989, A4.

15. Telephone interview with Juliet A. Leftwich, managing attorney, Legal Community Against Violence, 18 July 2002.

16. Telephone interview with Juliet A. Leftwich, 18 July 2002.

17. Telephone interview with Juliet A. Leftwich, 18 July 2002.

18. Marcia L. Godwin and Jean Reith Schroedel, "Policy Diffusion and Strategies for Promoting Policy Change: Evidence from California Local Gun Control Ordinances," *Policy Studies Journal* 28, no. 3 (2000): 760–775.

19. Legal Community Against Violence, "Communities on the Move" (San Francisco: LCAV, 2000), 3.

20. Legal Community Against Violence, "Communities," (2000), 4–8.

21. Legal Community Against Violence, "Communities," (2000), 2.

22. Legal Community Against Violence, "Addressing Gun Violence through Local Ordinances," (San Francisco: LCAV, 2000), 6–7.

23. Telephone interview with Juliet A. Leftwich, 18 July 2002.

24. Telephone interview with Juliet A. Leftwich, 18 July 2002.

25. Telephone interview with Sue Ann Schiff, executive director, Legal Community Against Violence, 20 June 2002.

26. Personal interview with Joshua Horwitz, executive director, Coalition to Stop Gun Violence, Washington, D.C., 14 January 2005.

27. This estimate is based on a search in the Lexis-Nexis database of regionally prominent newspapers for May 15, 2000 to November 1, 2002. The search turned up 2,344 stories, but I have rounded down to account for a small number of duplicate mentions resulting from syndicated articles' appearing in more than one newspaper. On the other hand, because the database does not include articles from most of the nation's small newspapers, the actual number of Million Mom March mentions is considerably higher than 2,344. It is important to note that not all these mentions represent a specific activity carried out by the march members— that is, this is not a count of Million Mom March events. Some mentions, for example, come in articles featuring gun rights forces criticizing the Million Mom March.

28. Personal interview with Brian Malte and Becca Knox, Brady Campaign to Prevent Gun Violence, Washington, D.C., 21 January 2005.

29. I attended Lobby Day (January 17, 2005) as an observer and witnessed this exchange.

30. Daniel Polsby, "The False Promise of Gun Control," *Atlantic Monthly*, March 1994, 57–70.

31. Norman Ornstein and Thomas Mann, *The Permanent Campaign and Its Future* (Washington, D.C.: American Enterprise Institute and Brookings Institution Press, 2000); Sidney Blumenthal, *The Permanent Campaign* (New York: Simon & Schuster, 1982).

32. "Bar Hidden Weapons on Sullivan's Plea," *New York Times*, 11 May 1911, 3.

33. Paul E. Peterson and Mark C. Rom, *Welfare Magnets* (Washington, D.C.: Brookings Institution Press, 1990).

34. D. Kahneman and A. Tversky, "Prospect Theory: An Analysis of Decision under Risk," *Econometrica* 47, no. 2 (1979): 263–291.

35. Kristin A. Goss, "Policy, Politics, and Paradox: The Institutional Origins of the Great American Gun War," *Fordham Law Review* 73, no. 2 (2004): 681–714.

36. This is the logic of the "race to the bottom" in the welfare debate, in which states with stingy public assistance programs force more generous states to lower their levels to keep the welfare rolls stable. See Peterson and Rom 1990.


CHAPTER SEVEN
CONCLUSION: POLITICS, PARTICIPATION AND PUBLIC GOODS

1. "Understanding Gun Control," *Wall Street Journal*, 7 June 1972.

2. James Q. Wilson, *Political Organizations* (Princeton, N.J.: Princeton University Press, 1995).

3. David S. Meyer, *A Winter of Discontent: The Nuclear Freeze and American Politics* (New York: Praeger, 1990).

4. For a discussion of the historical role of federated voluntary associations in American politics, see Theda Skocpol, *Diminished Democracy: From Membership to Management in American Civic Life* (Norman: University of Oklahoma Press 2003).

5. Jane J. Mansbridge, *Why We Lost the ERA* (Chicago: University of Chicago Press, 1986).

6. David A. Stockman, "The Triumph of Politics," *Newsweek*, 21 April 1986, 40. This is an excerpt from Stockman's book, *The Triumph of Politics: How the Reagan Revolution Failed* (New York: Harper & Row, 1986).

7. "Gun-Control Advocates Take Fight to Local Level," Join Together Online, 21 May 2002, http://news.tobaccofreekids.org/gv/news/summaries/reader/0,2061,551169,00.html (accessed 27 September 2005). This is a summary of the Fox News report.

8. Personal interview with Dennis Henigan, Legal Action Project, Brady Center to Prevent Handgun Violence, Washington, D.C., 28 January 2005.

Appendix B
Brief Case Studies of Other Social-Reform Movements

1. Ruth Bordin, *Woman and Temperance: The Quest for Power and Liberty, 1873–1900* (New Brunswick, N.J.: Rutgers University Press, 1990), 49.

2. Anne N. Costain, *Inviting Women's Rebellion: A Political Process Interpretation of the Women's Movement* (Baltimore: The Johns Hopkins University Press 1992).

3. Costain 1992, 45.

4. Craig Reinarman, "The Social Construction of an Alcohol Problem," *Theory and Society* 17 (1988): 91–120.

5. John D. McCarthy, "Activists, Authorities, and Media Framing of Drunk Driving," in *New Social Movements: From Ideology to Identity*, ed. Enrique Laraña, Hank Johnston, and Joseph R. Gusfield (Philadelphia: Temple University Press, 1994), 139.

6. Bordin 1990, 50.

7. Jack S. Blocker Jr., *American Temperance Movements: Cycles of Reform* (Boston: Twayne Publishers, 1989), 102–103.

8. John C. Burnham, *Bad Habits: Drinking, Smoking, Taking Drugs, Gambling, Sexual Misbehavior, and Swearing in American History* (New York: New York University Press, 1993), 90–91.

9. Richard Kluger, *Ashes to Ashes: America's Hundred-Year Cigarette War, the Public Health, and the Unabashed Triumph of Philip Morris* (New York: Alfred A. Knopf, 1996), 307.

10. Ronald J. Troyer and Gerald E. Markle, *Cigarettes: The Battle over Smoking* (New Brunswick, N.J.: Rutgers University Press, 1983). The terms "assimilative" and "coercive" are borrowed from Joseph R. Gusfield, *Symbolic Crusade: Status Politics and the American Temperance Movement* (Urbana: University of Illinois Press, 1963).

11. Troyer and Markle 1983, 80.

12. Troyer and Markle 1983, 80; Stanton A. Glantz and Edith D. Balbach, *Tobacco War: Inside the California Battles* (Berkeley: University of California Press, 2000).

13. Glantz and Balbach 2000, 22.

14. Glantz and Balbach 2000, 22.

15. Quoted in Glantz and Balbach 2000, 32.

16. National Cancer Institute, *State and Local Legislative Action to Reduce Tobacco Use*, Smoking and Tobacco Control Monograph No. 11 (Bethesda, Md.: U.S. Department of Health and Human Services, National Institutes of Health, National Cancer Institute, NIH Pub. No. 00–4904, August 2000), 21.

17. National Cancer Institute 2000, 33–34.

18. National Cancer Institute 2000, 28.

# References

"Act before It Is Too Late." *American Rifleman*, September 1974, 22.

"Action Alert: Will Your Hometown Be Next?" *American Rifleman*, February 1982, 57.

Adelson, Lester. "The Gun and the Sanctity of Human Life; or the Bullet as Pathogen." *Pharos* 43, no. 93 (1980): 15–25.

Alm, Rick. "Gun Proposal a 'Hot Potato' for Businesses; Many Groups Avoid Taking a Stance on Proposition B." *Kansas City Star*, 27 March 1999.

Americans for Gun Safety. "Colorado and Oregon Voters Approve Historic Voter Initiatives to Close the Gun Show Loophole." Press release, 7 November 2000, http://www.campaignadvantage.com/services/websites/archive/ags/press_110700 .html (accessed 27 September 2005).

"An 'Equalizer' in the Gun Fight." *Washington Star*, 18 May 1976.

Anderson, Curt. "Senators Try to Kill Funds for 'Anti-Gun' Health Group." *Chicago Sun-Times*, 4 November 1995.

Anderson, Jack. *Inside the NRA: Armed and Dangerous*. Beverly Hills, Cal.: Dove Books, 1996.

Anderson, Jervis. "A Reporter at Large: An Extraordinary People." *New Yorker*, 12 November 1984, 109.

"Anti-Gun Fight Heats Up at State and Local Levels." *American Rifleman*, February 1989, 43.

"Anti-Gun Groups Step Up Activities at State and Local Levels." *American Rifleman*, January 1985, 53.

Arias, Elizabeth, Robert N. Anderson, Hsiang-Ching Kung, Sherry L. Murphy, and Kenned Kochanek. *National Vital Statistics Reports* 52, no. 3 (18 September 2003).

Associated Press. "Gun Program Costs Millions." *Washington Post*, 16 August 1964.

Babcock, Charles R. "Firearms Rule Draws a Fusillade." *Washington Post*, 17 May 1978.

Bachrach, Peter, and Morton S. Baratz. "Two Faces of Power." *American Political Science Review* 56, no. 4 (1962): 947–952.

Bailey, Anne Lowrey. "Many Grant Makers Are No Longer Shy about Gun Control." *Chronicle of Philanthropy*, 7 September 1993, 11.

Bakal, Carl. "The Traffic in Guns: A Forgotten Lesson of the Assassination." *Harper's*, December 1964, 62–68.

———. *No Right to Bear Arms*. New York: Paperback Library, 1968.

Baldacci, Leslie. "Violence Called 'Emergency'; Medical Experts Push Gun Control as Health Issue." *Chicago Sun-Times*, 10 June 1992.

Balk, Alfred. "The Firearms Theater of the Absurd." *Saturday Review*, 22 July 1967, 28+.

"Ban the Bullet." *Time*. 3 March 1975, 8.

"Bar Hidden Weapons on Sullivan's Plea." *New York Times*, 11 May 1911, 3.

"BATF Abuses Exposed to Senators." *American Rifleman, NRA Official Journal*, September 1979, 7–8.

"BATF's Rex Davis Resigns." *American Rifleman*, August 1978, 77.

"The Battle to Disarm the Gunman." *Literary Digest*, 19 February 1927, 9.

Baumgartner, Frank R., and Bryan D. Jones. *Agendas and Instability in American Politics*. Chicago: University of Chicago Press, 1993.

Baumgartner, Frank R., and Beth L. Leech. *Basic Interests: The Importance of Groups in Politics and in Political Science*. Princeton, N.J.: Princeton University Press, 1998.

"Be Strong, Carry a Gun." *New Republic*, 14 December 1963.

Beggs, Charles E. "Gun Measure Battle Tops $2.5 Million." Associated Press, 3 November 2000.

Benford, Robert D., and David A. Snow. "Framing Processes and Social Movements: An Overview and Assessment." *Annual Review of Sociology* 26 (2000): 611–639.

Benjamin, Philip. "New Group Urges Laws to Curb Sale of Firearms." *New York Times*, 4 December 1963.

Berinsky, Adam J., and Donald R. Kinder. "Making Sense of Issues through Frames: Understanding the Kosovo Crisis." Paper presented at the Annual Meeting of the American Political Science Association, Washington, D.C., August 2000.

Berry, Jeffrey M. *Lobbying for the People*. Princeton, N.J.: Princeton University Press, 1977.

———. *The Interest Group Society*, 3rd ed. New York: Longman, 1997.

———. *The New Liberalism*. Washington, D.C.: Brookings Institution Press, 1999.

"Big New Drive for Gun Controls." *US News & World Report*, 10 February 1975, 25–27.

Black, Dan A., and Daniel S. Nagin. "Do 'Right-to-Carry' Laws Deter Violent Crime?" *Journal of Legal Studies* 27, no. 1 (1998): 209–213.

Blanchard, Dallas A. *The Anti-Abortion Movement and the Rise of the Religious Right*. New York: Twayne Publishers, 1994.

Block, Irwin. *Gun Control: One Way to Save Lives*. Public Affairs Pamphlet No. 536. New York: Public Affairs Committee, 1976.

Blocker, Jack S., Jr. *American Temperance Movements: Cycles of Reform*. Boston: Twayne Publishers, 1989.

Blumenthal, Sidney. *The Permanent Campaign*. New York: Simon & Schuster, 1982.

Blumstein, Alfred, and Joel Wallman, eds. *The Crime Drop in America*. New York: Cambridge University Press, 2000.

Bordin, Ruth. *Woman and Temperance: The Quest for Power and Liberty, 1873–1900*. New Brunswick, N.J.: Rutgers University Press, 1990.

Bordua, David J. "Gun Control and Opinion Measurement: Adversary Polling and the Construction of Social Meaning." In *Firearms and Violence: Issues of Public Policy*, ed. Don B. Kates Jr., 51–70. San Francisco: Pacific Institute for Public Policy Research, 1984.

Bradley, Donald. "Partnership for Children Seeks to Take Political Stands." *Kansas City Star*, 10 February 1999.

"Brady Bill Becomes U.S. Law." *St. Louis Post-Dispatch*, 1 December 1993.

Brady, Henry E. "Political Participation." In *Measures of Political Attitudes*, ed. John P. Robinson, Phillip R. Shaver, and Lawrence S. Wrightsman, 737–800. San Diego: Academic Press, 1999.

Brady, Henry E., Kay Lehman Schlozman, and Sidney Verba. "Prospecting for Participants: Rational Expectations and the Recruitment of Political Activists." *American Political Science Review* 93, no. 1 (1999): 153–168.

Brady, Sarah. "Gun Control: The Next Step." *Washington Post*, 21 September 1994.

Brill, Steven. "The Traffic (Legal and Illegal) in Guns." *Harper's*, September 1977, 37–44.

———. *Firearms Abuse: A Research and Policy Report*. Washington, D.C.: Police Foundation, 1977.

Bronner, Ethan. "With Richer Backers, Rights Groups Cash In." *Boston Globe*, 30 December 1989, 1.

Brown, Peter Harry, and Daniel G. Abel. *Outgunned: Up Against the NRA*. New York: Free Press, 2003.

Browning, Charles H. "Handguns and Homicide: A Public Health Problem." *Journal of the American Medical Association* 236, no. 19 (1976): 2198–2200.

Bruce, John M., and Clyde Wilcox. "Gun Control Laws in the States: Political and Apolitical Influences." in *The Changing Politics of Gun Control*, ed. John M. Bruce and Clyde Wilcox. Lanham, Md.: Rowman & Littlefield Publishers, 1998.

———. "Introduction." In *The Changing Politics of Gun Control*, ed. John M. Bruce and Clyde Wilcox. Lanham, Md.: Rowman & Littlefield Publishers, 1998.

Bruce-Briggs, B. "The Great American Gun War." *Public Interest* 45 (Fall 1976): 37–62.

Buckley, John J., and Judy Holmberg. Personal letter to David J. Steinberg. 15 May 1978 (on file with author).

Burnham, John C. *Bad Habits: Drinking, Smoking, Taking Drugs, Gambling, Sexual Misbehavior, and Swearing in American History*. New York: New York University Press, 1993.

Burns, Nancy, Kay Lehman Schlozman, and Sidney Verba. *The Private Roots of Public Action: Gender, Equality, and Political Participation*. Cambridge, Mass.: Harvard University Press, 2001.

Callaway, Ben. "Gun Control? Let's Crack Down on Criminals, Instead." *Philadelphia Inquirer*, 6 January 1981.

Campbell, Andrea Louise. *How Policies Make Citizens*. Princeton, N.J.: Princeton University Press, 2003.

Campbell, Angus, Philip E. Converse, Warren E. Miller, and Donald E. Stokes. *The American Voter*. New York: John Wiley & Sons, 1960.

Carter, Gregg Lee. *The Gun Control Movement*. New York: Twayne Publishers, 1997.

Carter, Harlon B. "The Hidden Dangers in Gun Control." *American Rifleman*, September 1976, 49.

Cassidy, Warren. "Morton Grove: The Next Step." *American Rifleman*, April 1983, 54.

Chisholm, Laura B. "Exempt Organization Advocacy: Matching the Rules to the Rationales." *Indiana Law Journal* 63, no. 201 (1987): 201–299.

"Club-Women Mapping War on Gangsters." *Literary Digest*, 16 June 1934, 19.

"Coalition to Stop Gun Violence Timeline." Washington, D.C.: Coalition to Stop Gun Violence, 1999.

Cobb, Roger W., and Charles D. Elder. *Participation in American Politics: The Dynamics of Agenda-Building*. Baltimore: The Johns Hopkins University Press, 1972.

*Congressional Quarterly Almanac*. Vol. XX. Washington, D.C.: CQ Service, 1964.

———. Vol. XXI. Washington, D.C.: CQ Service, 1965.

———. Vol. XXII. Washington, D.C.: CQ Service, 1966.

———. Vol. XXIII. Washington, D.C.: CQ Service, 1967.

———. Vol. XXIV. Washington, D.C.: CQ Service, 1968.

———. Vol. XXV. Washington, D.C.: CQ Service, 1969.

———. Vol. XXVI. Washington, D.C.: Congressional Quarterly, 1970.

———. Vol. XXVIII. Washington, D.C.: Congressional Quarterly, 1972.

———. Vol. XXX. Washington, D.C.: Congressional Quarterly, 1974.

———. Vol. XXXI. Washington, D.C.: Congressional Quarterly, 1975.

———. Vol. XXXII. Washington, D.C.: Congressional Quarterly, 1976.

———. Vol. XXXIV. Washington, D.C.: Congressional Quarterly, 1978.

———. Vol. XXXVII. Washington, D.C.: Congressional Quarterly, 1981.

———. Vol. XLVII. Washington, D.C.: Congressional Quarterly, 1991.

———. Vol. XLIX. Washington, D.C.: Congressional Quarterly, 1993.

*Congressional Record*. 90th Cong., 1st sess., 22 August 1967.

———. 92nd Cong., 1st sess., 9 September 1971.

———. 92nd Cong., 2nd sess., 24 May 1972.

———. 92nd Cong., 2nd sess., August 1972. Reprint of Senator Kennedy's statement "Firearms Control."

———. 94th Cong., 1st sess., 23 September 1975.

———. 95th Cong., 2nd sess., 5 June 1978.

———. 104th Cong., 2nd sess., 27 June 1996.

Conrad, Peter. "Medicalization and Social Control." *Annual Review of Sociology* 18 (1992): 209–232.

Converse, Philip E. "Changing Conceptions of Public Opinion in the Political Process." *Public Opinion Quarterly* 51, pt. 2: supplement (1987): S12–S24.

Cook, Philip J. "The Technology of Personal Violence." In *Crime and Justice: A Review of Research* 14, ed. Michael Tonry, 1–71. Chicago: University of Chicago Press, 1991.

Cook, Philip J., and Kristin A. Goss. "A Selective Review of the Social-Contagion Literature." Terry Sanford Institute of Public Policy Working Paper. Durham, N.C.: Duke University, 1996.

Cook, Philip J., and John H. Laub. "The Unprecedented Epidemic in Youth Violence." In *Youth Violence: Crime and Justice: A Review of Research* 24, ed. Michael Tonry and Mark H. Moore, 27–64. Chicago: University of Chicago Press, 1998.

Cook, Philip J., and James A. Leitzel. "'Perversity, Futility, Jeopardy': An Economic Analysis of the Attack on Gun Control." *Law and Contemporary Problems* 59, no. 1 (1996): 91–118.

Cook, Philip J., and Jens Ludwig. *Guns in America: Results of a Comprehensive National Survey on Firearms Ownership and Use.* Washington, D.C.: Police Foundation, 1997.

Cose, Ellis. "Gun-Control Coalition Primed: Mikva." *Chicago Sun-Times*, 7 October 1975, 21.

Costain, Anne N. *Inviting Women's Rebellion: A Political Process Interpretation of the Women's Movement.* Baltimore: The Johns Hopkins University Press, 1992.

Craig, Barbara Hinkson, and David M. O'Brien. *Abortion and American Politics.* Chatham, N.J.: Chatham House Publishers, 1993.

Crenson, Matthew A. *The Un-politics of Air Pollution: A Study of Non-decisionmaking in the Cities.* Baltimore: The Johns Hopkins University Press, 1971.

"Crimes in the Nation's Schools Declined in the 1990s According to Departments of Justice and Education." Department of Education press release, http://www.ed.gov/PressReleases/10–2000/102600a.html (accessed 13 February 2005).

Critchlow, Donald T., ed. *The Politics of Abortion and Birth Control in Historical Perspective.* University Park: The Pennsylvania State University Press, 1996.

Dahl, Robert A. *Who Governs?* New Haven, Conn.: Yale University Press, 1961.

Davidson, Osha Gray. *Under Fire: The NRA and the Battle for Gun Control.* Iowa City: University of Iowa Press, 1998.

DeConde, Alexander. *Gun Violence in America: The Struggle for Control.* Boston: Northeastern University Press, 2001.

de Tocqueville, Alexis. *Democracy in America.* New York: Knopf, 1994.

Dionne, E. J., "Gun Foes Show Muscle." *Denver Post*, 18 April 1999.

Donohue, John J. "The Impact of Concealed-Carry Laws." In *Evaluating Gun Policy: Effects on Crime and Violence*, ed. Jens Ludwig and Philip J. Cook, 287–325. Washington, D.C.: Brookings Institution Press, 2003.

Downs, Anthony. "Up and Down with Ecology: The Issue Attention Cycle." *Public Interest* 28 (Summer 1972): 789–804.

"Drawing Line on Handguns." *Chicago Tribune*, 21 December 1975.

Drew, Elizabeth Brenner. "The Gun Law That Didn't Go Off." *Reporter*, 8 October 1964, 33–35.

Dreyfuss, Robert. "Dark Days for Gun Control." *Rolling Stone*, 2 September 1999, 43–46.

Edelman, Murray. *The Symbolic Uses of Politics.* Urbana: University of Illinois Press 1964.

Eisinger, Peter. "The Conditions of Protest in American Cities." *American Political Science Review* 67, no. 1 (1973): 11–28.

Epstein, Aaron. "How Pentagon Boosted NRA." *Philadelphia Inquirer,* 14 May 1979.

Erskine, Hazel. "The Polls: Gun Control." *Public Opinion Quarterly* 36, no. 3 (1972): 455–469.

———. "The Polls: Fear of Violence and Crime." *Public Opinion Quarterly* 38, no. 1 (1974): 138–145.

Farrar, Darwin. "In Defense of Home Rule: California's Preemption of Local Firearms Regulation." *Stanford Law and Policy Review* 7, no. 1 (1996): 51–57.

"FEC Orders HCI to Pay Penalty and Re-structure Organization." *National Rifle Association Monitor,* 31 July 1984, 1.

Fineman, Herbert. "Analysis of N.R.A. Arguments against Weapons Control Legislation." Harrisburg, Pa.: Democratic Caucus Offices, Pennsylvania House of Representatives, 1968.

Fingerhut, Lois A., Christine S. Cox, and Margaret Warner. "International Comparative Analysis of Injury Mortality: Findings from the ICE on Injury Statistics." *Advance Data,* no. 303 (7 October 1998). Atlanta: Centers for Disease Control and Prevention.

Finney, John W. "Senate Opens Debate on a Bill to Curb Crime and Gun Sales." *New York Times,* 2 May 1968.

Fiorina, Morris P., and Paul E. Peterson. *The New American Democracy.* Needham Heights, Mass.: Allyn & Bacon, 1999.

"Firearms Facts." Washington, D.C.: Department of Justice, 1968.

"Four Years of the Carter Administration." *American Rifleman,* October 1980, 59.

Freeman, Jo. *The Politics of Women's Liberation.* New York: David McKay Co., 1975.

Frumkin, Peter. "More's the Pity: Not Every Victim Ought to Be a Charity Case." *Washington Post,* 17 November 2002.

Gailey, Phil, and Mary Thornton. "Beleaguered Bureau at Treasury Becomes the Target of the Pro-Pistol Lobby." *Washington Star,* 29 April 1981.

Gamson, William. *The Strategy of Social Protest,* 2nd ed. Belmont, Cal.: Wadsworth Publishing Co., 1990.

———. *Talking Politics.* Cambridge, U.K.: Cambridge University Press, 1992.

Gamson, William A., and David S. Meyer, "Framing Political Opportunity." In *Comparative Perspectives on Social Movements,* ed. Doug McAdam, John D. McCarthy, and Mayer N. Zald, 275–290. Cambridge, U.K.: Cambridge University Press, 1996.

Garner, Anne, and Michael Clancy. *Firearms Statutes in the United States.* Washington, D.C.: U.S. Conference of Mayors, 1979.

Garrow, David J. *Bearing the Cross: Martin Luther King, Jr., and the Southern Christian Leadership Conference.* New York: William Morrow & Co., 1986.

Gaventa, John. *Power and Powerlessness: Quiescence and Rebellion in an Appalachian Valley.* Urbana: University of Illinois Press, 1980.

Geddes, Barbara. "How the Cases You Choose Affect the Answers You Get: Selection Bias in Comparative Politics." In *Political Analysis* 2, ed. James A. Stimson, 131–150. Ann Arbor: University of Michigan Press, 1990.

"G.I.'s in Vietnam Mail 'Flood' of Guns to U.S." *New York Times*, 8 March 1970.

Gimpel, James G., and Robin M. Wolpert. "The Structure of Public Support for Gun Control: The 1988 Battle over Question 3 in Maryland." In *The Changing Politics of Gun Control*, ed. John M. Bruce and Clyde Wilcox, 111–124. Lanham, Md.: Rowman & Littlefield Publishers, 1998.

Giovino, Gary A., et al. "Surveillance for Selected Tobacco-Use Behaviors—United States, 1900–1994." *Morbidity and Mortality Weekly Report* 43, no. SS-3 (18 November 1994).

Gladwell, Malcolm. *The Tipping Point*. Boston: Little, Brown, 2000.

Glantz, Stanton A., and Edith D. Balbach. *Tobacco War: Inside the California Battles*. Berkeley: University of California Press, 2000.

Godwin, Marcia L., and Jean Reith Schroedel. "Gun Control Politics in California." In *The Changing Politics of Gun Control*, ed. John M. Bruce and Clyde Wilcox, 88–110. Lanham, Md.: Rowman & Littlefield Publishers, 1998.

———. "Policy Diffusion and Strategies for Promoting Policy Change: Evidence from California Local Gun Control Ordinances." *Policy Studies Journal* 28, no. 3 (2000): 760–775.

Gorney, Cynthia. *Articles of Faith: A Frontline History of the Abortion Wars*. New York: Simon & Schuster, 1998.

Gorovitz, Eric. "California Dreamin': The Myth of State Preemption of Local Firearm Regulation." *University of San Francisco Law Review* 30 (1996): 395–426.

Goss, Kristin A. "'We All Have to Come Together': Moms' Role in Disarming Kids in the Nation's Capital." Master's thesis, Duke University, 1996.

———. "The Smoking Gun: How Focusing Events Transform Politics." Paper presented at the Annual Meeting of the Western Political Science Association, Las Vegas, 15–18 March 2001.

———. "NOW Is Not the Time: Women & Gun Control in the United States." Paper presented at the Annual Meeting of the Midwest Political Science Association, Chicago, 25–28 April 2002; and at the "Alva Myrdal's Questions to Our Time" conference, Uppsala, Sweden, 6–8 March 2002.

———. "Rethinking the Political Participation Paradigm: The Case of Women and Gun Control." *Women & Politics* 25, no. 4 (2003): 83–118.

———. "Policy, Politics, and Paradox: The Institutional Origins of the Great American Gun War." *Fordham Law Review* 73, no. 2 (2004): 681–714.

"Gun-Control Advocates Take Fight to Local Level," Join Together Online, 21 May 2002, http://news.tobaccofreekids.org/gv/news/summaries/reader/0,2061,551169,00.html (accessed 27 September 2005).

"Gun Control Dispute Focuses on Handguns." *Congressional Quarterly*, 19 April 1975, 795–800.

"Gun Control—Ever?" *Christian Science Monitor*, 20 September 1976.

"Gun Control, 1975." *Christian Science Monitor*, 9 January 1975.

"The Gun Menace." *New York Times*, 18 May 1972, 46.

Gusfield, Joseph R. *Symbolic Crusade: Status Politics and the American Temperance Movement*. Urbana: University of Illinois Press, 1963.

———. *The Culture of Public Problems: Drinking-Driving and the Symbolic Order*. Chicago: University of Chicago Press, 1981.

———. *Contested Meanings: The Construction of Alcohol Problems*. Madison: University of Wisconsin Press, 1996.

Halbrook, Stephen P. "Guns and Prohibition, in Al Capone's Day and Now." *Wall Street Journal*, 11 April 1989.

Hall, Richard L., and Frank W. Wayman. "Buying Time: Moneyed Interests and the Mobilization of Bias in Congressional Committees." *American Political Science Review* 84, no. 3 (1990): 797–820.

Halsey, Ashley, Jr. "The President's Stand on Guns." *American Rifleman*, August 1975, 23.

"Handgun Controls to Save Lives." *Providence Journal Bulletin*, 20 April 1974.

Hansen, John Mark. "The Political Economy of Group Membership." *American Political Science Review* 79, no. 1 (1985): 79–96.

Hardin, Russell. *Collective Action*. Baltimore: The Johns Hopkins University Press/Resources for the Future, 1982.

Harrington, Michael J. "The Politics of Gun Control." *Nation*, 12 January 1974, 41–45.

Harris, Ellen Stern. "Handgun Control Coalition's Target in Statewide Legislative Campaign." *Los Angeles Times*, 5 January 1975.

Harris, Richard. "Annals of Legislation: If You Love Your Guns." *New Yorker*, 20 April 1968. Reprint.

Harris, Sydney J. "There's No Alternative to Gun-Control Laws." *Detroit Free Press*, 5 December 1974.

Hart, Peter D., and Doug Bailey. "Gun Control: What Went Wrong in California." *Wall Street Journal*, 1 March 1983.

Hartz, Louis. *The Liberal Tradition in America*. San Diego: Harvest, Harcourt Brace & Company, 1955.

Hayes, Michael T. "The Semi-sovereign Pressure Groups: A Critique of Current Theory and an Alternative Typology." *Journal of Politics* 40, no. 1 (1978): 134–161.

Hey, Robert P. "Many Gun owners Distrust Government." *Christian Science Monitor*, 1 June 1972.

Hicks, Nancy. "2d Threat against Ford Spurs New Action by House Panel to Curb Handguns." *New York Times*, 24 September 1975.

Hinchey, John. "The Handgun Ban Fiasco: How the Democrats Let Themselves in for a Thrashing." *Ann Arbor Observer*, January 1986, 29–35.

Hirsch, Charles S., Norman B. Rushforth, Amasa B. Ford, and Lester Adelson. "Homicide and Suicide in a Metropolitan County." *Journal of the American Medical Association* 223, no. 8 (19 February 1973): 900–905.

Hirschman, Albert O. *The Rhetoric of Reaction*. Cambridge, Mass.: The Belknap Press of Harvard University Press, 1991.

Hofstadter, Richard. "America as a Gun Culture." *American Heritage*, October 1970, 4.

Holmberg, Judith Vandell, and Michael Clancy. *People vs. Handguns: The Campaign to Ban Handguns in Massachusetts.* Washington, D.C.: U.S. Conference of Mayors, 1977.

Hoover, J. Edgar. "Memo to All Law Enforcement Officials." *FBI Law Enforcement Bulletin,* June 1963.

Ikeda, Robin M., et al. *Fatal Firearm Injuries in the United States, 1962–1994.* Atlanta: Centers for Disease Control, National Center for Injury Prevention and Control, 1997.

Inglehart, Ronald. *Culture Shift in Advanced Industrial Society.* Princeton, N.J.: Princeton University Press, 1990.

Isikoff, Michael. "The 'Brady Bill': Success and Growing Pains." *Washington Post,* 31 May 1991.

Jackson, Maurice, Eleanora Petersen, James Bull, Sverre Monsen, and Patricia Richmond. "The Failure of an Incipient Social Movement." *Pacific Sociological Review* 3, no. 1 (1960): 35–40.

Jacobson, Peter D., Jeffrey Wasserman, and Kristiana Raube. *The Political Evolution of Anti-smoking Legislation.* Santa Monica, Cal.: Rand Corporation, 1992.

Johnson, Hillary. "The Friendly Persuaders." *New York Sunday News,* 6 June 1976.

Jones, Bryan D. *Reconceiving Decision-Making in Democratic Politics.* Chicago: University of Chicago Press. 1994.

Jones, Clayton. "Gun-Control Forces Say U.S. Is Ready to Restrict Weapons." *Christian Science Monitor,* 27 December 1974.

Kahneman, D., and A. Tversky. "Prospect Theory: An Analysis of Decision under Risk." *Econometrica* 47, no. 2 (1979): 263–291.

Kates, Don B., Jr. "Bigotry, Symbolism and Ideology in the Battle over Gun Control." *Public Interest Law Review* 31 (1992): 31–46.

———. "Public Opinion: The Effects of Extremist Discourse on the Gun Debate." In *The Great American Gun Debate,* ed. Don B. Kates Jr. and Gary Kleck, 94–122. San Francisco: Pacific Research Institute for Public Policy, 1997.

Kellermann, Arthur L. "Obstacles to Firearm and Violence Research." *Health Affairs* 12, no. 4 (1993): 142–153.

Kennett, Lee, and James LaVerne Anderson. *The Gun in America: The Origins of a National Dilemma.* Westport, Conn.: Greenwood Press, 1975.

Kerr, K. Austin. *Organized for Prohibition: A New History of the Anti-Saloon League.* New Haven, Conn.: Yale University Press, 1985.

King, Anthony. "Ideas, Institutions and the Policies of Governments: A Comparative Analysis: Part III." *British Journal of Political Science* 3, no. 4 (1973): 409–423.

Kingdon, John W. *Agendas, Alternatives, and Public Policies.* Boston: Little, Brown and Company, 1984.

Kleck, Gary. "Crime, Culture Conflict and the Sources of Support for Gun Control." *American Behavioral Scientist* 39, no. 4 (1996): 387–404.

———. "Absolutist Politics in a Moderate Package." In *Armed,* ed. Gary Kleck and Don B. Kates, 129–172. Amherst, N.Y.: Prometheus Books, 2001.

Kleck, Gary, and Mark Gertz. "Armed Resistance to Crime: The Prevalence and Nature of Self-Defense with a Gun." *Journal of Criminal Law and Criminology* 86, no. 1 (1995): 150–187.

Klein, Ethel. *Gender Politics.* Cambridge, Mass.: Harvard University Press, 1984.

Kluger, Richard. *Ashes to Ashes: America's Hundred-Year Cigarette War, the Public Health, and the Unabashed Triumph of Philip Morris.* New York: Alfred A. Knopf, 1996.

"Knox Declares War on GCA '68." *American Rifleman,* April 1979, 7.

Knox, Neal. "ILA Pledges to Fight BATF Firearms Abuses." *American Rifleman,* March 1978, 59+.

Kranish, Michael. "Reagan Speaks Up for Handgun Bill." *Boston Globe,* 29 March 1991, 1.

Kugler, Sara. "Gun-Control Group Gains." *Denver Post,* 16 July 1999, A7.

League of Women Voters of the United States. "Proposed National Gun Control Position." LWVUS, 1990.

Leff, Carol Skalnik, and Mark H. Leff. "The Politics of Ineffectiveness: Federal Firearms Legislation, 1919–38." *Annals of the American Academy of Political and Social Science* 455 (1981): 48–62.

Leftwich, Juliet. "Americans Must Work for State, Local Reform of Firearm Laws." *Daily Journal (Cal.),* 2 December 2004.

Legal Community Against Violence. "Addressing Gun Violence through Local Ordinances." San Francisco: LCAV, 2000.

———. "Communities on the Move." San Francisco: LCAV, 2000.

Lender, Mark Edward, and James Kirby Martin. *Drinking in America: A History.* New York: Free Press, 1982.

Lesar, John. "Gun Opponents Battle Ammo." *Atlanta Journal,* 10 March 1975.

Levin, Felice Michaels. "Evaluation of the Handgun Control Project, U.S. Conference of Mayors." Report prepared for the George Gund Foundation, Cleveland, 1977.

Levy, Doug. "Doctors, NRA Take Aim at CDC's Anti-violence Program." *USA Today,* 25 August 1995.

Lipset, Seymour Martin, and Gary Marks. *It Didn't Happen Here: Why Socialism Failed in the United States.* New York: W. W. Norton & Co., 2001.

Locy, Toni. "Boston Group Launched to Fight for Handgun Control Law." *Boston Globe,* 21 July 1992, 22.

Lohman, Frank T., Director, National Board for the Promotion of Rifle Practice. Letter to David J. Steinberg, Executive Director, National Council for a Responsible Firearms Policy. 9 May 1974 (on file with author).

Loth, Renee. "Safe Choice, High Price." *Boston Globe,* 25 June 2000.

Lott, John R., Jr. *More Guns, Less Crime: Understanding Crime and Gun Control Laws.* Chicago: University of Chicago Press, 1998.

Lott, John R., Jr., and David B. Mustard. "Crime, Deterrence and Right-to-Carry Concealed Handguns." *Journal of Legal Studies* 16, no. 1 (1997): 1–68.

Lowi, Theodore. "American Business, Public Policy, Case-Studies, and Political Theory." *World Politics* 16, no. 4 (1964): 677–715.

Ludwig, Jens. "Concealed-Gun-Carrying Laws and Violent Crime: Evidence from State Panel Data." *International Review of Law and Economics* 18, no. 3 (1998): 239–254.

Luker, Kristin. *Abortion and the Politics of Motherhood*. Berkeley: University of California Press, 1984.

Lynch, Mitchell C. "Gun Control Backers Focus on Organizing at the Grass Roots." *Wall Street Journal*, 10 June 1975, 1.

MacKenzie, John P. "Dodd Says 'Almost Hysterical' Foes Have Killed Firearms Bill for Year." *Washington Post*, 13 August 1964.

Mahler, Anthony J., and Jonathan E. Fielding. "Firearms and Gun Control: A Public-Health Concern." *New England Journal of Medicine* 297, no. 10 (8 September 1977): 556–558.

Maillie, D. M. Speech before the National Alliance of Handgun Control Organizations conference, Cleveland, 11–13 March 1978.

———. Letter to David J. Steinberg. 4 February 1980.

———. Memo to Members of National Alliance of Handgun Control Organizations. 20 May 1980.

———. Memo to Members of the Alliance [of Handgun Control Organizations] and New Prospective Members. Subject: General—DUES—1981–82—Please Pay Now. 10 June 1981.

———. "Notes from the President" [National Alliance of Handgun Control Organizations]. April 1982.

Mansbridge, Jane J. *Why We Lost the ERA*. Chicago: University of Chicago Press, 1986.

Marro, Anthony. "Pro-Gun Lobby Opens Fire on Treasury Dept. Official." *Washington Star*, 2 October 1978.

Martin, Richard. "New Moves to Control Firearms Won't Go Far If the Past Is a Guide." *Wall Street Journal*, 19 May 1972, 1.

Martinek, Wendy L., Kenneth J. Meier, and Lael R. Keiser. "Jackboots or Lace Panties? The Bureau of Alcohol, Tobacco, and Firearms." In *The Changing Politics of Gun Control*, ed. John M. Bruce and Clyde Wilcox, 17–44. Lanham, Md.: Rowman & Littlefield, 1998.

Mathews, Jay. "Gun Control: What Was California Saying?" *Washington Post*, 14 November 1982.

Mauser, Gary A., and David Kopel. "'Sorry, Wrong Number': Why Media Polls on Gun Control Are So Often Unreliable." *Journal on Firearms and Public Policy* 6 (1994): 23–53.

McAdam, Doug. *Political Process and the Development of Black Insurgency, 1930–1970*. Chicago: University of Chicago Press, 1982.

———. "Conceptual Origins, Current Problems, Future Directions." In *Comparative Perspectives on Social Movements*, ed. Doug McAdam, John D. McCarthy, and Mayer N. Zald, 23–40. Cambridge, U.K.: Cambridge University Press, 1996.

McAdam, Doug, John D. McCarthy, and Mayer N. Zald, eds. *Comparative Perspectives on Social Movements*. Cambridge, U.K.: Cambridge University Press, 1996.

McCarthy, John D. "Activists, Authorities, and Media Framing of Drunk Driving." In *New Social Movements: From Ideology to Identity*, ed. Enrique Laraña, Hank Johnston, and Joseph R. Gusfield, 133–167. Philadelphia: Temple University Press, 1994.

———. "Constraints and Opportunities in Adopting, Adapting, and Inventing." In *Comparative Perspectives on Social Movements*, ed. Doug McAdam, John D. McCarthy, and Mayer N. Zald, 141–151. Cambridge, U.K.: Cambridge University Press, 1996.

McCarthy, John D., and Mark Wolfson. "Consensus Movements, Conflict Movements, and the Cooptation of Civic and State Infrastructures." In *Frontiers in Social Movement Theory*, ed. Aldon D. Morris and Carol McClurg Mueller, 273–297. New Haven, Conn.: Yale University Press, 1992.

McCarthy, John D., and Mayer N. Zald. "Resource Mobilization and Social Movements: A Partial Theory." *American Journal of Sociology* 82, no. 6 (1977): 1212–1241.

McDowall, David, and Brian Wiersema. "The Incidence of Defensive Firearm Use by U.S. Crime Victims, 1987 through 1990." *American Journal of Public Health* 84, no. 12 (1994): 1982–1984.

Meacham, Jon, Howard Fineman, and Matt Bai. "'I Think the Real Target Is the Second Amendment.'" *Newsweek*, 23 August 1999, 31.

Memorandum from Anonymous to the Leadership of the National Coalition to Ban Handguns, the United States Conference of Mayors Handgun Control Project, Handgun Control, Inc., and the National Council for a Responsible Firearms Policy, Inc. 14 September 1979.

Memorandum from Anonymous to United States Organizations Working for Handgun Control. September 1981.

Meredith, Nikki. "Public Health Officials Taking a New Approach to Homicide." *Chicago Tribune*, 30 December 1984.

Merry, George B., "Battle over Handguns Moves from Washington to State Capitals in 1981." *Christian Science Monitor*, 17 December 1980.

———. "Handgun Control: Both Sides Post Losses, Wins in Ongoing Battle, *Christian Science Monitor*, 26 May 1983, 10.

———. "Massachusetts Handgun Control Advocates Seek Local Regulation." *Christian Science Monitor*, 27 November 1984.

Metzger, Dianne, and Virginia C. Strand. "Violence Prevention: Trends in Foundation Funding." *Health Affairs* 12, no. 4 (1993): 209–229.

Meyer, David S. *A Winter of Discontent: The Nuclear Freeze and American Politics*. New York: Praeger, 1990.

Mill, John Stuart. *A System of Logic Ratiocinative and Inductive*. London: Longmans, Green, 1930.

Miller, Alan C. "Gallegly to Again Back Brady Bill." *Los Angeles Times*, 30 April 1991.

Minkoff, Debra C. *Organizing for Equality: The Evolution of Women's and Racial-Ethnic Organizations in America, 1955–1985*. New Brunswick, N.J.: Rutgers University Press, 1995.

Moore, Mark H. "What Sort of Ideas Become Public Ideas?" In *The Power of Public Ideas*, ed. Robert B. Reich, 55–83. Cambridge, Mass.: Ballinger Publishing Company, 1988.

Morris, Aldon D. *The Origins of the Civil Rights Movement: Black Communities Organizing for Change*. New York: Free Press, 1984.

Morris, Aldon D., and Carol McClurg Mueller. *Frontiers in Social Movement Theory*. New Haven, Conn.: Yale University Press, 1992.

Morris, Norval, and Gordon Hawkins. *Letter to the President on Crime Control*. Chicago: University of Chicago Press, 1977.

Munson, Ziad Wael. "Becoming an Activist: Believers, Sympathizers, and Mobilization in the American Pro-life Movement." Ph.D. diss., Harvard University, 2002.

Murphy, Sherry L. *National Vital Statistics Reports* 48, no. 11 (24 July 2000).

Murray, Douglas R. "Handguns, Gun Control Laws and Firearm Violence." *Social Problems* 23, no. 1 (1975): 81–93.

National Advisory Commission on Criminal Justice Standards and Goals. *A National Strategy to Reduce Crime*. Washington, D.C.: U.S. Government Printing Office, 1973.

National Alliance of Handgun Control Organizations. *Update 5*. May 1980.

———. *Update 6*. October 1980.

———. Treasurer's Report. 11 March 1983.

———. "Resolutions Approved by the Members, March 13, 1983."

———. "Articles Establishing the National Alliance of Handgun Control Organizations." n.d.

National Board of the YWCA of the U.S.A. "At This Point in Time: Report for the Period April 1, 1973 to August 31, 1974."

National Cancer Institute. *State and Local Legislative Action to Reduce Tobacco Use*. Smoking and Tobacco Control Monograph No. 11. Bethesda, Md.: U.S. Department of Health and Human Services, National Institutes of Health, National Cancer Institute, NIH Pub. No. 00–4904, August 2000.

National Coalition to Ban Handguns. "Program for the National Coalition to Ban Handguns." 1975.

———. "Statement by Bishop James Armstrong." 19 June 1975.

———. "Inter-agency Workshop October 13–14 Notes." 1977.

National Council for a Responsible Firearms Policy. "For Firearms Policies in the *Public* Interest: The Purpose and Program of the National Council for a Responsible Firearms Policy." 1967.

———. "Government Gun Subsidy Assisted Would-Be Assassins." 27 June 1967.

———. "Needed: A Cohesive, Nationwide Campaign for Firm and Fair Gun Control in the Total Public Interest. A Statement by David J. Steinberg, Executive Director." 8 January 1976.

———. "Gun-Control Pioneer Lashes President Bush's Response to Gun Crime: Council Being Terminated after 22 Years." Press release, 28 December 1989.

National Council for a Responsible Firearms Policy, Bay Area Chapter. "Newsletter," Fall 1969.

National Council to Control Handguns. "A Brief Case for Handgun Control and Doing Something about It Now." 1975.

National Council to Control Handguns. "Handgun Control . . . Report Prepared by the National Council to Control Handguns." September 1975.

———. "A Proposal for Support." 1975.

———. *Handgun Control*. 22 October 1975.

———. *Handgun Control*. 13. 30 June 1976.

———. "Proposed Plan of Coalescence for the Handgun Control Movement," 9 July 1976 (on file with author).

———. Memo to All State and Local Lobbying Groups of the Handgun Control Movement from Pete Shields, NCCH Executive Director and Member of the Special Committee on Coalescence. 12 July 1976.

———. "The NCCH Relationship with Other Handgun Control Groups." n.d.

National Rifle Association. "What Every Woman Should Know about Self-Defense." Washington, D.C.: NRA, circa 1970.

———. "Return of Organization Exempt from Income Tax" (Form 990). 2001.

———. "Fact Sheet: Civilian Marksmanship Program," http://www.nraila.org/Issues/FactSheets/Read.aspx?ID=104 (accessed 9 February 2005).

"The NCBH vs. the NRA." *Handgun Control News*, March/April 1979, 1.

Nelson, Barbara J. *Making an Issue of Child Abuse*. Chicago: University of Chicago Press, 1984.

Nesmith, Jeff. "CDC and Guns." *Atlanta Journal-Constitution*, 2 May 1996.

———. "Gun Violence Study Survives Budget Vote." *Atlanta Journal-Constitution*, 14 June 1996.

Newton, George D., and Franklin E. Zimring. *Firearms & Violence in American Life*. Washington, D.C.: National Commission on the Causes and Prevention of Violence, 1970.

"NRA-ILA Calls for BATF Hearings." *American Rifleman, NRA Official Journal*, March 1979, 5.

Nye, Joseph S., Philip D. Zelikow, and David C. King, eds. *Why People Don't Trust Government*. Cambridge, Mass.: Harvard University Press, 1997.

Odegard, Peter H. *Pressure Politics: The Story of the Anti-Saloon League*. New York: Octagon Books, 1966.

Oliphant, Jim. "How the Gun Debate Died." *Legal Times*, 22 October 2002.

Olson, Mancur. *The Logic of Collective Action*. Cambridge, Mass.: Harvard University Press, 1965.

Ornstein, Norman, and Thomas Mann. *The Permanent Campaign and Its Future*. Washington, D.C.: American Enterprise Institute and Brookings Institution Press, 2000.

Orren, Gary. "Fall from Grace: The Public's Loss of Faith in Government." In *Why People Don't Trust Government*, ed. Joseph S. Nye Jr., Philip D. Zelikow, and David C. King, 77–107. Cambridge, Mass.: Harvard University Press, 1997.

Paget, Karen. "The Big Chill." *American Prospect*, May–June 1999, http://www.prospect.org/print/V10/44/paget-k.html (accessed 7 February 2005).

Perez-Rivas, Manuel. "500 to Attend D.C. Anti-gun Rally." *Newsday*, 21 March 1991, 39.

Perlis, Leo. Letter to supporters of the AFL-CIO on the intimidation of united funds. 6 June 1973.

Peterson, Paul E. *The Price of Federalism*. Washington, D.C.: Brookings Institution Press, 1995.

Peterson, Paul E., and Mark C. Rom. *Welfare Magnets*. Washington, D.C.: Brookings Institution Press, 1990.

Pharr, Susan J., and Robert D. Putnam, eds. *Disaffected Democracies: What's Troubling the Trilateral Countries*. Princeton, N.J.: Princeton University Press, 2000.

Phillips, Richard. "U.S. Withdraws Support for Gun Turn-in Drive." *Chicago Tribune*, 22 May 1977.

"Pistols and Politics." *Washington Star*, 7 May 1981.

Piven, Frances Fox, and Richard A. Cloward. *Poor People's Movements: Why They Succeed, How They Fail*. New York: Vintage Books, 1979.

Polsby, Daniel D. "The False Promise of Gun Control." *Atlantic Monthly*, March 1994, 57–70.

Potter, Lillian. Personal letter to David Steinberg. 25 November 1972.

"Proposition 15 Campaign in Full Swing," *American Rifleman*, October 1982, 58.

Putnam, Robert D. *Bowling Alone: The Collapse and Revival of American Community*. New York: Simon & Schuster, 2000.

Rabin, Robert L., and Stephen D. Sugarman, eds. *Smoking Policy: Law, Politics, and Culture*. New York: Oxford University Press, 1993.

Ram, Madhira D., Juan J. Geldres, and Jose B. Bueno. "Health Care Costs of Gunshot Wounds." *Ohio State Medical Association Journal* 73, no. 7 (July 1977): 437–439.

Raspberry, William. "Sick People with Guns." *Washington Post*, 24 October 1994.

Reich, Robert B., ed. *The Power of Public Ideas* (Cambridge, Mass.: Ballinger Publishing Company, 1988).

Reinarman, Craig. "The Social Construction of an Alcohol Problem." *Theory and Society* 17 (1988): 91–120.

Renz, Loren, and Steven Lawrence. *Foundation Growth and Giving Estimates, 2003 Preview*. New York: Foundation Center, 2004.

Ripley, Josephine. "The Right to Bear Arms." *Christian Science Monitor*, 16 December 1963.

Roberts, Sam. "In Memory of Those Shot in Civilian Wars." *New York Times*, 28 March 1991, B1.

Rochefort, David A., and Roger W. Cobb. *The Politics of Problem Definition*. Lawrence: University of Kansas Press, 1994.

Rochon, Thomas R. *Culture Moves: Ideas, Activism, and Changing Values*. Princeton, N.J.: Princeton University Press, 1998.

Rosenberg, Gerald N. *The Hollow Hope*. Chicago: University of Chicago Press, 1991.

Rosenstone, Steven J., and John Mark Hansen. *Mobilization, Participation, and Democracy in America*. New York: Macmillan, 1993.

Ryan, Richard A. "Ban-the-Bullet Campaign Fizzles." *Detroit News*, 6 April 1975.

Sandel, Michael J. *Democracy's Discontent*. Cambridge, Mass.: The Belknap Press of Harvard University Press, 1996.

Satcher, David. "Gunning for Research: In the NRA Attack on Firearms Studies, the Scientific Truth Is the Most Important Casualty." *Washington Post*, 5 November 1995.

Schattschneider, E. E. *The Semi-sovereign People: A Realist's View of Democracy in America*. New York: Holt, Rinehart and Winston, 1960.

Schlozman, Kay Lehman, and John T. Tierney. *Organized Interests and American Democracy*. New York: Harper & Row, 1986.

Schuman, Howard, and Stanley Presser. "Attitude Measurement and the Gun Control Paradox." *Public Opinion Quarterly* 41, no. 4 (1977–1978): 427–438.

———. "The Attitude-Action Connection and the Issue of Gun Control." *Annals of the American Academy of Political and Social Science* 455 (1981): 40–47.

Scott, Anne Firor. *Natural Allies: Women's Associations in American History*. Urbana: University of Illinois Press, 1991.

Sears, David O. "Symbolic Politics: A Socio-psychological Theory." In *Explorations in Political Psychology*, ed. Shanto Iyengar and William J. McGuire, 113–149. Durham, N.C.: Duke University Press, 1993.

Seibert, Trent. "Groups Tally Donations in Amendment Contests." *Denver Post*, 19 September 2000.

"Senators Told of More BATF Abuses." *American Rifleman, NRA Official Journal*, June 1980, 15–16.

Shapiro, Robert Y., and Harpeet Mahajan. "Gender Differences in Policy Preferences: A Summary of Trends from the 1960s to the 1980s." *Public Opinion Quarterly* 50, no. 1 (1986): 42–61.

Sheppard, Nathaniel, Jr. "Illinois Faces Lawsuit after Limiting Pistol Use." *New York Times*, 4 July 1981.

Sherrill, Robert. "High Noon on Capitol Hill." *New York Times Magazine*, 23 June 1968, 7.

———. *The Saturday Night Special*. New York: Penguin Books, 1973.

Shields, Pete. *Guns Don't Die—People Do*. New York: Arbor House, 1981.

Skocpol, Theda. *Protecting Soldiers and Mothers*. Cambridge, Mass.: The Belknap Press of Harvard University Press, 1992.

———. *Boomerang: Clinton's Health Security Effort and the Turn against Government in U.S. Politics*. New York: W. W. Norton & Co., 1996.

———. "Unravelling from Above." *American Prospect*, March–April 1996, 20–25.

———. "Advocates without Members: The Recent Transformation of Civic Life." In *Civic Engagement in American Life*, ed. Theda Skocpol and Morris P. Fiorina, 461–509. Washington, D.C.: Brookings Institution Press, 1999.

———. *The Missing Middle*. New York: W. W. Norton & Co., 2001.

———. *Diminished Democracy: From Membership to Management in American Civic Life*. Norman: University of Oklahoma Press, 2003.

Skocpol, Theda, Marshall Ganz, and Ziad Munson. "A Nation of Organizers: The Institutional Origins of Civic Voluntarism in the United States." *American Political Science Review* 94, no. 3 (2000): 527–546.

Smith, C. Fraser. "Handgun Control Bill Gets Early Support." *Providence Sunday Journal*, 17 March 1974.

———."'A Stolen Handgun Took His Life. . . .' " *Providence Evening Bulletin*, 17 April 1974.

———. "Firearm Law Foes Speak." *Providence Journal*, 19 April 1974.

Smith, Tom W. "The 75% Solution: An Analysis of the Structure of Attitudes on Gun Control, 1959–1977." *Journal of Criminal Law & Criminology* 71, no. 3 (1980): 300–316.

———. "The Polls: Gender and Attitudes toward Violence." *Public Opinion Quarterly* 48, no. 1 (1984): 384–396.

———. "Outline of Major Findings on the 1996 National Gun Policy Survey of the National Opinion Research Center: Preliminary Draft, January 1997." Chicago: NORC, 1997.

Snow, David A., and Robert D. Benford. "Master Frames and Cycles of Protest." In *Frontiers of Social Movement Theory*, ed. Aldon Morris and Carol Mueller, 133–155. New Haven, Conn.: Yale University Press, 1992.

Snyder, Howard N., and Melissa Sickmunda. *Juvenile Offenders and Victims: 1999 National Report*. Washington: Office of Juvenile Justice and Delinquency Prevention, U.S. Department of Justice, 1999.

Snyder, John M. "NRA Registers as Lobby to Uphold Gun Ownership." *American Rifleman*, April 1974, 16.

Spitzer, Robert J. *The Politics of Gun Control*, 2nd ed. New York: Chatham House, 1998.

"States Spend Settlement to Snuff Out a Bad Habit." *USA Today*, 1 August 2000.

Steinberg, David J. Personal letter to Mrs. Patricia DeMeo. 25 November 1968.

———. Personal letter to Selig Sacks. 23 January 1969.

———. Personal letter to William Keith Thompson. 18 March 1970.

———. Personal letter to Mrs. Charles Potter. 3 April 1973.

———. Personal letter to James B. Sullivan. 12 September 1974.

———. Personal letter to Dee Helfgott. 16 September 1974.

———. Personal letter to Ethan Finley. 28 March 1975.

———. Unpublished letter to the editor of the *Washington Star*. 20 May 1976.

———. Personal letter to Edwin H. Feinberg. 29 November 1976.

———. Personal letter to D. M. Maillie. 22 May 1980.

———. Personal letter to Joe Clough. 31 December 1980.

———. Letter to Board of Directors, National Council for a Responsible Firearms Policy. 20 January 1981.

———. Unpublished letter to the editor of the *Washington Star*. 11 May 1981.

———. "Faults and Failings of Gun Control." *Washington Post*, 27 July 1985.

———. Personal letter to Kimberly D. Reed. 2 August 1993.

———. Unpublished letter to the editor of the *New York Times*. 2 August 1993.

———. Unpublished letter to the editor of the *Washington Post*, 13 December 1993.

———. Unpublished letter to the editor of the *New York Times*. 31 August 1994.

Steinmo, Sven. "American Exceptionalism Reconsidered: Culture or Institutions?" In *The Dynamics of American Politics: Approaches and Interpretations*, ed. Lawrence C. Dodd and Calvin Jillson, 106–131. Boulder, Colo.: Westview Press, 1994.

Stockman, David A. "The Triumph of Politics." *Newsweek*, 21 April 1986, 40.

Stone, Deborah A. *Policy Paradox and Political Reason*. Glenview, Ill.: Scott, Foresman and Company, 1988.

———. "Causal Stories and Policy Agendas." *Political Science Quarterly* 104, no. 2 (1989): 281–300.

Strout, Richard L. "Gun Control an 'Idealistic Dream,' Says Saxbe, but Growing Trend Favors It." *Christian Science Monitor*, 18 January 1974.

Stuart, Peter C. "Handgun Foes—Too Many Strategies?" *Christian Science Monitor*, 2 June 1976, 1.

———. "A Failure of Nerve; Shooting Down Gun Control." *New Leader*, 11 September 1978. Reprinted in *The Issue of Gun Control*, ed. Thomas Draper, 105–110. New York: H. W. Wilson, 1981.

Sugarmann, Josh. *National Rifle Association: Money, Firepower & Fear*. Washington, D.C.: National Press Books, 1992.

Swers, Michele. "From the Year of the Woman to the Republican Ascendancy: Evaluating the Policy Impact of Women in Congress." Ph.D. diss., Harvard University, 2000.

Tarrow, Sidney. *Power in Movement*, 2nd ed. Cambridge, U.K.: Cambridge University Press, 1998.

Tatalovich, Raymond, and Byron W. Daynes, eds. *The Politics of Abortion: A Study in Community Conflict in Public Policy Making*. New York: Praeger, 1981.

———. *Moral Controversies in American Politics: Cases in Social Regulatory Policy*. Armonk, N.Y.: M. E. Sharpe, 1998.

Tate, Cassandra. *Cigarette Wars*. New York: Oxford University Press, 1999.

Taubes, Gary. "Violence Epidemiologists Test the Hazards of Gun Ownership." *Science* 258, no. 5080 (9 October 1992): 215.

Taylor, Michael, and Sara Singleton. "The Communal Resource: Transaction Costs and the Solution of Collective Action Problems." *Politics and Society* 21, no. 2 (1993): 195–214.

Taylor, Paul. "Powder Burn: As Gun-Control Advocates Hit a Bull's Eye or Two, the NRA Tries to Sharpen Its Aim." *Washington Post*, 6 July 1982.

———. "Rolling Stone Publisher, Police Take Aim at Guns." *Washington Post*, 31 August 1982.

Taylor, Paul, and Jay Mathews. "Gun Control Jammed: Defeat of California Initiative Throws Proponents Back on the Defensive." *Washington Post*, 9 November 1982.

Teret, Stephen P., Daniel W. Webster, Jon S. Vernick, Tom W. Smith, Deborah Leff, Garen J. Wintemute, Philip J. Cook, Darnell F. Hawkins, Arthur L. Kellermann, Susan B. Sorenson, and Susan DeFrancesco. "Support for New Policies to Regulate Firearms: Results of Two National Surveys." *New England Journal of Medicine* 339, no. 12 (17 September 1998): 813–818.

Thorpe, Norman. "Gun Proposal Prompts Battle in California." *Wall Street Journal*, 20 October 1982.

Toner, Robin. "'Feeling Ashamed' on Gun Issue, Senator Is Moved to Act." *New York Times*, 17 May 1999.

Tonso, William R. "Social Problems and Sagecraft: Gun Control as a Case in Point." In *Firearms and Violence: Issues of Public Policy*, ed. Don B. Kates Jr., 71–95. San Francisco: Pacific Institute for Public Policy Research, 1984.

Trefethen, James B., and James E. Serven. *Americans and Their Guns: The National Rifle Association Story through Nearly a Century of Service to the Nation*. Harrisburg, Penn.: Stackpole Books, 1967.

Trosclair, A., et al. "Cigarette Smoking among Adults—United States, 2000." *Morbidity and Mortality Weekly Report* 51, no. 29 (29 July 2002): 642–645.

Troyer, Ronald J., and Gerald E. Markle. *Cigarettes: The Battle over Smoking*. New Brunswick, N.J.: Rutgers University Press, 1983.

Truman, David B. *The Governmental Process*. New York: Alfred A. Knopf, 1951.

Tversky, Amos, and Daniel Kahneman. "The Framing of Decisions and the Psychology of Choice." *Science* 211, no. 4481 (30 January 1981): 453–458.

"UF Held Hostage." *Grand Rapids Press*, 22 May 1973.

"Understanding Gun Control." *Wall Street Journal*, 7 June 1972.

United Press International. "Congress to Get Gun Bill in Wake of Ford Attack." *Chicago Tribune*, 24 September 1975.

U.S. Conference of Mayors. "Resolution 10: Firearms Control." Passed at annual meeting, Chicago, 15 June 1968.

———. "Resolution on Handgun Control." Passed at annual meeting, New Orleans, 21 June 1972.

———. "Issues and Alternatives 1975." Washington, D.C.: U.S. Conference of Mayors, 1975.

———. *Second National Forum on Handgun Control: Proceedings*. Washington, D.C.: U.S. Conference of Mayors, 1976.

———. *Targeting in on Handgun Control* 7, no. 2 (1981).

U.S. Congress. House. Committee on the Judiciary, Subcommittee on Crime. *Firearms Legislation*. 94th Cong., 1st sess., pt. 1, 18 February—9 April 1975.

U.S. Congress. Senate. Committee on Commerce. *To Regulate Commerce in Firearms*. 73rd Cong., 2nd sess., 28–29 May 1937.

U.S. Congress. Senate. Committee on the Judiciary, Subcommittee to Investigate Juvenile Delinquency. 88th Cong., 1st sess., 1 May 1963.

———. 90th Cong., 2nd sess., 26 June 1968.

U.S. Department of Agriculture. "Glickman Announces $340 Million to Aid Tobacco Farmers." Press Release 0245, 20 July 2000.

U.S. Department of Health, Education, and Welfare. Office of the Surgeon General. *Healthy People: The Surgeon General's Report on Health Promotion and Disease Prevention*. Rockville, Md.: Department of Health, Education, and Welfare, 1979.

U.S. Department of Health and Human Services. Centers for Disease Control and Prevention. *Investment in Tobacco Control: State Highlights 2001*. Atlanta: Centers for Disease Control and Prevention, 2001.

———. "History of the 1964 Surgeon General's Report on Smoking and Health," http://www.cdc.gov/tobacco/30yrsgen.htm (accessed 9 February 2005).

U.S. Department of Justice, Bureau of Justice Statistics. "Crimes Committed with Firearms, 1973–2003 (2003), http://www.ojp.usdoj.gov/bjs/glance/guncrime.htm (accessed 24 January 2005).

U.S. Department of the Treasury. Bureau of Alcohol, Tobacco, and Firearms. *State Laws and Published Ordinances—Firearms*. Washington, D.C.: Bureau of Alcohol, Tobacco and Firearms, 16th ed. (1984); 19th ed. (1989); 22nd ed. (2000).

Verba, Sidney, Kay Lehman Schlozman, and Henry E. Brady. *Voice and Equality*. Cambridge, Mass.: The Belknap Press of Harvard University Press, 1995.

Vernick, Jon S., and Lisa M. Hepburn. "State and Federal Gun Laws: Trends for 1970–99." In *Evaluating Gun Policy: Effects on Crime and Violence*, ed. Jens Ludwig and Philip J. Cook, 345–411. Washington, D.C.: Brookings Institution Press, 2003.

Vernick, Jon S., Stephen P. Teret, Kim Ammann Howard, Michael D. Teret, and Garen J. Wintemute. "Public Opinion Polling on Gun Policy." *Health Affairs* 12, no. 4 (1993): 198–208.

Vizzard, William J. *In the Crossfire: A Political History of the Bureau of Alcohol, Tobacco and Firearms*. Boulder, Colo.: Lynne Rienner, 1997.

———. *Shots in the Dark: The Policy, Politics, and Symbolism of Gun Control*. Lanham, Md.: Rowman & Littlefield Publishers, 2000.

Volland, Victor. "Clergy, Congregations Grapple with Guns Issue." *St. Louis Post-Dispatch*, 27 February 1999.

Walker, Jack L., Jr. *Mobilizing Interest Groups in America*. Ann Arbor: University of Michigan Press, 1991.

Walsh, Thomas E. "St Germain Explains Quitting 'Handgun.'" *Evening Bulletin (Providence)*, 6 July 1976.

Weed, Frank J. "Grass-Roots Activism and the Drunk Driving Issue: A Survey of MADD Chapters." *Law & Policy* 9, no. 3 (1987): 259–278.

———. "The Impact of Support Resources on Local Chapter Operations in the Antidrunk-Driving Movement." *Sociological Quarterly* 30, no. 1 (1989): 77–91.

Wildermuth, John. "Rampages Elicit Little Outcry for Gun Control." *San Francisco Chronicle*, 24 March 2001.

Wilensky, Harry. "Gun Control Bill May Be Near." *St. Louis Post-Dispatch*, 30 April 1975, A1.

Wilson, Harry L., and Mark J. Rozell. "Virginia: The Politics of Concealed Weapons." In *The Changing Politics of Gun Control*, ed. John M. Bruce and Clyde Wilcox, 125–138. Lanham, Md.: Rowman & Littlefield Publishers, 1998.

Wilson, James Q. *Bureaucracy: Why Government Agencies Do What They Do*. New York: Basic Books, 1989.

———. *Political Organizations*. Princeton, N.J.: Princeton University Press, 1995.

Wilson, James Q., and Mark H. Moore, "Enforcing the Laws We Have." *Washington Post*, 1 April 1981.

Wolf, Richard. "Many Factors Aided Gun Bill." *USA Today*, 10 May 1991.

Wolfinger, Raymond E. "Nondecisions and the Study of Local Politics." *American Political Science Review* 65, no. 4 (1971): 1063–1080.

Wolfson, Mark. *The Fight against Big Tobacco*. New York: Aldine de Gruyter, 2001.

Wolk, Ronald A. "Gun Control: An Emotional Problem." *Providence Journal*, 19 February 1973.

Wooddy, Carroll H., and Samuel A. Stouffer. "Local Option and Public Opinion." *American Journal of Sociology* 36, no. 2 (1930): 175–205.

Wright, James D., and Linda L. Marston. "The Ownership of the Means of Destruction: Weapons in the United States." *Social Problems* 23, no. 1 (1975): 93–107.

Wright, James D., Peter H. Rossi, and Kathleen Daly. *Under the Gun: Weapons, Crime, and Violence in America.* New York: Aldine de Gruyter, 1983.

Yost, Paula. "Permanent Import Ban on Assault Rifles: 43 Types Affected by Bush Order." *Washington Post,* 8 July 1989, A4.

Young, John T., David Hemenway, Robert J. Blendon, and John M. Benson. "Trends: Guns." *Public Opinion Quarterly* 60, no. 4 (1996): 634–649.

Zald, Mayer N. "Culture, Ideology, and Strategic Framing." In *Comparative Perspectives on Social Movements,* ed. Doug McAdam, John D. McCarthy, and Mayer N. Zald, 261–274. Cambridge, U.K.: Cambridge University Press, 1996.

Zartman, Katherine. Personal letter to Pete Shields. 12 October 1981.

———. Personal letter to Barbara Bell, Leader, Ban Handguns, 6 November 1981 (on file with author).

———. "Statement of Katherine Zartman, President, Illinois Citizens for Handgun Control, at Third Annual Walk against Handgun Violence, October 23, 1983" (on file with author).

Zimring, Franklin E. "Firearms and Federal Law: The Gun Control Act of 1968." *Journal of Legal Studies* 4, no. 133 (1975): 170–194.

Zuckoff, Mitchell. "Subdued NRA Shifts Gears as Calls for Gun Control Grow." *Boston Globe,* 30 April 1999, A1.

# Index

Page references followed by *fig* indicates an illustrated figure; followed by *t* indicates a table.

PRINCETON STUDIES IN AMERICAN POLITICS:
HISTORICAL, INTERNATIONAL, AND COMPARATIVE PERSPECTIVES